Japan and the World

Ishida Takeshi

Japan and the World

Essays on Japanese History and Politics in Honour of Ishida Takeshi

Edited by
Gail Lee Bernstein
and
Haruhiro Fukui

St. Martin's Press   New York

Library of
Japan and
honour of
Fukui.
p. cm.
Bibliograp
Includes in
ISBN 0–31
1. Japan—
I. Ishida T
Haruhiro,
DS881.9.J
952.03—d

Contents

List of Figures and Tables

Illustrations

Tables

Notes on the Contributors

Gail Lee Bernstein is Professor of Oriental Studies and History at the University of Arizona. She is the author of *Japanese Marxist, a Portrait of Kawakami Hajime* (1976) and *Haruko's World, a Japanese Farm Woman and Her Community* (1983).

Shigeko Nimiya Fukai teaches in the Political Science Department of Auburn University, in Alabama. She has contributed to *World Politics, Third World Quarterly, Asian Survey, Chūō Kōron* and *Current History*. She is currently writing a political biography of former Prime Minister Nobusuke Kishi.

Haruhiro Fukui is Professor of Political Science at the University of California, Santa Barbara. He has authored *Party in Power: The Japanese Liberal-Democrats and Policy-making* (1970); co-authored *Managing an Alliance: The Politics of U.S.–Japanese Relations* (1976), *The Textile Wrangle: Conflict in Japanese–American Relations, 1969– 1971* (1979), and *Japan and the New Ocean Regime* (1984); and edited the two-volume encyclopedia, *Political Parties of Asia and the Pacific* (1985).

Ehud Harari is at The Hebrew University of Jerusalem, where he is Senior Lecturer in Political Science and East Asian Studies, Senior Fellow of the Truman Institute and Director of the professional M.A. Program in Public Administration of the Department of Political Science. His publications include *The Politics of Labor Legislation in Japan: National–International Interactions* (1973) and numerous articles on Japanese politics and industrial relations.

Atsuko Hirai, Associate in Research at the Reischauer Institute of Japanese Studies, Harvard University, is interested in comparative political thought and intellectual history of modern Japan and the West. In addition to several scholarly articles, she is the author of *Individualism and Socialism: The Life and Thought of Kawai Eijirō (1891–1944)* (1986). Her current research explores the question of individualism in modern Japanese thought.

ix

Ellis S. Krauss is Professor of Political Science at the University of Pittsburgh, and the author of *Japanese Radicals Revisited: Student Protest in Postwar Japan* (1974) and the co-editor of *Political Opposition and Local Politics in Japan* (1980) and *Conflict in Japan* (1984). The author of over a dozen chapters and articles on Japanese politics, his latest project is a book on politics and the news industry in Japan.

S. J. Park is Vice-Dean of the Department of Philosophy and Social Sciences II, Free University of Berlin, and Professor for Japan's Economy, Society and International Relations. The author of seventeen monographs and over fifty articles, Professor Park was a Research Scholar at the Institute of Social Science, University of Tokyo, in 1985. His forthcoming book is *Industrial Democracy in Postwar Japan: U.S. Efforts and Strategies*.

F. Quei Quo is Professor of Political Science at Simon Fraser University in Canada. His many book chapters, journal articles, monographs and books have appeared in English, Chinese and Japanese. Professor Quo is the editor of *Politics Among the Pacific Nations* (1983) and the co-editor, with Zhao Fusan, of *The Future of Taiwan* (1984). He was a Japan Foundation Professional Fellow at the Institute of Social Science, University of Tokyo, in 1979–80, and a Visiting Professor at the Institute of Social Sciences, Tsukuba University, in 1985–7.

Henry D. Smith II is Professor of History at the University of California, Santa Barbara, and the author of *Japan's First Student Radicals* (1972) and *Hiroshie: One Hundred Famous Views of Edo* (1986) and the co-author of *The Modernization of Japan and Russia: a Comparative Study* (1975) and *Learning from SHOGUN: Japanese History and Western Fantasy* (1980). He has written on the Meiji artist Kobayashi Kiyochika, and he is currently engaged in a study of the changing structure of the early modern Japanese visual world as interpreted through pictorial views and maps of the city of Edo.

Thomas A. Stanley is Lecturer in Japanese History at the University of Hong Kong, and the author of *Ōsugi Sakae, Anarchist in Taishō Japan* (1982). Among his current research projects is a study of the Japanese police and their effect on political thought and social values in the Taishō period. Dr Stanley was a Research Fellow in the Research School of Pacific Studies, the Australian National University, from

Ellis S. Krauss is Professor of Political Science at the University of Pittsburgh, and the author of *Japanese Radicals Revisited: Student Protest in Postwar Japan* (1974) and the co-editor of *Political Opposition and Local Politics in Japan* (1980) and *Conflict in Japan* (1984). The author of over a dozen chapters and articles on Japanese politics, his latest project is a book on politics and the news industry in Japan.

S. J. Park is Vice-Dean of the Department of Philosophy and Social Sciences II, Free University of Berlin, and Professor for Japan's Economy, Society and International Relations. The author of seventeen monographs and over fifty articles, Professor Park was a Research Scholar at the Institute of Social Science, University of Tokyo, in 1985. His forthcoming book is *Industrial Democracy in Postwar Japan: U.S. Efforts and Strategies.*

F. Quei Quo is Professor of Political Science at Simon Fraser University in Canada. His many book chapters, journal articles, monographs and books have appeared in English, Chinese and Japanese. Professor Quo is the editor of *Politics Among the Pacific Nations* (1983) and the co-editor, with Zhao Fusan, of *The Future of Taiwan* (1984). He was a Japan Foundation Professional Fellow at the Institute of Social Science, University of Tokyo, in 1979–80, and a Visiting Professor at the Institute of Social Sciences, Tsukuba University, in 1985–7.

Henry D. Smith II is Professor of History at the University of California, Santa Barbara, and the author of *Japan's First Student Radicals* (1972) and *Hiroshie: One Hundred Famous Views of Edo* (1986) and the co-author of *The Modernization of Japan and Russia: a Comparative Study* (1975) and *Learning from SHOGUN: Japanese History and Western Fantasy* (1980). He has written on the Meiji artist Kobayashi Kiyochika, and he is currently engaged in a study of the changing structure of the early modern Japanese visual world as interpreted through pictorial views and maps of the city of Edo.

Thomas A. Stanley is Lecturer in Japanese History at the University of Hong Kong, and the author of *Ōsugi Sakae, Anarchist in Taishō Japan* (1982). Among his current research projects is a study of the Japanese police and their effect on political thought and social values in the Taishō period. Dr Stanley was a Research Fellow in the Research School of Pacific Studies, the Australian National University, from

Notes on the Contributors

Gail Lee Bernstein is Professor of Oriental Studies and History at the University of Arizona. She is the author of *Japanese Marxist, a Portrait of Kawakami Hajime* (1976) and *Haruko's World, a Japanese Farm Woman and Her Community* (1983).

Shigeko Nimiya Fukai teaches in the Political Science Department of Auburn University, in Alabama. She has contributed to *World Politics, Third World Quarterly, Asian Survey, Chūō Kōron* and *Current History*. She is currently writing a political biography of former Prime Minister Nobusuke Kishi.

Haruhiro Fukui is Professor of Political Science at the University of California, Santa Barbara. He has authored *Party in Power: The Japanese Liberal-Democrats and Policy-making* (1970); co-authored *Managing an Alliance: The Politics of U.S.–Japanese Relations* (1976), *The Textile Wrangle: Conflict in Japanese–American Relations, 1969–1971* (1979), and *Japan and the New Ocean Regime* (1984); and edited the two-volume encyclopedia, *Political Parties of Asia and the Pacific* (1985).

Ehud Harari is at The Hebrew University of Jerusalem, where he is Senior Lecturer in Political Science and East Asian Studies, Senior Fellow of the Truman Institute and Director of the professional M.A. Program in Public Administration of the Department of Political Science. His publications include *The Politics of Labor Legislation in Japan: National–International Interactions* (1973) and numerous articles on Japanese politics and industrial relations.

Atsuko Hirai, Associate in Research at the Reischauer Institute of Japanese Studies, Harvard University, is interested in comparative political thought and intellectual history of modern Japan and the West. In addition to several scholarly articles, she is the author of *Individualism and Socialism: The Life and Thought of Kawai Eijirō (1891–1944)* (1986). Her current research explores the question of individualism in modern Japanese thought.

ix

1985 to 1986, and from 1982 to 1985 he was on the faculty of the National University of Singapore.

Patricia G. Steinhoff is Professor of Sociology at the University of Hawaii, and a co-editor of *Conflict in Japan* (1984) and the author of several chapters and articles that explore the phenomena of *tenkō*, terrorism, student radicalism and conflict in modern Japan.

J. A. A. Stockwin is Nissan Professor of Modern Japanese Studies and Director of the Nissan Institute of Japanese Studies at the University of Oxford, England. Between 1964 and 1981 he taught in the Department of Political Science at the Australian National University in Canberra. He is the author of *The Japanese Socialist Party and Neutralism* (1968) and *Japan: Divided Politics in a Growth Economy* (1975, 1982).

Ezra F. Vogel is Professor of Sociology at Harvard University, and the author of numerous books on Japan, including *Japan's New Middle Class* (1965), *Japan as Number One* (1979) and *Comeback: Building the Resurgence of American Business* (1986); the editor of *Modern Japanese Organization and Decision Making* (1975); and the co-editor with C. V. Devan Nair, Nobuyoshi Namiki and Lim Chong-Yah, of *Learning from the Japanese Experience* (1982).

Notes on Names and Citations

Following East Asian practice, Chinese, Korean and Japanese surnames precede given names in this book, except in cases of East Asian scholars whose English-language works are cited and/or who reside in the West and observe the Western practice of giving surnames last.

Unless indicated otherwise, Tokyo is the place of publication for all Japanese publications cited in this book.

Notes on Names and Citations

Following East Asian practice, Chinese, Korean and Japanese surnames precede given names in this book, except in cases of East Asian
scholars whose English-language works are cited and/or who reside in
the West and observe the Western practice of giving surnames last.

Unless indicated otherwise, Tokyo is the place of publication for all
Japanese publications cited in this book.

1985 to 1986, and from 1982 to 1985 he was on the faculty of the National University of Singapore.

Patricia G. Steinhoff is Professor of Sociology at the University of Hawaii, and a co-editor of *Conflict in Japan* (1984) and the author of several chapters and articles that explore the phenomena of *tenkō*, terrorism, student radicalism and conflict in modern Japan.

J. A. A. Stockwin is Nissan Professor of Modern Japanese Studies and Director of the Nissan Institute of Japanese Studies at the University of Oxford, England. Between 1964 and 1981 he taught in the Department of Political Science at the Australian National University in Canberra. He is the author of *The Japanese Socialist Party and Neutralism* (1968) and *Japan: Divided Politics in a Growth Economy* (1975, 1982).

Ezra F. Vogel is Professor of Sociology at Harvard University, and the author of numerous books on Japan, including *Japan's New Middle Class* (1965), *Japan as Number One* (1979) and *Comeback: Building the Resurgence of American Business* (1986); the editor of *Modern Japanese Organization and Decision Making* (1975); and the co-editor with C. V. Devan Nair, Nobuyoshi Namiki and Lim Chong-Yah, of *Learning from the Japanese Experience* (1982).

Preface

This volume originated among a group of scholars wishing to honour Ishida Takeshi, the doyen of social science research in Japan and the leading facilitator of modern Japanese studies throughout the world. It represents a collective enterprise of considerable historical significance. To the best of our knowledge it is the first *Festschrift* ever published in honour of a Japanese scholar by a group of largely non-Japanese contributors. A great deal of co-operation on the part of the contributors and many others was required to bring such an enterprise to a successful conclusion. We cannot name all these individuals here, but we wish to acknowledge the particularly important assistance we have received from some of them.

The immediate inspiration for this collection of essays was Professor Ishida's 1983 Christmas letter, in which he announced his retirement from the University of Tokyo at the age of sixty. Galvanised into action, the co-editors conspired with Professor Ishida's wife, Reiko, and their son, Hiroshi, to acquire the mailing list for the family's annual Christmas letter, and contacted many of the names on it. In our initial planning for the *Festschrift*, we were far from certain that we would succeed, and preferred to keep it a secret from Professor Ishida himself. The members of his family responded with great understanding, dispatch and discretion to our somewhat unusual request.

Our first mailing produced enthusiastic responses from all over the world, demonstrating Professor Ishida's widespread impact on the study of modern Japan. Encouraged, we began seeking out potential publishers, with the aid of two of our contributors, Shigeko N. Fukai and J. A. A. Stockwin. At Professor Stockwin's initiative our plan was finally brought to the attention of Mr T. M. Farmiloe, editor of the distinguished British publishing house, Macmillan, and the typescript was soon tentatively accepted for publication in the series jointly run by Macmillan and St Antony's College, Oxford. The editorial board, chaired by Mrs Rosemary Thorp and including Professor Stockwin among its members, offered us a contract that contained only one hard-and-fast provision: the final typescript could not exceed 80 000 words. At the time this limitation sounded perfectly reasonable and realistic to us.

Before long, however, we discovered that our inquiries to potential contributors had elicited prompt and enthusiastic responses and promises of participation from more correspondents than we had anticipated. At that point we committed a miscalculation of some consequence: we assumed a normal rate of attrition would sufficiently reduce the number of contributions actually received on time and in acceptable form to keep the length of the completed typescript within the publisher's limits. We were wrong. Our contributors, scattered among several countries, proved to be far more faithful to their initial commitments than we had ever dared to hope, and we ended up with a manuscript of well over 120 000 words, or at least 50 per cent in excess of the prescribed length!

After a hard and anxious second look at each and every individual contribution, we concluded that we had already trimmed almost as much as we could and that it would be virtually impossible to reduce it down to 80 000 words. There were simply too many substantial contributions. For a while it looked as if we would either have to expunge several chapters *in toto* or seek another publisher. To our surprise and great relief, however, Mr Farmiloe and Mrs Thorp both agreed to accept the typescript in its considerably enlarged form, provided that we tried harder to prune it. This is what we did in the early summer of 1986, in the scorching heat of Tucson and the chilly rains of Oxford, working under the considerable pressure of time. That pressure prevented us from consulting as closely as we would have liked with each of the contributors whose drafts were being edited. All, however, responded to our urgent requests for clarification with much patience, tolerance and good humour. Our work was aided by Professor Stockwin, who, barely a week before leaving on a research trip to Australia, read the typescript chapter by chapter for the editorial board of the St Antony's/Macmillan Series and made a number of valuable editorial suggestions.

Meanwhile, on 30 May, at a party hosted by Professor Stockwin for Professor Ishida at the Nissan Institute of Japanese Studies, we made the first public announcement of the forthcoming publication of this *Festschrift*. In the audience on this memorable occasion were not only Mrs Thorp, Professor Stockwin and Professor Fukui, but a number of other friends and colleagues in the field of Japanese studies and also, rather miraculously, Professor Ishida's wife, Reiko, and two sons, Hiroshi and Ken.

This unique enterprise would never have been completed without the goodwill and assistance of all the individuals mentioned above and many others too numerous to include. We thank them all and hope they share our joy and satisfaction in seeing this work come to fruition.

mises of participation from more correspondents than we had anticipated. At that point we committed a miscalculation of some consequence: we assumed a normal rate of attrition would sufficiently reduce
the number of contributions actually received on time and in acceptable
form to keep the length of the completed typescript within the
publisher's limits. We were wrong. Our contributors, scattered among
several countries, proved to be far more faithful to their initial
commitments than we had ever dared to hope, and we ended up with a
manuscript of well over 120 000 words, or at least 50 per cent in excess
of the prescribed length!

After a hard and anxious second look at each and every individual
contribution, we concluded that we had already trimmed almost as
much as we could and that it would be virtually impossible to reduce it
down to 80 000 words. There were simply too many substantial
contributions. For a while it looked as if we would either have to
expunge several chapters *in toto* or seek another publisher. To our
surprise and great relief, however, Mr Farmiloe and Mrs Thorp both
agreed to accept the typescript in its considerably enlarged form,
provided that we tried harder to prune it. This is what we did in the
early summer of 1986, in the scorching heat of Tucson and the chilly
rains of Oxford, working under the considerable pressure of time. That
pressure prevented us from consulting as closely as we would have liked
with each of the contributors whose drafts were being edited. All,
however, responded to our urgent requests for clarification with much
patience, tolerance and good humour. Our work was aided by Professor Stockwin, who, barely a week before leaving on a research trip to
Australia, read the typescript chapter by chapter for the editorial board
of the St Antony's/Macmillan Series and made a number of valuable
editorial suggestions.

Meanwhile, on 30 May, at a party hosted by Professor Stockwin for
Professor Ishida at the Nissan Institute of Japanese Studies, we made
the first public announcement of the forthcoming publication of this
Festschrift. In the audience on this memorable occasion were not only
Mrs Thorp, Professor Stockwin and Professor Fukui, but a number of
other friends and colleagues in the field of Japanese studies and also,
rather miraculously, Professor Ishida's wife, Reiko, and two sons,
Hiroshi and Ken.

This unique enterprise would never have been completed without the
goodwill and assistance of all the individuals mentioned above and
many others too numerous to include. We thank them all and hope
they share our joy and satisfaction in seeing this work come to fruition.

Preface

This volume originated among a group of scholars wishing to honour Ishida Takeshi, the doyen of social science research in Japan and the leading facilitator of modern Japanese studies throughout the world. It represents a collective enterprise of considerable historical significance. To the best of our knowledge it is the first *Festschrift* ever published in honour of a Japanese scholar by a group of largely non-Japanese contributors. A great deal of co-operation on the part of the contributors and many others was required to bring such an enterprise to a successful conclusion. We cannot name all these individuals here, but we wish to acknowledge the particularly important assistance we have received from some of them.

The immediate inspiration for this collection of essays was Professor Ishida's 1983 Christmas letter, in which he announced his retirement from the University of Tokyo at the age of sixty. Galvanised into action, the co-editors conspired with Professor Ishida's wife, Reiko, and their son, Hiroshi, to acquire the mailing list for the family's annual Christmas letter, and contacted many of the names on it. In our initial planning for the *Festschrift*, we were far from certain that we would succeed, and preferred to keep it a secret from Professor Ishida himself. The members of his family responded with great understanding, dispatch and discretion to our somewhat unusual request.

Our first mailing produced enthusiastic responses from all over the world, demonstrating Professor Ishida's widespread impact on the study of modern Japan. Encouraged, we began seeking out potential publishers, with the aid of two of our contributors, Shigeko N. Fukai and J. A. A. Stockwin. At Professor Stockwin's initiative our plan was finally brought to the attention of Mr T. M. Farmiloe, editor of the distinguished British publishing house, Macmillan, and the typescript was soon tentatively accepted for publication in the series jointly run by Macmillan and St Antony's College, Oxford. The editorial board, chaired by Mrs Rosemary Thorp and including Professor Stockwin among its members, offered us a contract that contained only one hard-and-fast provision: the final typescript could not exceed 80 000 words. At the time this limitation sounded perfectly reasonable and realistic to us.

Before long, however, we discovered that our inquiries to potential contributors had elicited prompt and enthusiastic responses and pro-

We do wish to say a special word of thanks to Michael Patrick Sullivan and Junri Fukui, who, throughout the period we were working on this project, lent us their support simply by being where they were, doing what they were doing, and sharing our fondness and respect for the person to whom this book is dedicated.

Tucson, Arizona   GAIL LEE BERNSTEIN
Santa Barbara, California   HARUHIRO FUKUI

Introduction

Gail Lee Bernstein and Haruhiro Fukui

Ishida Takeshi's retirement from the University of Tokyo in 1983, on his sixtieth birthday, marked the end of an era, in many senses, for that university and, in particular, for its Institute of Social Science, on whose faculty he had served for more than thirty years. The event also marked the end of an era personally for each of the thirteen contributors to this *Festschrift* who have known him for a considerable portion of those years as mentor, colleague or friend. The conclusion of his long and distinguished service at the oldest and most prestigious of Japan's universities seemed a suitable occasion to express our deep sense of indebtedness and gratitude to this great teacher and scholar by dedicating our modest volume of essays to him.

Professor Ishida spent his youth in a turbulent era. He was born on 7 June 1923 in Aomori Prefecture, where his father, a prominent Home Ministry official, was director of the prefectural police department. Six months later his father's transfer took his family to Tokyo, and then on to a dozen different places in subsequent years. He entered kindergarten in Kyoto in 1928, the year of the 15 March Incident; he began the elementary division of Seikei School in Tokyo in 1936, the year of the 26 February Incident; and he entered the upper secondary division of the same school in 1941, the year of Pearl Harbor. Two months after being accepted into the humanities faculty of Tōhoku Imperial University, in October 1943, he was conscripted into the army, and for the next twenty months he served at an artillery regiment post in Tokyo Bay.

Following the end of the war and his demobilisation in August 1945 the 22-year-old veteran returned briefly to Tōhoku University before transferring, in May 1946, to the Law Faculty of Tokyo Imperial University. From then on his career was fixed on the academic world. Upon graduation in March 1949 he was appointed Assistant in the Law Faculty of the university, now renamed the University of Tokyo, and, in October 1953, he became Assistant Professor in its Institute of Social Science. Until his retirement in 1983, he remained a member of the Institute's faculty, as Professor after 1967 and as Director of the Institute from March 1978 to March 1980.

The driving force behind Ishida's decision to become a social scientist was his compelling personal need to understand the cause of

xvii

Japan's disastrous war and his own involvement in it. The starting-point for his research was the study of nationalist ideology in modern Japan, and when he resumed his studies at the University of Tokyo after the war what interested him most was, as he recently put it:[1]

> why we had been so deeply indoctrinated by ultranationalism that we had never questioned the cause of the war. This interest was the result of serious reflection on my wartime experience, rather than mere academic curiosity. In order to establish my own identity in the completely changed value orientation of the period immediately after the defeat, it was imperative to find the answer .. to why I had succumbed so easily to Japan's ultranationalist ideology.

Even while a secondary and upper secondary school student Ishida was an avid reader of works by liberal Japanese philosophers and historians, such as Miki Kiyoshi, Muraoka Tsunetsugu and Watsuji Tetsurō. It was probably Maruyama Masao, however, who had the greatest influence on Ishida both as a student and, subsequently, as an established scholar. His first encounter with Maruyama's writings apparently occurred when he was a fourth-year secondary-school student in 1940. Following his demobilisation at the end of the war he transferred from Tōhoku to Tokyo Imperial University partly in order to work with Maruyama, and, once there, he immediately enrolled in Maruyama's junior seminar in world history. Thereafter their teacher–student relationship evolved rapidly and soon became the basic intellectual anchor for Ishida's own scholarship.

Maruyama's influence is most visible in the first three of the twenty books Ishida had published by the end of 1983, which incorporated the first ten of the well over a hundred articles and book chapters published during the same period.[2] Like many of his mentor's works, these early studies by Ishida are characterised by a historical but highly conceptual approach, a strongly liberal normative orientation, and a concern with the peculiarities, if not uniqueness, of the Japanese political ideology and institutions that were presumed to account for the rise and triumph of fascism and militarisn in pre-war Japan. In their attitude toward Marxism and Marxists these works were, again much like Maruyama's, essentially ambivalent. On the one hand they were clearly sympathetic to and respectful of survivors among pre-war Japanese communists for their principled opposition to militarism and authoritarianism in the 1920s and 1930s; on the other hand, they were equally sceptical of many of the basic dogmas of Marxism and the policies of the Japan Communist Party based on those dogmas.

Such ambivalence toward Marxism notwithstanding, Ishida was involved during this decade in a variety of anti-government political and civic activities, beginning with the 1952–3 protest campaign against the construction of a shooting-range for use by the US military at Uchinada Town, Ishikawa Prefecture, and culminating in the 1959–60 demonstrations in Tokyo streets against the revision of the US–Japan Mutual Security Treaty. The involvement in the latter event would unexpectedly lead some fifteen months later to Ishida's first travel abroad to visit the USA, a development that had far-reaching effects on his professional life.

Before going abroad Ishida's scholarly attention had begun to shift by the late 1950s to political processes and institutions, especially the principles and patterns of interest aggregation and articulation in contemporary Japan. The two books published in 1961, which incorporate most of the fifteen or so articles published between 1958 and 1961, thus dealt with the structure and behaviour of Japanese pressure groups in general and of the major labour and farm groups in particular.[3] These works displayed Ishida's growing interest in the application of Western behavioural methodology and concepts to the study of Japanese politics. Ironically, however, this trend was interrupted by his visit to the US, where he would spend two years at three different universities–Michigan, Berkeley and Harvard.

The sojourn in the USA was an unexpected result of a letter Ishida wrote to a fellow Japanese political scientist visiting Berkeley at the time, Masumi Junnosuke. The letter, which was inspired by the resolve of a group of Ishida's colleagues to write their US friends about the causes and implications of the anti-Security Treaty riots in Tokyo, was apparently translated and distributed among interested scholars on the Berkeley campus, leading to an invitation to its author to visit the US as a Rockefeller Foundation fellow. Ishida's two-year stay in the US, which materialised almost by accident, had a profound impact, in both the short and long run, on his scholarship as well as on his personal view of and attitude toward the US and Americans and, more generally, toward the world and its inhabitants at large.

In the years following his first visit to the US Ishida was a visitor at a number of foreign universities – the East–West Center in Hawaii (1965), El Colegio de Mexico (1971–3), Oxford (1974), the University of Arizona (1976–7), the University of Dar es Salaam (1978) and the Free University of Berlin (1981). But for the Vietnam War and his objections to the US's role in it he might have visited US campuses a few more times in the late 1960s and early 1970s. In any event the experiences at several foreign universities and in their surrounding communities greatly influenced Ishida's scholarship and life in general.

During the early months of his first visit to the US Ishida was busy learning English, getting used to the US way of life and mastering the principles and methodology of the heavily behavioural political science as it was taught at the leading US graduate departments at the time. He was immensely impressed with much of what he saw and learned in Berkeley and Ann Arbor. As time passed and his English improved he remained deeply interested in and impressed with US democracy at the grass roots, but became less enamoured with, and increasingly critical of, behavioural political science as practised in ivory towers and, especially, modernisation theory and its methodology. He questioned, in particular, the assumption of a unilinear path of development definable simply in terms of quantitative socioeconomic indicators such as per capita income or exposure to mass media and proposed instead to emphasise the direction of change in values and social structure. What appears like a case of successful modernisation from the perspective of simply quantitative change may well turn out to be a case of failed modernisation, or one of 'demodernisation' as he put it, from the point of view of qualitative and structural change, as illustrated, for example, by the pattern of development of interest groups in modern Japan.[4] He seemed to believe that many if not all US specialists of Japanese politics failed to understand the complex and problematic nature of the changes involved in modernisation.[5]

Ishida's criticism of US foreign policy, especially US involvement in the Vietnam War, and his scepticism about behavioural political science in general and modernisation theory in particular were already apparent in the last months of his visit to the US, when he spent a considerable amount of time meeting with local peace movement and civil rights activists both on and off the Harvard campus. His views on these matters became even more explicit following his visits to El Colegio de Mexico in the early 1970s and to the University of Dar es Salaam in 1978. A short visit to Oxford in 1974 as a Visiting Fellow of St Antony's College and encounters with political theorists and historians there, followed by a one-year visit to the University of Arizona as a guest of one of the co-editors of this volume, apparently reawakened the theorist and historian in Ishida himself and accelerated his 'post-behaviouralism'.

By the time Ishida returned to Tokyo from Oxford, peace research and comparative political cultures had become the two dominant motifs of Ishida's writings.[6]

Peace and culture, however, have by no means been the sole and exclusive subjects of his research and publications in recent years. For one thing, following his return from Tanzania he was an active participant in a team research project on the epidemic of mercury poisoning (the Minamata disease) that had broken out in communities around Minamata Bay in Kumamoto prefecture.[7] For another thing, and consistent with the general shift in his approach and orientation during the two decades of frequent travel abroad, his earlier interest in political ideologies in pre-war Japan and political organisations in post-war Japan has not only survived but also deepened, as attested by a series of works on these subjects that have been published during the last decade.[8]

Ishida's long list of publications eloquently testifies to the enormity of his contributions to the study of Japanese political culture, ideologies and institutions in both historical and comparative perspectives. Of equal, if not greater importance to the authors who appear in this volume are his contributions as a teacher and promoter of scholarly exchange between Japan and other countries. As a leading Japanese social scientist and, especially, as a faculty member of the University of Tokyo's Institute of Social Science, over the years he had advised, assisted and collaborated in one way or another with numerous students and fellow scholars, both Japanese and foreign, including all the contributors to this *Festschrift*.

His help took many forms. He wrote the requisite letters of recommendation for research fellowships and visa applications. He arranged *kenkyūsei* status for scholars seeking to use the facilities of the Institute of Social Science. A note scrawled on the back of his name card gained access to important figures in the academic and political worlds and to library collections. In a society like Japan, which operates according to personal contacts and connections, the foreign researcher is especially helpless; with Ishida's support, the way was clear.

Professor Ishida's personal library collection was often the starting-point for our scholarly pursuits. Indeed, the range of topics and disciplines represented in this collection of essays attests to the scope of Ishida Takeshi's interests and bibliographic grasp. Equally at home in the disciplines of history and political science, whatever our proposed research topic he had at least half a dozen relevant books and articles piled on a chair in his office, awaiting our arrival. That office, on the fourth floor of the Institute, became a meeting-place for Japan scholars from all over the world – a mini-Japan Centre and a home-away-from-home where foreign scholars, weary of riding the Tokyo subways and bleary-eyed from reading Japanese language materials, could gain encouragement, sympathy and advice. Simply being able to describe our problems in our own language was a relief, and he obliged us by learning English, Spanish and German.

Our collective effort to acknowledge this extraordinary mentor and friend has taken several different forms. Some colleagues have chosen to contribute research that has engaged them for many years, while others have decided to share preliminary findings of research projects they have only recently launched. A few have written 'thought pieces', while others have reported on the results of empirical studies. The common thread tying the book together is the theme of Japan's relations with Europe, Asia and the USA over the past one hundred years or so – the cultural, economic and political influences that have helped to shape Japanese history for over a century.

It is a subject that has informed much of Ishida Takeshi's own life work. For a devoted advocate and practitioner of internationalism – someone whose indefatigable energy and endless zest has led him physically and intellectually to explore many regions of the world, and to help to develop Japanese studies wherever he has gone, it seems only fitting to dedicate a book that carries a title as broad as his own scholarly pursuits and life experiences.

Part I
Ways of Seeing the World

1 World Without Walls: Kuwagata Keisai's Panoramic Vision of Japan

Henry D. Smith II

The title of Donald Keene's survey of Tokugawa literature capsulises our dominant image of the Edo period as a 'world within walls'.[1] The intent was of course to indicate Japan's isolation from other nations, but the same phrase may be extended to encompass the pervasive image of early modern Japan as rigidly compartmentalised into a multiplicity of smaller 'worlds', whether the 'four classes' of society, the miscellaneous 'genres' of literature or the hereditary 'schools' of learning and the arts.

These structures of isolation and compartmentalisation have become deeply entrenched in our ways of thinking about Tokugawa culture. By suggesting that we may be better served by a counter-paradigm of a 'world without walls', I have no intention of denying the realities of status, lineage and legal category which were so central to the Tokugawa strategy of rule. But exceptions were many: despite the textbook image, which tends to reflect official ideology more than social reality, land *was* alienable, samurai did *not* uniformly outclass commoners, Japan *did* have regular contact with the outside world, and movement around the country was *not* rigidly controlled. By the early nineteenth century the exceptions had become so numerous that, far from proving the Tokugawa rule, they were coming to constitute a new order of rules.

I would thus propose that the image of 'walls' – or any such word suggesting an impenetrable barrier – can be misleading, and might better be replaced by an image such as 'fences' – barriers to be sure, but easily peeped through and often crossed. More importantly, I wish to suggest that in the cultural life of the nation it was precisely in crossing these 'fences' that some of the most creative energies were discharged. It is these 'border zones' between classes, between schools and between

3

Japan and the outside world, I would argue, that we must explore in order to grasp the inner dynamics of change within the culture as a whole. Rather than belabour this argument in the abstract let me offer a single piece of evidence, a colour woodblock print of the early nineteenth century.

'A PICTURE OF THE FAMOUS PLACES OF JAPAN'

This astonishing print [Fig. 1.1][2] immediately presents one intriguing border zone, between 'pictures' and 'maps'. Even in modern English these words which we so easily distinguish in daily experience are surprisingly resistant to precise definition. In early modern Japanese the linguistic distinction itself was blurred by the overlapping use of the Japanese *e* and the Sino-Japanese *zu*. In general an *e* tended to be a 'picture', while a *zu* could refer to either picture or map. When used in combination *e-zu* was the conventional term for 'map', while *zu-e* came to refer to topographical pictures. The language better accommodated, in other words, the conceptual overlap which must be provided for in any distinction between pictures and maps.

This print in particular must be seen as *both* picture *and* map, no matter what definition one uses. It is more likely, however, to give the initial impression of a picture, in the sense of a representation suggestive of common visual experience. From a vantage-point high in (what we now call) space, we gaze out to the west over the islands of Japan, which sweep in a great jagged arc from the southern tip of Hokkaidō (to the upper right), down to the Kantō region in the centre below, and up out through west Japan to the upper left. Whereas the Tōhoku area to the right seems to climb precipitously up the surface of the paper, the western extremity to the left is depicted with a strong illusion of recession into the distance, towards a far horizon capped by the crescent of a waning moon that sinks slowly into a bank of clouds above the South China Sea. The mountainous silhouette hovering above the horizon to the right, according to a tiny label, is Korea ('Chōsen'). Looking more closely into the land of Japan itself, we see a serrated coast swarming with tiny boats, and inland mountains range interspersed with tiny settlements – many capped by castle towers [Fig. 1.2]. The entire nation of Japan is presented in one homogeneous vision as a work of landscape art – an accomplishment with no precedents and only later imitations.

At the same time this picture is also a map, both in the sense that it represents a region of the earth's surface too large to comprehend in ordinary vision, and in the sense that it relies on symbols which must be 'read'. Each one of the sixty-eight ancient provinces of Japan is labelled with a rectangular cartouche, and over seven hundred smaller places – mountains, towns, islands, temples, hot springs – are carefully identified in minuscule *katakana* notation. Some of these named places are also rendered pictorially, but many are identified only by the *katakana* text.

The ambiguous character of this print is further suggested by the title, which appeared on the wrapper in which it was sold: 'A Picture of the Famous Places of Japan' (*Nihon meisho no e*) [Fig. 1.3]. The title thus clearly identifies the print as a picture rather than a map, but at the same time it draws our attention less to the whole than to the parts, less to Japan as a totality than to the assembly of particular 'famous places'. This emphasises its map-like character, for one must 'read' the picture, often relying on the *katakana* text, in order to locate places with which one is familiar. And yet in the end we come back to its quality as a picture of all Japan, existing in three-dimensional space and linked in turn to the distant continent. One aphoristic distinction holds that a picture is what we see, while a map is what we know. Such a distinction here yields, however, to an inextricable fusion of both perception and knowledge.

Where did this remarkable vision come from, and what did it mean? Let us turn first to the artist.

A Problem of Names

The difficulty begins with naming our artist, identified on the print as 'Keisai Shōshin of Edo'. All Tokugawa men of culture bore a variety of names, different 'hats', which enabled them to move with ease from one social situation or cultural milieu to another. Yet most ended their lives with a dominant identity and a single name by which later generations might know them. Not so with the man who began his career as Kitao Masayoshi, an illustrator of popular fiction in the *ukiyo-e* style, and who in his early 30s was transformed into Kuwagata Tsuguzane, a privileged official painter in the retinue of a *daimyō* from west Japan. Such passages from commoner to quasi-samurai status were less unusual than we are often led to believe, but the particular conversion from *ukiyo-e* artisan to 'true artist' (*hon'eshi*) seems to be limited to this one case. It is precisely this zone of transition that is critical for an understanding of the picture-map that is our concern.

The bare facts are these.[3] He was born in Edo in 1764 as Akabane Sanjirō, son of a *tatami*-maker, and apprenticed in his early teens to the celebrated *ukiyo-e* artist Kitao Shigemasa. As early as 1780, at the age of 16 he began as 'Sanjirō' to illustrate popular comic-book works of parodic fiction known as *kibyōshi* (after what were originally 'yellow covers'), and in the following year he took the school name of 'Kitao Masayoshi'. Over the next decade and a half he became the most prolific illustrator of *kibyōshi* known, responsible for over 170 titles.[4]

The circumstances of Masayoshi's sudden and unusual change of status are unclear, but in the summer of 1794 he was appointed official painter, with a generous stipend, to Matsudaira Yasuchika, the *fudai daimyō* of Tsuyama. Apparently an avid amateur painter, Yasuchika died three months after Masayoshi's appointment, at the age of 43. This may explain an uncertain interval of three years, during which the artist was active both as 'Masayoshi' and as 'Keisai', an art name (*gō*) which he had been using since as early as 1785 and which was confirmed as his formal art name upon his appointment in 1794.

The critical change in name came in 1797, at age 33, when he took a legal surname – something previously denied him as a commoner – and a proper samurai-style personal name (*na*). For the former he chose his paternal grandmother's maiden name of Kuwagata, and for the latter Tsuguzane, which he came also to use as an art name – a function most conveniently distinguished by the Sino-Japanese reading 'Shōshin'. At the same time he was bidden to take the tonsure – an important convention of life-cycle transition – and to undertake Kano school training under the master Korenobu. Within three years he had phased out both the name 'Masayoshi' and the *kibyōshi* illustration with which it was associated,[5] and came to use the names Keisai and Shōshin in various combinations, although 'Shōshin' seems to have predominated in his later work.

The shifting status of the artist was thus reflected in his changing names – but only roughly. 'Masayoshi' tended to be a popular illustrator and 'Shōshin' a privileged painter, but even these lines were blurred, since we can find 'Masayoshi' on elegant paintings [Fig. 1.6] and 'Shōshin' on illustrative prints [Fig. 1.13]. And in between was 'Keisai' as the name which linked the two, a kind of transformational identity which we will see reflected in his artistic evolution. It seems appropriate that we refer to him historically as Keisai. He died in 1824 at the age of 60.

The World of Kitao Masayoshi

The genre of *kibyōshi* in which Masayoshi was active in his early years presents another problem of separate 'worlds': were these text-filled picture-books art, or were they literature? Obviously they were a fusion of the two, but at least until recently, serious consideration of this 'special genre halfway between literature and art'[6] has been obstructed by the disciplinary walls of modern scholarship, which tend to divide the literary and visual arts into separate camps. The problem is not unlike that of picture-maps, which fall between the concerns of art historians and map specialists.

Kibyōshi, however, must be understood as an intricate interweaving of text and picture. In the example here [Fig. 1.4] both text and picture work together to produce a constant shifting of viewpoint as we move through the narrative from top to bottom, right to left. The sections of text alternate between an unseen narrator and individual figures within the picture; some of the texts refer to the three pictures hanging above, which themselves have texts; some of the texts are comments by the figures about each other, which are supplemented by their gazes and expressions; and within the texts themselves are punning references to still other texts and legends. This interweaving of image and text within an overall pictorial unity bears an obvious structural relationship to the picture-map of Japan.

The literary style of *kibyōshi* takes from the aesthetics of linked-verse composition the concept of *shukō*, the particular 'twist' which a poet imparts to the general theme dictated by the prior verse in an on-going chain. The proper metaphor for the corresponding visual structure might be 'angle', and it was through Masayoshi's extended practice at the manipulation of viewpoint in *kibyōshi* illustration that we can see the making of an artist who would in time become famous for his visual 'contrivances' (*kufū*), of which the view of all Japan is the supreme example.

Although Masayoshi was engaged primarily in *kibyōshi* illustration in his early years, he also executed a number of works in the quite different medium of single-sheet colour prints. Particularly relevant here were those of the type known as *uki-e* ('floating pictures'), compositions executed in Western-style linear perspective. The term itself appears to have referred to the distancing effect of such pictures, particularly in the naïvely exaggerated form in which it was introduced to Japan. The first *uki-e* appeared in Edo in about 1739–40, probably by way of still-unidentified Chinese prototypes, in the form of large theatre and brothel interiors.[7]

Until the 1760s the effect of horizontal recession in Edo *uki-e* was limited to architectural spaces, whether interiors or streets, while natural landscapes continued to be depicted in the traditional horizonless manner. In the meanwhile, however, a critical development was taking place in Kyoto, where in the 1750s a struggling young painter by the name of Maruyama Ōkyo (1733–95) had been commissioned by a toy dealer to execute landscapes for the *optique* (in Japanese, *nozoki-megane*, 'peeping eyepiece'), a lens-equipped picture-viewing device which was very popular in Europe and probably introduced to Japan by way of China.[8] With these paintings Ōkyo became the first in Japan regularly to apply Western techniques of landscape perspective, a method he apparently learned from Chinese adaptations of European originals. Ōkyo's views were also issued as woodblock prints, and it was through their influence that a new type of *uki-e* appeared in Edo in about the late 1760s, combining a strong sense of recession in both landscape and architecture.[9]

Figure 1.5 shows one of a series of *uki-e* landscapes of Edo which Masayoshi produced some time in the 1780s.[10] It was in single-sheet prints like this that the artist was able to express a sense of unified spatial expanse that was denied him by the enclosed and text-bound world of *kibyōshi* illustration. Yet even here Masayoshi indulges in the obvious manipulation of viewpoint, by using wholly separate lines of recession for the street on the right and the river on the left. One is almost invited to 'read' the picture like a *kibyōshi*, from the towers of Edo Castle to the distant right, down through the crowded fish market, across the stage-like centre space to the boats unloading their cargo of fish, then up the river, under the traffic on Nihonbashi Bridge and finally on to the form of Fuji in the far distance.

Broadening Vistas

Our artist's earliest datable venture out of the witty, stagy world of *kibyōshi* and *uki-e* was a fan painting [Fig. 1.6] with a bird's-eye view of Nakazu, a narrow strip of landfill along the Sumida River which from the early 1770s until its demise in 1789 was Edo's premier summer entertainment district.[11] The painting is signed 'Kitao Masayoshi' and dated 'Tenmei 3 [1783] midsummer'. The view here shows the nighttime bustle of Nakazu under the light of a new moon, with a variety of pleasure boats below, some setting off fireworks and others taking on and letting off passengers from the long row of riverside teahouses. This painting is remarkable for two reasons. First, it demonstrates that Masayoshi was already a skilled painter, producing works of much more elegance and subtlety than were allowed in the medium of the woodblock print. This simultaneous activity in prints and painting represents another kind of fertile 'border zone' in Tokugawa art. Second, it shows that from a very early point the artist was evolving a new type of vision, not the fragmentation of viewpoint which we have seen in his *kibyōshi* and *uki-e*, but rather the expansion of a single viewpoint to encompass a wide range of topography. Here, for example, in a single well-integrated space, he has managed to curve the Sumida River on the right in such a way that the view covers a geographical span of close to 180 degrees. It seems possible that this 'panoramic' reach was inspired by the structure of the fan itself, marking the first step in the mode of vision that would expand to encompass all Japan.[12]

Masayoshi's interest in topographical depiction became even clearer two years later, in 1785, when he designed an elegant printed handscroll entitled 'Views of the Famous Places of Edo' (*Edo meisho zue*) [Fig. 1.7]. Only 6½ inches high and over 40 feet in length, the scroll presents fifty different scenes separated by title cartouches with poems, alternating between very wide views and sequences of narrower views. The wide landscapes in particular are flowing and expansive, unframed and generous in the use of long unlined cloud bands in the *Yamato-e* style. As in the earlier fan panorama of Nakazu, we see here a very different world from the tightly framed and crowded spaces of the *kibyōshi* which Masayoshi was producing at the rate of over one per month in these same years. As if to emphasise the difference, he ended the scroll with a new name – or rather a new middle name: Kitao 'Keisai' Masayoshi.

The term *meisho zue* appearing in the title of this handscroll is revealing, since it suggests the inspiration of the genre of illustrated topographical gazetteers which had begun in Kyoto five years earlier with the famous *Miyako meisho zue* ('Views of the famous places of the capital', 1780). There is no doubt that Masayoshi was familiar with this work, since he used it as the compositional model for the twelve views of Kyoto which he designed for *Ehon miyako no nishiki* ('Brocade of the Capital'), a beautiful colour-printed book of 1787. His own earlier handscroll '*meisho zue*' of Edo, however, was a far more original work in terms of landscape design, with a sense of spatial expanse that was virtually absent from the conventional *meisho zue* genre.[13]

Masayoshi meanwhile continued his prolific production of *kibyōshi* illustration, but in 1789 the genre itself was dealt a heavy blow under the Kansei Reforms of Matsudaira Sadanobu. It was in fact Masayoshi himself who had illustrated Koikawa Harumachi's *Ōmugaeshi bunbu no futamichi* ('Parroting the twin path of arms and letters'; see Fig. 1.4), the *kibyōshi* which most stirred the wrath of Sabanobu for its satire of his policy urging the balanced cultivation of 'arms and letters' and which led to the censure and possibly the suicide of the author. As illustrator, however, Masayoshi seems to have escaped attention and continued to illustrate *kibyōshi* over the next several years. We may imagine, however, that the dampening of satirical spirit effected by the Kansei reforms encouraged the artist's turn in directions in which he was already headed, towards more refined and more simplified forms of expression.

In this turn towards a more elevated art, Masayoshi perhaps actively sought out an aristocratic patron, although the exact circumstances of his 1794 appointment by the *daimyō* of Tsuyama are obscure.[14] The most plausible connection involves another man of several names: Katsuragawa Hosan (1754–1808), equally well known as Morishima Chūryō and Shinra Banshō, a multi-talented writer and scholar for whom Masayoshi had illustrated several *kibyōshi* and who in turn had written introductions to two of Masayoshi's landscape books in 1787. A further link between the two men was provided by Rangaku ('Dutch learning'), the study of Western science, which would become one critical element in the conception of the view of all Japan. It was in the same year, 1787, that Morishima Chūryō (as I shall call him) edited *Kōmō zatsuwa* ('Red-hair miscellany'), a landmark anthology of bits of Western learning gleaned from Dutch emissaries to Edo. Masayoshi provided one of the illustrations to *Kōmō zatsuwa*, the depiction of an experiment with a static electricity generator.

The final link in this complex (and admittedly conjectural) set of connenctions was a Western-style doctor by the name of Udagawa Genzui (1755–97), a disciple of Hosan's distinguished elder brother Hoshū and the author of one of the postscripts to *Kōmō zatsuwa*. Genzui, as it happens, was an official doctor of the Tsuyama domain, and hence the most likely person to have intervened on behalf of the upwardly mobile Masayoshi. Whatever the exact circumstances, such an appointment could have only been made by the interaction of several of the many not-so-isolated 'worlds' of late Edo culture.

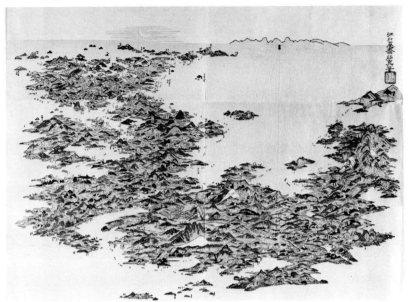

1.1 'A Picture of the Famous Places of Japan' (*Nihon meisho no e*). Colour woodblock print, 41.5×56.1 cm. Signed, 'Painted by Keisai Shōshin of Edo' [seal: 'Shōshin']. Mitsui Bunko, Tokyo.

1.2 Detail from 'A Picture of the Famous Places of Japan', showing the area of present Hyōgo, Tottori and Okayama prefectures. The exaggerated depiction of Tsuyama Castle in the centre is a witty personal boast of Keisai's position at the time as an official painter of the Tsuyama domain.

1.3　Wrapper of 'A Picture of the Famous Places of Japan'. 35.8×47.8 cm.

1.4　Viewing votive paintings (*ema*) at Asakusa Kannon Temple, from *Ōmugaeshi bunbu no futamachi* (Parroting the twin path of arms and letters, 1789), *kibyōshi* written by Koikawa Harumachi and illustrated by Kitao Masayoshi. Tokyo Metropolitan Library.

1.5 'Uki-e of Edo: View of the Fish Market at Nihonbashi Odawara-chō' (*Uki-e Edo Nihonbashi Odawara-chō uoichi no zu*). Colour woodblock print, 22.1×32.2 cm. Signed, 'Painted by Kitao Masayoshi'. 1780s. Kanagawa Prefectural Museum, Yokohama.

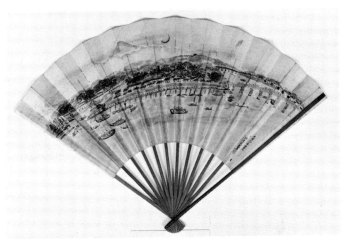

1.6 Fan painting of bird's-eye view of Nakazu at night. Signed, 'Painted by Kitao Masayoshi, midsummer of Tenmei 3 [1783].' Kōnoike Collection, Ōta Memorial Museum of Art, Tokyo.

1.7 'Nihonbashi', from *Edo meisho zue* (Famous Places of Edo). Colour-printed handscroll by 'Kitao Keisai Masayoshi'. 16.7 cm high. Published by Noda Shichibei, Edo, 1785. Mitsui Bunko, Tokyo.

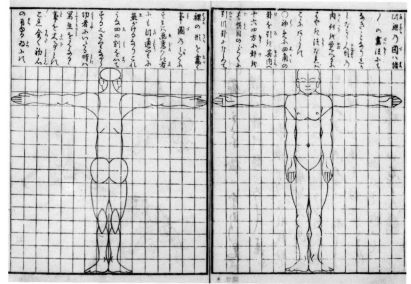

1.8 Illustration of method for copying a nude figure, from *Ryakugashiki* (abbreviated picture style). Illustrated book by 'Keisai Kitao Masayoshi', published by Suwaraya Ichibei, 1795. National Diet Library, Tokyo.

1.9 Wrestlers, from *Ryakugashiki* (1795).

1.10 Views of Edo, from *Sansui ryakugashiki* (Landscapes in the abbreviated picture style). Illustrated book, 1800, signed, 'Painted by Keisai' [seal: 'Shōshin'].
Ravicz Collection.

1.11 'A Picture of the Famous Places of Edo' (*Edo meisho no e*). Colour woodblock print. 42.1×58 cm. Signed, 'Painted by Kuwagata Shōshin of Edo' and 'Carved by Noshiro Ryūko'. *Ca*. 1803. Mitsui Bunko, Tokyo.

1.12 Kō [Yokoyama] Kazan, 'Panoramic View of the Capital' (*Karaku ichiranzu*). 41.3×64.0 cm. Published in Kyoto, 1808 or 1809. Mitsui Bunko, Tokyo.

1.13 Maruyama Ōkyo, View of Kyoto (Title on box: *Kyōraku fukanzu* [Bird's-eye view of the Capital]). Colour on silk, 67.3×110.4 cm. Signed, 'Ōkyo' [seal: 'Ōkyo']. Dated 1791 on box. Kobe City Museum.

1.14 Maruyama Ōkyo, Restaurant on Maruyama Hill. *Megane-e*, hand-coloured woodblock print, 20.7×27.2 cm. *Ca.* late 1750s. Kobe City Museum.

1.15 'View of the Precincts of Kanda Myōjin Shrine' (*Kanda Daimyōjin on-shachi no zu*). Colour woodblock print, 32.6×47.5 cm. Signed, 'Painted by Shōshin' [seal: 'Shōshin']. After 1797.

1.16 Teahouse with telescope, detail from 'View of the Precincts of Kanda Myōjin Shrine'.

Ryakuga-shiki: The Artifice of Simplicity

Keisai (as we may hereafter refer to him) undertook an important stylistic innovation in 1795, the year after his appointment by Tsuyama. This was the book entitled *Ryakugashiki* ('Abbreviated picture style'), which together with several later volumes in a similar style would earn him his most lasting fame as an artist. The preface by Kanda-an Shujin ('Master of Kanda Hermitage' – possibly Keisai himself) explains the idea:

> An old man next door had a plum tree. He manipulated it into the shape of a boat, taking great care that it still bloom every spring. I have no taste for this sort of thing. For one who truly loves flowers, a wild plum is the best. Without contrivance or manipulation, it has the taste of nature (*tennen no fumi*). These views are of the same sort. They depict the spirit without relying on form. This is called *ryakuga-shiki*, in which things are abbreviated without manipulating the form.

Given Keisai's particular circumstances this statement may at first appear to be a calculated repudiation of the artifice which distinguished so much of his past work as an illustrator of *kibyōshi*. A closer look at the contents of *Ryakugashiki*, however, suggests that the preface is merely a statement of the ideology that was conventional to such Chinese-influenced painting schools as that of the Kano line in which Keisai was soon to receive formal training. Following the preface, for example, appeared a curious two-page diagram demonstrating a method of copying (in this case, the form of a human figure) by the use of a superimposed grid pattern [Fig. 1.8], a technique probably learned from a Western text on drawing.[15] It is a mechanical approach which seems strangely at odds with the commitment to nature asserted in the preface, although the accompanying explanation (presumably by Keisai himself) stresses that while such a method can enable 'even those with no talent at pictures' to draw a nude, it is strictly for beginners. This didactic pose is another hint of Keisai's new status, for he is now a 'teacher', not a mere artisan.

There follow fifty-eight pages of examples of the 'abbreviated style', essentially a method of quick sketching which is here applied to figures, birds, flowers and landscapes. The volume is of a type that was to become common in years to follow, less in Edo than in Nagoya, Kyoto and Osaka, intended as much for enjoyment as instruction, whereby miscellaneous works by well-known painters would be reproduced in the woodblock medium, often enhancing the painterly effect by the use of unlined areas of colour. This style would come to be known among Western collectors as 'impressionistic'.

Yet a closer look at Keisai's volume suggests a certain artifice behind the very idea of 'simplicity'. While many of the human figures, in particular, are indeed simplified, they are far from natural, showing wildly and wittily exaggerated poses [Fig. 1.9]. In effect it is a style of caricature, one which would have a considerable influence on the later *Manga* of Hokusai. While naturalistic in effect the whole effort is carefully contrived.

The implications of the 'abbrievated' style for Keisai's view of all Japan did not become clear until his *Sansui ryakugashiki* ('Landscape in the abbreviated picture style') of 1800, in which he systematically applied his principles to the depiction of landscapes. It is an exquisite book, beautifully printed, and suggests that Keisai had achieved a new synthesis, combining the taste for visual wit of the *ukiyo-e* artist with a new feel for the broad and 'impressionistic' space of books in the painterly style. The landscapes are executed in a brush style with few outlines, and printed in light, elegant tones of brown and grey.

The naturalness of execution in *Sansui ryakugashiki* is complemented by the systematic manipulation of viewpoint, both in angle and in expanse. The album begins, for example, with two illustrations on each page, but gradually, the views begin to span two pages, and finally proceed to single views over a two-page spread [Fig. 1.10]. Although clearly 'abbrievated', these lovely landscapes nevertheless give a sense of a uniform and extensive space reaching horizontally into the distance. Here we can see the logic which would in time lead to the view of all Japan.

Keisai's View of Edo – A Kyoto Connection?

The critical intermediate stage between the broad vistas of the *Sansui ryakugashiki* and the view of all Japan was a dramatic bird's-eye view of the entire city of Edo [Fig. 1.11].[16] It is a single-sheet woodblock print of the same size as the view of Japan, about 16 inches high and 22 inches wide. It is signed 'Edo Kuwagata Shōshin' (the latter being the name he took in 1797) and was sold in a wrapper which provided, together with the names and addresses of the three Suwaraya-house publishers that issued it, a title: 'A Picture of the Famous Places of Edo'

(*Edo meisho no e*).[17] As in the view of all Japan, individual places are identified in tiny *katakana* script, over 250 names in all.

Although this view of Edo is undated, there survives a record of an application in 8/1803 for a licence (*kabu*) to publish such a title; presumably the actual print appeared shortly after.[18] It is particularly revealing that this system of licensing was for maps of Edo, and did not extend to landscape prints. Legally, in other words, it was considered a map, although its title identified it as a picture. The novelty of the view was such that the authorities were probably unsure how to classify it.

Where did Keisai find the idea for a bird's-eye view of an entire city?[19] We can largely discount the tradition of the huge screens depicting the city of Kyoto in the late sixteenth and early seventeenth centuries. Although these 'Views In and Out of the Capital' (*Rakuchū rakugai zu*) did offer a precedent of an assemblage of named 'famous places', they gave no such sense of a unified visual experience, as though one were actually looking down over the city from a high vantage-point. A more plausible source of inspiration from the same era would be European bird's-eye views of cities, some of which were in fact copied on to screens from printed albums brought by Jesuit missionaries.[20] There is no evidence, however, that this brief and circumscribed contact was transmitted to the common culture of Edo, nor that any such pictures were reintroduced to Japan in the later Tokugawa period.

We must thus delve into late Edo culture itself for the immediate source of Keisai's vision. A key piece of evidence is the allegation by Edo chronicler Saitō Gesshin (1804–78) that Keisai had taken the idea from 'Bird's-Eye View of the Capital' (*Karaku ichiranzu*), a colour-printed view of the entire city of Kyoto by Shijō school artist Kō [Yokoyama] Kazan (1784–1837) [Fig. 1.12].[21] Kyoto publishing records, however, indicate that this print was issued in 1808 or 1809, several years after Keisai's Edo view.[22] Even more importantly it is now evident that Kō Kazan himself was following an earlier model, that of a large painting now in the Kobe City Museum [Fig. 1.13]. It bears a date of 1791 on its storage box and is signed by none other than Maruyama Ōkyo, the Kyoto artist whom we encountered earlier as a young designer of Western-style views for the *optique*.[23]

Although some three decades separate Ōkyo's *optique* views (known in Japanese as *megane-e*, 'eye-piece pictures') from the 1791 depiction of all Kyoto, the link is clear in such a work as Fig. 1.14, a view of a restaurant overlooking Kyoto to the west from Maruyama Hill – perhaps the first Japanese picture ever to give a realistic sense of looking down over a city. Ōkyo's art in the meantime had matured and deepened, and as he discovered more pedigreed patrons he left behind *megane-e* as a youthful experiment and restricted himself more to the traditional elegance of the Kano school in which he was trained. Yet as art historian Sasaki Jōhei has demonstrated, he never abandoned the feel for a unified pictorial space which he learned from the West, although he developed this continuing concern in a manner that owes as much to traditional Chinese and Japanese painting as to Western inspiration.[24] The result was the superbly eclectic vision of his late view of all Kyoto, which combined his insistence on close observation of nature (here the city of Kyoto itself, rich in recognisable detail), a viewpoint that in the Chinese manner seems to be at once high and low, a Western-derived use of white clouds in a blue sky, and overall the same sense of unified space seen in his early *megane-e*.[25]

Comparing Ōkyo's Kyoto with Keisai's Edo the influence seems persuasive – if not by way of this particular painting, then perhaps by others like it, for Ōkyo also did a similar view of Osaka and perhaps of other cities as well.[26] Both cities are backed by their protective peaks, Mt Hiei and Mt Fuji respectively, and the city below is tipped upward, maplike, to show maximum detail. Where necessary, the city plan is distorted to achieve overall compositional balance, as in Ōkyo's curvature of the straight avenues of Kyoto – echoed in the S-curves which Keisai uses to depict the linear canals east of the Sumida River.

Decisive evidence of Keisai's exposure to the work of Ōkyo remains to be found. Such a connection was asserted many years ago by Louise Norton-Brown, but her evidence is suspect.[27] It is certainly plausible, however, that Keisai's privileged status after 1794 gave him access to paintings by Ōkyo if not to the artist himself, who died the following year. Although Keisai's appointment involved serving the *daimyō* at his Edo mansion, he is known to have travelled to Tsuyama in 1810,[28] and may well have made earlier visits as well, surely stopping at Kyoto along the way.

Even if Keisai was familiar with the work of Ōkyo, however, his urban view differs from that of the Kyoto master in revealing ways. First, it is more dense and filled in, with none of the elegant gold mists which periodically interrupt Ōkyo's Kyoto: Keisai's only concession to this convention is a token cloud pattern along the very bottom. And while Keisai takes from Ōkyo the urge to show the city as an impressive whole, he has a far greater interest in the systematic cataloguing of all its separate parts, the individual *meisho*.

Another – and particularly revealing – difference is the panoramic breadth of Keisai's vision, by which he has introduced a depiction of the sun rising over the province of Kazusa (which is identified by a tiny label on the skirt of the mountain to the far left).[29] This involves a remarkable breadth of vision, since both Kazusa (the central part of the Bōsō Peninsula) and the rising sun lay to the south-east of Edo – geographically, over 90 degrees left of centre in this Fuji-facing view. Keisai has thus mobilised his panoramic range to integrate this crucial eastern vignette into a westward view, thereby implying a greater wholeness of Edo by the symbolic incorporation of all Japan (*Nihon*, 'source of the sun'). The pride in the city which Keisai reveals in the 'Edo' prefix to his signature on the right is balanced by the pride in Japan which he reveals in his 'contrivance' to the left. Indeed, the whole view is one remarkable contrivance in terms of the pictorial conventions of the time, as suggested by the text of the wrapper in which it was sold:

> Master Keisai has contrived anew (*arata ni kufū shite*) to produce this unusual view of the bustling scenic and historic sites of the capital of Edo, fanning out from a single viewpoint (*hitome ni miwataseru*). It offers the delights of wandering from one place to another, and is suitable for framing or mounting as a scroll, or for presentation as a timely gift or souvenir. We offer for your display this wondrous view, one of the rarest of all times.

The vaunted rarity of Keisai's view of Edo was to be confirmed by its history, for it became the model for virtually all later bird's-eye views of Edo. Keisai himself later re-created the view from a slightly different angle in a superb *fusuma* painting dated 1809 which he made for Tsuyama Castle and which survives in Tsuyama today.[30] He never repeated the printed version, however, which was left to various later imitators.[31]

The Leap of Vision

Keisai's next feat of imagination, from a view of all Edo to a view of all Japan, was truly a quantum leap, one for which I have been unable to find any precedents, either in Tokugawa Japan or indeed anywhere else in the early modern world.[32] It is easy enough to conceive of a single-point depiction of an entire city, particularly in Japan, where adjacent hills provide just such a prospect of most settlements. But a view of the entire nation of Japan, with Korea perched on the far horizon! This would have no experiential counterpart until the space age. How did Keisai make the leap?

At least part of the explanation lies, I believe, in two important developments in late eighteenth-century Japan. One was a growing interest in devices with magnifying lens. In *Kōmō zatsuwa* of 1787, for example, we find illustrations of a microscope – an instrument probably first imported within the previous decade – and of the sorts of new visibility (mostly of insects and seeds) which it afforded.

For Keisai, however, the preoccupation was rather telescopic. The instrument itself had been known in Japan for many years, but there is little evidence of interest by artists – with the important exception of (once again) Maruyama Ōkyo, who recommended the telescope as a tool for correcting natural vision.[33] Keisai's interest in the telescope seems rather to have been topographical, as revealed in an intricately constructed 'View of the Grounds of Kanda Myōjin Shrine' (*Kanda Daimyōjin onshachi no zu*) [Fig. 1.15]. The dominant half to the lower left depicts the shrine precincts in conventional parallel perspective. Stretching out in a wholly separate space to the upper right, however, is a panoramic view, complete with labels of the major sights. When plotted on a map the arrangement of these place-names reveals that the view depicted can actually be seen from one – and only one – place: the elevated rise of Kanda Myōjin Shrine itself.

Still closer study yields the instrument [Fig. 1.16], a huge telescope peering out from one of the teahouses located on the east-facing bluff beside the shrine. A later gazetteer confirms that these teahouses rented out telescopes as a way of 'admiring the landscape' (*fūkei o moteasobu*).[34] In Keisai's view one guest peers through the telescope while his companion and the teahouse owner point eastward to identify the sights. The seventeen labelled places span a panorama of 160 degrees.

How might this interest in telescopic observation lead to the view of all Japan? I would propose that the close study of a distant landscape through a telescope, enabling the identification of named places not visible to the naked eye, could with the proper sense of manipulative viewpoint and spatial breadth – precisely the types of vision which Keisai had long been cultivating – lead to the idea of looking at the entire country of Japan from a great distance and identifying its separate places.

The other relevant development of Keisai's time was a mounting interest in mapping the borders of Japan, in defining the place of the nation, as it were, on the globe. This effort was at once scientific, impelled by the eagerness of astronomers to calculate the meridian and magnitude of the earth, and strategic, triggered by the growing Russian presence in the north. The global interests of the scientists merged with the national interests of the *bakufu* to enable the famous surveying career of Inō Tadataka from 1795 until his death in 1818 – precisely the era of Keisai's own expanding maplike vision. It is difficult to say whether Keisai knew of Inō or his surveys, but both seem to share a common spirit of the age, an effort both to ascertain Japan's borders and to affirm its place on the earth.

This mapping mentality also brings us back to Matsudaira Sadanobu, whom we previously encountered as the vengeful enemy of *kibyōshi*. Masayoshi's opponent, however, would prove in the end to be Keisai's ally.[35] It was Sadanobu, for example, who took along the artist Tani Bunchō to record views of the coast of the Izu Peninsula in 1793, producing a series of landscapes which perfectly balanced the strategic interests of Sadanobu and the artistic interests of Bunchō.[36] It was also Sadanobu who after his retirement as politician sponsored copperplate artist Aōdō Denzen to produce a great map of the entire world.[37] Keisai himself had personal ties with Sadanobu, who commissioned what is universally acclaimed as Keisai's masterpiece as a painter, a series of three handscrolls depicting Edo trades (*Shokunin-zukushi ekotoba*).[38] The accompanying text was written, revealingly, by three leading men of Edo light fiction, all of whom had earlier felt the sting of Sadanobu's Kansei reforms: Ōta Nanpo, Santō Kyōden and Hoseidō Kisanji.[39] This suggests that by the early nineteenth century there had been a certain reconciliation of the playful vision of *gesaku* with the pragmatic vision of the *bakufu*.

And so the issue returns to the playful vision of Edo. However much the concerns of magnified vision, global measurement and strategic mapping may have provided an essential environment for Keisai's leap of vision to the view of all Japan, that leap was ultimately a leap of wit rather than science. Look once again at Figure 1.1. As in the view of Edo we are looking to the west and slightly south, and the artist has indulged in a similar spatial manipulation, curving the elongated form of Japan in order to accommodate a panoramic range. But unlike the view of Edo, there is no rising sun. The answer is simple: what Keisai has depicted is a view of Japan *as seen by the rising sun*. It is admittedly difficult to prove that this is the intent, since conventional maps of Japan were oriented with the west above. But in an age that still could not conceive of flight beyond the range of a bird (even Icarus, after all, was but an impetuous bird), only a heavenly body could provide the

proper inspiration. And in the land of the rising sun, it could only be a
'sun's-eye view'.

Keisai's World

Over a generation before Keisai, another Japanese of remarkable
imagination had devised his own view of Japan from space:[40]

> *Inazuma ya*   A flash of lightning:
> *Nami mote yueru*   Bound in by waves
> *Akizushima*   The Dragonfly Isles

The poet was Yosa Buson (1713–83), and the verse was composed at a
haiku party in Kyoto in the late summer of 1768. The image shares with
Keisai the astonishing sense of a view of all Japan, here designated by
the ancient name of Akizushima, the 'Dragonfly Isles.' And yet the
vision is in a critical sense a limited one, first in the ephemerality of the
lightning flash and second in the 'binding' effect of the sea, yielding an
image which is truly a 'world within walls'.

By the time of Keisai's view over three decades later, however, things
had clearly changed. To be sure, Japan is still envisioned as both
manageable and beautiful, reminding us that the National Learning
(Kokugaku) movement was growing in tandem with that of Western
Learning in the late eighteenth century. But in Keisai's vision the sea
serves less to hem in the isles of Japan than to link them to the adjacent
continent, and the momentary flash of lightning gives way to the steady
illumination of both moon and sun.

More broadly we can see between Buson and Keisai the transition
which Haga distinguishes, from a culture of 'appreciation' (*kanshō*) to
one of 'observation' (*kansatsu*). In Keisai's view the element of appreciation remains strong: as the Meiji gardening expert Ōzawa Suien
remarked, the view of Japan would serve nicely as a model for *bonkei*, a
miniature tray landscape.[41] Yet at the same time there is a new element
of objectivity, in the close observation of Japan, as though it were seen
through the distancing effect of a lens.

Keisai's panoramic 'sun's-eye view' of Japan was thus the result of
cross-fertilisation *across* different 'walls' – those between samurai and
commoner, between maps and pictures, between artifice and nature,
between paintings and prints, between Edo and Kyoto, and between
Japan and the rest of the world. Keisai's creative activity occupied a

'border zone' in all of these respects. To be sure, the creative accomplishment of the view of all Japan was not to be duplicated: like Keisai's view of Edo, it was later copied but never surpassed. Such creative blending was going on in many different ways in late Tokugawa Japan, however, as the rapidly unfolding events of the succeeding decades would continue to demonstrate.

2 Anglo-American Influences on Nishida Kitarō

Atsuko Hirai

In non-Marxist scholarship in both Japan and the West, Nishida Kitarō (1870–1945) enjoys the reputation of being the most important philosopher of modern Japan as well as the most 'Oriental' and original one. He earned this renown by teaching philosophy at Kyoto Imperial University (1910–28), intensely practising Zen meditation and writing scores of treatises with concepts that did not always conform to the Western categories of thought he used. Partly for this reason, and partly because of his Hegel-like state theory, Nishida *tetsugaku* ('Nishida philosophy') held a canonical status in the nationalistic Japan of the 1930s.

It is no surprise, then, that the least-known aspect of Nishida's thought is its relationship to the ideas of Thomas Hill Green (1836–82), the English Idealist who has virtually disappeared from the world's roster of philosophers today. To be sure, several scholars have suggested a link between Nishida's *Zen no kenkyū* (Study of good) and Green's *Prolegomena to Ethics*. In 1961 Yamada Munemutsu proposed that future Nishida studies consider why his early letters often mention Green.[1] Takeuchi Yoshitomo responded to the call by addressing the question in his biography of Nishida.[2] Among Western scholars, Valdo Viglielmo promptly followed the lead of the Japanese in acknowledging the possible influence of Green on Nishida.[3] None, however, has fully discussed or explained the nature of Nishida's indebtedness to Green.

If the world is unaware of the importance of Green to Nishida, it may be because past research on this subject was fraught with elementary problems. First, investigators failed to examine Nishida's thought in the context of the general concern with Green among Japanese scholars at that time. True, Takeuchi parenthetically stated the need for a study of Green's role in modern Japanese philosophy.[4] Yet, concerning the origin of Nishida's interest in Green, Takeuchi merely raised the possibility that Nishida read about Green 'through someone's introductory writing' and pointed out that Nakajima Rikizō, Professor of Philosophy at Tokyo Imperial University, used the *Prolegomena* in 1894 as a textbook for his class in ethics, which was attended by a friend of Nishida's.[5] Viglielmo ignored altogether the question of the genesis of Nishida's interest in Green.

Second, not a single earlier writer accurately explained the nature of Green's influence on Nishida. All were agreed that *Zen* probably 'assimilated' the major ideas of the *Prolegomena*, and they also observed that, of these ideas, the ethical doctrine of self-realisation was of the utmost importance to Nishida. Yamada boldly speculated that 'self-realisation' was a theory of 'communication society' which early modern philosophers characterised by the theory of social contract.[6] Takeuchi suggested that what Nishida called *tōitsuteki arumono* was 'basically the same' as Green's spiritual principle.[7] But in what way? Regrettably, none of these scholars articulated the complex nexus between Nishida and Green that extended far beyond those which they mentioned and are summarised here.

Third, neither Takeuchi nor Viglielmo identified the ultimate goal of Nishida's philosophical endeavour. That is, they did not recognise those problems of Green's philosophy which Nishida tried to solve. It is only from the perspective of this goal that we can make sense out of Nishida's simultaneous involvement in Green and William James, the latter being the widely acknowledged partner in Nishida's philosophical journey.

This chapter undertakes to elucidate these neglected problems in the study of Nishida's philosophy.

GREEN AND NISHIDA'S EARLIEST WORKS

Nishida's interest in Green must be viewed in the context of the scholarly trends fashionable in his student days, for even as a young man on the periphery of the academic world, he aspired to respectability as a professional philosopher. At Tokyo Imperial University, where Nishida was a much despised 'special student' in the years between 1891 and 1894, one of his first professors was Nakajima Rikizō, the harbinger of Green study in Japan. Nakajima's eleven-page article on Green was published in the venerable *Tetsugaku zasshi* during Nishida's second year at the university.[8] By the time Nakajima adopted the *Prolegomena* as a classroom text, Nishida had already graduated. But he began studying the book on his own only a month after Nakajima had assigned it to his class. The result of this study was Nishida's first scholarly publication, an article entitled 'An Outline of Green's Moral Philosophy', published in 1895 in *Kyōiku jiron*[9]

In assaying a publishable work on Green, Nishida was by no means alone, even at this early date. While he was writing the article in a country town in Ishikawa prefecture, the effect of Nakajima's teaching was being felt persistently in publications in Tokyo. Almost every other month between December 1894 and July 1895, *Tetsugaku zasshi* carried a Green-related article by authors personally known to Nishida. Nakajima Tokuzō's article on Green's epistemology appeared in the December 1894 issue, followed in February 1895 by Mizoguchi Shinma's translation and critique of Book I of the *Prolegomena*. While publishing Mizoguchi's work in three parts, *Tetsugaku zasshi* also published Takayama Rinjirō's article praising self-realisation as the highest moral ideal. Nishida's work appeared within a month of the last portion of Mizoguchi's and the first instalment of Takayama's. Although *Kyōiku jiron* was not as prestigious as *Tetsugaku zasshi*, Nishida had reason to feel that his 'long-cherished wish' for scholarly recognition was fulfilled.[10]

The 'Outline' was published in three parts in May 1895. The first part, which outlines Green's theory of knowledge and corresponds to 'Introduction' and Book I of the *Prolegomena*, appeared in the 5 May issue. The second part, a summary of Green's theory of the will presented in Book II, followed ten days later. The last part, giving the gist of Book III of the *Prolegomena*, appeared in the journal's 25 May issue. Altogether, the article consists of approximately twelve pages of printed Japanese (as opposed to 469 pages of Green's work). It includes no comments or evaluations by Nishida himself and reveals flaws in his English comprehension.[11] Otherwise, it is the most articulate, comprehensive and readable summary of the *Prolegomena* that any Japanese had written to that date.

What light does the 'Outline' shed on our second question, namely, how Nishida assimilated Green's philosophy? Unlike the other writings on Green mentioned above, being strictly a summary of his work, the article itself offers no clue. In his letter to Yamamoto Ryōkichi, Nishida related his immediate reactions, which were so negative that he seemed to be totally unsusceptible to Green's thought. To Nishida, Book I of the *Prolegomena*, or Green's ontology and epistemology, was little more than a 'rehashing' of Kant's and Hegel's. Green's views on will, the topic of Book II, were 'worthless', and his thought on the practical application of moral philosophy discussed in Book III was even 'less worthwhile'. 'The only thing new to me', Nishida wrote, was 'the distinction Green introduced between "blind impulse" and "desire"'; the only part of the *Prolegomena* that Nishida esteemed was Green's agreement with the German philosophers concerning the existence of an *a priori* knowledge.[12]

Like the 'Outline', these remarks help little in our inquiry. They are not only cryptic but sound like the bragging of a young man (Nishida was 25 at the time) and a second-class citizen in the profession. On the other hand, they intimate that, by the time he finished reading Book I of the *Prolegomena*, he had accepted some basic tenets of Idealism as represented by Kant, Hegel and Green. Nishida's subsequent publications confirm this impression. In 1896 he published a short article on Hume, presumably an offshoot of his senior thesis at the university, in which he maintained a stoic neutrality on the issue of Idealism versus Empiricism.[13] Two years after the 'Outline', he published an article entitled 'Senten chishiki no umu o ronzuru'. (Does an *a priori* knowledge exist?) In this work Nishida unequivocally declared his allegiance to Idealism.[14] At this point, then, it is reasonable to conclude that Green's arguments had had an effect in bringing Nishida into the Idealist camp.

'ZEN NO KENKYŪ': THE PROBLEMS

The most critical area in which Nishida's assimilation of Green must be tested is his celebrated work, *Zen no kenkyū*, a collection of four articles published between 1906 and 1909. This is by no means an easy book. Nishida's writing is replete with inconclusive thoughts, contradictory statements and flimsy reasoning. Some difficulties arise from Nishida's peculiar manner of exposition, which does not indicate whose ideas he is discussing at a given moment. Others result from the economy of exposition and lack of explanation. Yet other difficulties are related to his unconventional use of important terms. Even with care and patience, a reader may still fail to obtain a clear vision of the process and structure of Nishida's thought.

These observations amount to a warning that no matter what one may write about Nishida's thought in *Zen*, it can be argued that the opposite is true. In the following exposition certain interpretations will be presented, and no effort will be made to argue 'the opposite'. I will closely adhere to the question of the possible effect of Green's *Prolego-*

mena on Nishida's *Zen*, and the thesis will be presented in a bold outline, omitting as many 'on the other hands' as possible.

Zen no kenkyū poses two major intellectual problems for its readers. These are Nishida's presentation of the 'philosophical-thematic' question he sought to solve and his interpretation of William James. The philosophical-thematic problem pertains to the epistemological quarrels fought in the West between the Rationalists and Empiricists in the eighteenth and nineteenth centuries. The essence of these quarrels was how the knowledge of things was formed from the sensations they caused upon man's senses. More specifically, the question was: If there was any relation between one sensation and another to render them to cognition, how was the relation established? Was there a transcendental agent, the Reason, as the Rationalists claimed, that united sensations which would otherwise remain disjointed atoms devoid of meaning? Or, as the Empiricists argued, was there no such rational agent and, moreover, as Hume maintained, even union of sensations as such was inconceivable?

Among Scottish and English philosophers, into whose tradition Green was born, the Empiricist view of the origin of knowledge enjoyed almost a monopolistic influence throughout the eighteenth century and the first half of the nineteenth. It is, then, no exaggeration to say that Green, following Kant, almost single-handedly created a place for Rationalist epistemology in British philosophy. In the last quarter of the nineteenth century Green's position commanded sufficient adherents to come to be identified both by his contemporaries and latter-day students as 'the Oxford Movement', a philosophical movement which in fact encompassed broader areas than epistemology. *The Prolegomena to Ethics* was the outstanding testimonial to this new trend in British philosophy.

Green's rationalist view, however, did not win in Britain the kind of monopoly influence that the Empiricists had enjoyed. Objections arose even before the publication of the *Prolegomena*. Noteworthy criticisms came from William James, a native of New England. James sought to liberate man's consciousness from the metaphysical cast of Green's doctrine of the Universal Self-Consciousness – the Reason – into the realm of 'pure experience'. The consequence was his famous concept of the stream of consciousness, which posited that one consciousness – the 'sensation' of the erstwhile philosophical battles – was joined to another through its halo-like 'fringe'. The process was devoid of the supervention of an extra-conscious being.[15]

What was referred to above as the philosophical-thematic problem which Nishida tried to solve in *Zen no kenkyū* was, then, this age-old feud among Western philosophers, the feud revived by Green and James and fought in Japan by their respective followers and critics. The second problem of *Zen* is Nishida's interpretation of James. In an article published in *Tetsugaku zasshi* in 1911, Nishida wrote:

> Mr. James seems to think that various experiences, which are independent from each other, are united from the *outside* by the experience of the relations, that the relations are something like a hinge that unites things from *outside*. What Mr. James calls the relation between one experience and another appears *external* to me. (italic added)[16]

The above quotation indicates that Nishida misunderstood not only James but also the heart of the controversy between the Rationalists and Empiricists. It is true that, according to James, the relations between things were as much experiential events as were the things themselves and that some areas of consciousness were experienced as a relation or joining of the consciousness. It was, however, the Rationalists who postulated a unifying agent existing *outside* the consciousness, while James opposed this view and considered the unifying action as originating from *inside* the consciousness. Reversing James's position meant reversing the Rationalist conception.

'ZEN NO KENKYŪ: THE ARGUMENTS

The temptation to dismiss Green's influence on *Zen* is strong. Not once in the entire book does Nishida mention Green. This silence is forbidding if for no other reason than that he acknowledges scores of other Western philosophers from ancient to modern times. Furthermore, Nishida discourages a reader from associating his work with Idealism by invoking profusely in Book I ('Pure Experience'), and persistently in other books, the names and works of such Empiricist-psychologist philosophers as Wilhelm Wundt and William James. It is understandable that Shimomura Toratarō, the revered perpetuator of Nishida's ideas, called the master's philosophy 'not ... rationalist but ... empiricist' of a 'radical' kind,[17] just as James 'nicknamed' his philosophical position 'Radical Empiricism'.[18]

One possible way to demonstrate Green's influence on *Zen no kenkyū* is not to begin from Book I, the theory of pure experience, but first to

examine Nishida's discourses on reality and good, the subjects respectively of Books II and III, and then to consider Book I in their light as well
as in the light of other information. (In fact this approach coincides
with Nishida's advice to readers to skip Book I when reading *Zen* for
the first time.)[19] To be sure, even this method is not free of pitfalls, for
both Books II and III unavoidably carry the overtones of Book I. None
the less, it is easier to recognise in them the fundamental characteristics
best explained in reference to Green.

Three topics of Nishida's theory of reality have been selected for
discussion: reality-in-consciousness, *tōitsuteki arumono* and the self.

Reality-in-Consciousness. The most readily cited thesis of Nishida's
theory of reality reads: 'The phenomena of consciousness are the only
reality.'[20] This statement contains two points that require clarification.
Nishida's 'phenomena' are not exclusively spatio-temporal events.
They freely and casually move out of this world of empirically
observable facts, into one that transcends it, and back into this world
again. To posit the conventional distinction between 'this world' and
'the one outside it', however, is to misunderstand Nishida's philosophy.
The world *he* envisages not only encompasses both phenomena and
nonphenomena (that is, 'noumena' in the standard vocabulary, which
Nishida refuses to use)[21] but also destroys all walls that the Western
philosophers have for centuries maintained between them. In his
promiscuous cosmos, a phenomenon *is* a nonphenomenal reality
which, contrary to Kant's teaching, renders itself to experience and
experiment. Spacelessness or timelessness often appears in Nishida's
writings as no less legitimate a phenomenon than an aching tooth or a
falling star. In short, the word 'phenomena' has no discriminating
meaning in *Zen*.

The second point requiring clarification is that the principle of
indiscrimination applies equally to 'consciousness'. By this term Nishida does point to the events related to the physical and psychological
faculties of man, such as the seeing of a lamp or the hearing of thunder.
His 'consciousness', however, seeps out of its human confines, like air
flying out of the lungs, at first imperceptibly but soon at an explosive
speed, until it suddenly pervades the entire universe. Thus, the chapter
which begins with the statement quoted above ('the phenomena of
consciousness are the only reality') and contains merely fourteen
paragraphs, ends with what appears a wholly incongruous statement:
'Consciousness is . . . what Hegel calls *das Unendliche* [the infinite]' and
'neither stands under the qualitative limitations of time, space, and
force, nor is subject to the law of causality.'[22]

Neither the statement in question nor the related theorem that matter independent from and in addition to consciousness cannot be postulated conveys empirical knowledge.[23] The points of reference are more than man's consciousnesses. At issue are the principles regarding the methodology of the metaphysics of consciousness. These principles may be stated as follows: only what exists and occurs in man's consciousness is 'that which *is*', and by examining one's consciousness, one discovers the character of the cosmic reality. Whatever that reality is, human consciousness is but its finite form of 'self-development'.[24]

Furthermore, viewed in terms of the fundamental philosophical question of whether there is a spiritual principle in nature or whether nature itself is the ultimate reality, Nishida's 'consciousness' presents a position decidedly in favour of the spiritualists. Nishida maintains: 'Natural phenomena are the phenomena of consciousness and come into existence by ... the union of our sense of sight, sense of touch, etc.'[25] The graphic example of this line of thinking is his comparison of body to consciousness. 'Consciousness does not exist in the body', he contends, 'but it is the body that exists in consciousness.'[26] In other words, the existence of one's body is ascertained only by the fact that one is aware of that body. Supplemented by Nishida's pan-psychic cosmology, the problem reduces to a simple formula: Consciousness (spirit) makes nature. For a positivist this is an impossible position.

Tōitsuteki Arumono. This is the term Nishida uses most frequently to indicate the equivalent of the Infinite. It cannot easily be rendered into English, and translating it inevitably involves interpreting Nishida's philosophy. Depending on its content and on what one believes Nishida's thought to be, the term seems to mean literally either 'unified certain one' or 'unifying certain one'.[27] What is more, Nishida refuses to draw a distinction between 'the one that unifies' and 'the one that is unified', while at the same time he admits that there does exist a unifying action and that something becomes unified because of it. He abhors such differentiation, calling it in effect a figment of imagination, 'the result of abstract thinking'.[28] Nevertheless, the question of whether *tōitsuteki arumono* is merely a self-contained unity or has a unifying property which acts upon things other than itself affects Nishida's entire theory of consciousness. Is *tōitsuteki arumono* 'unified certain one', 'unifying certain one', or possibly 'unified unifying certain one'? How is it related to the finite consciousness?

Following the order of Nishida's discourse, the point of departure is his reflection that consciousness necessarily has unity.[29] A unified consciousness in turn presupposes a unifying action by which the contents of consciousness, or what takes place in consciousness, such as memories and perceptions, are connected with one another by a unifying power so as to become a meaningful whole. The question is whether consciousness unifies itself or depends on a unifying influence external to it.

To some extent the answer depends on which consciousness one is talking about. Nishida divides consciousness into two categories, active and passive. The active consciousness attains unity from within itself, whereas passive consciousness is susceptible to an external agent that gives it unity. Consciousness, therefore, may be either the unifier or the unified.[30] Nishida, however, does not consider the active-passive dichotomy to be absolute. The difference between the two is 'a matter of degree',[31] and ultimately the passive consciousness, too, is found to become unified independently of external influences. The kind of unity that pervades all consciousnesses can then be described as in the following quotation: 'The fundamental fact is the unifying action which is the *direct union* of the content of consciousness'[32] (italic added). Using the imagery of an axis, Nishida writes: Consciousness adheres to the axis composed of similar ideas and emotions.[33] This is to say that no heterogeneous element is involved in the act of unification.

It is necessary to recall Nishida's interpretation of James. He thought that James attributed to a factor, the 'hinge', external to consciousness, the function of unifying it. In Nishida's inverted vision of the Western philosophies, the 'direct union' was thus postulated not by James, but by his Rationalist opponents. When Nishida speaks of 'direct union', he should not be interpreted as supporting James's theory. For the same reason, Nishida's 'active consciousness', for which unity is an internal occurrence, must be viewed as having no relation to Empiricist theories of knowledge. In fact, Nishida derides Empiricist schools by comparing their position to the cultivation of inviable seeds. Such seeds do not germinate no matter how much external stimulus they receive.[34]

If consciousness achieves unity independently from the external stimulus of the empirically observable world, is it also free from other influences comparable to the one that the Rationalists claimed, namely, the concept-giving eternal principle? That this is by no means the case is shown by this statement of Nishida's: 'The unifying function of consciousness is not ruled by time . . . [but] at the base of consciousness exists a certain immutable one that is transcendent outside time.'[35] Nishida lets us know what this 'certain immutable one' is: 'At work behind reality (consciousness!) is *tōitsuteki arumono*.'[36] Furthermore, 'the unifying action does not come into existence caused by reality, but reality comes into existence by the unifying action'.[37] Finally, and most revealingly, Nishida conceives of a law that regulates the union of matter such as atoms, which necessarily have a 'function'. The law says: 'When one thing functions, it always works upon another thing, and there must be a third thing that unites them and enables them to work upon each other.'[38]

By internal and direct union of consciousness, therefore, Nishida actually means that man's consciousness is acted upon by a unifying influence, not entirely of its own, and that this latter influence originates in *tōitsuteki arumono*. It is inescapable, then, that despite Nishida's refusal to call it either the unifier or the unified, *tōitsuteki arumono* is the 'certain unifying one'. It is the reason that the objects reflected on consciousness are transformed from mere sensations into thoughts and concepts.

This interpretation is supported by Nishida's comparison of the unifying power of *tōitsuteki arumono* with *ri*, 'something that people believe to exist in the universe'.[39] Since he writes *ri* in the Chinese character 理 (li) he no doubt means by it the cosmic principle of Neo-Confucian metaphysics. According to Nishida, *ri* is an independent and self-sufficient entity that is beyond change by 'time, place and man'. It is also ubiquitous in the universe, and its presence 'brings into existence' all things, material as well as spiritual. *Ri* 'creates'. Man, therefore, knows the principle that governs the universe 'by means of the *ri* that is inside of him'. As for its unifying action, Nishida makes some unambiguous statements. First, '*ri* is the unifying force of all things and at the same time the unifying force of consciousness'. Second, 'the footprints of the activity of *ri* control the perceptual union of man's subjective consciousness'. Finally, 'the unifying force of the objective world and the unifying force of the subjective consciousness is the same ... *ri*'. If *ri* is the universal unifier that works upon man's consciousness and *tōitsuteki arumono* is compared to it, then the latter must also be such a 'unifying one' that generates unity *for* consciousness.

Although Neo-Confucian metaphysics is helpful in understanding Nishida's thought, how can the unifier be described not by analogy but in and of itself? Nishida uses two kinds of language for this purpose. In the one he writes that, in addition to possessing all the properties of *ri* enumerated above, the unifier is the self-activating, ceaseless and eternal activity.[40] Being a pure activity it does not reflect upon itself and, in this sense, possesses no consciousness.[41] It is the only cause for the universe to become what it is: the self-manifestation of the only reality in myriad things which, by virtue of the unifier, exist not individually and separately but united among themselves, related to each other. The universe is 'the eternal activity of the only reality',[42] the unifier.

In the other language, which contains Nishida's last word on the subject, the unifier is God, the great nothingness, creator of all things, and the universal spirit that also stays 'hidden in the small bosom' of man. Nishida designates three areas in which God's unifying action affects man: learning, art and morality. Because of God's inherent presence in man's intellectual faculty, man can investigate and understand the truth about the universe. For the same reason, man expresses the 'great spirit' in his art. In the realm of morality, man loves others and becomes united with them because God in him is the unifying power among all men. Nishida ends Book II on a messianic note: 'God is cosmic unity, infinite love, infinite joy, and peace.'[43]

The Self. The last area of Nishida's theory to be examined is the self. There are three modes: man's self, nature's self and *tōitsuteki* self. Nishida rejects purely positivistic psychological theories which, according to him, maintain that the self of man is 'merely a mass of ideas and emotions'.[44] Like consciousness, Nishida's human self partakes of a cosmic order. As such it receives two levels of explanation. In relation to the actual events of consciousness, be they perception or thought, the self is 'the action to compare and differentiate the objects' that cause these events.[45] In the cosmic context the same self is the manifestation of the unifying force of the universal reality; it is 'the eternal and immutable power'.[46] Compared with the universal reality, man's self is small. It has the capacity to grow larger, however, and, within limits, to become more like its cosmic counterpart. The small self upholds the universal reality as the ideal of its development.[47]

Nishida attributes 'a kind of self' to nature, too.[48] His conception is teleological. 'Every form and movement of a natural object is closely and meaningfully related to the overall end of that object.'[49] For example, every anatomical organ of an animal is designed to conform to the purpose of its existence. The final goal of a thing and its conditions in the evolutionary process are co-ordinated because the thing is governed by a unifying power. This unifier is the self of this thing and the same cosmic unifier that appears in consciousness. Nishida finds the self not only in animals, but also in plants and inorganic objects. In his eye even a piece of crystal has a self common to the self of man.[50]

The puzzle of Nishida's theory of the self is what he calls *tōitsuteki* self. As in the case of *tōitsuteki arumono*, Nishida's statements on *tōitsuteki* self are open to various interpretations. One might contend that it is adjectival in nature, appended to the other modes of the self which are characterised by an internal unity – *tōitsu*. This interpretation seems plausible in the light of the statement that *tōitsuteki* self is 'not the unknowable something that has no relation to our consciousness but the unifying action of our consciousness'.[51] On the other hand, how should one interpret Nishida's utterance that 'even a plant and an animal . . . must be considered as a manifestation of *tōitsuteki* self'?[52] Or note his oblique mention of the relationship of this mystifying self to a bronze statue that 'expresses our ideal . . ., the unifying force of our ideal'.[53] Viewed as a whole, Nishida's arguments reveal that *tōitsuteki* self is the Self written large. It is the cosmic Self of which man's self is a part, and it is the ideal in accordance with which the small self 'develops and realises itself'.[54]

If Nishida's theory of the self sounds animistic, he saves it from primitive atavism by introducing the idea of self-conscious spirituality. Spirituality is also the unifying action of reality which, like the self of man, compares and differentiates the objects of unification. It is, however, the unifying action transformed into a spiritual phenomenon as the self 'takes it out and poses it against the object of its operation'.[55] The capacity to 'take out' the unifying action is equivalent to the awareness which the self has of its own unifying action. The more fully developed this awareness, the more spiritual the self. The self of the unifying action is in a tree, but the tree is not aware of it.[56] Likewise, an infant's self resembles that of nature, and it is only after the child grows and becomes 'aware of his mind distinguished from nature'[57] that he attains spirituality which is conscious of itself.

'ZEN NO KENKYU': GREEN'S CONTRIBUTIONS

It is now possible to show how Nishida took the material and structure of his thought from Green. Green's first noteworthy contribution was methodology. He proposed that observation of consciousness through self-reflection was the necessary, although not the only, means of acquiring knowledge of the eternal spiritual principle. Emphasis on an empirical method to arrive at a metaphysical truth was his significant concession to science and was the means by which he tried to harmonise science with his unswerving faith in God. In *Zen* Nishida displayed a keen methodological awareness, although he did not practise the skill as rigorously as did Green. This awareness as well as Nishida's dependence on consciousness must primarily be attributed to his reading of the *Prolegomena*.

Second, the idea that consciousness was the 'self-development' of *tōitsuteki arumono* was a thinly disguised translation of the fundamental idea of Green's philosophy, which held that man's consciousness was the 'self-realisation' of an eternal spiritual principle called 'a self-distinguishing consciousness'. By the latter term, Green conveyed the notion that the eternal principle was itself a consciousness which 'distinguished itself' from natural phenomena, presenting them to itself for recognition.[58] What is loosely called 'our' consciousness, according to Green, might mean either of two things.[59] One is 'a function of the animal organism, which is being made ... a vehicle of the eternal consciousness'. The other is the eternal consciousness itself 'making the animal organism its vehicle and subject to certain limitations in so doing, but retaining its essential characteristic as independent of time ...'. Consciousness in the first sense, which varies from moment to moment, is a phenomenon as well as 'media for the realisation of an eternal consciousness'.

While rejecting Green's view that the eternal principle had consciousness, Nishida nevertheless adopted its twin concept that the immutable one was the condition of cognition. That is, being 'self-realisation' of the Eternal Consciousness, man's consciousness carried in it the action of the parent consciousness that united into knowledge the natural phenomena which it perceived. In Green's own words, the non-natural consciousness, 'as so far realised in or communicated to us ... constitutes our knowledge, with the relations, characteristic of knowledge, into which time does not enter'.[60] In Nishida's parlance, consciousness attains 'direct union' because at its 'bottom' exists 'a transcendent and immutable something'. Certainly, Nishida spoke differently from Green. Whereas Green stated that consciousness was *not* 'a phenomenon among the phenomena' which it unified,[61] Nishida argued that consciousness *was* a phenomenon *par excellence*. In substance, however, Nishida's position did not differ from Green's once he argued that consciousness was as much outside nature as inside it.

Nishida's metaphysics of consciousness also contained Green's adaptation of Kant's famous dictum: 'Understanding makes nature.' To reiterate, Nishida held that natural phenomena were conscious phenomena ensuing from the unity of consciousness. According to Green, Kant's doctrine meant that it is through understanding that there is for *us* an objective world, that we *conceive* an order of nature. Understanding 'makes nature in the sense of enabling us to conceive that there is such a thing'.[62] In adopting Kant, Green substituted 'consciousness' for 'understanding' on the implicitly stated grounds that consciousness was a generic activity inclusive of understanding. From the vantage-point of Kant's Idealism innovated by Green, nature existed only in relation to consciousness. The proposition was rewritten by Nishida as: Natural phenomena exist only as conscious phenomena.

Green's ideas on 'the objective world', the universe, were also faithfully installed in *Zen*, especially in Nishida's view that nothing in the universe exists in isolation and that there is an unchangeable relationship among phenomena. One of Green's original ideas, as opposed to those adopted from his predecessors, including Kant and Hegel, was the interpretation of facts as relationships among things. The objective world which man's mind, the subject, knew was for Green a single and all-inclusive system of relations among things. The universe consists of unalterably related objects, and if reality is seen in the light of this fact, its essence is definable as relations. In this formulation Green emphasised the importance of the 'unalterableness' of the relationship as much as 'relatedness'. If anything is real, the qualities ascribed to it are unchangeable, and if reality is truly real, its relationship is *always the same*.[63] Nishida's writings reflect these views in such statements as 'reality consists in mutual relationship' and 'there is an unalterable relationship among phenomena'.

It can also be argued persuasively that Nishida's concept of the self – the term as well as the notion of the Unifying Self – derived from Green's Universal Consciousness to which was attributed an ego, the Self. Similarly, the idea that man's self was a 'manifestation' of the eternal self came from Green. Green thought that, along with the capacity to distinguish itself from nature, the spiritual principle trans-mitted its Selfness to man's consciousness. Consequently, man not only became capable of distinguishing himself from *his* natural surroundings but received the faculty to know himself, to make himself the object of his own consciousness. This faculty of self-consciousness was special to him in the sense that it was absent in both inorganic nature and in organisms other than man; it was his hallmark as a spiritual being.[64]

Nishida used the theory of self-distinguishing consciousness to differentiate the self of man from the self of nature. In so doing, he used the words *chūshō* and *jikaku*, which translate as 'take-out' and 'self-awareness'.[65] As quoted earlier, man 'takes out the unifying action, the self, and poses it against the object which is being unified'; the statement reflects the self-distinguishing function of Green's 'consciousness'. This interpretation is supported by Nishida's own admission that by being 'abstracted', the self acquired a 'self-conscious' spirituality that separated it from other forms of the self, just as Green's consciousness differentiated itself from the animal kingdom by its self-distinguishing action.

Finally, if one wonders why, in Book II, Nishida lavishly used poetry to support his philosophy, one might consult the first few paragraphs of the Introduction to the *Prolegomena*. There Green admires the Romantic poets for grasping the truth far more accurately than the philosophers he criticised, citing Tennyson, Browning and Wordsworth. For essentially the same reason, Nishida cites Goethe, Schiller and Heine. Just as Green was not a poet simply because he mentioned Tennyson's *In Memoriam*, so Nishida was not a poet because he appealed to 'poetic truth'.[66] He sought to use poetry to facilitate reasoning and understanding, but, unfortunately, by so doing he created rather than solved problems, as in the case of his reference to Goethe's *Das Veilchen*.[67]

THE MEANING OF 'PURE EXPERIENCE'

If in writing Book II of *Zen no kenkyū* Nishida depended heavily on Idealism, on its various streams as they converged in Green, what place in his thought did James's psychological theory of 'pure experience' fill? To answer this question, one must restate James's position and the meaning of pure experience in that context.

In reviewing James's struggles against Idealism it is worth noting that, in the Empiricist camp, his enemies were widely spread (he was no more sympathetic with the Mills than with Hume) while among the Rationalists the immediate target of his criticism was none other than Green. James was only seven years younger than Green, and, when, in the 1880s, he began to formulate his theories, he was keenly aware of Green's influence upon the philosophical circle of Oxford. In his lecture at Oxford in 1908, twenty-six years after Green's death, James was still objecting adamantly to Green: to Green's refusal to admit that there was any relation between one sensation and another; to his insistence that sensations contained in themselves no element that made them susceptible to cognition; to his recourse to a 'self-distinguishing' absolute and eternal mind to relate sensations into a meaningful whole.[68] These and more came under James's attack. Green's critique of Locke was 'pathetic', and his theory of knowledge a tissue of 'verbality' with no benefit of empirical investigation.[69]

James's objection to Rationalism found a highly appreciative reception in Book I, 'Pure Experience', of *Zen no kenkyū*. Referring to James, Nishida held at one point: 'Abstract concepts are not of the transcendental ...; they are a kind of feeling.'[70] At another point, Nishida invoked James again: 'If we consider the so-called fringe of consciousness as a fact of direct experience, the consciousness of various relations among empirical facts also ... falls into this category (of direct experience).'[71] At yet another juncture, Nishida extrapolated James's observation on the conjunctive relation of consciousness, concluding that 'thought, traditionally regarded as a spiritual function categorically different from pure experience', was in fact 'a kind of pure experience'.[72] Nishida's most succinct statement of Jamesian anti-Rationalism was the following:

> Ordinarily it is believed that pure experiences acquire meaning and become discernment when they are united by an objective reality. Seen from the standpoint of the theory of pure experience, however, we are unable to leave the confines of pure experience. Both meaning and discernment arise from the union of the present consciousness with the consciousness of the past.[73]

The 'objective reality' which Nishida rejected in this passage was the extrasensory cognitive agent 'ordinarily' essential to the Rationalist theory of knowledge.

Nishida's rapprochement with 'Radical Empiricism' extended to the theory of will as well. In a Jamesian vein Nishida contended that will was an 'experience of the shifting of attention from one mental image to another'.[74] Seen in this light, will was a mode of consciousness and differed from its other modes only by being the most prevailing one. As for its freedom, the much-debated topic in the philosophy of the West, Nishida asserted that it was free only in the sense that man *felt* free when there was no obstruction between his will and its realisation.[75] In point of its relationship to moral imperatives, Nishida maintained that the law of reason, on the one hand, and man's desire (that is, the tendency of will desiring fulfilment), on the other, derived from the same 'root'. To support this view he called upon the Oxford critic of Rationalism, F. C. S. Schiller, who suggested that axiomatic postulates had the same 'mode of genesis' as 'the crudest cravings of individual caprice' devoid of a transcendental base.[76]

It might seem that Nishida was either confused or that he changed his mind between the writing of Book II in 1906 and Book I two years later. That he did not exactly change his mind was shown by the continued presence of *toitsuteki arumono* in his thought. The old theme appeared under various labels, such as 'the latent', 'the universal', and 'the unconscious', but it unfailingly held the same unifying capacity discussed above. Compared with Book II, Book I underplayed the extra-conscious character of the 'unifying certain one'. None the less, Nishida's unifier never became a matter *of* empirical consciousness in the same way that James's 'fringe' was *of* it. How subtly but decidedly Rationalist Nishida's conception of the unifier was can be seen in the following passage, taken from the chapter which contends that 'pure experience is thought itself': 'Viewed from concrete thoughts, concepts possess universality not because they are abstractions of similar qualities, as is commonly said, but because they contain that power which unifies concrete facts. Hegel, too, stated that the universe is the spirit of the concrete. The unifying power which is at work at the basis of pure experience is none other than the universality of concepts. Pure Experience, therefore, is the self-realisation of the so-called universal.'[77]

By holding that 'the concrete is the spirit of the universal', Hegel did not mean that the concrete existed logically prior to the universal, and Nishida knew Hegel's position. Nishida also knew that Hegel's unflinchingly Idealist deductionism, no less than Green's philosophy, contradicted James's psychological theories. Is it possible that warring philosophical factions can both be right? Nishida obviously believed that such was the case. Instead of thinking that Radical Empiricism and 'Radical Idealism' conflicted with each other, Nishida viewed their relationship as complementary; what convention held to be irreconcilable could, in fact, be reconciled. Nishida's point of conciliation was 'pure experience'.

Nevertheless, Nishida's 'pure experience' presented in Book I bore little resemblance to that of James. Whereas James pitted his against the supervention of the rational concept-giving Principle, Nishida conceived purity of experience merely as 'the strict unity of consciousness in the concrete', no matter whence the unity rose.[78] By 'unity', moreover, Nishida did not envision the joining of the consciousness of one moment with that of another, as James did. Nishida's 'unity of consciousness' meant the kind of union of the knower and the known wherein existed only the activity of the knower, who had neither consciousness of, nor reflection upon, his own activity. It was a state of consciousness of the knower's utter self-oblivion. To Nishida the consciousness of a new-born baby epitomised pure experience because it did not even differentiate light from darkness.[79] As another example, one who mastered the art of tea ceremony can make and serve tea unconsciously but meticulously following every rule prescribed for a perfect ceremony. For such an accomplished tea master, there is neither self-consciousness nor the thought of his action during the ceremony, but simply action, 'pure experience', itself.[80] Nishida's 'pure experience', therefore, was synonymous with 'pure action'.

'Unity of consciousness' and 'purity of experience' were not events antithetical to that which James regarded as beyond experience and, for that reason, non-existent. They merely represented the opposites of thought and knowledge, the very elements that came to exist in James's case through the conjoining of consciousness. Seen from Nishida's vantage-point, James's 'pure experience' merely referred to 'that which can be experienced', consciousness as well as its relation.

Nishida's construct of pure experience included the idea of intellectual intuition, which incorporated into pure experience what James believed was beyond experience and non-existent. If pure experience is the complete fusion of the object and the subject of knowledge, intellectual intuition is its most 'deepened and enriched' form.[81] By means of this rarified capacity, man, the knower, experiences the known, 'the so-called ideal, or that which is ordinarily said to be above experience'. In the moment of intellectual intuition, there is 'neither the I nor the thing but only one world, one spectacle' of the total fusion of the I, the knower, with the objective reality, 'the mystical something'. After the breakdown of the fusion this 'something emerges into the consciousness as something intimately and unmistakably known to the I.[82] This pure experience is also a mode of 'self-realisation of the so-called universal',[83] and to experience this mode is to know the universal. As the opening sentence of *Zen no kenkyū* reads, 'to experience is to know things directly', and the Unifier itself is no exception to this method of knowing.

Nishida's view that the philosophies of Green and James were not contradictory but complementary could hold on the assumption that James's theory proved the direct union of consciousness but did not disprove Green's Universal Consciousness. To use James's illuminating analogy, Radical Empiricism was a 'mosaic philosophy' in which the pieces were held together by their edges without the support of the bedding that could be compared to the Absolute.[84] Nishida's philosophical exercises meant that although James showed how the pieces of the mosaic did not need a bedding to hold them together, he had not demonstrated that the bedding did not exist. Those who believed in the bedding, therefore, could presumably sustain their position without contesting James's stand on 'the edges'.

THE IMPORTANCE OF 'PURE EXPERIENCE'

If Nishida's obliteration of the distinction between the subject and the object of knowledge echoed Hegel's philosophy, his attempt to synthesise Idealism in general and Rationalist epistemology in particular with Jamesian Radical Empiricism was certainly original. The students of his philosophy who praise him for originality may be credited for their insight if it is this to which they are referring. Whether or not by being original Nishida's philosophy was also true is beyond the capacity of this writer to determine. Further inquiry, therefore, may be directed merely to the question of why Nishida tried such a synthesis, which Western philosophy could acknowledge as possible only if one believed the dictum that absolute opposites are absolutely identical. To ask this question is to reconsider *Zen no kenkyū* in relation to the Meiji scholarship on Green, which leads us to the third observation made at the beginning of this chapter.

Meiji writings on Green generally viewed his philosophy as consisting of two separable entities: ethics, and ontology and epistemology. On the whole the Japanese discarded the latter and used the former extensively. However, they raised two objections.[85] First, they maintained that Green's proof for the existence of the Self-Distinguishing Consciousness was invalid because it contradicted the law of causality. Second, they argued that his theory of knowledge touched only on half of the truth by examining relationships among things and ignoring the things themselves. The first objection resulted from the rigorous application of the law of causality to what was believed to be the trans-experiential realm of thought; the second stemmed from the first as well as from adherence to Kant's philosophy, which dealt with things in exclusion of their mutual relationship.

A few writers took exception to this separation of ethics from metaphysics. The most notable was Nakajima Rikizo, who acquiesced in the prevailing criticism against Green; in fact, it was he who predisposed students against the 'inadequacies' of Green's philosophy.[86] But he stopped short of rejecting Green's fundamental metaphysical presupposition, the eternal Self. Unlike his own students, who came to write some of the earliest Japanese works on Green, and many of those who followed, Nakajima steered a middle course. He urged philosophers to formulate a theory of knowledge capable not only of providing the existence of the Absolute, but also of accounting for things and their relationship in connection with man's cognitive faculty.[87]

In studying Green's *Prolegomena* and trying thereby to make a place for himself as a philosopher, Nishida had a choice of joining the separatists or adopting Nakajima's course. He sided with the latter. As mentioned above, his commitment to Idealism was finalised in 'Does *priori* Knowledge Exist?', written two years after he published a summary of the *Prolegomena*. With this commitment he faced the task of denying the law of causality and/or of finding a way of explaining the genesis and nature of knowledge in terms acceptable to positivists.

James's Radical Empiricism thus entered Nishida's Idealist picture. In all likelihood his discovery of James was accidental (a friend happened to write from America calling his attention to James's *The Varieties of Religious Experiences*).[88] Once the discovery was made, however, James's psychological findings and, in a perverse way, his philosophical outlook itself proved congenial to the concerns caused by Nakajima.

The kinship between Nishida and James lay in the irony of James's position. Despite the ruthless debunking of Green, James could ill afford to ignore his adversary's contributions. He candidly admitted that the world owed to Green 'more than anyone' the recognition that knowledge about things was knowledge of their relations.[89] Needless to say, James's interest was not confined to the 'relations' as such. The point is that acknowledgement of Green's contribution must be read in conjunction with the major concern of his works, such as *The Stream of Consciousness*, in which he emphatically directed his inquiry into the 'conjunctive and disjunctive relation of consciousness'. His opposition to Green came virtually to form the substance of his philosophy, the feat achieved by turning around Green's Rationalist theory to stand on an Empiricist ground, in much the same way that Marx claimed to set Hegel's dialectics on its feet.

Ultimately, Nishida did not desert Idealism in favour of James's psychological theory. Yet it is not correct to suggest, as Takeuchi did, that Nishida was inclined to reject, rather than accept, James.[90] Paradoxically, Nishida fully availed himself of the radically empiricist theory of consciousness to buttress Idealism against positivistic objections: James *scientifically* proved the relations among things which

Green, in the opinion of his Meiji critics, merely fancied to exist, much to their dissatisfaction.

How did Nishida handle the law of causality, which caught Green in the dilemma of asserting that human consciousness was the effect of the universal consciousness and then finding that the universal had no cause? Nishida simply negated the validity of causal thinking itself, demoting it from the status of law to that of man's 'habit of thought'.[91] Man formulated the law on the basis of the recurrence of similar events under certain conditions. Being a mental artifice, this formulation itself was the function of the unifying action of the universal. In short, Nishida substituted for causal law pure experience in the form of intellectual intuition.

Incidentally, in the end, Nishida stood on the same ground with Green concerning the evidence of God. In the writings to which neither Nishida nor his contemporaries paid any attention, Green admitted that God's existence was a matter of faith and could not be proven scientifically.[92] For Green, God was something he personally lived as a schoolboy at Rugby, not in the school's chapel, but on solitary walks in the green meadows near by. For him it was the nature of faith to believe in that which could not be scientifically or even logically proven. In fact, he believed that faith itself was evidence of God. On his part Nishida contended that to decry God's existence was the mark of mediocrity and spiritual shallowness. Those who had an eye to see could 'witness' God, and that eye was the soul to experience God directly.[93]

CONCLUSION

To point out Nishida's indebtedness to Green is not to deny the importance of other philosophers in the formulation of his thought. I harbour no objection to the conventional interpretation that Kant and Hegel, on the one hand, and Bergson and James, on the other, contributed to the making of the philosopher Nishida. My point is rather that, by neglecting Green's influence, one misses an important link in the evolution of Nishida's philosophy.

Of course, one might argue that, being an English exponent of German Idealism, Green can properly be subsumed under Kant and Hegel. In the context of Nishida's early thought as related to these Western thinkers, however, such a position undermines a full under-standing of Nishida's writings. Not only was Green significantly different from the Germans, but that difference became a point of departure for Nishida's philosophy. Even if Nishida himself did, in fact, believe that Green was a mere 'rehashing' of Kant and Hegel, his oversight does not excuse the same mistake on the part of students of his thought.

It does remain puzzling why Nishida refused even to mention Green's name in *Zen no kenkyū*. Whether or not he genuinely believed that Green was an English copy of Hegel might be determined if one examined his knowledge of Hegel at that point. Unfortunately that is a separate assignment. Another possibility might be to delve deeply into Nishida's psychology, but that, too, is another of the many areas of study this chapter refrains from entering.[94]

Part II
Development, Authority and Conformity

3 A Non-traditional View of Japanese Modernisation

Ezra F. Vogel

As someone concerned with changes in Japanese society since the Second World War I have been struck by the adaptability of Japanese society and by the capacity of its leaders to introduce new practices that quickly become 'the Japanese way'. I am persuaded that many so-called Japanese practices, like permanent employment and quality control circles, are better understood as conscious efforts to respond to new problems than as reflections of tradition. Groups of government and business élites broader than current office-holders pay close attention to changing circumstances and become actively involved in the process of defining patterns of thought and organisation to respond to the needs of the society as a whole.

In the Tokugawa (1600–1868) and Meiji (1868–1912) periods the dominant patterns of thought and institutions were not so much reflections of tradition as conscious efforts to cope rationally with the problems of governance. While some have argued that Japan's strength is based on the adaptability of its tradition, I would venture to say that Japan's strength is based on its tradition of adaptability. A few examples from Japanese history illustrate this theme.

STRATEGIES OF TOKUGAWA RULE

Once Tokugawa Ieyasu gained hegemony over the other feudal clans the key problem was to establish a pattern of rule to maintain effective control over them. The strategies that evolved, while not entirely new, were none the less extraordinarily well adapted to this basic problem. Allies were given land at critical locations, while the largest potential rivals were located at greater distances from the Tokugawa heartland. The Tokugawa themselves kept direct control over key localities.

Recognising the limits of their effective rule, however, they gave the clans considerable leeway to manage affairs within their own jurisdiction, just as superiors in contemporary Japanese organisations allow lower-level sections a great deal of discretion. This method of rule avoided the intrusiveness characteristic of many centralised governments, which in the long run interfere with efficient governance. At the same time, by requiring the *daimyō* to leave their families hostage in Edo whenever they were in their home fiefs and to spend every other year in Edo, the Tokugawa enforced a brilliant system for preserving their hegemony over the other clans.

The handling of foreigners likewise was not so much a result of traditional behaviour as it was a consciously developed method to cope with the problem of order. When the European Christians first arrived, the central government was weak and could not easily restrain them. Once the government was centralised, and it became clear that Christians could be disruptive to rule, because opponents of the status quo rallied to their side, they were of course banned. It is little wonder that the state should have banished Christianity, which taught a belief in a supernatural God who could challenge state authority. By limiting foreign residence to a single port at a great distance from Edo, however, the Tokugawa devised a safe way to continue gathering information about and exchanging goods with the rest of the world.

The enforcement of a fixed four-class social system also assured stability. As one Confucian scholar wrote

> There are four classes of men: samurai, peasants, artisans, and merchants. The samurai use their minds, the peasants and those below them use their muscles. Those who use their minds are superior; those who use their muscles are inferior. Those who use their minds have broad visions, high ideals, and profound wisdom. ... If these positions were reversed, there would be, at best, discontent in the land and, at worst, chaos.[1]

A further measure designed to promote a stable feudal social structure was the removal of the warrior class from the land and its relocation in castletowns. Although warriors preserved their right to carry swords, they were expected to apply themselves to the civil arts. Tokugawa Ieyasu, in the words of the official history of the Tokugawa period, 'realised early that the land could not be governed from a horse. ... Therefore, from the beginning he encouraged learning.'[2]

The kind of learning promoted by the Tokugawa shoguns – Chinese

Neo-Confucianism as developed by Chu Hsi – had been found to serve the cause of the stable state in Sung dynasty China. It is hard to imagine a teaching more appropriate for maintaining a stable feudal order. The fundamental virtue taught by Japanese Neo-Confucianism was loyalty of the subject to his lord. At the same time that teachers were given honoured positions and philosophers supported by the rulers, persons who expressed heterodox thought were reported by censors in order to catch potentially disruptive ideas before they sprouted.

Neo-Confucianism was clearly oriented to answer the needs of the state for a rational theory of rule. The role of the state was discussed by many Confucian philosophers, including Ogyū Sorai (1666–1728), who, citing the case of a peasant driven by poverty to abandon his mother for the priesthood, argued that in order to maintain order the state should deal with the basic problems of poverty that caused individuals to become unfilial. The most fundamental issue for samurai scholars like Ogyū, in short, was social harmony, not individual morality.

Tokugawa rulers thus devised a social system, a philosophy and a set of political practices that constituted excellent solutions to the basic problems they confronted in ruling Japan. Their efforts could be interpreted as reflecting strong ideological leanings, but they could also be seen as highly rational responses to the problems of governing Japan in that era.

THE STRATEGY OF MODERN JAPAN

It was only in the late Tokugawa period that a strong sense of modern-type nationalism, with very deep roots among the people, began to develop in Japan. Modern nationalism requires a high level of aware-ness of cultural distinctiveness. It is heightened by a sense of threat that spreads throughout the population and leads to a broader basis of political participation. This sense of nationalism became widespread in Japan shortly before the middle of the nineteenth century. It could be argued that the new outside threats stimulated a revival of traditional ideology, centred on Shintō beliefs about the sacredness and unique-ness of Japan, but it could be argued as well that the outside threat led to a willingness to change ways of thinking and adapt to crisis by developing a more modern form of nationalism. Meiji leaders, despite their considerable nostalgia for the past and their attempts to preserve the Japanese spirit, in fact were even more concerned with developing a rational response to the new threat.

Leaders in both Edo and in the major outer clans, despite the official policy of seclusion, closely followed the Opium War and quickly responded to the shocking British victory over China by increasing their intelligence-gathering activities and taking steps to strengthen Japan's defences. The initial reluctance to comply with Commodore Perry's demand for trade in 1853 likewise can be seen as essentially a rational response – rejecting foreign pressure. The Japanese yielded only when they had no choice, and then used whatever leverage they had to minimise the foreign impact.

In comparative perspective, one of the most striking attributes of the Meiji leaders was their willingness to jettison one of their most basic values, loyalty to the clan, for the sake of allegiance to the nation. Few clans offered forcible resistance to the abolition of the *han*. In contrast, state loyalty at the time of the American Revolutionary War, while hardly as deep and long-lasting as clan loyalty in Japan, proved remarkably resistant to central authority. When one considers how reluctant Americans are to transfer even a few functions of state government to the national level in matters of education, the Japanese flexibility in doing away with tradition is all the more striking.

The Japanese were similarly willing to give up the most fundamental features of their traditional social structure, the formal class system. In how many countries have the members of the leading class been willing to renounce the privileges of their entire class? To be sure, some samurai resisted the abolition of their prerogatives, and they were 'bought off' with payments. But even when their payments were converted to bonds and lost their value, resistance to the new state was surprisingly limited.

A similar pattern was to follow after the Second World War. At that time, one of the most fundamental features of the traditional social structure was the relationship between landlords and tenants in the countryside. Yet landlords acquiesced in the land reforms, which required them to sell some of their land at low price to their tenants. More remarkable, their tenants continued to treat them as prominent members of the village. To be sure, land reform was greatly facilitated by the authority of the Allied Occupation. None the less, even after the Occupation ended, the former landlord class peacefully accepted its losses, just as the daimyo had, and unlike the case in China, where hundreds of thousands died during the course of land reform.

Some might argue that, despite the abolition of the class system, the Meiji government did not adopt a system that was fully and formally democratic in the Western sense. The principle of élitism remained.

People still had duties, not rights, and bureaucrats were 'above the clouds', not subject to popular approval. The constitution was legitimated not as representing the will of the people but as a 'gift' from the Emperor. Yet, at the very least, as Ronald P. Dore and others have argued, there was a fundamental shift from élitism based on inherited status to élitism based on meritocracy, and in Meiji even the content of what constituted élitist meritocracy underwent radical change. In contrast, Americans have clung far more to their tradition of democratic forms even when it has become clear that some more sharply meritocratic élite system is necessary to attract the ablest people to high levels of government and to perform the complex functions of governing the modern state.

Admittedly, a traditional respect for learning formed the basis of the search for knowledge and the respect for education during the Meiji period. Yet this masks fundamental changes in the content of education. The willingness to renounnce old kinds of learning and beliefs and to accept foreign learning, not only in science and technology but also in organisation and practice, cannot be explained by reference to Japanese tradition, unless it is the tradition of flexible accommodation to new circumstances challenging the polity.

It is true that there have been ongoing debates about the need to preserve tradition, and the process of learning has been marked by historical accidents and peculiar distortions. Yet Japanese in every walk of life have shown a continual willingness to abandon their traditional way of doing things and to adopt what appeared to be more modern and efficient ways of bringing the fruits of civilisation to the Japanese, whether it was the constitution, the central government administration, the military, the school system or the technology of industry. Although they never veered from the Meiji goal of 'enriching the country and strengthening the military', they were always willing to reorganise, to readjust lower level loyalties, and to change customs in pursuit of these goals.

This willingness to change can also be seen in the realm of commerce. Though commerce had grown considerably during the Tokugawa period, merchant activity had been carefully circumscribed under the feudal order. The new freedom and know-how derived from the West during the Meiji period led to vastly new ways of organising commercial activity, also with remarkably little resistance. In mining and manufacturing the Japanese bought not simply new technology, but entirely different patterns of organisation and thinking. Former samurai entrepreneurs spearheaded entirely new combinations of organisation and finance; they developed entirely new patterns of staff development and training; and government leaders were ready to consider entirely new forms of sponsorship and organisation.

The innovative efforts of famous Meiji intellectual and business leaders like Fukuzawa Yukichi and Shibusawa Eiichi to strengthen the nation are especially noteworthy. Shibusawa readily tried new patterns of organisation like the joint-stock company to accumulate capital quickly. His readiness to put up his own funds when he judged an activity important for the national good, regardless of the risk or the profit margin, may have been in keeping with earlier feudal values, but in the light of these values it is perhaps more surprising that he and others accepted profit as an important goal and granted power to stockholders who would measure success by how much money a company was making.

Japanese companies undeniably were still bounded by a web of social and political obligations that contrasted with the raw independence of nineteenth-century American entrepreneurs. But it could be argued that this difference was less a reflection of tradition than it was a product of latecomer development, where government and banks typically played a larger role in financing priority sectors, making entrepreneurs inevitably bound to them.

Japanese and Western scholars have demonstrated numerous other examples of conscious problem-solving among business leaders. Even permanent employment and the seniority system were not simply remnants of tradition. They resulted from conscious efforts by employers to develop a stable supply of labour and to retain those who had been given expensive training in new techniques. Similarly, Japan's commitment to international trade, the key feature of 'the Japanese way', was hardly a simple reflection of historical patterns. It would be hard to describe Tokugawa thought as primarily oriented to international trade and the promotion of exports. Rather, the late nineteenth century was characterised by strenuous efforts to promote exports, necessitated by the trade imposed on Japan, and, in the face of crisis, the Japanese demonstrated great resourcefulness in uncovering markets for their goods. The adaptation to a colonial economy that accompanied Japan's late nineteenth-century empire-building was not only entirely new – Japan had never before been a colonial power – but it was different from the pattern of global marketing and global competitiveness that became the hallmark of Japanese economic expansion after the Second World War.

Another example of Japan's flexibility lies in the country's changing attitudes towards the military establishment. Considering Japan's firm commitment to developing a powerful military in the one hundred years from the middle of the nineteenth century until 1945, foreigners find it difficult to believe how completely Japanese have been willing to renounce a strong military after the Second World War. I have no doubt that if Japanese leaders and influential private citizens in Japan were thoroughly convinced of the need for a strong military, the Japanese would be willing to develop one again. But Japanese leaders are convinced that their country's interests are better served by a modest military budget. They do not believe there is a serious military threat as long as they remain firm but non-provocative towards the Soviet Union. A modest military does not provoke the anger of East Asian neighbours and therefore makes it possible to sell them Japanese products. It keeps down the tax burden of Japanese companies, thus helping their international competitiveness, and it enables national energies and resources to go where they are really important – to commercial competiton for global markets. There are admittedly disagreements about the level of desirable military spending, but more significant is the readiness of a world super-power to give up military institutions that had been central to the nation for almost a century and that had strong roots in the Tokugawa period and even beyond.

The process of democratisation of Japan since Meiji is often treated by historians as the struggle between different groups representing different ways of thought. It could also be seen as a problem of management of pluralism by national leaders. The central problem from their point of view has been how to maintain a central government with enough strength to govern effectively, while granting enough initiative to gain the involvement and commitment of broader sections of the public. The management of a transition from a more traditional autocratic government to a more modern democratic government has been difficult for most countries of the world, and it is possible that Japan could not have managed this transition itself without the Second World War and the Occupation. Yet until the military pressures became overwhelming in the 1930s Japanese leaders were working hard to guide this transition, and similar efforts to retain a strong state continued under the Occupation as well as after it. Again, the most salient feature of Japan's modern history is not the commitment to any traditional belief or to Western beliefs but the pragmatic commitment to finding a balance that would sustain a strong and effective nation.

Education policy offers an excellent example of this pattern of pragmatic accommodation to societal needs. Traditional Confucianism very much valued education, but it was for morality and ruling, and limited to a small élite of rulers. Since the Meiji period, education policy has been geared to preparing people to fill positions in modern society, where everyone needs literacy and, in addition, many kinds of specialists are required. The educational programmes developed in Japan represented a pragmatic response to these needs, and even the moral training in the school curriculum before the Second World War aimed at developing a dedicated citizenry rather than preserving any particular moral tradition.

Even at lower levels of society, where social practices have not resulted primarily from national policy, Japanese have shown a striking ability to form new social structures, like agricultural co-operatives, Parent–Teachers' Associations, political support groups, recreational associations and new religous associations to replace the kinship and village organisations which have now vastly declined in importance. Although these associations have roots in traditional society, their purpose, organisational structure, basis of membership and pattern of activities could hardly be described as traditional.

CONCLUSION

In short, it may be argued that the search by many Japanese and Western scholars for the traditional roots of Japanese modernisation has led to an over-emphasis on the importance and maintenance of Japanese tradition. If there is a continuity that characterises Japan in the course of modernisation it is the extraordinary adaptability of the society to rapid changes. Perhaps what needs to be explained is not the persistence of traditional ideas and patterns, but the source of the enduring adaptability. If one wishes to consider this in itself a tradition, it might be called the 'tradition of adaptability'.

One source of this 'tradition of adaptability' is the commitment of leaders in every group to communicate well with each other and to explore all possible options for solving their problems. Another is the commitment of the leaders to the general well-being of the members of the group and the confidence that the upgrading of the skills of the members is in the interest of the society as a whole. A third is the readiness to curtail individual self-assertiveness in the interests of the group as a whole while simultaneously allowing for lower-level initiatives.

Whatever the sources, surely what is striking in the course of Japan's modernisation during the last century is precisely this willingness of leaders everywhere to consider what needs to be done to promote the welfare of the Japanese people and to preserve a moral base of the society as a whole even if it means swiftly doing away with traditional social structures and patterns of thinking.

4 Women in the Silk-reeling Industry in Nineteenth-century Japan

Gail Lee Bernstein

As the first and only country in Asia to industrialise in the nineteenth century Japan holds special fascination for theorists of development.[1] Scholars have tried to explain Japan's industrialisation by exploring numerous factors such as the role of the government's industrial policy, the formation of a business ethos linked to nationalist ideology, and the availability of an agricultural surplus. However, few Western-language studies have focused on the crucial role of female labour in the early years of industrialisation from around the 1870s to the First World War.[2] During this period there were more women in the industrial labour force in Japan than in any other country for which we have comparable figures. In the textiles industry, which formed the basis of the Industrial Revolution, over 80 per cent of the workers were female.

The domination of female labour in the textiles industry and the distinguishing characteristics of that labour are two important elements that belong in any model of Japan's economic development. Why did women and, in particular, young rural women comprise the bulk of the labour force in the textiles industry? And how did this special aspect of the labour force affect both the course of Japan's industrial efforts and the position of female workers?

This study concentrates on the silk-reeling industry, which was critically important for Japan's industrialisation because silk thread was the major Japanese export commodity from the late nineteenth century to the 1920s and as such it earned valuable foreign currency used to purchase the raw materials and machinery needed to launch the mechanisation of other industries, such as cotton, iron and steel.[3] Initially, the Meiji government played a role in promoting silk, but the industry remained largely in private hands. By the turn of the century Japanese silk thread dominated the international market, and by the First World War, Japan was the world's largest exporter of silk.

In the success of the silk industry and therefore the success of Japan's

54

industrialisation, a crucial role was played by the young women who worked in the silk filatures, and in whose hands to a very great extent, the fate of the industry rested. Their presence in large numbers in the silk industry, while explained away by some authors in terms of their being 'cheap labour', 'unskilled labour', or 'excess daughters of the countryside', in fact had more complicated roots in the pre-Meiji period.

THE TECHNOLOGY OF SERICULTURE AND SILK REELING IN TOKUGAWA JAPAN

As early as the seventeenth century sericulture had become a thriving industry in the northern and western parts of the Kantō region (the area around present-day Saitama prefecture), and by early nineteenth century, silk markets flourished in Fukushima and Gumma prefectures.[4] Whereas commercial silk production before Tokugawa times had been mainly an urban activity confined largely to artisans in Kyoto and its environs, by the end of the Tokugawa period, it provided by-employment opportunities in rural areas where, unencumbered by guild restrictions and aided by low labour costs, farmers engaged in silk production to supplement their farm incomes.

Silk in most of its phases of rural production was almost exclusively women's work.[5] Although men planted and cultivated the mulberry trees whose leaves were fed to the silkworms and handled the marketing of the thread, women were responsible for raising the silkworms, reeling thread from the cocoons and weaving silk cloth.[6] In areas where the silk industry thrived, girls were trained to spin from the age of 6.[7] Indeed, in the Osaka area, both cotton- and silk-weaving skills 'became a prerequisite for marriage, with brides expected prior to marriage to weave their own clothing and bedding from yarns they had dyed themselves'.[8]

Women reeled and wove not only for home consumption, but for the *han* tribute and the market as well.[9] Consequently, they became recognised as valuable workers. Wage scales for female agricultural workers show that weaving ability in particular was a major determinant of women's wages.[10] According to the recollections of an eighteenth-century Buddhist monk, 'Buyers in the market, when they pick up a piece of cloth, can tell immediately that it was woven by so-and-so's wife or daughter in such and such a village'.[11]

By the end of the eighteenth century women were finding employment as reelers for merchants or neighbouring farmers. The earliest record of paid female labour is 1766, when thirty girls were brought together in one room and paid wages to reel for a *han* official in charge of promoting sericulture and mulberry cultivation in Kumamoto *han*.[12] Women's value as reelers was so great in cotton and silk regions that, as one edict complained, female farm and day labour became 'exceedingly scarce'.[13] In 1794 when the *han* government officially forbade women from working away from home in the town of Suwa (Nagano prefecture), merchants and farmers avoided the ban by giving women individual reels, which they used in their own homes on a contract basis.[14]

Experienced sericulturists and reelers were prized because each stage of the process of silk production demanded technical knowledge, patience and manual dexterity. The cocoon spun by a silkworm consists of a single filament that measures 1/100 of a millimetre thin and 1500 metres long. The reeler had to exercise great skill to unravel this delicate filament without breaking it. Pulling the filament from the cocoon, which was soaked in a basin of hot water to loosen the gluey substance that binds the fibres, she united it with several other filaments to make a single continuous thread. The finest grade of silk is 'like a spider web and a single pound would stretch 280 miles'.[15]

The level of endogenous technology in sericulture was both high and well diffused, including as it did systematic techniques of silkworm breeding, sanitation and temperature control in the breeding rooms, and 'uniquely Japanese' cultivation and harvest methods for mulberry-tree plantations.[16] Reeling equipment, however, was still primitive throughout much of the Tokugawa period, further challenging the manual dexterity of the silk worker. The oldest method of reeling, *doguri*, dates back to pre-Tokugawa times and involved winding thread on to a cylindrical piece of wood. The reeler turned the cylinder with the palm of her right hand while pulling filaments from the cocoon with her left. This simple device allowed her to spin only one thread at a time, and because her right hand was engaged at the reel, she could not add new thread while reeling. The thread produced was inevitably coarse, and it lacked that special quality of lustre so prized in fine silk, for the slow rotation of the reel prevented the thread from drying and caused filaments to stick together.[17]

Another method also developed prior to the Tokugawa period used a wooden frame with a handle affixed to it (*tebiki*). The reeler turned the frame with her left hand, while her right hand was free to add filaments without stopping. However, further improvement in both quality and quantity depended upon completely freeing the reeler from the need to turn the reel manually.

The first step in this direction came with the invention of the Gumma *zaguri* (sitting-type reel). This new method, developed in the Tokugawa period, used axles connected by cogwheels. The reeler rotated the thread frame by turning a handle attached to the large axle. The cogwheels facilitated a faster rotation, while the indirect rotation of the thread frame produced greater uniformity in the quality of the thread.[18]

Towards the very end of the Tokugawa period, and especially after 1858, when trade with the West began, entrepreneurs among the farm class began to experiment with various kinds of mechanical reels, including some driven by water wheels, to satisfy the new foreign market's demand for silk.[19] However, it was not until the mechanisation of the silk-reel industry in the early Meiji period that the reeler's hands were at last freed to concentrate on the task of uniting the filaments into a single thread and connecting it to the thread already on the reel.

Technological innovation seems to have originated among the male owners of silk-reel cottage industries, but throughout the history of silk reeling in rural Japan, the teachers of the new techniques, which usually consisted of relatively simple changes, were invariably experienced female reelers. Nagano producers in the Tokugawa period, for example, commonly hired female reelers from Gifu to teach reeling techniques. It was not unusual to bring a female reeler from another province or send one's own reelers, including one's wife, elsewhere to acquire new production methods. In the early Meiji period as well, women served as disseminators of new reeling methods.[20]

THE ORGANISATION OF LABOUR IN THE SILK-REELING INDUSTRY IN TOKUGAWA JAPAN

Although the invention of the *zaguri* encouraged farmers to expand their operations, the basic organisation of silk manufacture remained largely unchanged throughout the Tokugawa period. A typical reeling operation employed thirty to forty women.[21] Hired on a seasonal basis during the farm slack season, they lived at home and received an annual, fixed wage, usually working for the same neighbour over a period of many years.

Silk reeling under these conditions probably was not overly arduous. Employed close to home in familiar surroundings with other women from their village, reelers may have even welcomed the respite from the ordinary isolation of their lives. One account describes how, 'their sleeves tied back with a sash, and their white arms exposed', female reelers drew the attention of passers-by, 'which must have lifted their spirits, for they sang while working'.[22]

At least two separate sources claim that early female reelers were not from poor farm families, but from the 'owner-cultivator' class of peasants. Records of farmer-entrepreneurs list the women workers' names in such respectful terms as 'O-Hichi-sa' or 'O-tomo-sa', or in familiar terms like 'So-and-So's daughter'. Some names continue year after year, though others change, suggesting that some of the women were either no longer needed to supplement their family's wages or that, if young women, they stopped working after they were married. The age of the female reelers varied from the daughters to the wives and mothers of household heads.[23]

In the latter part of the Tokugawa period, work conditions in the silk-reeling industry began to change. More successful entrepreneurs, increasing the scope of their operations, hired larger numbers of female operatives. This was true of the weaving industry as well. In one case, in Kiryū (Gumma prefecture), a master weaver employed 132 weavers, fully half of whom came from outside the province. Girls worked away from home, indentured to employers under a system of bond labour, and returned home during slack times, a practice that paved the way for the factory system established in the middle of the Meiji period.[24]

This long history of sericulture in rural Japan suggests the reason why the silk industry was targeted for development in the early Meiji period and why rural girls were employed as the major part of the workforce. Japanese government and industrial leaders correctly estimated that Japanese raw silk could successfully compete on the international market with French, Italian and Chinese silk, and could bring in the foreign currencies urgently required to support the modernisation of other industries, such as cotton textiles and armaments. Starting with the establishment in 1872 of the Tomioka Silk Mill, which imported French equipment and hired French technicians to teach the latest techniques of silk reeling, the Meiji government advertised the important mission of promoting the nation's economic development through the export of silk thread – one of Japan's few export commodities.

Significantly the Tomioka pilot factory was located in Gumma prefecture, the centre of the traditional silk-reeling industry, and the government appealed to families in that prefecture and others where silk reeling flourished to supply female trainees. The women sent to Tomioka were mainly *shizoku* daughters whose families were already engaged in the silk industry in the rural areas and were eager to acquire the new technology. One famous example is Yokota Hide, author of *Tomioka Nikki*, whose father, a former samurai, had a silk business. At the age of 15, Hide donned her father's *haori* and *hakama* and went to work in Tomioka. A year later she returned to her native town to become a 'technical leader' of the newly established silk mill there. After her marriage she taught at her father-in-law's new filature, the Rokkōsha.[25] Other trainees were sent elsewhere in Japan to teach the new reeling techniques.[26] Before the pilot factory was sold to private hands it had trained five thousand women.[27]

It was natural for industrialists to rely on female labour for both cotton and silk production. This is not necessarily because women had 'nothing else to do' or because, as at least one scholar has argued, women were 'unskilled'.[28] On the contrary, women were hired because they had acquired the techniques of reeling as part of their farm and household responsibilities and, moreover, because even before the Meiji period, they had become accustomed to working for wages and even to migrating for work in the flourishing silk industry. Rural women were also accustomed to teaching reeling techniques to others. In their zeal to industrialise rapidly, private entrepreneurs drew on this experienced labour force to an extraordinary degree. Indeed, as the industry developed, stimulated by the opening of trade to the West, there was heated competition among mill owners to recruit and retain experienced female workers.

THE EVOLUTION OF THE FEMALE LABOUR FORCE

The rapid development of the silk-reeling industry produced major changes in the nature of Meiji Japan's female labour force and their work conditions. First, silk reeling became separated from sericulture. Second, instead of serving as a form of by-employment for farmers, in many instances silk reeling became a full-time occupation for a separate group of farmers-turned-mill-owners. As the demand for silk thread grew, the number of filatures increased, and competition among mill owners for experienced reelers became intense.

The leading raw-silk producer in Japan by 1891 was Nagano prefecture. The area spawned six of present-day Japan's eight largest silk filatures. At the heart of Nagano's silk-thread industry, Suwa, in the village of Hirano (Okaya City), drew a large number of factory girls to work in its silk mills and so may be considered representative of the private, relatively large-scale, 'modern' silk-reel industry that developed in Meiji Japan.[29]

In Suwa alone the number of silk filatures rose rapidly from 2600 in 1883 to 21 000 in 1910.[30] To meet the increased demand for labour, employers began recruiting workers from greater distances, lodging them in company dormitories, and employing them on a full-time, year-round basis, under contracts that typically lasted three to five years. In the 1880s more than half of the female workers came from outside Suwa; by 1900, when the number of filatures had increased by more than fourfold, 60 per cent of the workers came from outside the county and another 10 per cent were recruited from other prefectures.[31] By the end of the Meiji period (1911), 35 per cent of the workers came from other prefectures, primarily Yamanashi and Gifu, but also Fukushima and Niigata.[32]

Under these new circumstances older married women were no longer available for hire, and employers began recruiting unmarried women instead. Accordingly, the starting age of workers dropped; even children of 10 years of age were enticed into the mills.[33] The draining-off of young women from the countryside became so extreme in some regions that, after the First World War, severely affected villages took measures either to prohibit the recruitment of women or to encourage early marriages.[34] Not surprisingly, the new working class was recruited from poorer farm families. According to Nakamura Masanori's study of the Yamanashi silk-reeling industry in the late Meiji period, 81 per cent of the factory girls came from families owning less than three-quarters of an acre or from tenant-farm families.[35]

Changes in the nature of the workforce were accompanied by changes in working conditions. Factory girls worked from twelve to fifteen hours a day, seven days a week, and for most of the year, except for the period around New Year, when cocoons were out of season, and they were allowed to return home. They worked under the close supervision of foremen in poorly ventilated filatures, where the accumulated steam from the basins and the stench from the drying cocoons caused special health problems: respiratory ailments, skin rashes and, with the introduction of new machinery, serious accidents resulting in the loss of limbs.

Changes in the nature of the workforce were also accompanied by innovations in the wage system. Competition for new recruits led to the evolution of a variety of different kinds of payments, such as money advances (*zenshakukin*), paid to parents as a kind of loan, and earnest money (*tezukekin*). With the exception of pocket money, wages were either sent home to the girls' parents or garnisheed to repay loans made earlier to their parents when they signed contracts with the mill.[36] If a girl quit before fulfilling the full term of her contract, her family was obliged to repay the loan, and if a girl got sick and returned home, her family was expected to send a substitute worker to replace her.[37] Thus, the female labour force that emerged in the textiles industry in the last two decades of the nineteenth century – the era of the mechanisation of the textiles industry – was not so much an independent, urban working class as a class of temporary indentured servants or debtors, tied to their farm families on the one hand and to rural mill owners on the other.

While we cannot determine with any degree of certainty what the factory girl's earnings meant to her family, we can gain some idea of the worth of her labour by examining figures on wages and other payments made by the filatures and comparing these with the average small cultivator's annual income. In Yamanashi prefecture in 1892 filatures paid two *yen* per factory worker as *zenshakukin*. By 1906, in response to recruitment competition, they were advancing loans in the amount of five or ten *yen* or even more, depending upon the length of service specified in the contract.[38] According to Nakamura Masanori's estimates in 1908 the net income of a small rice cultivator (cultivating about 1.25 acres) was approximately seventy-two *yen*. Hence, a loan of five *yen* might constitute about 7 per cent of the farm family's annual income from rice.[39]

Factory girls' actual wages, as opposed to loans and advances, are difficult to compute because they were based on the quality of their work and also because the wage scales showed considerable regional and temporal variation. Wages in Suwa in 1902 ranged from ten to sixty *sen* per day or roughly between three and nine *yen* per month.[40] Not all of this money was sent home. A worker might remit half of her pay to her parents and use the rest for daily needs.[41] Some workers, especially in their first year of employment, may not have earned any wages at all. Still, assuming a girl earned five *yen* per month and sent half of that amount home, her annual contribution to her family, based on a ten-month work year, could have been as much as twenty-five *yen*, or, somewhere around one-third of their cash expenditures.[42] At the very minimum, this amount, while not sufficient to raise the family's socioeconomic status, could help the family to survive on the land. In extraordinary cases, such as the one reported in *Aa Nomugi tōge*, a family with several skilled daughters considerably increased their landholdings.[43]

To be sure, these wages would not have sustained factory workers if they had not lived in the factory dormitories or if they had been raising children in separate households, like female silk-reel workers in nineteenth-century France.[44] French reelers in times of unemployment resorted to begging and prostitution; Japanese reelers simply returned home to the farm. This difference reflects an important aspect of Japan's modern economic history, namely, the intimate relationship between the Industrial Revolution (especially in the textiles industry), women's work and agriculture. The evolution of Japan's distinctive industrial labour force – a young, female, unmarried, 'rural proletariat' – may be explained by the continuing close ties between the silk industry and the farming regions.

The silk industry, the rural areas and female labour were linked in several ways. First, they were tied through a circular flow of cash. By helping to meet rent payments to landlords, the factory girls' earnings, however meagre, often made the difference between the survival and starvation of their families. Most factory girls came from poor tenant-farmer families who rented not only rice paddy land but mulberry-groves as well. More than half of the sericulturists in Yamanashi prefecture cultivated mulberry-trees as tenants, and landlords strictly regulated access to the trees.[45] Some Japanese scholars have argued that, without the factory girls' earnings, faithfully remitted home, the institution of tenancy, with its concomitant high land rents, would not have survived.[46]

Landlords, in turn, directly and indirectly provided investment capital for silk and other industries either by establishing their own silk mills or, more typically, by placing their savings in local banks, where the money was recycled in the form of loans to mill owners needing capital to purchase equipment and cocoons.[47] Hence, cash flowed from landlord to mill owner and back again through the mediation of the factory girls' wages.

Ties between the silk industry and agriculture were further strengthened by the concentration of filatures in the countryside, especially in Nagano and Yamanashi. Entrepreneurs located their filatures in rural areas in order to recruit experienced female reelers, to be close to the supply of required raw materials, and to take advantage of low wage scales. Silk reelers' wages were pegged to the wages of agricultural day-labourers and varied according to the region.[48]

As a consequence of these links between the rural areas and the emergent silk industry, the failure of a filature affected numerous rural interests, including landlords, sericulturists, local merchant middlemen, bankers and industrialists involved in the various stages of silk production. The whole system was vulnerable to fluctuations in the world market and so interrelated that, to take one example, if the price of cocoons fell, tenant farmers might not be able to pay their land rent. This intimate connection between the silk-reeling industry and agriculture in Meiji Japan helps explain the nature of work conditions in filatures employing rural women.

WORK CONDITIONS AND RATIONALISATION OF THE SILK-REELING INDUSTRY

The deplorable conditions of factory life have already been documented in a number of Japanese and English sources.[49] Factory girls were housed in company dormitories, sleeping together with as many as fifty girls in one large room and sharing bedding. Many contracted tuberculosis and pleurisy. The girls were locked in and had to have a guard open the gate to leave company grounds. (This was allegedly for their own protection.) 'Working in a factory was [like] working in a jail', said one woman.[50] The songs they now sang, with titles such as 'Prison Lament' and 'Song of the Living Corpses', capture something of the suffering they must have experienced.[51]

That these child labour conditions were tolerated by government leaders and factory owners can be explained, though surely never justified, by a number of factors in addition to sheer greed. There was an atmosphere of desperation about much of Japan's early efforts to industrialise. Whipped on by patriotic slogans and by fears for the nation's survival, business and government leaders pushed themselves and their underlings to exhaustion. New silk mills were highly vulnerable to price fluctuations on the international market, caused by world economic conditions, sepculation or changing fashions. Many silk mills failed.[52]

The success of the Japanese silk-reeling industry depended primarily on outpricing major international competitors in the production of good thread in ample quantity. Despite the fact that the technology of silk production lagged behind China, Italy and France, Japan managed to capture the international market in the Meiji period by producing thread that cost one-half the international price.[53] As a result, silk exports increased sixfold between 1877 and 1897. By 1909 Japan was the world's chief exporter of raw silk.[54]

The Japanese silk-reeling industry was successful for many reasons. First, mill owners secured comparatively inexpensive raw materials. Cocoons accounted for as much as 80 per cent of the total costs of production.[55] In order to buy low-priced cocoons in great volume the mill owner needed large amounts of capital during the cocoon season. At first this kind of financing came from local merchants and landlords, who pooled their capital. Eventually, with the establishment of banking institutions, loans became available to mill owners to purchase cocoons in large volume at low cost from sericulture farmers.[56] The price of cocoons was considerably lower in Japan than in Europe or even in China, where cocoons were subject to heavy provincial taxes.[57]

Second, the Japanese benefited from the plight of the Italian and French industry, which was afflicted by pebine, a protozoan disease that killed silkworm eggs and nearly ruined European sericulture in the 1870s.[58] The Japanese also held a competitive advantage over the Chinese silk-thread industry, which, while still able to produce superior thread, was plagued by anarchic political conditions and a reputation for dishonest business practices.[59]

Japanese mill owners further enhanced their competitive edge by introducing improved equipment, such as reels with three and four spools, which came into operation between 1900 and 1905.[60] Reeling machines and equipment, based on modified versions of French and Italian equipment, but adapted to local needs and made from cheaper materials, drastically reduced capital costs while increasing productivity.[61]

The Meiji government directly and indirectly promoted the diffusion of foreign technology in Japan through its pilot factory, research institute and financial institutions, in particular, the Bank of Japan and the Yokohama Specie Bank, which helped Yokohama silk wholesalers make loans to silk reelers. The government's role stands in sharp contrast to the Italian government, which 'could not implement an effective policy of assistance for the faltering Italian silk reeling industry',[62] and to China, where 'silk reeling suffered from inadequate financing and inadequate, or at least inappropriate, government support'.[63]

Finally, in examining the reasons why the Japanese silk-reeling industry captured the world market, it is important to look at labour costs. French, Italian and Japanese filatures all relied on female workers. However, whereas Italian and French reelers by the end of the nineteenth century worked eleven- or twelve-hour days, 205 days a year, Japanese factory girls were pushed to work fourteen hours or more each day, and they too began working over 200 days each year.[64] Moreover, their hourly wages were approximately half that of the Italian or French workers.[65]

At first, gains in productivity were made by sacrificing quality. The increase in working hours frequently resulted in less fine thread.[66] The final hurdle for Japanese silk filatures selling their thread in the overseas market, therefore, was to achieve a consistently uniform product. By paying sedulous attention to the demands of foreign (especially American) buyers for consistency in the quality of thread, Japanese industrialists at last overtook all other competitors. By the 1920s 90 per cent of the raw silk exported from Japan was sold in the USA.[67]

The unfortunate irony is that each new mechanical or organisational innovation designed to rationalise production had a detrimental effect on the factory workers. Rather than freeing them from the more arduous tasks associated with silk-reeling, innovations in the industry often had the opposite effect of increasing their burden. This is because, unlike cotton textiles, the silk-reeling industry was not fully mechanised until after the Second World War. In the Meiji period the major mechanical advance was the introduction of water or steam power to turn the reels and the increase in the number of porcelain bottoms, corresponding to the number of spools a reeler could work at one time. Other innovations included using steam instead of a wood fire to heat the water in which the cocoons were boiled. But the hardest part of the job remained unmechanised: factory girls still had to use their fingers to pull wispy filaments from cocoons and to thread them through the porcelain eyelets. The introduction of mechancial energy to turn the reels in effect harnessed the factory girls to the machines, forcing them to work faster at this delicate operation, upon which the quality of the final product depended. If they failed to keep up with the turning of the reel, their thread broke and they lost valuable time splicing it. In other words, to increase profits in the silk-reeling industry, which was not highly mechanised, the mill owners had to put pressure on the factory girls.

Whereas women in the cottage industries of the Tokugawa period could reel only one thread at a time, mechanically-turned reels both enabled and required reelers in the late Meiji period to reel two, three and, by the end of the Meiji period, four threads at a time. According to a late 1920s' account, 'Reeling girls at work appear like so many machines. Their eyes are riveted on the cocoons being unwound, and their nimble fingers are always attending to any mishap that may interfere with the production of even-sized, defect-free raw silk.'[68] Sitting over steaming pans of cocoons, their bodies dripping with sweat, their fingers flying, factory girls worked at a frenzied pace.

Adding to the arduousness of the work was the introduction of new techniques for measuring the quality of the thread. Silk-reelers, unlike workers in other industries and also unlike silk-reelers in Italy or France, were paid according to the quality and quantity of the thread they produced. The quality of thread was determined by a number of criteria, such as evenness of colour, length, thickness, lustre and absence of patches. In the 1880s, quality was standardised throughout the Suwa region. After the First World War a device known as a seriplane (*seripuren*), issued by the Silk Association of America, evaluated workers' thread presumably in a more scientific way by comparing it to seven pictures of thread graded on a scale from one to seven.[69] This method of inspection and grading led to further competition among the workers, who stood in constant danger of being penalised by low wages for inadequate performance. Girls failing to meet minimum standards received no wage at all, had to pay the company for their lodgings, and were required to stay extra hours to receive further instruction. The inspection system was the most hateful part of factory life for many girls, though it did produce some comic moments. When one young worker wrote home complaining that 'the *seripuren* is making me cry', her father, unfamiliar with the word, assumed it was the local dialect for pregnancy and wrote back, 'Don't get mixed up with that man.'[70]

Still another way in which the rationalisation of the silk-reeling industry negatively affected workers was the organisation of a league of mill owners to regulate competition for employees. The formation of the Suwa Silk Reel League in the first decade of the twentieth century led to the enforcement of a number of regulations designed to eliminate the raiding of workers. Among these was the forced registration of workers and stipulations in workers' contracts threatening litigation or loss of forced savings if they did not remain loyal to their employer. In addition, common working hours and quality standards were established. These regulations had the effect of severely curtailing economic mobility, because in various ways they prevented silk-reelers from changing jobs to improve their work situation.[71]

Above all, to understand why women workers were hired in such large numbers and treated the way they were, however, we must again refer to the intimate link between farming and early industry in Japan. The chronic poverty of the farm community gave struggling tenants few options: one of their options was, in essence, to sell their daughters to the mills for wages that were viewed by all concerned as merely supplemental farm income. 'The impoverishment of the tenant farmer and small landowner', as Ishida Takeshi has written, was 'itself an indirect result of the government's encouragement of industrialisation, because the heavy land taxes imposed by the new Meiji government in order to pay for its strenuous campaign of economic development fell on the shoulders of poor farmers', who were reduced to tenancy when they could not raise the cash to meet their tax burden.[72]

The deplorable conditions of factory life, in short, were merely a reflection of the even worse conditions that existed among small landowners and tenants in the Meiji period. Indeed, some Japanese factory girls – it is impossible to say how many – may have been better off, or at least no worse off, in the mills than they had been on the farms, and even if their skills never progressed sufficiently to enable them to earn high wages, they had the consolation of knowing that their families had a little more food because there was one mouth less to feed at home.[73] While dormitory fare was meagre, it was none the less superior to the diet at home, where rice was a luxury. Girls with expert reeling skills were paid substantial wages by the standards of the day and there is some evidence that, at least in the Taishō period, their wages helped increase the landholdings of their families.[74]

Moreover, factory work, however tedious, may have been easier than the farm work girls were called upon to do at home. Although factory workers described the factory as a jail or likened it to hell, some farm women wished they had gone to work in the filatures. As one such woman explained, 'I stayed ... without friends, and ... burned the hillside to open up some farmland to grow grass and millet. ... I used to walk 2 *ri* [about 5 miles] on a mountain road, covered with snow up to my hips, with a sack of rice and a box of flour on my back. ...'[75]

Both factory work and farming were superior to one of the only other options available to young farm girls from impoverished regions – prostitution. Thousands of young rural women were virtually sold into prostitution – some to overseas brothels – in the Meiji period.

The memoirs of one factory worker, whose book, *Aa Nomugi tōge*, is a major source of information on factory life in the silk industry, describes the ways in which factory girls received recognition for their work from family and officials. The satisfaction of turning over money to grateful parents was often the high point of their return home. Those with highly paid skills were greeted by family members and neighbours as '100 *yen*' factory girls and strenuously wooed by recruiters. The factories were occasionally visited by high Meiji officials dressed in Western uniforms, who publicly praised the girls' contribution to the nation's goal of industrialisation (and then threw up from the sulphur-like stench of the putrefied cocoons).

To be sure, other sources suggest that the position of factory girls in their home villages declined as a result of their experience as migrant factory workers. Yanagida Kunio explained that, 'As a rule, even when the girls returned home to their parents they became the targets of much criticism. Actually they had by no means grown accustomed to luxury in the cities, as the country people often said, but they had indeed often grown so unaccustomed to the rhythm of village life that they found it difficult to adjust. Too, they had often missed out on much of the training in housework that a young woman was expected to have received, and it was consequently difficult to find husbands for them.'[76]

Women interviewed about their lives in the factory rarely complained about their experiences. Nakamura Masanori found that they considered the work conditions 'normal' or 'natural'. They helped their families and pleased their parents by going to work. Everyone was poor and everyone suffered.[77]

Elderly women interviewed about experiences that occurred earlier in their lives, and socialised not to complain, might gloss over the more painful aspects. They may have also deliberately chosen to forget or suppress the worst part of those experiences. Still, their personal recollections offer insights into some of the rewards tempering the harshness of silk-reeling.

One such woman is Utsunomiya Tamiko, who worked in a silk filature in Ehime prefecture from 1919 to 1934, beginning work right after graduating from primary school at the age of 12 and continuing until shortly before her marriage at the age of 28. The eldest child and only daughter of a farm family, Tamiko was one of forty female workers in the filature. She commuted daily to the factory, working for an hour before eating breakfast at 7 o'clock in the morning. With the exception of lunch at noon and a snack at 3 o'clock in the afternoon, the factory girls worked continuously until 5 p.m. At first her wages were only three *yen*, thirty *sen* per month. This gradually increased to seven *yen*. She gave her wages to her parents, who put aside a portion in savings for her.

Tamiko described the work of reeling as 'interesting' and not difficult, though the hot water in the cocoon basin caused the skin on her hands to wrinkle. The most pleasurable part of the job was the friends she made. What made the work memorable, however, was the recognition she received from government officials. Every year one girl from each factory in the area was chosen for official commendation at a ceremony held on the third floor of the local police station. When Tamiko was 20 years old, she was selected from among all the workers in her factory and invited to the police station, where she was lavishly praised and presented with a certificate of merit, a gift and three *yen*. Fifty-five years later, she confided that she 'can never forget the memory of that day'.[78]

FACTORY GIRLS AND THE EARLY LABOUR MOVEMENT

Not all factory workers were as docile as Tamiko. Many rebelled against the harsh work conditions of silk filatures. Their opposition took several forms, all of which aggravated the labour shortage and diminished the pool of labour required to meet constantly expanding production quotas. Factory girls committed suicide or they deserted, returning home or getting jobs in other factories (an option only until 1900, when the association of mill owners took measures to end raiding).

Along more assertive lines, the factory girls organised strikes – tactics which, until recently, have been largely neglected in the labour history of Japan. Although factory girls have been depicted as docile, cheap labour, or as ignorant farm girls, they appear to have been, in fact, the pioneers of Japan's modern labour movement, and their opposition to exploitative conditions eventually inspired the famed Japanese company paternalism, designed to keep factory workers on the job.

The first-recorded strike in modern Japanese history was by female silk-reelers of the Amamiya Kiito Bōsekijō (Amamiya Silk Spinning Mill), a fairly large filature in Kōfu, the heart of Yamanashi's silk-reeling industry. However, one year before the Amamiya strike, in August 1885, there was a walkout of female silk-reelers in another mill in Kōfu that set the stage for the more famous labour dispute at Amamiya. The women protested against discriminatory practices, complaining that mill owners favoured the prettier factory girls when doling out loans.[79] Earlier Japanese historians have tended to view the strike as 'emotional' and 'impulsive', rather than rational and economic, and therefore to minimise its importance as a genuine labour dispute. Marxist historians argue that the workers probably did not have a 'class consciousness'. Their arguments were 'non-ideological, practical, commonsensical and reminiscent of farmers' protest'. Their strike was not the 'inevitable result of the machine stage of development'.[80]

For these reasons and because the strike was not reported in the newspapers, the 1885 walkout in Kōfu has been largely neglected. The fact remains, however, that the women workers were striking over inequality of treatment, and they were sufficiently well organised to make a stand in large numbers. They undoubtedly realised that work stoppage was harmful to production schedules, for they themselves worked under the pressure of time, and it was obvious that walkouts could be extremely damaging to factories that operated around the clock.

The Amamiya strike one year later, on 12 June 1886, involved about one hundred women workers (out of about 140 to 200 registered employees – the exact number cannot be determined from the records). They walked out of the filature in protest over the owner's decision to increase daily working hours by thirty minutes and to decrease daily wages of the highest-paid workers by ten *sen* in order to bring his mill into conformity with regulations governing work conditions in other mills. Since this particular company did not supply lodgings, woman workers were commuting for as much as one hour each way, and in order to start at the new hour of 4.30 in the morning, they would have had to leave their homes as early as 3.30. The longer working day, they argued, would impose extreme hardships on them and they would not 'have time to drink even a glass of water'. The company agreed to allow women commuting long distances to start work later and to consider ways of improving work conditions for other workers.[81]

The Amamiya strike was followed by several others in the same year, a year in which the newspaper *Jiji shimpō* reported that in Japan the 'strike is still a foreign thing'.[82] All were opposed to the new regulations imposed by the amalgamation of mill owners in Yamanashi. In one case, twenty women workers walked out, saying 'Because we have been treated in this way, you can't expect us to reel good thread ... our health cannot endure [these new regulations]'.[83]

Although the 'workers movement' is usually considered a post-First World War phenomenon in Japan, silk industry workers, despite the constraints under which they operated, did not remain uniformly acquiescent. In a typical strike, factory workers in large numbers (as many as four to eight hundred in some instances) would walk out of the factory and gather at a local Buddhist temple or other public area, waiting for the company to send negotiators. The walkout was damaging to the company's production schedule and, because these strikes were reported in the newspapers, they might also prove damaging to the company's reputation, though public support was not necessarily on the side of the factory girls. Far from being spontaneous, such large-scale labour activities must have required considerable planning and co-ordination.

There were four or five such incidents of labour conflict each year. Most of these are not well-studied. Almost half occurred in Yamanashi prefecture; in 1906, approximately 60 per cent occurred there. In contrast, Nagano prefecture – the location of the Suwa complex of silk reels – witnessed far fewer incidents of strikes.[84]

Several factors may account for the greater incidence of labour conflict in Yamanashi. Almost three-quarters of the large-scale mills were concentrated in Kōfu, the main city in the county. The Kōfu factories stayed open longer and consequently produced more thread. Although they constituted only one-quarter of the total number of factories in the prefecture, they produced 60 per cent of the silk thread and also they led in the introduction of new technology.[85]

Women workers in the Kōfu mills commuted to work in large numbers, 'carrying their *bentō*', and were paid a fixed daily wage. Consequently they enjoyed greater mobility and freedom than Suwa workers, who lived in company dormitories.[86] In addition, the *batten* (grade) system of wages instituted in Suwa may have created a competitive consciousness among the women workers that militated against the development of a feeling of solidarity. Finally, the 'medium of resistance' – a local newspaper – was established earlier in Yamanashi than in Suwa.[87]

Factory girls' protests occasionally were supported by their rural communities which, upon hearing about working conditions in the mills, refused to allow recruiters into their communities.[88] In some instances, parents tried to redeem their daughters or they complained to the factories about the girls' treatment.[89] When the burgeoning socialist movement became interested in labour conditions around the turn of the century, the Ministry of Agriculture and Commerce began considering some form of protective factory legislation. Members of the All-Japan Cotton Spinning Association (Dai Nihon Bōseki Rengōkai) responded by launching a major investigation of work conditions in their own mills. The results of their survey of 71 000 workers in seventy-five mills appeared in 1897. The Ministry of Agriculture and Commerce drew largely on this study for its own report, *Shokkō jijō* (Factory conditions), published six years later.[90]

The information contained in the three-volume *Shokkō jijō*, gathered from interviews with factory workers, personnel agencies and factory owners, remains a basic source for the study of work conditions in not only the textiles industry but in many other Meiji industries, including cement, glass and light-bulb manufacturing plants, iron works and printing, tobacco and match enterprises. The interviews covered such sensitive subjects as love affairs, rapes and runaway attempts, and it frankly discussed rivalry among female workers, schisms between female supervisors and workers, and favouritism on the part of management. The interviewers evidently gained the confidence of the workers, who openly talked about their efforts to run away (usually during a storm, when they were less likely to be seen outside) and described their greatest difficulties on the job (having the thread tear) and their greatest pleasure (not having the thread tear). Their other pleasures included days 'when everyone shows up for work', buying things to eat, and having a boyfriend. One informant confided that, if workers complained to the company about mistreatment, the company representative would reply, 'You don't have any place to go. You can't even get three decent meals a day at your own home.' Another woman worker described how the bodies of factory girls who had died on the job were treated like 'horse bones'.[91]

As a result of this thorough and candid disclosure of factory conditions, the plight of workers became well known to Japan's political elite. Yet, despite the well-documented evidence of abuse of factory workers, the Factory Act of 1911, passed in the face of opposition from the business community, gave only minimal protection to women and children (defined as workers under the age of 15). Although it limited the work day to twelve hours, it contained provisions for extending the work day another hour or two when necessary. The law applied only to factories with fifteen or more workers. Whereas night shifts for women were prohibited, this provision did not go into effect until 1929.[92]

Silk filatures made minimal efforts to improve the lives of their workers by organising educational activities, usually in the form of morally edifying lectures. The larger mills also provided classes in the tea ceremony, flower arrangement, sewing, etiquette and ethics, though these were available only in the evening, after work. For the most part, factory girls received scant relief from the government, private industry or the labour movement itself.

In comparing the trade-union movement among textiles workers in Japan with the situation among silk workers in France and Italy, several differences appear salient. Despite the low wages, long hours and harsh work conditions, there were comparatively fewer strikes in Japan among silk workers than there were among their Italian counterparts. Corrado Molteni reports that, between 1896 and 1913, there were 500 officially recorded strikes in the Italian silk-reel industry, but only forty-eight in the same period in Japan.[93] In France, by the middle of the nineteenth century, silkworkers in Lyon, the heart of the industry, had successfully obtained various kinds of assistance from the government, as well as from local merchants and silk entrepreneurs. In the revolutionary background of French political life, Lyonnais silk entrepreneurs, fearing urban riots, instituted a system of doles to unemployed workers, while a Bureau de Bienfaissance in the 1840s distributed food, clothing and money to needy workers, and a Society for Mutual Aid and Retirement Fund, funded by city leaders and the Chamber of Commerce of Lyon, aided both male and female silk workers. Women also succeeded in winning other concessions from the government, such as national workshops for female silk workers, and they readily engaged in litigation against employers who reneged on wage agreements.[94]

In all three countries the majority of the silk workers were female, and, at least in the case of the French workers, they were, like Japanese women, excluded from men's labour organisations. Nevertheless, the French women centred as they were in the city of Lyon and not indentured or under contract, could more easily organise. Significantly, many of the French female silk workers were urban dwellers, permanently separated from their rural roots, and either married or, if single, on their own. They were more inclined to develop female solidarity groups, probably because, unlike the Japanese silk workers, they were not a temporary workforce, and also because the Japanese mill owners encouraged competition among silk reel workers.

These differences in the nature of the workforce may further help explain the competitive advantage the Japanese gained on the world market. Japanese mill owners appear to have made fewer concessions to their workers, suffered fewer strikes and given fewer benefits than their European competitors in the nineteenth and early twentieth centuries. Surely the Japanese textile industrialists were less constrained by labour laws than were English textile enterprises. By 1844 England had passed a law restricting adult female labour to twelve hours daily. Five years later Parliament passed a bill limiting the hours of labour to ten a day for women and young persons. These bills, though opposed by factory owners, were strenuously supported by Members of Parliament like Lord Ashley, by writers such as Charles Dickens and by numerous reform groups, and were enforced in India as well as in Great Britain.[95]

FACTORY GIRLS AND THE MODEL OF JAPAN'S INDUSTRIALISATION

Farm girls from impoverished families formed the backbone of Japan's Industrial Revolution. The countryside served as a reservoir of female labourers who were willing to work away from home for low wages and were able to master the techniques of silk-reeling. Whether this was an economically efficient way to industrialise is open to question: a heavy labour turnover and high rate of absenteeism can be expensive. Better-trained workers, working fewer hours daily and remaining longer on the job, might have been economically more rational in the long run.[96] It certainly would have been more humane. The object here, however, is not to question the ethics of Meiji entrepreneurs nor to challenge their capitalist strategies but simply to point out that any model of Japan's industrialisation must include a description of the labour force and employment conditions in major industries. One of the ingredients of Japan's 'success' was a labour pool of teenage girls locked into filatures. When historians of Japan's economic development describe, as one of the Tokugawa legacies for industrialisation, a disciplined, reliable workforce, they gloss over the real nature of the early factory class.

The explanation of Japan's ability to industrialise in the nineteenth century should also include reasons why this particular labour pool was available. One reason is that the traditional sericulture and silk-reeling industry was also dominated by women. Unlike France, where for centuries before the mechanisation of silk production, male artisan weavers, assisted by their wives, children and apprentices, spun and wove silk at home in family workshops, in Japan women were the major silk-reelers and weavers in areas outside the traditional guild centres. Whereas French women displaced master craftsmen as silk production was mechanised in the 1830s and 1840s, Japanese women, when they moved into the factories, merely continued a century-long tradition of female labour. As far as wages were concerned, however, the effect in both countries was the same: women were expected to content themselves with lower wages than men.[97]

Another reason why farm women formed the labour pool for the textiles industry is that desperate conditions in the rural areas forced farmers to sell their daughters to the filatures. Not all societies are willing to send their young women to work away from home, however. A study of migrants in one area of China in the late nineteenth century found that women could not easily move for work, because 'social norms of traditional China did not allow women to work outside the home'.[98] In India, 'even the dispossessed peasants' daughters did not aspire to be mill workers'.[99] When talking about women's contribution to economic development, therefore, we should look at not only young women's high rate of economic participation, but the cultural reasons that made their economic role possible.

There were few major cultural factors inhibiting Japanese women's work either on the farm or away from home. The availability of female labour, unconstrained by such religious taboos or cultural inhibitions as bound feet or purdah, or by extreme constraints against sexual promiscuity, made women a highly mobile, marketable commodity, at least in the lower classes in Japan.

In addition, traditional Japanese family institutions reinforced women's active role in the economy. The stem family system pushed women and younger sons out of the house to relieve the financial burden of hard-pressed farm families. While it is commonly believed that women in pre-industrial societies are less mobile than men, in Japan such was not the case, and the high rate of female migration in nineteenth-century Japan paved the way for the recruitment of factory girls.[100]

A number of scholars have already speculated about the implications of female mobility for Japanese history. They suggest, first, that migration of female agricultural workers before their marriage tended to raise the marriage age and hence reduce their child-bearing years. This phenomenon, if it was widespread, would help explain the remarkably static population over the last half of the Tokugawa period, a fact that in turn may help explain the rise of per capita income or surplus accumulation necessary for industrialisation.[101]

A second implication of female mobility is that the girls' wages enhanced the overall income of their farm families, enabling the number of farm families, for better or for worse, to remain constant as industrialisation progressed. This pattern of migration, where individuals rather than whole families left the rural areas, continued into the industrial period. At the same time, because they never broke their ties with their families, and because they worked not as individuals but as family members supplementing family income, women were paid less than men. To this day, women continue to provide a flexible workforce, willing to work for low wages and irregular time periods, accommodating themselves to the needs of both their families and Japanese industry. Women's manual dexterity, mobility and flexibility, while nowhere more apparent than in the silk-reeling industry, served many other areas of economic life as well.

Although we have ample evidence of the hardships faced by factory girls, unlike the histories of other developing countries, Meiji Japanese women made the transition from cottage industry to factory without losing out to male workers, who frequently have sole access to the new technology. Having dominated the traditional silk-reeling industry, women also dominated the labour force of modern industry which, though mechanised, did not introduce the kind of heavy power equipment that might have required male workers. Indeed, some have argued that the presence in large numbers of female workers in the silk-reeling industry discouraged the introduction of further mechanisation (and slowed the development of the productive power of the industry).

While female reelers were not displaced by men or machines, their status plummeted in the course of the Industrial Revolution as technology cancelled out the uniqueness of the contribution of the individual worker to the finished product. The observations of Alice Bacon, a late nineteenth-century American teacher in Japan, capture the changed position of the Japanese women within the silk industry. Describing women who still worked at home sericulture, she wrote:

> It is almost safe to say that this largest and most productive industry of Japan is in the hands of the women; and it is to their care and skill that the silk product of the islands is due. In the silk districts one finds the woman on terms of equality with the man, for she is an important factor in the wealth-producing power of the family, and is thus able to make herself felt. . . [102]

If the Japanese female silk-reeler's labour was devalued when she entered the filature, her labour participation none the less remained crucial to the success of industrialisation. This lesson has not been lost on present-day developing countries, whose young, poor, rural women, paid 'supplementary' rather than 'primary' wages, provide 'the cheapest labour available in the world.'[103] The predominently female labour force composition in the early years of Japan's industrialisation is typical of Third World countries today, as is the age and marital status distribution of that work-force: most are under the age of 25 and single. Not only in nineteenth-century Japan but throughout the Third World today, a typical household survival strategy is to send a daughter to the factory.

5 Tenkō and Thought Control

Patricia G. Steinhoff

The word '*tenkō*' has been applied at various times to everything from the Meiji intellectual's rediscovery of Japanese culture to the post-war student activist's acceptance of a job with Mitsubishi.[1] It refers to the act of renouncing an ideological commitment under pressure. The current usage of the term originated in the 1930s, when the majority of imprisoned members of the Japan Communist Party publicly renounced their party affiliations. The fact that an ideological commitment was given up, and the fact that the persons involved were in prison because of that commitment, suggests that *tenkō* is related to thought control.

The term 'thought control' is bandied about even more than the word '*tenkō*'. In general it refers to a power relationship in which one party deliberately attempts to limit or direct the thoughts and beliefs of some other party. Thought control may be directed only towards overt acts and external expressions of thought, or it may aim to penetrate into the internal state of the individual's mind, reaching even his unexpressed thoughts and beliefs. In addition, thought control may focus on inculcating good thoughts, on eradicating bad thoughts or on some combination of the two.

Labelling something as 'thought control' also subtly directs attention to the perpetrators of control. Thought control is something people or agencies do to others. *Tenkōsha* may be seen as the other actors in the drama, the objects, targets or victims of thought control. This connection may seem obvious in the abstract, but it remains to be seen whether the objects of thought control, *tenkōsha*, actually made their conversions solely because of the thought-control policies of the government.

THE PEACE PRESERVATION LAW

The *tenkō* phenomenon of the 1930s is a particularly interesting

78

problem because the people involved were already Japan's last holdouts from other, more generalised processes of thought control.[2] Meiji and Taishō Japan's educational system, military training system, publications policies, regulation of political organisations and general police surveillance practices all operated at least in part as instruments of thought control. They indoctrinated certain desirable ideas in the populace, and attempted to screen out or isolate other undesirable ideas.

Despite all of these hurdles, a tiny fraction of the population became involved in a political organisation which was illegal precisely because it advocated ideas that the government wished to proscribe. The Japanese Communists who became *tenkōsha* were arrested for violations of the 1925 Peace Preservation Law, which made it illegal to organise or knowingly participate in an association for the purpose of changing the national polity or repudiating the private property system.

The Peace Preservation Law was concerned with thought, but its approach was indirect. The crime was participation in an organisation, and the organisation was defined in terms of the beliefs it advocated. On the surface the concern was only with overt actions which were the consequences of particular ideologies. As a 1939 legal commentary on the law by Ikeda Katsu explained, 'The object of punishment in this law is always a practical act for an illegal purpose, and this act is a consequence of a certain practical theory or thought. . . . The peculiarity of this law is that it makes acts based on certain practical thoughts the object of punishment. The thoughts in thought crimes are not simple, theoretical, abstract thoughts, but practical, concrete thoughts.'[3]

Within the Justice Ministry, however, the administration of the Peace Preservation Law emphasised thought quite directly. Peace Preservation Law violations were prosecuted by thought procurators (*shisō gakari kenji*) assigned to the thought bureau (*shisō bu*), whose province was a broad collection of specific criminal statutes, plus crimes of any sort committed by persons involved with particular social movements.[4] These crimes, particularly violations of the Peace Preservation Law, were known officially as thought crimes (*shisō-teki hanzai*, later *shisōhan*). The people who committed them were known as 'thought criminals'. Although the legal means focused on organisational activity, the activity was perceived as the overt expression of particular dangerous thoughts.

The Justice Ministry's policy of suppressing overt acts which were expressions of proscribed ideas resulted in the arrest of over 57 000 persons for suspected Peace Preservation Law violations from 1928 to 1934.[5] The figures were considerably inflated by the practice of making sudden raids on whole organisations and later sifting through the arrestees and pressing charges against only a small number of persons. During the years 1928–34 Peace Preservation Law charges were seriously considered against 48 545 people, but only 8.4 per cent of the charges were actually indicted.[6] All of these were for activities related to the Japan Communist Party. By 1935 the Party had been effectively eliminated, although several small attempts were made to re-establish it. From 1935 to 1945 arrests for Peace Preservation Law violations continued against a broader spectrum of ideological positions on the dwindling Left.

The vast discrepancy between arrest rates and charge rates, which is much greater than for other crimes, suggests that the Peace Preservation Law was utilised for harassment purposes. This suspicion is strengthened by evidence that the Justice Ministry invented a new case disposition called 'charges withheld' (*ryūhō shobun*), which permitted them to place certain suspected Peace Preservation Law violators under court supervision even if they did not formally charge them with the violation. This disposition was used from 1931 to 1935 on about 4.5 per cent of those arrested but not charged. Another 6.7 per cent of the arrestees were released with the indictment suspended, which was still another way of maintaining some control over a person who was not actually charged with a thought crime. These two dispositions combined accounted for 11 per cent of those arrested, which is 50 per cent more than the number who were actually indicted.[7]

Quasi-legal harassment and surveillance tactics aside, a substantial number of persons were charged, tried and convicted under the Peace Preservation Law. During the 1928–34 period virtually all of these people were members of the Japan Communist Party. Conversely, the persons who were tried and convicted under the Peace Preservation Law comprised virtually all of the Party's membership. The high point of the legal activity against the Party was a major public trial of nearly two hundred Japan Communist Party leaders, which ran from June 1931 to October 1932.

Since the intention of the Peace Preservation Law was to prohibit acts which stemmed directly from certain political ideas, the aim can fairly be termed 'thought control'. However, the reach of the law was limited to action proceeding from thought. The law could not exercise effective jurisdiction over what a person thought.

FIRST GESTURES TOWARDS TENKŌ

Prior to 1933 there does not appear to have been an explicit policy aimed at getting arrestees or defendants to change their beliefs. The first job of the Justice Ministry was to prosecute the offenders. Yet the authorities were certainly predisposed to regard favourably an individual prisoner's desire to break with the Party. Several Japanese cultural traditions, undoubtedly shared by court and prison officials, suggest an implicit orientation towards encouraging thought criminals to change their beliefs.

The traditional consensus orientation in Japanese society stemmed from philosophical ideas of harmony and unity, and was reinforced at the practical level of consensus decision-making procedures. It strongly encouraged efforts to bring the wayward back into the fold, and viewed uniformity of thought as a natural and desirable state. Japanese tradition also emphasised the welfare of the group above the desires of individuals. While this tradition certainly recognised the depth and power of personal emotions, it declared quite unequivocally that the difficult but correct choice was to sacrifice personal beliefs and feelings for the good of the larger social unit.

In addition to these general cultural orientations there was a long-standing Japanese legal tradition, derived from ancient Chinese law, that repentant persons need not be punished further for their crimes. By this logic the aim of punishment was to deter the person from criminal activities, and if he already displayed repentance no further action by the state was necessary. The traditional means of establishing repentance was through voluntary confession. This principle appears throughout the Meiji criminal code in the form of sentence reductions. In the Peace Preservation Law itself sentences were to be reduced if the person voluntarily came forward to report the crime before it came to the attention of the authorities. This provision may be read as an immunity protection for informers, but its intent was also consistent with the tradition of encouraging confession and repentance.[8]

All of these traditions in concert would suggest that thought criminals ought to give up their dangerous beliefs for the sake of Japanese society, that they could be persuaded to accept the general ideological consensus and that it would be proper to encourage and reward them for doing so. This view would also suggest that an unrepentant thought criminal would be regarded as a piece of unfinished business, and that persons administering thought criminals would be particularly sensitive to signs of a change of heart. Even though thought-control policies in the early years officially stopped with the suppression of overt acts through the punishment of their perpetrators, there is every reason to believe that officials were highly receptive to the idea of altering thoughts directly by inducing the believer to repent.

There are several overt indications of Justice Ministry interest in the thought criminals' states of mind. The intake procedures for persons arrested for Peace Preservation Law violations required an assessment of the suspect's 'state of repentance'. In addition, all Japan Communist Party defendants were asked to write an essay on their 'process of transition in thinking'.[9] This material was initially used to help Justice Ministry officials understand how Japanese, particularly young people, came to believe in Marxism and Communism.

At various times between the first mass arrest of Communists in 1928 and the major trial of party leaders in 1931–2, individuals and small groups of arrestees indicated their repentance and were released from custody. Except for Mizuno Shigeo's faction (Kaitōha), which announced its break with the Japan Communist Party in 1929, most were isolated individuals with very minor party roles. Each case was handled more or less individually. There apparently was no general policy of soliciting statements of repentance; the officials were simply ready to reward them when they occurred spontaneously.

Officials also were prepared to capitalise on spontaneous repentance by encouraging the defectors themselves to convince their comrades. Mizuno Shigeo, for example, was permitted to circulate a statement urging the dissolution of the Party to other imprisoned party members.[10] He was also permitted to meet with his closest friends in order to persuade them to join his new group. Mizuno's influence was limited and prisoner morale was reasonably high at the time, so only a handful of his close associates rallied to his new cause. In 1931 Mizuno's small group was permitted to leave prison and form a new political group, under close police supervision.[11]

SANO AND NABEYAMA

Initially the case of Sano Manabu and Nabeyama Sadachika was no different than these earlier, isolated instances. In January 1933 Sano and Nabeyama independently indicated to the authorities that they were having some misgivings about party policies. Sano had confided his feelings to his wife, who mentioned them to a jailer. Nabeyama apparently said something directly to a friendly warden. Since it was already established practice to encourage such feelings, Sano and Nabeyama were brought together to reinforce one another's doubts.[12] The fact that they were having misgivings was also not too surprising, since directions from Moscow, as well as the behaviour of Japanese Communists outside of prison, were becoming rather erratic at that time. The 1932 Theses from Moscow represented a sharp change of direction in official party policy, which seemed to reflect Stalin's interests more than an understanding of Japan. Moreover, after five years of heavy arrests, the inexperienced and desperate party members left outside of prison were increasingly different from those inside. The Party's 1932 Ōmori bank robbery, which was intended to obtain operating funds for the Party, had deeply shocked the members in prison. Then, too, the violent 1933 arrest of Tanaka Seigen, who was armed with a machine-gun and wearing a bullet-proof vest, was a far cry from the earlier raids on election campaign offices and study group meetings that had put most members in prison.

The only difference in this case of misgivings was that Sano and Nabeyama were two of the very top leaders of the Party. They had been members of the Central Committee, and after their arrest had served on the Prison Central Committee which organised the collective defence at the leaders' trial. Sano was an intellectual and one of the Party's chief theoreticians and organisers. Nabeyama was one of the very few labourers who had risen to the highest ranks of leadership. Both had received life sentences at the conclusion of the Party leadership's trial in October 1932.

After meeting together regularly for six months, Sano and Nabeyama produced a joint statement announcing their defection from the Japan Communist Party, explaining their reasons, and urging their comrades to follow them. Much of the rationale for Sano and Nabeyama's break with the Party involved specific, rather narrow complaints about party doctrine and organisation. Most important from the point of view of the authorities was their conviction that Japan was unique and should not have its revolution conducted by the Comintern in Moscow. They called their action a *tenkō*, or change of direction.

This split in the party's highest leadership was just what the Justice Ministry needed. *Tenkō*, which began as a spontaneous invention of two disgruntled party leaders, suddenly became a policy objective of court and prison officials. Official support followed the pattern established in the Mizuno (Kaitōha) case, but since the defectors this time were leaders of the entire Party, every other party member was now viewed as a potential *tenkōsha*.

The *tenkō* statement was published at government expense and distributed to all of the nearly 1800 party members then in custody. Sano and Nabeyama were allowed to meet with individuals who might be persuaded to *tenkō* because of previous personal connections with them. Prison officials leaned hard on the prisoners, forcing them to study the *tenkō* statement and offering them various incentives if they would agree to join with Sano and Nabeyama. The Marxist scholar Kawakami Hajime, who had only recently joined the Party and still more recently had been arrested for that act, was urged to *tenkō* in order to add his intellectual prestige to the efforts of the practical politician and the labour leader. Kawakami refused to give up his ideological belief, but later agreed to stop his party activity.[13]

Even without him the impact of the Sano and Nabeyama *tenkō* was enormous. Within a month 548 others had formally renounced their ties to the Party. They comprised 35.8 per cent of the party members already convicted, and 30 per cent of those awaiting trial. Over the next several years two-thirds to three-quarters of all Peace Preservation Law violators formally renounced their commitment to the Communist Party by making a *tenkō*.[14]

THE JUSTICE MINISTRY'S VIEW

While the Peace Preservation Law had technically drawn the line at the overt expression of ideas through organisational activity, *tenkō* went beyond this, to focus on belief in ideas directly. A *tenkō* was a change in belief, from which a change in organisational activity would necessarily follow. It was thus the logical extension of the Justice Ministry's focus on thought crimes and thought criminals.

Within six months of the inception of *tenkō* an official classification system had been devised to evaluate thought criminals' degree of repentance. The first three classes, called *tenkōsha*, all involved the prisoner's renunciation of ideological beliefs.

A. The person renounces revolutionary thought and pledges to give up all social movements.
B. The person renounces revolutionary thought and in the future plans to work in legal movements.
C. The person has renounced revolutionary thought, but is undecided about his position regarding legal social movements.

Two other categories reflected incipient change and were classified only as '*Jun-tenkōsha*':

D. The person's revolutionary thought has been shaken and it is anticipated that he will renounce it in the future
E. The person does not renounce revolutionary thought, but he has pledged to give up all social movements in the future

The final category was also listed under '*Jun-tenkōsha*':

F. The person is still recalcitrant.[15]

The classification system reveals several features of administrative thinking. First, primary emphasis was placed on the renunciation of ideological belief. Although a person could renounce organisational activity without giving up his ideology, as Kawakami and many others eventually did, he was not considered a genuine *tenkōsha* until he had changed his beliefs. It was not sufficient to repent of illegal organisational activity. True repentance necessarily involved the rejection of the ideology which was the motivation for that activity.

Both the general consensus orientation and the immediate optimism of the *tenkō* successes appear to be reflected in the fact that category F, 'The person is still recalcitrant', is included in the classification as a potential *tenkō*. If Communist Party members in general were the last holdouts of thought control, the phenomenon of mass *tenkō* could only have encouraged the authorities to view every last Communist as a potential prodigal son.

Yet the classification system also reveals the authorities' second look at *tenkō* and the attempt to routinise and institutionalise what was initially a spontaneous and rather chaotic situation. In the first flush of success, in July 1933, many lower-level prison officials exercised excessive zeal in extracting *tenkō* commitments. Subsequently, as higher officials gained more experience in the new phenomenon, less emphasis was placed on the extraction of *tenkō* and more on the commitment involved. More time was devoted to making sure that the person was sincere, and the methods of persuasion became more subtle.[16]

There is no doubt that from mid-1933 on, the Justice Ministry's explicit policy was to get Communists to abandon their ideological commitment. However, it would be a gross oversimplification to presume that because there was such a thought-control policy the desired result was automatically obtained, or that the Communists were passive, helpless victims of thought control or terror.

The initial cases of *tenkō* were spontaneous changes of heart on the part of individual prisoners. It was the Communists themselves who invented *tenkō*, not the Justice Ministry. What the Ministry did was latch on to a good thing at the appropriate moment, and carry it to its logical limits. Even then, it took some time before the officials comprehended what *tenkō* was really about and how it might be developed.

The Ministry's view of the Communists can be characterised as theoretical, abstract and ideological. The Peace Preservation Law delineated what specific ideological tenets were proscribed for organisations. The investigation and prosecution of violators rested heavily on the documentation of the ideas they advocated by quoting from their policy statements and publications. In their trial the Japan Communist Party leaders were permitted to elaborate at great length on their ideology. They saw it as a forum for propagandising their ideas, but to the prosecution, they were simply establishing their guilt more thoroughly. The defendants were frequently the social and educational equals and even former classmates of the Ministry officials who interrogated, prosecuted and judged them. The only visible difference between them was ideology. The early formal renunciations of the Party, including both the 1929 Kaitōha and Sano and Nabeyama's very similar 1933 *tenkō*, were couched as narrow theoretical arguments with party doctrine and policy. Thus, it was quite natural for the authorities to promote *tenkō* by seeking new pledges of agreement with the Sano–Nabeyama statement, and to believe initially that they were succeeding by dint of the superiority of their ideological arguments.

THE *TENKŌSHA*'S PERSPECTIVE

The reality was quite different. The vast majority of the new *tenkōsha* who pledged their agreement with the Sano-Nabeyama statement did not care at all about its content. Many did not comprehend the detailed, insider's arguments, while others were not convinced by them. Each prisoner had his own personal doubts and frustrations. Sano and Nabeyama simply provided an opportunity to act on them.

This does not mean that *tenkō* was a sham. Quite the contrary, it was more genuine than the officials themselves at first comprehended. It was simply a change of a different quality than they thought. The documents on *tenkōsha* amply demonstrate that *tenkō* was an internal struggle between a commitment to a particular abstract ideology and some other emotional tie which came to be more and more salient to the individual.[17] It was not a mental struggle between two competing ideologies.

For some there was not even one ideology involved in the conflict because their primary commitment to Communism was to a particular individual or group, and the ideology was simply a function of that personal relation. Even where initially there was a genuine direct commitment to the Party and its ideology, *tenkō* happened because that commitment paled beside some more powerful emotional tie with which it had become incompatible. Ideology may have been the prize, but it was not the arena in which the contest was waged.

Most previous studies of *tenkō*, including the Science of Thought group's pathbreaking work and Hoston's more recent study,[18] have been based on the political writings of a small group of party leaders, with the assumption that all *tenkōsha* thought as these leaders did. In fact most of the people involved in *tenkō* did not share their leaders' preoccupation with the niceties of ideology, and did not write political theory. When the broad corpus of *tenkō* statements and the literary as well as political writings of *tenkōsha* are examined, it becomes clear that the political *tenkōsha* form a distinct subgroup precisely because they struggled over specific points of their ideological commitment.

Many *tenkōsha* have described the point of *tenkō* as the moment when they realised that theoretical arguments were irrelevant to the problem. Some experienced a particularly acute sense of emotional connection which precipitated a decision to *tenkō*. Others slipped into a state of emotional longing and only some time later realised that they had forgotten about the ideological conviction which put them into prison.

The conflict was made more difficult by the presence of emotional ties binding the person to the Party, or to particular comrades. Many refused to *tenkō* for a long period after they no longer believed in the ideology because they did not want to betray their comrades. Since the prisoners were kept in solitary confinement, they often attributed a stronger faith to their absent comrades than actually existed. Yet in the long run, isolation weakened the ties to the Party. They felt cut off and alone. Many said wistfully that they could have maintained their faith with the support of the group, but could not sustain it alone. The silent comrade became less salient over time than the letter from home, or the kind and persuasive chaplain.

To some extent the state of emotion conducive to *tenkō* was itself a product of thought-control policies. People were in prison essentially because of their beliefs. The treatment they received and their physical and mental condition made it more difficult to sustain an ideological commitment. Yet that is precisely the point of ideological commitments. A person can believe anything he wants when nobody cares what he thinks. The only real test of the strength of such a belief is the extent to which it can be sustained under pressure. The Japanese prison of the 1930s provided a relatively severe test, although the world – and Japan – have seen far worse. The reasons that so many Japanese Communists failed the test have as much to do with Japanese culture and personality, with the content of the ideology and with Communist Party organisational structure[19] as they do with the severity of thought-control policies of the Japanese authorities.

TENKŌ AND JAPANESE SOCIAL STRUCTURE

The emotional ties which drew the *tenkōsha* away from the Party and its ideology were the social bonds linking that person to Japanese society. The critical areas were his sense of identity as a Japanese; his sense of belonging within his family; and his sense of connection to social groups through commitment to particular persons. Viewed from the perspective of the individual these three kinds of links constituted the main elements of Japanese social structure. From a societal point of view, these links formed a national political and symbolic structure centring around the Emperor system and resting on a common cultural heritage, a strong family system and a strong group structure based on factional linkages.[20] A fourth critical factor for some *tenkōsha* was a concern over individual identity, or sense of self, which at the time of *tenkō* was not particularly related to any of the first three areas. (*Tenkōsha* of the latter type often became deeply interested in Japan's cultural heritage after *tenkō*, but this was not a factor in the actual decision to break with Communism.)

These four areas of emotional concern distinguish four quite different types of *tenkō*. In each case the pressure to *tenkō* stemmed not only from the sheer strength of these emotional forces in Japanese society, but also from their relationship to the organisation and doctrines of the Party. Which social tie proved most important to any particular individual seems to have been related to personality factors, the social background of the individual and his position in the Party.[21]

Among the most highly political and theoretical party members, particularly those who had held positions of responsibility and had received higher education, the critical pull was a sense of national identity. This sentiment conflicted not only with the Party's universalistic, international ideology, but also with the Party's doctrine of opposition to the Emperor system.

Both of these issues became more salient in 1932. The Manchurian Incident aroused feelings of nationalism in many Japanese Communists who had hitherto espoused a universalistic view of world political developments and who had initially opposed Japanese military adventures on the continent. At the same time the 1932 Theses from Moscow raised the policy of opposition to the Emperor from a minor issue to the first priority of the Party, and contained a new and more elaborate rationale for this policy which explicitly linked imperialism abroad with the Emperor system at home. The implications of an ideological commitment to Communism contrasted more and more sharply with the newly aroused sense of national identity, and the result was *tenkō*.

The actual shift of belief was usually couched in terms of specific elements of party doctrine or practice which the *tenkōsha* could no longer accept due to his new analysis of Japanese society. This type can be termed 'political *tenkō*' because the *tenkōsha* maintained a sense of himself as a political actor. He shifted from one ideological position to another, but the impetus for the shift was the emotional recognition of his national identity.

Family ties became the critical factor for a very different group of party members. They were predominantly the less-educated workers who had been brought into the Party during a period of hasty expansion after 1928. They tended to have had less theoretical and ideological commitment from the beginning, and were attracted to the Party more because of its promise of concrete improvement in the lot of workers.

The Party had never paid much attention to the Japanese family system, except to demand that party loyalties take precedence over other personal commitments. The family system was never singled out as an area of party policy. At the worst an individual party member might have been estranged from his family and too busy with party work to feel guilty about it. At best he might have been living with his family and keeping his illegal party life secret.

Although family ties were incidental to party ideology and activity, they remained a source of potential conflict. The circumstances of arrest and prolonged imprisonment in solitary confinement brought out their latent emotional force. On the one hand, arrest brought disgrace to the Party member's family and aroused very powerful feelings of family obligation. On the other hand, the isolation of prison life aroused strong memories of the warmth and security of family life. Since the prisoner was also isolated from his party comrades, and had no ideological doctrine to apply to the situation, he had no defence against these feelings. Commitment to the Party simply dissolved.

The persons most prone to this type of *tenkō* were relatively low-level party members whose violations were considered to be less serious, so *tenkō* usually resulted in immediate release from custody. Consequently this type of *tenkō* involved only minimal cross-pressures. The powerful emotional pull of family ties, together with the direct incentive of being able to return to the family if one made a *tenkō*, greatly outweighed an ideological commitment which was vague to begin with, and had been weakened further by isolation from party social support. The people involved usually retired permanently from political activity.

A third form of *tenkō* involved primarily persons who had held middle-level positions of responsibility in the Party and had been personally involved with higher-level party leaders. Personal relations in the Party were primarily vertical and extremely limited in range. A party member at the very bottom might know his own contact and nobody else. Higher up, a person might know the one or two people who were his immediate superiors, and the few people below him whom he had recruited himself. Only at the very top were there horizontal relationships among members who actually made collective decisions.

The pattern of party organisation was identical to the factional structure found throughout Japanese organisations. Consequently, personal relations within the Communist Party tended to carry the same obligations of personal loyalty as did other relationships in Japanese society. When a leader made a *tenkō* his personal followers felt a strong emotional pressure to follow his direction.

The authorities encouraged this by permitting important *tenkōsha* to meet with their followers and attempt to persuade them. The leader himself might have made a political *tenkō*, and his aim was to convince his former associate that his new political perspective was correct. From the subordinate's point of view his leader was asking him to follow. He felt a strong personal moral obligation to do so, regardless of whether he agreed with the specific ideological points involved. The strength of the individual's commitment to communist ideology *per se* thus competed with his loyalty to the organisational structure of the Party as symbolised by his personal relationship to his superior. Factional *tenkōsha* were able to remain politically active as followers in the faction leader's new political line, but their personal motivations stemmed from the leader–follower bond rather than from the strength of an ideological commitment in and of itself.

The fourth type of *tenkō* affected primarily the writers and other creative artists who had been involved in the Party's various cultural front organisations. They had contributed to the Party by bringing proletarian culture to the masses through dramatic and musical performances and proletarian literature. They believed in the Party's political ideology, and they believed – at least in the abstract – in the concept of using art to promote politics.

However, they were also deeply committed to their own personal aesthetic standards and the validity of their personal creative expression. Conflict arose when the two sets of standards, aesthetic and ideological, yielded differing judgements about a particular work. As the conflict deepened, the artist began to feel that the Party was stifling his creativity. The Party's answer was that he was succumbing to bourgeois sentimentalism. His attempts to suppress his feelings only made them more insistent. Such problems frequently had developed long before the person was arrested, particularly since the cultural front was not hit by mass arrests until 1933.

Once such a person was imprisoned, his feeling that the Party was stifling his creativity became intertwined with a growing fear that he would die in prison. The only way to avoid this certain death was to give up the ideology. He then agonised over whether he cared enough about the Party to die a miserable, unsung death for it. The emotional force which brought about a *tenkō* in such cases was both an elemental desire to live, and a more specific desire to live in order to express one's personal creative self.

Unlike the emotions involved in the other three types of *tenkō*, this one did not immediately reintegrate the *tenkōsha* into Japanese society. His *tenkō* did not produce a direct transition back into the nation or the family, nor did it maintain an important personal relationship. Rather, this type of *tenkōsha* was left even more isolated and alone after his break with the Party. His subsequent efforts to find a sense of identity often led to religion, to the study of traditional Japanese culture, and to literary creativity in such forms as the I novel and the personal essay.

THE *HI-TENKŌ* ALTERNATIVE

The experience of *tenkō* has been explained as the result of emotional commitments which became more salient to the *tenkōsha* than their commitments to the Communist Party and its ideology. The emotions in question involved fundamental elements of Japanese culture and social structure as well as basic human needs. They also touched on critical problems in the doctrine and structure of the Party. Taking all of this into consideration, *tenkō* appears to be an extremely natural and probable response. The phenomenon harder to understand is *hi-tenkō*, or the refusal to *tenkō*.

It is clear that *tenkō* was a far more frequent occurrence than *hi-tenkō*, but it is difficult to produce exact figures. Many low-level party members managed to finish their short prison terms without making a *tenkō*, but they did not engage in any further party activity after their release. Technically, they were *hi-tenkōsha*, but no one really knows what happened to their beliefs during the rest of the war. The real, acknowledged *hi-tenkōsha* are the handful of men who remained in prison until 1945 without ever making a *tenkō*. There were less than two dozen of them, out of the approximately 5000 persons who were convicted of violations of the Peace Preservation Law for Communist Party activity. Probably an equivalent number perished in prison without ever agreeing to *tenkō*.

From the few cases for which evidence is available it appears that the *hi-tenkōsha* possessed some special characteristics that enabled them to resist or avoid the emotional pressures to which other party members succumbed. Circumstances sometimes favoured them, but in addition they seemed to have a different mental approach to their situation.[22]

In some cases *hi-tenkōsha* were immune to a particular pressure because that structural problem simply did not apply to them. For example, some were not members of someone else's faction, but were high enough leaders to feel a direct sense of loyalty to the Comintern leadership in Moscow. Tokuda Kyūichi, as the descendant of a long line of Okinawan prostitutes and sailors, was relatively impervious to the pressures of both Japanese nationalism and family ties. Miyamoto Kenji's wife was also in the movement, so family ties were not a pressure towards *tenkō* for him. On the other hand, Nabeyama's wife was also in the movement, but did not *tenkō* when he did.

In other cases the *hi-tenkōsha* possessed an alternative emotional commitment of greater strength. Shiga Yoshio held an idealised image of the Soviet Union and the Communist International as the nation to which he owed his loyalty. Likewise, for Tokuda, the Party itself was both his family and his only larger social identity.[23]

Beyond these specific alternative commitments, the *hi-tenkōsha* seem to have maintained their sense of continuing the Party's work and being part of the action even while they were in prison. They felt they had important work to do in prison, and they did not believe they had been abandoned there. This made them far less vulnerable to the sense of isolation and imminent death which heightened the impact of other emotional pressures. They appear to have had a greater capacity to maintain their sense of connection to the Party mentally, without the reinforcement of immediate social contact.

Despite these clear differences between *tenkōsha* and *hi-tenkōsha*, it should not be assumed that to be a *hi-tenkōsha* was primarily an ideological commitment. For some it was a matter of will, pride and the struggle for a sense of self at all costs. They would never have made a *tenkō* even if they had completely changed their beliefs, simply as a matter of principle. Whereas some *tenkōsha* had had to break with the Party to preserve their sense of personal integrity, some *hi-tenkōsha* maintained their sense of self in precisely the opposite way. This, too, was a primarily emotional rather than ideological experience.

TENKŌ, HI-TENKŌ AND THOUGHT CONTROL

When *tenkō* is viewed solely from the perspective of the Japanese government, or through the hagiography of the post-war Japanese Left, it appears to have been a clever and highly successful instrument of thought control. However, when the experiences of the recipients of this thought control are examined, the problem becomes more complicated.

Tenkō was not a simple matter of applying direct pressure until a person capitulated and agreed to give up his beliefs. The pressure applied was indirect, and the actual response was still more indirect. *Tenkō* was actually a response to something fundamental within the individual, which revealed its potency as an indirect result of the various pressures placed on the prisoner. Thought control may have been the intent and the result, but what intervened was a psychological process of far greater complexity than a simple stimulus-response.

The key intervening variables were the unifying forces within Japanese society, which the individual experienced as personal emotional ties. In a sense *tenkōsha* were not responding to the particular efforts at thought control directed at them, but rather they were responding to the same broad, cultural patterns and values which had kept the rest of the population from joining the Communist movement in the first place. These forces existed both in the society at large and within the individuals who tried to break away from it.

This suggests that something similar to *tenkō* might well have happened even if there had been no thought-control policy of encouraging it. When *tenkō* is examined closely it turns out to have been only the most extreme case of recognition of social and cultural ties by the small minority who had ever questioned them. Much of this recognition was relatively spontaneous, or at least was due to structural elements of the situation rather than to particular actions or persuasions of the officials. It follows, then, that many *tenkōsha* would have made the same painful emotional discoveries about themselves even if no one had given the process a name.

Certainly there would have been exceptions. Some would have maintained at least their belief that they still believed in the ideology, because they would have been able to avoid confronting the inconsistencies. Others might have made the transition less completely if they had not been required to be so explicit about it. On the other hand, some *hi-tenkōsha* derived the strength to maintain their beliefs because the demand was explicit. Some of them might have made a private *tenkō* if they had not had such a clear alternative to fight against. It is reasonable to conclude that a great deal of *tenkō* would have occurred anyway, but perhaps the individual roll call would have read somewhat differently.

6 The 1960s' Japanese Student Movement in Retrospect

Ellis S. Krauss

In June of 1985 Japan passed a historic milestone – the twenty-fifth anniversary of the peak of the 1960 demonstrations against the US–Japan Mutual Security Treaty (Anpo).[1] These demonstrations, called 'the greatest mass movement in her [Japan's] political history',[2] featured the leftist student movement and individual radicals playing a significant, if not crucial, role.[3]

Yet, intellectual and popular journals contained only a few articles commemorating the event, and some of these were written by famous former student leaders who have since converted to the right.[4] Privately, and more as if they had been part of a college fraternity than a political movement, ex-student radicals held nostalgia parties and reunions with former comrades. All of this took place in a Japan ruled by the same party that was in power in 1960, now under the leadership of its most conservative prime minister in decades, with the same security treaty still in effect. The student movement, having briefly played a major role in politics in the widespread campus movements of the late 1960s, had long since degenerated into a small, fractionalised, often violent shadow of its former self, lacking in both campus and public support.[5]

Witnessing the subdued commemoration of the Anpo demonstrations a quarter of a century later in the affluent, high-tech, urban-middle-class and politically conservative Japan of the 1980s, I could not help but feel that the 1960s' student movement had become arcane and irrelevant. This surely must be the way most of the high-fashion teenagers feel as, equipped with stereo walkmans, they stroll along the same streets on which their predecessors had snake-danced only a generation earlier.

Of course, I knew that not all former student radicals had converted,[6] that the 1960 movement had been instrumental in bringing down a hawkish prime minister and turning the Liberal Democratic Party

95

more towards the non-controversial policy of rapid economic growth, and that the late-1960s' movements had led to a few reforms in higher education. None the less, for an American who had done research on the 1960s' movement and had personally observed the student protests in the latter part of the decade, the toned-down observance of the anniversary of the Anpo movement provoked several vexing questions. What was the long-term significance, if any, of the 1960 Anpo movement and the campus movements of the late 1960s? Did they have a common political and sociological meaning, one that transcended their obviously 'failed' objectives of ending the US–Japan treaty or fundamentally restructuring Japanese society and higher education? Did they have any connection to the present? What has happened to the spirit and beliefs that motivated those idealistic students two decades ago?

THE SOCIALISATION OF STUDENT ACTIVISTS OF THE 1960s: EMPIRICAL FINDINGS

Sufficient data exist on students who were politically active in the 1960s to enable us to draw a portrait of them in terms of their backgrounds, motivation and values.[7] First, however, it is necessary to distinguish among several different types of student activists. Those who played a major role in the 1960 Anpo movement may be called 'committed activists'. These students rebelled against the authoritarianism and 'revisionism' of the Communist Party and captured the leadership of Zengakuren (All Japan Student Federation), the nationwide organisation of student governments. Their descendants, organised into various factions, along with 'non-sect' radicals, were prominent in the campus protests of the late 1960s.

By contrast, 'non-committed activists' were those who had briefly been mobilised to participate in the movement during the Anpo crisis, but were otherwise not committed participants in student organisations. Finally, students who remained part of the Communist Party's Minsei (Democratic Youth) organisations, as we shall see, were separate from the radical student movements in this decade.

The typical anti-Yoyogi (i.e. anti-Japan Communist Party) 'committed activist' of the 1960 Anpo generation came from a family in which the father was employed in management or administration, white-collar work or the professions. The 'non-committed activists', on the other hand, were more likely to come from families in which the father was a small shopkeeper. In other words, the non-committed activists tended to come from the old middle class.

Further, committed activists' parents had above-average educations, with the father tending to have gone to college and the mother at least to senior high school. These are especially high levels of education when we consider that in the pre-war generation of these parents a college education for men and a high school education or above for women were confined to a much smaller élite than in the post-war period.

In terms of family atmosphere anti-JCP radical activists came from more permissive families. They were likely to have become sensitive to social and political conditions and events quite young, usually by middle school or high school. And through recognition of conditions in society which violated their anti-war, democratic and egalitarian values, they also became politicised during these same years. In addition, they were more strongly oriented towards personal expression in middle and high school classes and toward participation in extra-curricular school activities than students who later were not to become committed to the student movement.[8]

These students seemed to be searching for philosophies to express their social concern and anger towards a society they viewed as contradicting their ideas. In college they came into contact with and embraced Marxism because it appealed to both their intellect and to their values: it was both a 'scientific' and a humanistic ideology suited to the purpose of changing a society which they felt was far removed from the universalistic values of peace, democracy and equality they espoused. Many, however, took an eclectic approach to Marxism, reading many types of Marxist theorists and the early 'humanistic Marx', as well as attempting to combine Marxism with other philosophies, such as existentialism.

For these students, as Robert Lifton has noted, their college years were a period of search for *shutaisei*, a concept that implies a combination of personal identity, 'holding and living by personal convictions', and socio-political commitment – 'having the capacity to act in a way that is effective in furthering historical goals'.[9] Personal and political goals and expression, in other words, were inseparable. A student leader of the 1960 Anpo movement interviewed by Tsurumi Kazuko contrasted his generation with the Communists of the pre-war days: 'Their primary motivation was a spirit of martyrdom. In contrast, emancipation of ourselves as human beings has become our primary concern since the time of the anti-security treaty campaign.'[10] Because of the close connection between personal expression and identity and commitment, Tsurumi calls this generation 'hedonistic revolutionaries'.[11]

When we turn to the major anti-JCP sects and non-sect radicals of the late 1960s, we find a remarkable continuity in background and goals with the 1960 student activists. The late 1960s' radical students also tended to come from families of the new middle class who raised them permissively. They, too, experienced early in their lives a period of sensitisation to the contradictions of society and became oriented towards direct participation. Marxism appealed to them too as a 'humanistic revolutionary ideology'.

By contrast, JCP-affiliated Minsei students were more oriented towards Marxist ideology as a scientific theory of historical materialism to be used for the purpose of bringing about social reform.[12] A survey among Tokyo University students in February, 1969 revealed that, while almost all of those who supported the JCP-affiliated groups saw the campus struggle as one of democratisation of the university, a majority of those who supported Zenkyōtō (the non-sect radical organisation) saw it as a struggle to 'change oneself' and to 'establish selfhood'.[13] In other words, late 1960s anti-JCP activists sought personal identity through a simultaneous process of internal change and external social action.[14]

A comparative survey of university students in eleven countries, including Japan, conducted in 1969–70 at the time of the widespread campus unrest in Japan and elsewhere, further underlines the characteristics of this portrait.[15] When asked about career aspirations, far-left Japanese students most frequently chose one of two responses: 'to avoid entering the bureaucracy' and 'to have many free hours'. They also chose these responses in higher proportions than centre, moderate leftist or political students.[16]

The survey also investigated students' relationships with their parents. When asked about their emotional, moral and political closeness to their parents, only 28 per cent of Japanese students said they felt close to their parents politically, the lowest proportion of any of the eleven nations. When students were queried as to the specific areas upon which they diverged from their parents, the Japanese chose the issues of 'success', 'art', 'individualism', and 'leisure' most frequently. Again, it was the far-left students, compared to other types of Japanese students, who most consistently disagreed with their parents on these items. For the late 1960s' generation of committed activists in Japan, the issue thus centred on the rejection of conventional success as a goal, and the espousal of aesthetic, individualist, and life-style values in addition to political ones.[17]

In terms of student evaluations of their university and the educational system, Japanese students' attitudes were consonant with the 'generation gap' that existed between them and their parents. Japanese students scored among the highest of the eleven nations in seeing the goals of the university as being: (1) to allow students to pursue personal interests without specialisation, (2) to stimulate personal development rather than technical competence, and (3) to provide a basic general education. They were among the lowest of the eleven nations in seeing the purpose of the university as providing students with the means to achieve higher income and status and with training in specialised skills. Again, although the differences here were not as great as along other dimensions, far-left Japanese students exhibited these tendencies as much as or to a greater degree than other types of students.[18]

A further connection between generational values and university life was shown in the area of freedom of expression. A higher proportion of Japanese students than in any of the other countries but one believed that censorship should be abolished. Conversely, Japanese scored lowest of the advanced industrial nations in feeling personally free to express their political point of view within the university. Typically, far-left students scored higher on these dimensions than other Japanese students.[19]

The results of this very comprehensive cross-national survey of student attitudes thus buttress my contention that, whatever other differences they may have had, late 1960s' non-Communist radical students and the 1960 Anpo generation of student activists shared very similar backgrounds and values. They were predominantly from new middle-class, educated and permissive families and were sensitised to humanistic, expressionistic and participatory values early in their youth. By the time they were in college and radicalised, they were particularly alienated from their families' political values and from a society that emphasised status, success and élite bureaucratic careers. They perceived the university's goals and environment as clashing with their strong individualistic, egalitarian and expressionist values. Non-radical and non-activist students as well as Communist Party organisation students shared only some of the background and socialisation characteristics of the radicals, and these values they shared to a lesser degree. Radical activists of the 1960s thus emerged from a widespread generational culture, but were the most consistent and extreme bearers of that culture.

AFTER UNIVERSITY: MARXISM AND THE 1960 STUDENT
RADICAL

As we have seen, the 1960s' generation of activists had a more eclectic
approach to Marxism than their leftist predecessors and also attempted
to combine ideology with personal value goals. How did their ideology
weather the transition to occupation and adulthood?

To answer this question, in 1969 and 1970, I conducted a follow-up
study of the members of the 1960 Anpo generation who had been
interviewed eight years earlier by Professor Tsurumi.[20] The results
indicated that many student radicals of this generation continued their
search for personal identity and self-expression even after graduation.
Many entered occupations in the professions, particularly the 'intellectual' professions of teaching, journalism, publishing and research,
rather than entering the business world, as did most Japanese college
graduates.[21] Many told me in interviews that they had picked their jobs
in the hope of finding environments allowing for more personal
autonomy and opportunities to observe or participate in political and
social events.[22]

My sample included three types of former students: LEADERS of the
1960 student movement, COMMITTED ACTIVISTS who belonged to the
various factions of the student movement,[23] and INTERMITTENT AND
NON-ACTIVISTS, i.e. completely non-active students along with those
who did not ordinarily belong to the student movement, but who were
mobilised only briefly to participate in demonstrations.

The Decline and Maintenance of Belief in Marxism

Did the appeal of Marxism change among former student activists?
The question of the increase or decline in the appeal of Marxism
embraces two related problems. First, changes in the appeal of Marxism as an ideology – the importance of Marxism as a whole in our
respondents' specific thought and belief, and second the changes in the
appeal of certain tenets of Marxist theory. The former indicates change
in the intensity of belief and the latter in the comprehensiveness of
belief.

I repeated three questions from the original Tsurumi study to gauge
changes in the importance of Marxism as a whole. The first question
asked the respondent whether he considered himself a Marxist to tap
the most intense level of appeal – a willingness to identify oneself in

terms of the ideology. The second question presented the respondent with a list of fourteen philosophical or ideological viewpoints ranging from Marxism through liberalism, existentialism, and nationalism, and asked him to choose those to which he felt closest. This question thus measures whether or not the respondent had an affinity to Marxism. The third question simply asked whether the respondent was interested in Marxism.

A comparison of the answers to these questions in the two surveys eight years apart is presented in Table 6.1. As expected, the less intense the level, from identification through affinity to interest, the larger the proportion of the sample who responded positively. This was true in both surveys. Also as expected, the appeal of Marxism along each of

Table 6.1 Change in identifications as Marxist by activity in the student movement

Identification	Activity in the student movement			
	leaders (n = 10)	Activists (n = 18)	int. & non-activists (n = 25)	Total % sample (n = 53)
% in 1962	70	55	4	34
decline	30	22	4	15
increase	–	–	16	7
% in 1970	40	33	16	26
Net change	– 30	– 22	+ 12	– 8
	Change in affinity to Marxism by activity in the student movement			
AFFINITY				
% in 1962	100	89	24	61
decline	30	22	16	21
increase	–	5	12	8
% in 1972	70	72	20	48
net change	– 30	– 17	– 4	– 13
	Change in interest in Marxism by activity in the student movement			
INTEREST				
% in 1962	100	100	52	77
decline	30	–	20	15
increase	–	–	8	4
% in 1970	70	100	40	66
net change	– 30	–	– 12	– 11

these dimensions in 1962 varied greatly with the type of student, leaders being more likely than activists, and activists more likely than non-activists, to be Marxist-oriented.

What changes occurred in the eight-year period? For the sample as a whole there was an overall decline in the appeal of Marxism on each dimension. Interest in Marxism was down to 66 per cent of the sample, a decline of 11 per cent; affinity to Marxism declined to less than half the sample (48 per cent), a decrease of 13 per cent since 1962; identification with Marxism declined to about one-quarter of the sample, a loss of 8 per cent.

A look at each category of student and the basis for decline, however, reveals that a straight comparison of the appeal of Marxism on each of these dimensions for the sample as a whole actually masks an interesting pattern of change. One reason the net change was so low is that part of the decline in each case was offset by a smaller but not insignificant *increase* in the appeal of Marxism over the eight-year period among some of the respondents, mostly the non-activists. Also the leaders seem to have been more susceptible to a change in belief and interest than the activists were. Two reasons for the relatively small net decline in the appeal of Marxism after eight years thus emerge: (1) a larger decline actually occurred but was offset by an increase in the appeal of Marxism among former uninterested and non-believing students, and (2) the activists seem to maintain more interest and belief than the former leaders do.

Changes in Belief in Specific Tenets of Marxism

The results of the survey indicate a moderate decline in the importance of Marxism between 1962 and 1970, though this change varied with the type of former student, and was partially compensated for by an increase in the importance of Marxism among former non-believers. Was the attrition of ideology also reflected in an across-the-board decline in belief in the major tenets of Marxism, or was the change reflected in a loss of faith in only certain tenets?

All respondents were asked in 1962 and again in 1970 whether they thought the following points of Marxism were correct: the proposition that history until now has been the history of class struggles, the analysis of the contradictions in capitalism, the inevitability of the collapse of capitalism and the advent of socialism, and the inevitability of the dictatorship of the proletariat. The first two represent two of the main premises of Marxian theory and the latter are two predictions based on these premises. Did each of these tenets suffer the fate of the ideology as a whole – a partial decline? Or, were the students selective, albeit un-Marxian, in their rejection? A glance at Table 6.2 supplies the answer. In 1962 the students were already eclectic in their agreement with different aspects of Marxist theory. History as class struggle and the contradictions in capitalism were the two most accepted tenets in the first survey, gaining large support from the leaders and activists and fair support from the non-activists. The inevitability of the collapse of capitalism and of the dictatorship of the proletariat seemed less certain to all categories, but particularly to the non-activists. An unwillingness to subscribe to what were to Marx consequences of his basic premises was common among all students, especially the non-activists.

In addition, far from rejecting all of these elements in the ideology, by the second survey a greater number agreed with the first two (history as a class struggle and the contradictions in capitalism). Besides a slight decline in the number agreeing with the dictatorship of the proletariat, only in the case of the inevitability of socialism was there a sharp decline. All categories of former students had lost faith in this tenet. Thus, this sample of former students not only was still eclectic in its agreement with the various propositions of Marxism, but the number believing in the methodological premises of the Marxian world view increased, while more came to reject Marx's predictions based on those premises.

The Role of Adult Occupation in Bringing about Ideological Change

A detailed explication of the reasons for the above changes is beyond the scope of this chapter. However, I would like to discuss briefly one of the most salient factors – occupation.

Those entering certain occupations were more likely to maintain or increase their belief, while those who entered other professions were more likely to maintain no belief, or lose the belief they once had. For example, on the dimension of affinity to Marxism, those who entered teaching, research, medicine or law were five times as likely to maintain or acquire an affinity to Marxism as to continue without or lose that affinity. Those who entered large enterprise or government, on the other hand, were five times as likely to lose an affinity or continue without belief as to maintain or acquire a positive belief.

Table 6.2 . Change in agreement with history as class struggle by activity in the student movement

Agreement with proposition	Activity in the student movement			
	leaders (n = 10)	activists (n = 18)	int. & non-activists (n = 25)	TOTAL % SAMPLE (n = 53)
% in 1962	80	89	48	67
decline	–	11	8	7
increase	–	11	16	11
% in 1970	80	89	56	71
Net change	–	–	+ 8	+ 4

Change in agreement with theory of contradictions of capitalism by activity in the student movement

% in 1962	60	89	56	67
decline	–	11	12	9
increase	40	11	24	23
% in 1970	100	89	68	81
Net change	+ 40	–	+ 12	+ 14

Change in agreement with inevitability of collapse of capitalism, and advent of socialism by activity in student movement

% in 1962	70	67	20	45
decline	10	17	16	15
increase	–	11	12	9
% in 1970	60	61	16	39
net change	– 10	– 6	– 4	– 6

Change in agreement with dictatorship of the proletariat by activity in the student movement

% in 1962	70	61	16	42
decline	40	17	12	19
increase	10	22	16	17
% in 1970	40	66	20	40
Net change	– 30	+ 5	+ 4	– 2

Affinity to Marxism is only one of a number of dimensions that might have been used to illustrate this pattern. For example, we saw that the inevitability of socialism was the tenet of Marxist belief that showed the most decline over eight years. Here too, those who gave up the belief were twice as likely to be in business as in the intellectual professions. The few who have since come to agree with the tenet were engaged in teaching and research, medicine or law.

Second, through my depth interviews with many of the former students, I noticed that, regardless of the occupation entered, their job played a key mediating role in the process of change for those who had rejected or begun to have doubts about Marxism. As the following examples of types of negative change make clear, the process involved a complex interaction between the individual's ideological beliefs and experience in the student movement in college, the manner in which he attempted to reconcile his ideological principles with his career goals, and his political and occupational experience as an adult.

Type I: 'Cognitive [Knowledge] Change'

'M' was a former leader in the Zengakuren at the time of the 1960 Anpo struggle, high enough in the leadership to serve as Zengakuren's representative at the funeral of Kamba Michiko, the coed who died during the clash with the police at the Diet on 15 June. After graduation he worked as a sales engineer for two years until his superiors discovered his record as a student activist. Unemployed for four years, in 1970 he found work in a publishing company in Tokyo, where he applied his interest in economics to the editing of a monthly magazine about labour problems and workers. Of his experience with Marxism he says:

> I went into Marxism and became familiar with its major theorists when relatively young. I studied it for ten years. The age from fifteen to twenty-five is the prime of a human being. In the prime of my youth, I didn't go with girls, I didn't go to the mountains, I didn't go to the seashore, I committed myself thoroughly to the study of Marxism and became completely familiar with it. ... The greatest change [in my thought about Marxism] has been to arrive at the conclusion that it is indeed childish by the standards of knowledge in the latter half of the twentieth century. Thus, while at that time Marxism satisfied my intellectual desires, it can no longer satisfy them at all. You could say that now, when I see only the faults in Marxism, it's because I know it well. When you go into it thoroughly, you also see its weaknesses. Even when I was a Marxist, I saw various weaknesses in Marxism, but now, I see them more clearly, even in economics.

'M''s change of heart typifies what I call 'cognitive' change, since it came about mainly through study and further knowledge, particularly of Marxist theory and of economics. I also interviewed 'K', another former leader in the student movement and now a university professor of 'futureology'. He had also rejected Marxism, having 'come to recognize clearly the contradictions in its theoretical structure'. Reports of the experience of others indicate that this type of change has been quite prevalent among the leaders of 1960.[24] Motivated by their interest in and commitment to Marxism, and sometimes by their desire to account for the failure of the 1960 struggle to result in revolution, they entered professions in which they could study Marxist economics. More thorough study and contact with 'modern' economics (i.e. US quantitative economic theory) often convinced them that Marxism was outmoded. I believe the frequency of this type of 'conversion' among leaders helps account for the often higher rate of change in belief among leaders than among other activists.

Type 2: 'Personal Value-Change'

This type of change among leaders and activists often represents not a complete rejection of Marxism, but rather just the beginning of doubts as to its premises or tenets. This type is prevalent among those who continued their activity in the left-wing movement and who entered professions or changed to jobs that allowed them greater freedom to participate. Even while continuing their radical activity and without forsaking their radical beliefs, they began to realise that Marxism's assumptions and categories conflicted with either their other beliefs about human nature or with the realities of their everyday life. Often these doubts occurred owing to their postgraduate experiences in their political activity or occupation.

Time had not diminished at all the extraordinary intensity of 'S''s commitment to political activity which characterised him during his student days as a leader of Zengakuren. But now, as a Tokyo University tutor, he said, 'I myself have been active in political organisations and have had doubts about Marxism–Leninism. During the Tokyo University struggle (1968–9), I realized that Marxism itself is an extension of the modern enlightenment. How to go beyond that is now the problem. . . .'

Proud of his individualism, 'S' went on to discuss his doubts about

Marxism and in the process revealed personal, individualistic values which were beginning to take precedence over ideology:

> Marxism is scientific socialism which says that a human being's rational consciousness rules his action. That's sort of limited. There definitely are things in action which can't be explained by such rationality, by science. ... I'm thinking quite a bit now about individual human beings who can't be lumped together quantitatively. I'm beginning to think that if the 'proletariat' or 'bourgeoisie' becomes just a 'mass' – well, I'm sorry, you just can't leave it like that!

Many of those who demonstrate an increased interest or belief in Marxism experienced changes that parallel the 'value' type and the 'cognitive' type, but with opposite results, as the following examples will show. Here, especially, postgraduate experience in college environments, journalism and law play a key role.

'O''s father was purged by the Occupation for his wartime role and he grew up with strong anti-Communist beliefs. Now a reporter for a major Tokyo newspaper, he labelled himself 'ideologically free', but he accepted the contradictions in capitalism as a correct analysis, voted for the Communist Party, and admitted to an increase of interest in and agreement with Marxism, sparked by his experiences as a reporter, which deepened his interest in society.

At the time of the first survey in 1962 'J' did not consider himself a Marxist nor did he have an affinity to Marxism. Eight years later he identified himself as a Marxist, choosing Marxism because it was the only philosophy he felt close to, and wanting to relate Marxism to present conditions in the world. A researcher in Asian economics, he came to Marxism about the time he entered graduate school, and credited reading primarily for his conversion.

Type 3: 'Career Change'

The 'Career Change' type is found in all categories from leader to intermittent activist. One of their major characteristics is a concern for their future place in society and this often results in a mid-college cessation of participation in demonstrations. The shock of arrest or suspension from school often leads to a period of re-evaluation of their goals and concern about their future. Change in belief about Marxism may occur at this time (i.e. prior to graduation) or gradually after employment. Their choice of business or government as a career is an expression of strong achievement drives. Their change in ideology is closely linked to their changed personal relationships after quitting the student movement. Receiving no reinforcement for their ideological beliefs among their few friends in school and/or at the workplace, their former attachment to Marxism wanes. A subcategory of this type consists of those who stop going to demonstrations in their senior year so as not to jeopardise their chances for employment in large enterprise.

'I', a former leader, was suspended from school for three years for his activity in Zengakuren. During that time he decided to refrain from political activity so that he could go back to school. When he went to look for a job he was accepted by the company of his choice, only to be suddenly rejected the next day. He finally got a job as an accountant, but left it to start his own very successful trading and real estate company with a college friend. Talking about the change in his outlook since college, he considered the starting-point to be his suspension, but the crucial decision was the occupational one:

> My goals now are different than they were in college. Life and work have become all mixed together for me and work comes before life. In my student days, politics was primary. ... I don't even know when it changed. I think I took the final decisive step when I graduated from college and decided to look for work. If I had remained in school and gone on to graduate school, politics would have probably stayed primary. However, when I decided to make a living by being a salary man and support a family, it changed.

'I''s views of Marxism paralleled the change in his goals. He no longer regarded Marxism as a political problem but found its economic aspects 'interesting'. Although he now felt he could talk freely about his past, in his former job he was afraid he would be fired if he did. Whenever he went outside his company, he cautiously refrained from talking about politics.

What is crucial to note about this threefold typology of change in ideological belief is that only the last category, the 'career-change' type, conforms to the commonly held view of student radicals as almost universally inclined to eschew their past beliefs and behaviour out of self-interest or fear, join 'establishment' organisations and become more conservative. In fact, among former leaders and activists the first two types of change, 'cognitive' and 'value' change, was more common.

The first represents doubts about the intellectual and logical structure of Marxism, while the second represents the questioning of the basic values underlying the ideology. In other words, former activists were more inclined to alter their ideological beliefs as a result of adult experience, which undermined one of the two major appeals that attracted them to the ideology in the first place – its scientific or its humanistic values.

Furthermore, while former believers may have jettisoned certain tenets of Marxism they did not necessarily abandon the entire ideology. They did not find it inconsistent or contradictory to accept some of Marxism's principal tenets but to reject others. Ideology for these former activists was never a 'closed structure' of thought that must be accepted or rejected *in toto*. Just as in their student days they had combined Marxist belief with other philosophies and maintained a questioning attitude, so in their adult years they continued to take a syncretic and sceptical approach to ideology.

STUDENT MOVEMENTS IN PERSPECTIVE

This composite portrait of the 1960s activist student can provide us with explanations of the subsequent development of the student movement if we see it as an early and politicised part of an emerging generation of 'post-industrial' youth appearing throughout Western Europe and the US as well. Ronald Inglehart's analysis of generations in Western Europe described the emergence by the 1970s of younger middle-class cohorts with 'postbourgeois values' stressing aesthetic and intellectual needs rather than the 'bourgeois' acquisitive orientation of their parents' generation. He further found that such postbourgeois values were associated with support for leftist parties.[25]

Similar studies of intergenerational change have been conducted in Japan. Scott Flanagan, slightly modifying Inglehart's framework, tested for a set of 'libertarian' values found in the mass consumption, affluent and welfare societies of Western Europe, North America and Japan. He identifies these values as self-indulgence, secularism, permissiveness, independence, cynicism and individualistic, assertive attitudes. Significantly, he found such are most closely associated in Japan with younger age and higher education and politically are closely associated with voting for the opposition parties and supporting political protest (specifically the 1960 demonstrations, student strikes and other protest activities). Moreover, when Flanagan compared differences between generations in six industrialised European countries and Japan and correlated this with rate of economic growth, he found that the faster the rate of economic development from the early 1950s to 1970, the greater the value differences separating generations. Thus, with its highest rates of economic growth during this period, Japan also had the largest generation gap between 'traditional' and 'libertarian' (postindustrial) values, a finding consistent with the cross-national data we presented above on university students.[26]

In a similar study Nobutaka Ike found that the decline in acquisitive values among the younger generation in Inglehart's European study was less pronounced in Japan, but a large generation gap existed regarding the value of leading a life that suits one's taste. Ike associates this finding with the search for *shutaisei*, selfhood or individuation, that Lifton saw in the protesting youth of the 1960 Anpo crisis.[27]

Our findings on the 1960s' student activists and, in particular, our discussion of their attempt to combine political action with individualistic self-expression; humanistic values; and rebellion against bureaucratic heirarchy, specialisation and authority correspond closely with these more general findings on the emergence of 'postindustrial' youth cohorts in Japan by the 1970s. By viewing the Japanese post-war student movement in the context of an emerging 'postindustrial' generation, the origins, nature and fate of the student movement in Japan in the last quarter-century become clearer, and some of the apparent differences between the activist students of twenty-five years ago and their non-political and self-indulgent descendants of today are lessened.

Social Change and the Two Student Movements of the 1960s in Japan

Social scientists have identified major differences between student movements in developing societies and those that arose in the already industrialised societies of the West in the 1960s. In developing, non-Western societies undergoing modernisation and involved in contact with, or colonised by, Western countries, student movements represent the emergence of a small group of educated youth who experience a gap between the modern and Western values of democracy, nationalism, rationalism and so forth, and the values of their traditional families. This intellectual élite typically rebels against both their traditional families and the colonial or authoritarian regime's establishment. They ally themselves with other 'modern' political groups – independence movements, military groups or leftist parties. Often in the later stages of industrialisation, they join wider socialist or trade-union movements for the advancement of political and economic rights. These students in late industrialising societies are strongly oriented towards social reform and believe in leftist ideologies like orthodox Marxism.

In 'postindustrial' societies,[28] a new kind of student activist appears – 'postmodern' youth. These are the sons and daughters of professional and new middle-class families rebelling against bureaucratic, mass society and seeking to replace it with a society more in line with the humanistic, egalitarian, self-expressive and personally autonomous values they acquired early in their youth. Postmodern youth typically feel strongly the contradictions between their ideals and reality, between their self-expressive needs on the one hand and the nature of bureaucratic politics and occupations on the other. Alienated from bureaucratic organisations, they usually reject all forms of adult political organisations in favour of independent movements emphasising personal contact, non-hierarchical organisation and grass-roots participation.

While in college they often adopt the rhetoric of an older ideology like Marxism in order to criticise contemporary society, because they are deeply involved in a search for new human relationships and identities, postmodern youth reject that ideology's orthodoxy and attempt to mould it to their more humanistic concerns. Although they share the social and political goals of their predecessors' ('modernizing youth'), they seek in addition personal identity and self-transformation through their activities.

Looking at Japan in this historical and comparative perspective, we find a society that has made the transition from traditional and modernising society to postindustrial society in less than the forty years of the post-war era. Japanese society under the American Occupation in some aspects resembled the situation in developing nations: it was poor, it lacked employment opportunities, it contained many traditional social relationships that had survived pre-war modernisation (and, indeed, had been reinforced in some instances by the pre-war élite to justify modernisation and their own authority) and it was under the control of a foreign occupying power that, as in many colonial societies, was disseminating Western values of democracy and equality. From the end of the Occupation to the present, Japan has rapidly experienced, first, reindustrialisation and, then, the transition to a mass-consumer, affluent and 'postindustrial' society.

My point here is one often made about Japan: owing to the rapidity of economic growth and reindustrialisation in the post-war period, the usual stages of development often experienced serially in other societies have been 'telescoped' into a short period with overlapping stages. This post-war modernisation process by the 1960s had given rise to two simultaneously existing types of student movements, one representing the 'modernising' experience, and the other the 'postindustrial' or 'postmodern' experience. The JCP-dominated student movement (Minsei) closely resembled a modernising student movement oriented towards the same political and social goals as student movements in developing non-Western nations and industrialising Western democracies. JCP students in the immediate post-war period rebelled against their parents' 'feudal' pre-war values, challenged the foreign 'colonial' occupation with its own modern values, and fought against the poor conditions of society and student life. Subsequently, succeeding generations of Minsei students continued to manifest characteristics of students in non-Western developing nations: an emphasis on nationalist themes, on anti-American imperialism and on the material welfare of students and the working class.

With Japan's economic recovery and the legitimation of post-war peace and democratic ideals, the JCP-affiliated student movement has also increasingly exhibited the characteristics of modernising student movements in democratic industrial societies: alliance with an adult leftist organisation for the preservation and expansion of political and economic rights, for the reform of social institutions and for political power.

The anti-Yoyogi (anti-JCP) movement, on the other hand, clearly represented the emergence of postindustrial youth. They came from similar backgrounds as the student activists of the 1960s in the West and rejected adult bureaucratic political organisations in favour of their own independent political movement. They rejected Marxist orthodoxy in favour of more eclectic, less economically rationalistic and more humanistic versions of the ideology which satisfied their search for self-expression and personal identity. They emphasised universal rather than nationalistic themes.

If my analysis of the nature and causes of these two Japanese student movements of the 1960s is valid, then the 1960 Anpo crisis, in retrospect, must be viewed as the crucial transition period to a generation of postindustrial radical youth. This crisis, which joined thousands of leftist adults and normally non-active students in the movement to preserve 'peace and democracy', demonstrated the old left's strength and represented the apex of the modernising student movement. But, at the same time, it foreshadowed the appearance of 'postindustrial' youth – the anti-JCP activists whose adult fates I analysed above. As the 'postindustrial' characteristics of Japanese society developed, the numbers of youths on campuses with 'postindustrial' and 'libertarian' values increased. The themes that first emerged in the 1960 Anpo generation of activists – autonomy, anti-bureaucratism, direct participation, individualism, search for personal identity, eclectic Marxism, expressive politics and anger at the gap between the ideal and the actual – became even more characteristic of the late 1960s student generation, and particularly of the radical activist component of that generation that created so much campus conflict in 1968–9.

WHERE HAVE ALL THE STUDENT ACTIVISTS GONE?

Where are they now – these 'postmodern' youth? Why doesn't the present generation of youth follow in their footsteps? Some would argue that the oil shocks of the early 1970s and the contraction of job opportunities made the 'postindustrial' protest era a very short one and changed the values of subsequent generations of students. Undoubtedly there is some truth in this view.

But I think that the nature of individual 'change' in postindustrial societies is different. The analysis of the ideological fates of the 1960 Anpo activists gives us a clue to the nature of this difference. Most of the activists did not 'change' in the conventional sense of rejecting their previously held values and adopting new ones; rather, with the exception of the practical, 'career-change' type who fits the stereotype of conformity in adulthood to values different from those in one's youth, 'change' paradoxically came about as a result of *conformity to the same values that motivated their student activism*: the 'cognitive change' and 'personal change' types lost faith in Marxism or some Marxist tenets precisely because they continued the same search for personal identity, commitment to intellectual 'scientific' understanding, individuation and humanistic values that had led them to Marxism in the first place. Their basic values did not change; what did change was the extent to which they perceived that Marxism expressed and fulfilled those values.

Has not a similar process occurred in the student movement and intergenerationally among youth in Japan in the last fifteen years? The degeneration of the student movement of the 1960s into small splinter factions engaging in internecine struggles, in retrospect, appears to be as much a manifestation of the development of the same 'postindustrial' values that motivated the 1960s' generation. At least in part this degeneration appears due to the clashing of postindustrial values with the organisational necessity of a movement. In the 1970s, as the values of autonomy, individualism, direct participation and expressionism that characterised postindustrial youth became even more prevalent, it became almost impossible to maintain cohesive movement organisations because these require collective will, discipline, authority and self-sacrifice. Formal and large organisations have difficulty maintaining themselves in the face of students who prefer community to hierarchy, expression to discipline, direct participation to obedience to a larger cause and individual autonomy to the authority of leaders. Factionalism inevitably resulted. Extreme splinter groups, which seek the ultimate form of self-expression, find community in personal leadership and locate individual identity in the small group will, might also be expected to resort to violence and terrorism.[29]

The majority of Japanese students in the late 1970s and early 1980s, however, continued to seek the same values as their 1960s' predecessors. The difference is that they sought postindustrial values through other means – privatised rather than public action. As Ike, citing Masao Maruyama, indicates, there is evidence that generations of Japanese youth after the 1960s have become increasingly individuated:

> One of the several ways in which this individuation process can proceed is 'privatization', which Maruyama defines as an orientation towards the 'achievement of self-gratification rather than public goals' and a 'withdrawal' or 'retreatism' as a 'conscious reaction against the increasing bureaucratization of the system and against the complexities of the social and political process in which he [youth] finds himself involved'.[30]

In other words, is it not possible that today's self-indulgent, non-political, conservative youth in Japan actually share many of the same 'postindustrial' values as the student activists of the 1960s? Is it possible that there has not been so much an intergenerational value change as a change, similar to the adult changes of the 1960 Anpo activists, *in the objects through which they seek to achieve and manifest those values*? The expression of many of these values today through material self-indulgence, of course, was made more possible by the fact that, unlike youth in Western Europe, Japanese youth have never rebelled against acquisitiveness *per se*, but rather they have railed against bureaucratisation. The increasing affluence and pluralisation of Japanese society make this option more appealing and possible than in the past.[31] Individual withdrawal into leisure pursuits and personal fulfilment to escape bureaucratisation and authority now substitutes for public protest against it.

In other words, whereas political commitment and protest activism traditionally have involved the adoption of a whole *Weltanschauung* of ideology and the individual's subjection of self to the political cause, in postindustrial society, they involve eclectic values and rationales and the goal of self-fulfilment. Those who undergo *tenkō* (ideological conversion),[32] or subsequent generations that choose to fulfil their values and selves through other than political means, do not 'change' so much as 'adapt' their values in a different way. Perhaps the 40-year-olds who attended the twenty-fifth anniversary reunions of the Anpo movement, and the teenagers who considered it ancient history, have more in common than they think.

Part III

Political Institutions and Practices

7 Electoral Laws and the Japanese Party System

Haruhiro Fukui*

People learn from and build on each other's successes and failures, often across racial, ethnic and national boundaries, for a variety of reasons and purposes. The Japanese may not have done so more often than other peoples, but they have arguably done so more selectively than many, largely thanks to their country's peripheral position on the world map. Throughout its recorded history Japan's physical distance and separation from other countries has provided its people with a natural barrier that filters products of foreign civilisations and cultures for selective importation and adoption. With few exceptions, such as the Occupation period, the Japanese have thus consciously 'internationalised' at their own pace and on their own terms.

It may appear that, by and large, the filtration mechanism and process have contributed to the effective digestion and absorption of the ideas and institutions, as well as goods and services, imported from abroad, whether from China or Korea in the pre-Heian period, or from China and Europe in the brief pre-Tokugawa 'Christian era', or from Europe and the USA after the Meiji Restoration of the mid-nineteenth century. It may appear, in other words, that the Japanese have developed, refined and effectively applied the technology of cross-cultural idea-hunting and institution-borrowing to a remarkable extent.

But have the Japanese been really so successful in their selective search for and adoption of foreign ideas and institutions? If so, how did they correctly evaluate the usefulness of an alien idea or institution? How, in particular, did they anticipate the long-term consequences and impact of an imported idea or institution on Japanese society and mores? What rules or tools of discrimination and evaluation enabled them to discern the appropriateness of the targeted foreign idea or institution? How accurate and dependable was their judgement?

It is impossible to provide empirical answers to these questions. So numerous and varied have been the foreign ideas and institutions borrowed and adopted by the Japanese over the last two millennia that it is futile even to try to identify all of them. Moreover, even if it were possible to identify and sample all of them, it would still be impossible to document the process through which each idea or institution in the sample was actually selected, imported and utilised. Nor would it be possible to evaluate, objectively and accurately, how useful the imported idea or institution proved to be. This would be the case because, first, utility is by definition a highly subjective value that varies, often quite widely, from one user of the subject involved to another and, therefore, the same imported idea or institution must have inevitably been more useful to some Japanese than to others. Second, it is obviously impossible to identify all users of any of the countless ideas and institutions involved, not to mention measure, add up and average their widely varying utilities.

Nevertheless, it may be useful to subject to detailed analysis the process of the importation of one specific idea or institution and its outcome. The results of such analysis should reveal at least some aspects of a process which may well be common to all or most processes of cross-national idea-hunting and institution-borrowing as practised by the Japanese.

This study focuses on the Meiji electoral institution – specifically, the mixed single- and double-member constituency (electoral district) system combined with the plurality (first-past-the-post) formula – and its subsequent evolution and impact on the development of another, and closely related, political institution, the competitive party system, in pre-war and post-war Japan. This is a particularly appropriate case for two reasons: the election of legislators was an indisputably foreign import in Meiji Japan and, despite its foreign origin, the electoral institution quickly became, and has remained to this day, a permanent and critically important, though not always the dominant, component of the Japanese polity. It is an exceptionally interesting case because an electoral system is, perhaps even more than most other political institutions, a culture-bound and culture-sensitive institution with significantly dissimilar effects on different political systems. Finally, it is a good case to investigate in terms of our broader theoretical concerns because a respectable body of relevant theoretical and cross-national comparative literature exists.

SOME THEORETICAL GUIDEPOSTS BASED ON CROSS-NATIONAL EXPERIENCES

In all competitive electoral systems most, though usually not all, candidates run, at least nominally, in the name and as representatives of political parties. Competition thus takes place at two levels – between individual candidates and between parties – and the latter kind of competition counts more than the former kind, at least in theory. In other words, a competitive electoral system is always accompanied by a competitive party system, and vice versa. But how are the two systems causally related to each other?

In the mid-1950s Maurice Duverger, one of the most respected political scientists of the period, argued that an electoral system causally influences a party system.[1] Since then, however, the validity of this simple view has been questioned by a number of others, notably by Stein Rokkan and, more recently, by contributors to a 1983 volume edited by Vernon Bogdanor and David E. Butler.[2] It would now seem reasonable and prudent to argue that a party system is the cause and an electoral system is the result, rather than the other way round. 'When one looks at the ways in which the electoral systems have developed in the four [Scandinavian] countries, it becomes apparent that changes in the electoral order have always come about as a result of a change in the balance of forces or in the structure of the party systems. Electoral systems are devised by political parties in response to political circumstances.'[3]

It is thus tempting to dismiss categorically the causal impact of a country's electoral system on its party system. Common sense suggests, however, that the truth is probably close to what Bogdanor has argued is the case: 'The relationship between electoral systems, party systems and the process of social change are . . . reciprocal and highly complex.'[4]

This must be true as well for the two components of an electoral system that I have chosen to study, the constituency system and the electoral formula. These are, as Douglas W. Rae has suggested, the two components that determine the relationship between the percentage share of votes which a party wins in a free and competitive election and the percentage share of seats which that share of votes earns that party.[5] Rae demonstrated, on the basis of a careful analysis of the electoral performance of 664 parties in twenty Western democracies in 115 elections, that nearly all electoral systems favour larger elective parties – i.e. those with larger numbers of members and/or supporters – and penalise smaller ones.[6] He also demonstrated, however, that some electoral systems are more conspicuously biased in such a direction than others: for example, single-member constituency systems tend to be more biased than multi-member constituency systems.[7] The general rule is: in a one-man, one-vote system, the larger the number of seats per constituency (which Rae called the 'magnitude' of the constituency), the less advantaged a large party is *vis-à-vis* a small party and the more proportional the distribution of seats to the distribution of votes, although this relationship is not linear but curvilinear.[8] Important corollaries of this rule are: the larger the number of seats per constituency, the larger the number of parties represented in the legislature, the smaller the largest party's or parties' shares of votes and seats, the larger the number of parties needed to form a legislative majority and the more fractionalised the legislature.[9]

Electoral formulae also make an important difference in the degree of fit between various parties' share of votes and seats and, therefore, in the overall profile of a party system. Not surprisingly, proportional representation (PR) formulae tend to yield closer fit and greater proportionality than either majority or plurality formulae. Different kinds of PR formulae, however, produce different degrees of fit: the d'Hondt formula currently used, for example, in Israel as well as in the national-level allocations in West Germany and the constituency-level allocations in Iceland gives more advantage to larger parties than the Sainte-Laguë formula used, for example, in Norway as well as in the constituency-level allocations in Denmark and Sweden, or the largest remainder formula used in Italy as well as in the national-level allocations in Denmark and Sweden, or the Hare formula used in Austria and Belgium.[10]

By comparison, both the majority formula used, for example, in Third and Fifth Republic France with the two-ballot system and in Australia since 1918 with the alternative vote system, and the simple plurality (first-past-the-post) formula, used in Canada, New Zealand, the US, and the UK should in theory produce, and in practice do tend to produce, greater disproportions than PR formulae. When combined with a single-member constituency system, the latter formula, in particular, can produce 'disproportions of cubic proportions', as Rae put it.[11] A significant, though not entirely consistent, difference in the performance of PR and plurality systems in this regard is shown in a recent study by Richard Rose.[12] Combination with a multi-member constituency system may either exaggerate or neutralise the large-party bias of the plurality formula, depending on how many ballots each voter has. If each voter can cast as many ballots as the number of candidates to be elected from the constituency and if all or most voters cast their ballots strictly along partisan lines, a large party, especially the largest one, should enjoy enormous advantage. If, on the other hand, each voter has fewer ballots than the number of seats to be filled, as in a limited vote system, the large party's advantage is reduced and a minor party can win representation relatively easily, at least in theory. In such a system a minority party will win a seat if it runs only as many candidates as or fewer than the number of ballots allowed each voter and, in addition, it manages to win a percentage share of votes larger than the quotient of the number of ballots per voter divided by the sum of that number and the total number of candidates to be elected. For example, if each voter has two ballots and as many as five candidates are to be elected from the constituency, any party that runs no more than two candidates and wins more than 28.6 per cent of the vote (2 divided by $2 + 5$) should win at least one seat.[13]

If each voter has only one non-transferable ballot in a multi-member plurality system, the small-party advantage should increase so much that the effects will be similar to those of a PR system. In fact, at least one scholar calls this version of the limited vote system 'semi-proportional'.[14] In practice such a system in its unadulterated form has been in use only in two cases – in Japan's House of Representatives elections since 1925, except in the first post-Second World War election of 1946, and in Spain's Senate elections since 1977.[15] Japan's is thus the only case that has been in use long enough to generate a body of data sufficiently large to test the long-term effects of such an electoral system upon a party system. As we shall see in a later section of this chapter, the Japanese experience leads us to question the validity of the theoretical inference mentioned above. Unfortunately, however, it does not permit an unequivocal conclusion partly because the system has in it an inherent element of uncertainty and unpredictability and partly because the Japanese system has been contaminated by gross *de facto* gerrymander in the last three decades.[16]

Despite its ambiguities the Japanese case is interesting and valuable for its uniqueness. It is also interesting, as I have already mentioned, as an example of a complex and culture-sensitive institution originally imported from abroad and subsequently modified and adapted to suit the country's circumstances and needs as defined by its leaders. How and why has the unique system been chosen? We will now try to answer that question by retracing the history of electoral laws in pre-war and post-war Japan in some detail.

The Evolution of the Japanese Electoral System

The first official effort to introduce an electoral system in Meiji Japan apparently preceded by about a year and a half the inception of the People's Rights Movement (*Jiyū Minken Undō*). Initiated in the Department of the Left (*Sain*) in the summer of 1872 as part of a broader effort to draft a constitution, this effort culminated in *The Rules of the National Assembly (Kokkai Giin Kisoku)* submitted to the *Dajōkan* in August 1872.[17] Japan's first electoral law, however, was not actually promulgated until 1878, some four years after Itagaki Taisuke and his comrades petitioned the Department of the Left for the establishment of a popularly elected national assembly. This law, entitled *The Rules of Prefectural Assemblies (Fukenkai Kisoku)*, applied only to prefectural and local elections, although it set an important precedent for the law to govern national assembly elections that was soon to follow. The efforts to draft the latter kind of electoral law, as well as a constitution, continued throughout this period, with the assistance of several foreign advisers, such as the Frenchman Albert Charles du Bousquet, and the American Guido Fridolin Verbeck.[18] However, they did not lead to an immediate success.

The ultimately successful effort to draft an electoral law for national assembly elections was undertaken, again simultaneously with a renewed effort to draft a constitution, in the late 1880s. The task was led by Kaneko Kentarō with the assistance, directly, of Itō Miyoji and Inoue Kowashi and, indirectly, of several foreign advisers, notably the German jurist, K. F. Hermann Roessler, and culminated in the House of Representatives Members Election Law promulgated in 1889 simultaneously with the Meiji Constitution.[19]

Many details of the process by which the 1889 electoral law was drafted are missing. It is known, however, that the original draft was revised at least twice, by Itō Hirobumi and Inoue Kowashi, respectively, before it was accepted by the Kuroda Cabinet in or around May 1888, but that it was agreed from the beginning that the system to be chosen would be one with a plurality formula, with one ballot per voter and single-member constituencies of between 80 000 to 100 000 inhabitants each as a rule and, possibly, with some multi-member constituencies as exceptions.[20] When actually enacted after further revision by the Privy Council, the 1889 law provided for the election by the plurality formula of 300 House of Representatives members from 214 single-member and 43 double-member constituencies, all quite small in area, with the seats distributed roughly at the ratio of one per 120 000

Table 7.1 Japanese House of Representatives Members election laws

Law	Franchise	Voters	Districts	Members per District	Ballots per Voter	Formula	Members in house
1889	25 years or older payers of Y15+ direct national taxes	c. 450 000	257	1 as norm; some 2	1–2	Plurality	360
1900	25 years or older payers of Y10+ land or direct natio-nal taxes	c. 1 000 000	97	1–11 per prefecture; 4–13 per city	1	Plurality	360
1919	25 years or older payers of Y3+ direct national taxes	c. 3 000 000	374	1 as norm; some 2 or 3	1	Plurality	464
1925	All 25 years or older males	c. 12 400 000	122	3–5	1	Plurality	466
1945	All 20 years or older	c. 37 000 000	54	4–14 per prefecture as norm; some prefectures divided into 2 districts	1–3	Plurality	468
1947	All 20 years or older	c. 41 000 000	117	3–5	1	Plurality	466
1950	All 20 years or older	c. 42 000 000	118	3–5	1	Plurality	467

Source: Shūgiin and Sangiin (eds) *Gikai Seido Shichijūnen-shi: Shiryō-hen* (Tokyo; Okurashō Insatsu-kyoku, 1962) pp. 199–202.

inhabitants.[21] Suffrage was limited to those males 25 years of age or older who paid at least fifteen *yen* in direct national taxes – or about 1.2 per cent of Japan's total population at the time.

The first House of Representatives electoral law of Japan thus adopted a highly restrictive franchise, combined with a constituency system and an electoral formula that would in theory reward larger parties and punish smaller ones. This is not particularly surprising, considering that this was the first electoral law enacted in the country; it is none the less interesting, considering the fact that it was authored by and on behalf of leading oligarchs known then for their hostility to the 'people's parties' that were likely to dominate the House of Representatives, at least in the short run. This apparent paradox can be explained by the oligarchs' decision, dictated partly by their inexperience and partly by the mounting pressure of the People's Rights Movement, to borrow and adopt a respectable European model or models in a great hurry. And, in fact, the law was a remarkably faithful, though eclectic, replica of the existing British and, to a lesser extent, German, electoral laws. This was true even in its fundamental ideological orientation.

It must be remembered that restriction of franchise by property (tax payment) requirements was a standard practice in Europe in the nineteenth century. Even in the cradle of modern democracy, England, from which the founding fathers of Meiji Japan learned and borrowed in a variety of areas, the vote was granted to only 2.1 per cent of the total population before the passage of the Reform Act of 1832 and 3.3 per cent after that. The secret ballot was introduced as late as 1872; a majority of adult males, accounting for 15.6 per cent of the total population, gained the vote only after the Reform Act of 1884; and, finally, universal male suffrage was not introduced until 1918.[22]

In Germany, which provided another, and in some areas even more attractive, model for Meiji Japan's institution-hunters, the rules governing the election of members to its federal legislature in the late nineteenth century were at least superficially more liberal. The historic Frankfurt Assembly passed in 1849 an electoral law that introduced universal male suffrage and direct, secret voting, though the law was not implemented until Bismarck used a modified version for the election of members to the Reichstag or Imperial Diet, first, of the Northern German Confederation in 1867 and, subsequently, of the newly established Reich in 1871.[23] This law granted universal adult male suffrage, but the voting was not secret and, moreover, elected members of the Reichstag were explicitly forbidden to be paid salaries and therefore had to be men of substantial wealth.[24] The latter provision acted as a *de facto* property requirement for candidates, though not for voters.

It should also be noted that the Reichstag's powers were extremely limited, especially in the early years, with no legal competence to pass on issues of foreign or military policy or to influence, not to mention bind, the actions of either the emperor or members of the Bundesrat, or Federal Council, who conducted the affairs of the state with little regard to Reichstag members' views or interests. It was a Parliament, as one observer put it, 'without a government' and condemned 'to deliver monologues'.[25] Moreover, the Bundesrat represented the governments of the twenty-five states comprising the empire and after 1849 the most influential of them, Prussia, and after 1896 Saxony as well, elected members of their state Diets by the rigidly property-based three-class franchise system, which granted to voters varying numbers of ballots depending on the amounts of taxes paid.[26]

The 1889 Japanese electoral law followed the precedents set by the European models with regard to the constituency system and electoral formula. In England until 1885 double-member constituencies had been the norm and, in fact, the last constituency of this type survived until as recently as 1950.[27] Moreover, thirteen constituencies had elected three members each under the Representation of the People Act of 1867 until they reverted to the two-member norm under the Redistribution Act of 1885.[28] On the other hand, the 1871 German law for the election of Reichstag members adopted a strictly single-member constituency system, combined, however, with the second-ballot majority rule: in order to win, a candidate had to win an absolute majority either in the first or the second ballot, the latter fought between the two who scored the largest and second-largest numbers of votes in the first ballot.[29]

It is thus clear that the Japanese House of Representatives electoral law of 1889 was modelled largely on the English and German laws of the times and was theoretically biased in favour of the larger anti-oligarchic 'people's' parties (the Liberals and the Progressives). The theoretical bias was corrected to a large extent by the extremely restrictive franchise and, although, as we shall see in the next section, the bias did show in an exaggerated way in the first two general elections, it gave way to what appeared to be an opposite bias in favour of smaller parties in the next four elections. None the less, the government revised the law in 1900 in a bold but theoretically correct direction.

The 1900 law retained the plurality formula and single-ballot rule but introduced a highly complex system of constituencies electing variable numbers of representatives. Ninety-seven very large constituencies with boundaries coinciding with those of prefectures or cities would thus elect one to thirteen members each.[30] This represented a critical point of take-off in the process of the adaptation, or Japanisation, of the European model, setting a precedent for the so-called medium-sized constituency system of three to five members per district that would become the norm after 1925.

An important objective of the revision was to boost the weight of urban interests and reduce that of rural interests in order to overcome the latter's continuing opposition to an increase in land-tax rates that was deemed essential for meeting the growing fiscal needs. That was what Prime Minister Yamagata Aritomo meant when he emphasised the need to give urban voters fair and equal representation in the Diet.[31]

Another, and in the long run more important, objective was to weaken the major 'people's' parties and nurture the pro-government minor parties, such as the Kokumin Kyōkai, and independents. A government spokesman thus argued, theoretically correctly, that the proposed system of multi-member constituencies combined with single ballots would ensure 'proportional representation'.[32]

The move was initially opposed by both major parties, but their positions subsequently changed, for reasons of shifting partisan interests. It is significant to note here that during the Diet debates on the bill, a Kenseitō member cited, though not entirely correctly, European experiences and precedents. Saibara Seitō thus argued:

> Large [multi-member] constituencies combined with single ballots would cause much confusion within each party, even to the extent of threatening its survival. . . . Even in the more advanced countries of Western Europe, large constituency systems used to be the norm. . . . Most of them, however, have switched by now to small (single-member) constituency systems. . . . This has been the case in France, Britain, and Germany. [This shows that] even in countries with well-developed party systems, large constituencies combined with single ballots make a difficult system to manage. . . .[33]

Ironically, no sooner had the law been revised to the advantage of the oligarchs and minor parties allied with them than the era of party government began to unfold. In fact, nearly two years before the 1900 revision of the electoral law, Japan's first, although extremely short-lived, party government had been formed by the majority party, the Kenseikai, and barely six months after the revision of the law a new and far more durable major party, the Rikken Seiyūkai, was created under the leadership of the most influential oligarch, Itō Hirobumi.[34] As the Seiyūkai and its main rival, the Kenseihontō (later Rikken Koku-mintō), subsequently established increasingly effective control over government, they began to press for another revision of the law in the opposite direction. Bills to replace the existing mixed system with a simple single-member system were introduced to the Diet by the Seiyūkai government in early 1912 and again by a group of Seiyūkai members in early 1918.[35] Neither passed the Diet at the time, but a similar Seiyūkai-backed bill carried in 1919.

Under the 1919 law 295 very small constituencies elected one member apiece, sixty-eight somewhat larger constituencies of two members apiece, and eleven constituencies three members apiece.[36] This may appear to represent reversion to the British model, but it is obvious that by this time the Japanese electoral and party systems both had long since begun to evolve according to the pressure and logic of domestic politics rather than in emulation of a foreign model, British or otherwise. This was to become even more obvious several years later when yet another revision was undertaken, successfully, to introduce an internationally unique system of 'medium-sized' (larger than those under either the 1889 or 1919 law but smaller than those under the 1900 law) multi-member constituencies with single ballots. This one has proved to be the most viable of the electoral systems with which Japan has experimented to date, surviving the tremendous political vicissitudes of the next sixty years with only one short interruption.

As I suggested in the preceding section, either a single-member constituency and single-ballot system or a multi-member constituency and plural ballot system – requiring either a majority or plurality of votes for election in either case – is a good one to choose if one wants to give advantage to larger parties. If, on the other hand, one wants to give advantage to smaller parties, the most logical choice will be a PR system, particularly of the Sainte-Laguë variety. Under the first Japanese universal adult male-suffrage law enacted in 1925, however, 466 medium-sized constituencies were to elect three, four or five members apiece, each voter casting only one ballot. Such a system would give substantial advantage to each of the several large parties, rather than the largest or two largest parties. It would thus encourage, theoretically, moderate degrees of cohesion and competition in the party system without the risk of either one-party dominance or extreme fragmentation. That may have entered the thoughts of the authors of the 1925 law. A far more important consideration was, however, the partisan interests of the three parties that had successfully engineered the enactment of the universal male-suffrage law.

The campaign for the enactment of the 1925 law was led by the ruling coalition of the Kenseikai, the Seiyūkai and the Kakushin Club. Of the three allied parties in government, the Kenseikai, which had been the second-ranking party more frequently than the first-ranking party in the Diet, and the Kakushin Club, which was a much smaller party than either of its two partners, both preferred a multi-member system; on the other hand, the Seiyūkai, which had until early 1924 been by far the largest party, pressed for a single-member system. A medium-sized, multi-member system of between three and five members per constituency was apparently a logical compromise solution.[37]

The 1925 law survived until 1945 and, when it was finally revised in the wake of the devastating war at the Cabinet's initiative, presumably under the pressure of the Supreme Commander for the Allied Powers,[38] it was replaced by a complicated system of multi-member (2–14) constituencies as large as those under the 1900 law, but with each voter casting one to three ballots depending on the number of members to be elected from his or her constituency. This limited-vote system was expected to give advantage to smaller parties and independents and the government defended it as a 'substitute for a PR system' and as a device designed to 'maximize the voter's' freedom of choice and help new candidates run and get elected.[39] In fact, in the April 1946 House of Representatives general election 81 per cent of those elected were new members and thirty-nine women candidates also won in this election in which women voted for the first time in Japan's history.[40] After only one election, however, Yoshida Shigeru's Liberal Party Cabinet abandoned the system in 1947 in favour of the 1925 system despite fierce resistance put up by the opposition. The Public Office Election Law of 1950 retained intact the law as revised in 1947 for the election of House of Representatives members. Since then, the medium-sized, multi-member, single-ballot system has survived periodic attempts by the conservatives in power to replace it with a simple single-member system that would give them a greater advantage.[41]

During the last hundred years the Japanese have thus studied Western models of electoral system, imported some, quickly modified and adapted them, and within about forty years fabricated a unique model of their own. We have traced this process of institution-borrowing and adaptation and identified pragmatic partisan interests and calculations as the principal motive force at work. It remains to examine the actual impact of the succession of electoral laws on the Japanese party system.

IMPACT OF ELECTORAL LAWS ON THE JAPANESE PARTY SYSTEM

How useful and satisfactory did the succession of Japanese electoral laws enacted so far prove to be in achieving the objectives set by their authors, whatever they were? What short-term and long-term impact did they have on the performance of various parties and the party system as a whole? For the reasons mentioned in the introductory section of this chapter, it is impossible to answer such questions definitively and unequivocally. It is possible, however, to answer them partially but none the less very usefully, if terms like 'impact' and 'useful' are defined sufficiently restrictively and certain qualifications and assumptions are accepted. In this section I shall attempt to find partial and qualified answers to the questions with the aid of methods used, *inter alia*, by Rae in his 1967 work.[42]

First, let us place the questions in the specific context of our study. As pointed out in the preceding section, Japan's first House of Representatives electoral law of 1889 was drafted under pressure and in a great hurry, most probably with little clear anticipation of its specific effects either on the incipient parties or on the by then well-entrenched oligarchy. What effects did the law have on either, if any? All the later laws, on the other hand, were enacted with specific partisan or political objectives in mind: the 1900 law to hurt the large 'people's' parties and aid the pro-government minor parties; the 1919 law to aid the larger parties at the expense of the minor ones; the 1925 law apparently to reward the three allied parties in power; the 1945 law to punish the dominant parties of pre-war vintage and nurture new groups; and the 1947 and 1950 laws to revert to the 1925 system of controlled interparty competition and collaboration. To what extent did each of these laws fulfil its authors' expectations?

The advantage enjoyed by large parties under a particular electoral law can be indirectly and partially measured either by the percentage shares of votes and seats that go to the largest (or the two largest) parties or by the degrees to which the distribution of votes and seats is concentrated or dispersed. Rae defined the latter as the degrees of 'fractionalisation'.[42] This concept applies both to the distribution of votes among contending parties at the polls (fractionalisation among 'elective' parties, or *Fe*) and the distribution of seats among parties represented in Parliament (fractionalisation among 'parliamentary parties, or *Fp*). For simplicity, *Fe* (or *Fp*) can be defined as the value derived from the equation:

$$Fe = 1 - \sum_{i=1}^{n} Pi^2 \qquad (7.1)$$

where *Pi* is Party *i*'s decimal share of votes (or seats). To borrow Rae's examples: System *A* with *Pa* (Party *a*'s share of votes or seats) of 1.0 will give *Fe* (or *Fp*) of zero; System *B* with *Pa* = 0.9 and *Pb* = 0.1 will give *Fe* (or *Fp*) = 0.18; System *C* with *Pa* = 0.5, *Pb* = 0.4, and *Pc* = 0.1 will give *Fe* (or *Fp*) = 0.58; System *D* with *Pa* = 0.25, *Pb* = 0.25, *Pc* = 0.25, and *Pd* = 0.25 will give *Fe* (or *Fp*) = 0.75; and so on. An electoral law aimed at helping smaller parties should increase the degree of fractionalisation thus defined; conversely, a law intended to help large parties should decrease the degree of fractionalisation.

Table 7.2 presents the average percentage share of votes and seats won by the largest parties in elections held under each electoral law, the differences between such parties' share of votes and share of seats and the degrees of fractionalisation both among elective and parliamentary parties.[43] Looking first at the largest parties' share of votes and seats it turns out that such parties did worst in the first two elections under the 1889 law and, as expected, under the 1945 law. Why they did so poorly under the 1889 law can be explained by the tremendous instability of the party system and fluidity of party memberships in the first few years of electoral and parliamentary politics in the country. As a result of the instability and fluidity the largest elective party in Japan's first House of Representatives election, the Liberal Club, won 23.1 per cent of the vote but 42.0 of the seats, while the largest elective party in the second election, the Liberal Party, won 20.5 per cent of the vote but only 1.3 per cent of the seats.[44] The 1945 law, on the other hand, may appear to have fulfilled its authors' expectations in so far as it apparently helped small parties and independents, thus increasing the degree of fractionalisation. It should be noted, however, that it also gave substantial advantage to the largest parties as well, as suggested by the figure for the difference between the largest party's percentage share of votes and percentage share of seats in Table 7.2. The largest parties seem, however, to have done even better under the medium-sized constituency, multi-member system introduced by the 1925 law and reintro-

Table 7.2 Indicators of largest party advantage and degree of fractionalisation

Law	Years of elections	Largest party's share		%S-%V	Fe	Fp
		% Votes	%Seats			
1889	2 (1890–1892)	21.8	21.6	− 0.2	831.00	746.00
	4 (1894–1898)	41.2	37.7	− 3.5	721.25	735.00
1900	7 (1902–1917)	41.8	45.7	3.9	700.57	692.57
1919	2 (1920–1924)	42.5	46.2	3.7	661.00	665.50
1925	6 (1928–1942)	49.3	55.5	6.2	607.66	538.66
1945	1 (1946)	24.3	30.2	5.9	817.30	796.23
1947	15 (1947–1983)	45.8	51.8	6.0	700.06	646.66

Sources: Asahi Shimbun, 20 December, 1983; Kōmei Senkyo Renmei (ed.), Shūgiingiin Senkyo no Jisseki: Dai 1-kai – Dai 30-kai (Tokyo: Kōmei Senkyo Renmei, 1967); Nishihira Shigeki (ed.), Naigai SenkyoDēta 1978 ('78 Mainichi Nenkan Bessatsu) (Tokyo: Mainichi Shimbunsha, 1978) pp. 10–11; Shūgiin and Sangiin Gikai Seido Shichijūnen-shi: Shiryō-hen (Tokyo: Okurashō Insatsu-kyoku, 1962) pp. 210–2; J.A.A. Stockwin, Japan: Divided Politics in a Growth Economy, 2nd ed (London: Weidenfeld & Nicolson, 1982) pp. 112–13, table 11.

duced in 1947 that was intended to benefit several parties more or less equally. On the other hand, the 1889 law, after the dust had settled, and the 1919 law, both of which were supposed to benefit the largest parties, did not help such parties significantly more than the 1900 law, which was expected to aid minor pro-government parties and independents.

The indexes of fractionalisation, especially those for parliamentary parties, confirm the same trend: the 1889 law in the first two elections and the 1945 law produced the highest degrees of dispersion, while the 1925 and 1947 laws brought about the highest degrees of concentration. The 1900 law, intended to increase dispersion, actually resulted in increased concentration, while the 1919 law, intended to encourage concentration, had only moderate impact in the intended direction, impact even less significant than that of the 1925 and 1947 laws.

What we have seen above is the performances of parties of various strengths under the succession of electoral laws which contradict the predictions of theory based on cross-national data. The contradictions, essentially of the same kind and magnitude, however, have been observed in the performances of both elective and parliamentary parties, suggesting that those in the performances of the latter may have merely reflected those in the performances of the former. In other words, one may infer from the data presented so far that each electoral law directly influenced the distribution of votes among elective parties, that the distribution of votes was translated more or less proportionally into the distribution of seats among the parliamentary parties, and that, therefore, there was essentially no distortion in the vote-to-seat conversion process. If substantiated, however, this interpretation would do very serious damage to the theory, a central contention of which has been systematic distortion resulting from the conversion process.

Before we jump to a conclusion on this issue let us look more closely at the pattern of relationships between the distribution of votes and that of seats under the succession of electoral laws. Theory predicts, it will be recalled, that in converting shares of votes into shares of seats all electoral systems favour large, especially the largest, parties but that some systems do so more than others. In other words the largest party may win 40 per cent of the vote and be awarded 50 per cent of seats under one system but only 45 per cent of seats under another system. If the theory is correct, the advantage accruing to large parties from this kind of bias should have been more substantial under the essentially single-member constituency systems introduced in 1889 and, again, in 1919 than either under the 1900 and 1945 multi-member constituency, limited vote systems or the 1925 and 1947 multi-member constituency, single-ballot systems. Do the data prove or disprove the theory?

In order to answer the question we now look at the patterns of relationships between shares of votes and shares of seats earned by all parties under each of the several electoral laws. A scatterplot and a regression equation based on the least-squares principle succinctly summarise the pattern under each system.[45] For our purposes the equation can be written as:

$$S = aV + b \qquad (7.2)$$

where S is any party's percentage share of seats and V its percentage share of votes. A scatterplot with dots concentrated along the regression line represents a large proportion of variation in the dependent variable S explained by the independent variable V, yielding a high (close to 1) coefficient of determination, R^2; conversely, a scatterplot showing dots widely scattered away from the regression line indicates a weak explanatory power of the independent variable V and yields a low R^2. If the shares of seats are exactly proportional to the shares of votes for all parties, then, by definition $a = 1$, $b = 0$, and therefore $S = V$. The closer to 1 coefficient a and the smaller the absolute value of coefficient b, the more proportional one kind of percentage share is to the other kind, and, conversely, the more a departs from unity and the larger the absolute value of b, the more disproportional the relationship is. If b (intercept) is positive the smallest parties enjoy advantage in the conversion of vote shares to seat shares; if it is negative, such parties suffer disadvantage.

A glance at Figures 7.1 to 7.7 reveals several interesting facts about the distribution of vote share/seat share ratios for all parties under the different electoral laws. First of all, R^2 in Figure 7.1 for the first two elections held under the original 1889 law is totally out of line at 0.392, confirming the effects of the general instability and fluidity of the incipient party system which we have already mentioned. Second, R^2 for all other equations are impressively large – all being 0.967 or larger, indicating great consistency in the distribution pattern of vote share/ seat share ratios under each electoral law. Third, we note that the coefficient a is smaller than 1 (0.907) only in Figure 7.2, suggesting that, as we have also pointed out, the 1889 law was relatively advantageous to the smaller parties rather than to the largest, contrary to the prediction based on theory. Fourth, the deviation of coefficient a from 1 (defined as $a - 1$) and the absolute value of coefficient b are both the

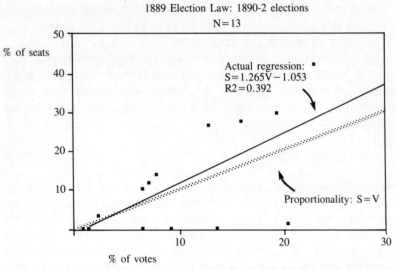

Figure 7.1

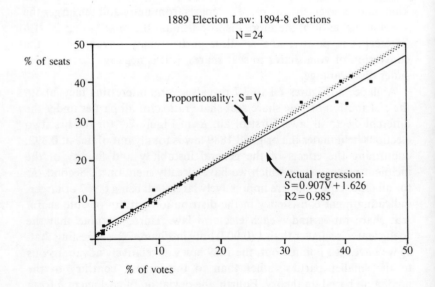

Figure 7.2

smallest in Figure 7.3 for the 1900 law, indicating the greatest proportionality, while they are the largest in Figure 7.6 for the 1945 law, indicating the greatest disproportionality, the rest falling between these two extremes. Fifth and last, *b* is positive in Figure 7.2 for the four elections held under the 1889 law and Figure 7.3 for those under the 1900 law, the former again contradicting the prediction of theory and the latter frustrating, at least partially, the partisan expectations of the law's sponsors. The relevant data in Figures 7.1–7.7 are summarised in Table 7.3.

The analysis of the scatterplots and regressions thus leads us to a conclusion in broad agreement with that previously reached by the examination of the largest party's share of votes and seats and the indexes of fractionalisation. Both sets of data point up interesting deviations of the Japanese case from outcomes either predicted by theory or expected by the authors or sponsors of the particular electoral laws concerned. The 1889 law thus proved advantageous to minor parties, contrary to theory, while the 1900 law failed to help minor parties much, contrary to its sponsors' presumed expectations. Just as surprisingly and interestingly, the 1945 law and, to a lesser extent, the 1925 and 1947 laws turned out to be most advantageous to the largest parties. The 1919 law should perhaps be said to have

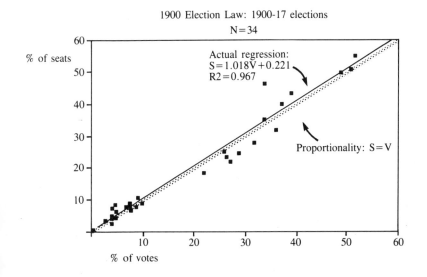

Figure 7.3

138

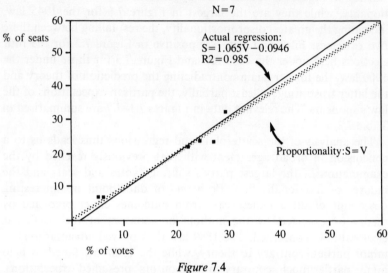

Figure 7.4

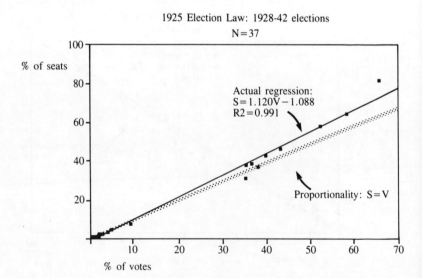

Figure 7.5

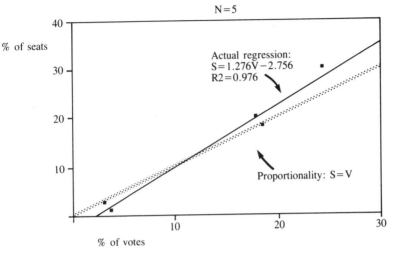

Figure 7.6

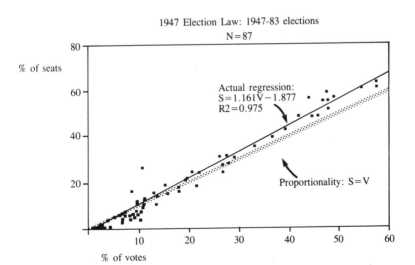

Figure 7.7

Table 7.3 Values of coefficients in regressions in Figures 7.1–7.7

Law	Elections	Equation	R^2	Coefficient $a-1$	Coefficient b
1889	1890–1892	$S = 1.1265V - 1.053$	0.392	0.265	−1.053
	1894–1898	$S = 0.907V - 1.626$	0.985	−0.093	1.626
1900	1902–1917	$S = 1.018V + 0.221$	0.967	0.018	0.221
1919	1920–1924	$S = 1.065V - 0.946$	0.985	0.065	−0.946
1925	1928–1942	$S = 1.120V - 1.088$	0.991	0.120	−1.088
1945	1946	$S = 1.276V - 2.756$	0.976	0.276	−2.756
1947	1947–1983	$S = 1.161V - 1.877$	0.975	0.161	−1.877

sources: See sources cited in Table 7.2.

performed closer to its intentions – to benefit the largest parties, but it did not do as well on this score as any of its three successors. Why should this have been the case? A definitive answer to the question will have to wait for the completion of the larger study of which this chapter is only a beginning. A tentative answer, however, will be presented in the conclusion that follows.

CONCLUSION

The simplest, and an essentially correct, answer to the question posed above would be that, as Bogdanor has pointed out: '[T]he same electoral system can have quite dissimilar effects in different countries; or even in the same country at different periods of its history'.[46] It should not be surprising in the least if the same electoral system had different effects in a European country and in Japan. It should be no more surprising if the leaders of Meiji Japan and their successors failed to anticipate and guard against this inherent risk of cross-national institution-borrowing. We may simply conclude that they were neither as far-sighted nor as successful in their enterprise as we may have been led to believe. Such a formalistic answer is, however, neither very interesting nor illuminating because it fails to address the substantive question: why did the Japanese electoral laws yield outcomes so regularly and consistently contrary to both theory and to the theoretically sound expectations of Japan's own institution-borrowers and adapters?

There are two plausible reasons for the 'anomalies' in the Japanese experience with electoral laws. One has to do with behaviour of the Japanese electorate that goes against the basic assumption of electoral competition in a Western democracy mentioned in the 'Theoretical Guideposts' section of the chapter – that electoral competition takes place primarily among political parties and not among individual candidates. Japanese voters, particularly those who reside in rural areas and support conservative politicians, tend to choose their candidates on the basis of personal relationship with little regard to their party affiliations or policy positions.[47] The essentially non-partisan orientation of the majority of Japanese voters cannot but spoil predictions based on a theory of electoral competition that assumes the central role of partisanship in voting behaviour. The orientation of the Japanese electorate should also give considerable stability to the distribution pattern of votes among candidates, and therefore indirectly among parties, not only across elections but also across electoral systems. In short, a candidate and his supporters stick together no matter what electoral law is in effect, thus minimising, if not totally eliminating, the impact of a change in the law.

We can attribute the persistence of personal ties as a major factor of voting behaviour among the Japanese electorate at least partially to the multi-member constituency, single-ballot electoral system itself. In his 1930 commentary on the system, the well-known constitutional scholar of the period, Minobe Tatsukichi, forcefully argued such a view:

> The main purpose of an electoral system in this age of party politics is to measure the degrees of trust the public places in different parties. In parliamentary competition, parties are the sole actors and individual members of parliament are significant only as members of a party. The existing electoral system, however, ignores the parties and recognises only individual candidates ... as the principals in electoral competition, thus leading voters to cast their ballots for particular candidates rather than for parties. ...
>
> Under an electoral system that ignores political parties, as the present system does, whether a small (single-member) constituency or a large (multi-member) constituency format is in place makes little difference; in either case, the results of an election fail to reflect public opinion accurately.[48]

The other and related reason concerns certain ambiguities in the pattern of inter-party competition under the medium-sized constituency system introduced in 1925. As we pointed out earlier, the unusual multi-member constituency, single-ballot system was set up originally with a view to making it theoretically possible for the three allied parties in power at the time to have a more or less equal chance to have their candidates elected from each and every constituency. The system does appear to have betrayed its authors by letting the largest party, rather than the three largest parties, win in most constituencies. That, however, is a matter of how one looks at the situation.

For one thing, a few years after the enactment of the 1925 law the three-party pattern was replaced not by a predominant party pattern, but by a fairly stable two-party pattern, until one of the two major parties, the Seiyūkai, split in 1939 into three separate parties and, then, merged with the other major party, the Minseitō, and others to form the wartime grand coalition party.[49] Under the post-war 1947 law a three-party pattern briefly reappeared before it gave way to one-party dominance by the Liberals in 1949, followed in the mid-1950s by a brief period of two-party competition between the Liberals and the Democrats. Finally, the merger of the Liberals and the Democrats and the reunification of the Right and Left Socialists in 1955, rather than ushering in an era of clear-cut one-party dominance, led to the 'one-and-a-half party system'. It is therefore not entirely correct to say that the 1925 law gave advantage only to the largest party; it did help the second-largest party as well.

Even more relevant here is the role of the factions in the ruling conservative party. As is well known, the Liberal Democratic Party (LDP) that has been in power without interruption since 1955 is a coalition of several entrenched factions which compete with each other at election time almost like separate parties.[50] Although they are called 'factions', however, they might as well be called 'parties'. In fact, in many constituencies they boast electoral support fully equal to that of the Socialists' and far broader and more stable than that of any other party, and they vigorously, and often successfully, compete with candidates of other parties as well as among themselves. What appears to be an LDP sweep in a three-member constituency can be seen instead as a case of victory by each of three allied conservative parties quite similar to those in the 1925 ruling coalition.

8 The Institutionalisation of Policy Consultation in Japan: Public Advisory Bodies

Ehud Harari

Samuel P. Huntington has defined institutionalisation as a 'process by which organisations and processes acquire value and stability'. That process may be measured by four criteria: *adaptability* (ability to cope with environmental challenges and maintain continuity despite turnover in leadership and membership), *complexity* of structure and functions, *autonomy* of environmental forces, and *coherence* (integration facilitated by agreement on principles, at least those regarding the rules of the game).[1] The Japanese state bureaucracy, measured against these four criteria, has been institutionalised since prewar days. In contrast, other organisations, such as the Diet; the Liberal Democratic Party; the Cabinet; and several interest organisations, including those representing doctors, farmers and textile workers, have become institutionalised much more recently. In this chapter I argue that, contrary to conventional wisdom, public policy consultation in Japan has also reached a notable level of institutionalisation.

Government consultation with individuals and groups from outside the government is an important measure of a political system's democratic character. Ideally, the process involves an equitable and interactive exchange of ideas between the government and society to facilitate the making of responsive, innovative and implementable policies. In the course of this exchange the government acquires information, expertise, ideas and vision that contribute to both its 'theoretical judgement', i.e. the ability to evaluate data and their implications for policy alternatives, and its 'political judgement', i.e. the understanding of the impact of policies on various segments of society. The government can use policy consultation to inform society of official views of and judgement on a variety of issues. If the process is

144

truly equitable, all individuals and groups concerned are given the opportunity to participate.[2]

Government consultation can take various forms, such as consultancy and research contracts with individuals, firms and university and non-university organisations; informal contacts with individuals and groups advocating certain positions; and statutory and non-statutory public advisory bodies established by government and composed either partially or exclusively of members recruited from outside the government. Each of these forms of government consultation shares at least one of the characteristics of policy consultation in democratic societies, but only advisory bodies, at least ideally, have all the characteristics; therefore, the evolution of public advisory bodies (hereafter 'advisory bodies' or 'ABs') is a central aspect of the institutionalisation of policy consultation in Japan.

There are two kinds of advisory bodies in Japan: statutory and non-statutory. The non-statutory ABs are most commonly known as *kondankai, kenkyūkai* or *konwakai*. These are informally established by the prime minister, cabinet members, other heads of government agencies or high-ranking government officials to act as their advisers and are collectively referred to as the 'private advisory bodies' (*shiteki shimon kikan*). According to the latest official estimate, in 1984 approximately 232 private ABs were in existence.[3]

Statutory ABs are known primarily as *shingikai*, but also, in descending order of frequency, as *chōsakai, shinsakai, iinkai, kyōgikai* and *kaigi*. Here I shall refer to all statutory ABs as *shingikai*, in both the singular and plural usage. *Shingikai* are established by various laws or, since 1983, by cabinet ordinances. In 1983 213 *shingikai* were authorised, though only 206 had been actually appointed.[4]

Public advisory bodies may be either *ad hoc* or 'permanent'. *Ad hoc* ABs are entrusted with a policy problem; once they have completed their task or reached their deadline they are disbanded. The Commission on the Constitution (Kempō Chōsakai) and the present Temporary Investigation Council on Education (Kyōiku Rinchō) are famous examples of *ad hoc shingikai*; the Economic Structure Adjustment Group for International Harmony (the so-called Maekawa Study Group) is an example of a recent *ad hoc* private AB. The permanent ABs deal with problems either as they are referred to them by the authority in question, or as they arise or are identified by their members. Members of permanent ABs are appointed for fixed periods (usually two years), but memberships are renewable.

Shingikai are assigned six types of tasks. In descending order of frequency these are: (1) studying and deliberating upon important policy measures, (2) examining administrative measures for licensing and standards for application of laws; (3) considering examinations, qualifications, and related matters; (4) examining administrative malpractices; (5) arbitrating and conciliating disputes; and (6) investigating matters requiring scientific expertise. The private ABs are primarily assigned the tasks of studying and deliberating upon important policy measures, investigating matters requiring scientific expertise and conciliating disputes.

Official pronouncements concerning public advisory bodies imply their importance in the democratic process by stating their goals as (1) introducing new expertise into government, (2) reflecting views and ideas of interests concerned in public policies, (3) promoting fair and equitable implementation of public policies, and (4) helping to co-ordinate related programmes of various government organisations. A widespread view of ABs in Japan, however, is that the state bureaucracy – the dominant force in policy processes – actually uses them to legitimise its own policy positions. Official pronouncements about the goals of the ABs are thus merely the *tatemae* (principles) called for by the spirit of the new, democratic constitution, while the *honne* (reality) remains bureaucratic domination. The state bureaucracy, so the argument goes, continues to control or at least manipulate society according to its own perception of the public interest and continues to maintain and further increase its own organisational power resources.

The argument I wish to make in this chapter is that, although this view may have been true of the majority of ABs in Japan in the past, it tends to ignore or unjustifiably dismiss as window-dressing recent indications that ABs have actually made dents in the unrivalled predominance of the state bureaucracy in policy-making. Indeed, the growing role of ABs parallels developments in other aspects of the political system, such as the increased weight of the LDP in policy-making and the growing importance of the Diet as a forum where meaningful policy discussions are conducted and legislative decisions made, not merely ratified. Taken together, these trends suggest that the Japanese political system is becoming more pluralistic. The analysis of the evolution of ABs and their increasing importance in policy consultation is one way of assessing this process of 'pluralisation' in contemporary Japan.

THE PRE-OCCUPATION ERA

Advisory bodies were established as early as the Meiji era. During the 1890s, the first decade under the Meiji Constitution, ABs were involved in such famous reforms as those of the legal system (Hōten Chōsakai) and the monetary system (Kahei Seido Chōsakai);[5] in the process that led to the passage of the Factory Act of 1911 (Nōshōkōtō Kaigi);[6] and in the formation of education policy (Kōtō Kyōiku Kaigi).[7] Since then and until the consultation system was changed under the auspices of the US Occupation authorities, other ABs were established in these and various other policy areas. Well-known examples include welfare (Kyūsai Jigyō Chōsakai, 1918),[8] labour relations (Shihon Rōdō Mondai Kyōgikai, 1918; Rinji Sangyō Chōsakai, Shakai Seisaku Shingikai, 1929),[9] land reform (Kosaku Seido Chōsakai, 1920),[10] the *burakumin* (outcasts) (Shakai Jigyō Chōsakai, 1921),[11] economic and industrial policy (Shōkō Shingikai, 1927; Sangyō Gōrika Shingikai, 1929),[12] and reform of the administrative structure and the financial and taxation systems (Rinji Gyōsei Zaisei Zeisei Shingikai, 1930).[13] Another famous example is the Cabinet Advisory Council (Naikaku Shingikai) formed in 1935 to deal with various 'basic policies'.[14]

I have not found a list of all ABs in existence prior to the Occupation period, nor have I found quantitative analyses of the legal status, structures, tasks, functions, manner of operation, sources of information and other characteristics of the ABs during that period. There are indications, however, that the number of ABs was not inconsiderable, especially from the 1920s onward. For example, a survey conducted in the mid-1930s for the Okada Cabinet identified 'over one hundred';[15] and in 1941 thirty-four ABs were listed among the organisations attached to the Ministry of Commerce and Industry.[16] What follows is a composite picture of some general trends identified on the basis of information sifted from various sources.[17]

First, ABs in the pre-Occupation period were formed by prime ministers, cabinets, individual ministers or high-level bureaucrats (hereafter 'bureaucrats'). Second, the legal instruments for their establishment were mainly imperial edicts, cabinet orders and ministerial ordinances, though several were formed by legislation. Third, while some were formed in response to requests from outside the government, generally ABs were established at the initiative of the particular administrative unit concerned. Fourth, while most ABs were *ad hoc*, some were permanent, including a few, such as the Hōsei Shingikai (legal system), that are still operating today. Fifth, more often than not

ABs were chaired by bureaucrats. The rest were chaired by prime ministers, other cabinet ministers, or *gakushiki keikensha* (persons of learning and experience); in most cases these were Tokyo Imperial University professors and leading industrialists. Sixth, membership was dominated by bureaucrats from relevant ministries; other salient categories of members were university professors and leaders of industrial and agricultural interests. A small number of labour leaders – and only those on the right wing of the labour movement – served on a negligible number of advisory bodies.

During the nineteenth century there was some interactive learning through ABs, mostly between the bureaucracy and professors and industrialists, but the consultation process was highly biased in favour of the mobilisation of support and consent. Examples are the Council on Education and the Council on the Monetary System. From late Meiji until the mid-1930s the process struck a better balance between interactive learning from more diversified groups in society on the one hand, and mobilisation of the support and consent of such groups on the other. Examples include ABs involved in the preparation of the Factory Act of 1911 and in the Council on Labor Legislation, the Commerce and Industry Deliberation Council and the Investigative Council on Relief Works.

From the mid-1930s until Japan's surrender to the Allies in 1945 the period of 'state corporatism', policy-making became more unidirectional, with ABs used primarily to mobilise the support and consent of the populace. Often ABs were also used to educate and mobilise the support of various units within the state bureaucracy in order to overcome bureaucratic sectionalism. For example, the Cabinet Advisory Council and more specifically the Temporary Investigative Council on Industry were established to examine two separate drafts of a trade-union bill, one prepared by the Ministry of Agriculture and the other by the Home Ministry.

REFORM UNDER THE US OCCUPATION

The US Occupation of Japan marked a turning-point in the evolution of Japanese advisory bodies in one important respect: as part of a series of democratic reforms, the Supreme Commander for the Allied Powers (SCAP) helped lay the statutory foundation for a system of advisory bodies[18] and set guidelines regarding their tenure, membership composition, support staffs, modes of operation and reporting, and government response to their reports.[19]

The reform of ABs was enacted with several objectives in mind: (1) to limit the powers of the bureaucracy, (2) to promote competent and equitable participation, (3) to make state administration more open and better integrated, (4) to increase ABs' autonomy by providing them with access to relevant and adequate information inside and outside government, and (5) to increase AB's genuine influence by calling on government to pay close attention to their reports. In short, the general intention was to prevent ABs from turning into mere instruments in the hands of the bureaucracy for the mobilisation of public support and consent.

This formal framework for the creation and operation of *shingikai* has been in effect, with various modifications, until the present. In this sense, and only in this sense, can one argue, as did Trezise and Suzuki, that 'One of Japan's inheritances from the American occupation is the institution of public committees and councils in an advisory capacity to the government.'[20] As I have described above, the use of ABs was not an innovation introduced by the Occupation. In fact, at SCAP's instigation ('suggestion,' in the diplomatic terminology of the time), the legal reform of the consultation system was accompanied by a drastic cut in the number of ABs, some of which were carry-overs from pre-surrender times.

Pruning the AB system was part of SCAP's more general policy of administrative rationalisation initiated by the Hoover Mission, which first visited Japan in late 1945, and later reinforced by the Nine-Point Plan for Economic Stabilization, designed to promote simplicity, efficiency and clarity in the responsibilities and organisation of state administration. It is by now widely recognised that, contrary to SCAP's initial intentions and despite the measures taken under SCAP's auspices, the Japanese bureaucracy emerged at the end of the Occupation not weaker but stronger than it had previously been.

POST-OCCUPATION DEVELOPMENTS

The state bureaucracy has retained its predominance in the policy process to the present. Throughout the 1950s and 1960s that predominance was largely unchallenged. The period also saw steady yearly net increases in the number of *shingikai* to the all-time high of 277 in 1965 (the only exception was 1963, when the number temporarily decreased by 2), and bureaucrats were instrumental in the formation of most of them. Several *shingikai*, especially those dealing with issues in agriculture and regional development with high salience among the electorate, were formed by individual Diet members' bills or in response to demands by interest groups.

A series of studies, first undertaken in the mid-1960s by the Provisional Investigative Council on Administrative Reform (nowadays known as the First Rinchō) and subsequently by scholars[21] and journalists,[22] concluded that to a large extent bureaucrats have subverted the spirit of SCAP's reform of the consultation system by turning the *shingikai* into instruments for obscuring rather than clarifying administrative responsibility, and for mobilising support and consent for policies formulated by particular bureaucratic units rather than for facilitating genuine learning by both government and society. This has been accomplished in the following ways.[23]

First, *shingikai* chairmanships and memberships have been dominated by persons on whom bureaucrats could rely to represent or unquestionably ratify the policies formulated by the bureaucrats. These persons, in decreasing order of reliability were: (a) acting bureaucrats; (b) retired bureaucrats currently holding positions in private occupations, interest-group organisations, local governments, universities, etc. (the so-called *amakudari kanryō*); and (c) persons without bureaucratic background who were none the less under the strong influence of the appointing authority, if not under its control. The last category includes: (1) officials of 'public policy companies' (*tokushu hōjin*), (2) members of government research institutes, (3) members of other research institutes, known as *ninka hōjin*, established under the auspices of, and at least partly financed by, particular ministries, and (4) trusted university professors and members of the mass media. Members who proved 'unsuitable' were not reappointed.

Second, *shingikai* membership did not reflect the whole gamut of relevant economic interests and social groupings. Rather, memberships were dominated by leaders of such 'established' organisations as the four *zaikai* associations (Keidanren, Nikkeiren, Nisshō and Keizai Dōyūkai) and major trade- and industry-specific associations (*gyōkai*), who were under the strong influence, if not always the control, of respective ministries. The less well-established groups, such as labour, women and consumers, were included in the memberships of a small number of *shingikai* in which they formed small minorities; at the most they could offer only token resistance to the bureaucrats and their sympathisers on the *shingikai*. By limiting effective participation to the established groups, bureaucrats used *shingikai* deliberations to hammer out consensus among them in support of government policies.

Third, chairmen and members who were not active bureaucrats were chosen mostly from among 'big-name personalities' whose established reputations lent prestige to the *shingikai*; at the same time, these appointees were relatively old, out of touch with the technological, professional and scientific state of the art, less than keen on innovating, and lacking the zeal to make their mark on *shingikai* deliberations. Moreover, being very busy in other fields of endeavour, these appointees could devote to the *shingikai* only a very short span of their attention; this was particularly true in the numerous cases where such individuals served simultaneously on several *shingikai*.

Fourth, bureaucrats determined *shingikai*'s frames of reference and set the agenda and time frame to suit their advantage.

Fifth, even where they did not serve as chairmen or members, bureaucrats played an active part in and often led *shingikai* deliberations.

Sixth, the information, evidence and data used by *shingikai* originated mostly from the bureaucracy; and where research was done especially for the *shingikai*, it was the bureaucrats who determined the research fields, carried out the research and analysed and interpreted the findings.

Seventh, *shingikai* were provided with neither independent budgets nor independent support staffs. Those assigned to 'service' the *shingikai* were officials of the appointing authority, for whom work with the respective *shingikai* was part of their regular assignments in their departments. In addition to secretarial and research work, the staffs routinely drafted *shingikai* reports.

Eighth, the membership of many *shingikai* was too large (over forty in most cases and over one hundred in some) to operate effectively without the guidance of the bureaucrats.

The system of advisory bodies has taken three other turns contrary to SCAP intentions. One concerns their duration. One of the principles established in 1951 in compliance with SCAP's suggestion was that *shingikai* be *ad hoc*; in the case of *shingikai* concerned with economic policy, they were to be disbanded not later than six months after their formation.[24] In fact, some very well-known ABs have indeed been *ad hoc* (such as the Commission on the Constitution and the First Rinchō). Most, however, have become permanent, that is, they were not disbanded after submitting their reports but were kept alive to deal with questions as they subsequently arose and were referred to them by the relevant authority. Their members were appointed for fixed terms, usually two years, but memberships were renewable; and in fact there has been a great deal of continuity in membership from one term to the next. In many cases *shingikai* were formally entitled to identify, study, deliberate and report on problems at their own initiative, but in practice few have actually done so.

The second departure from SCAP intentions is the informal way in which many advisory bodies have been appointed by prime ministers, cabinet members, heads of other government agencies and bureaucrats.[25] These non-statutory ABs or 'private' advisory bodies (*shiteki shimon kikan*) like the *shingikai*, are dominated by bureaucrats who make decisions regarding their structures and modes of operation without even the few constraints set by legislation for some *shingikai*, such as the specification of the categories of members to be appointed.

The third contravention of SCAP intentions is the use ministries and their sub-units have made of 'their' *shingikai* to promote their particularistic sectional interests and to expand their spheres of influence (*nawabari*) – most visibly in the budgetary process – rather than to better co-ordinate the work of the state bureaucracy as a whole.

Finally, one additional characteristic of several *shingikai* that has been the subject of sharp criticism from various quarters since the mid-1960s is the prevalence of Diet members' participation in them. In the pre-Occupation era, Diet members served on several advisory bodies, and SCAP reforms did not specifically prohibit this practice. After Japan regained its independence a small number of *shingikai* (less than 10 per cent at any given time) included Diet members. Dealing mostly with subjects closely related to pork-barrel politics (notably regional development, rail transportation and agriculture) or to party politics (notably the election system), many of those *shingikai* were formed by members' bills; membership of Diet members in this type of *shingikai* was distributed among the political parties proportionately to their respective shares of Diet seats.[26]

Diet members' participation has been criticised by bureaucrats, by the First Rinchō, and by scholars on the constitutional grounds that it contravenes the spirit of the separation of powers and that it runs counter to the principle that *shingikai* ought to supplement electorally based representation rather than duplicate it or substitute for it. In addition, the Diet members concerned have been criticised for tending to dominate the deliberations and to base their positions solely on consideration of party politics and their own constituency's support.[27]

INSTITUTIONALISATION

Criticism of Japanese advisory bodies dies hard.[28] Critics, however, tend to lose sight of or minimise several significant changes that have taken place in the system of advisory bodies, especially in the 1970s and 1980s, partly in response to past criticism and partly in line with other changes that have taken place in Japanese society and politics which, among other things, have made inroads into the unrivalled predominance of the state bureaucracy in public policy-making.[29] In combination these changes denote significant increases in the four measures of institutionalisation posited by Huntington: adaptability, complexity, autonomy and coherence.[30]

First, the scope and diversity of the subjects handled by public advisory bodies have expanded. Although there has been a net decrease in the number of *shingikai* from 277 in 1965 to 213 in 1983, the decline is explained by the fact that several inoperative *shingikai* have been abolished altogether and several performing similar tasks in the same or related policy areas have been merged.[31] Some of the new subjects addressed by ABs, such as electronic communication and DNA experimentation, reflect respectively public policy commitment to scientific and technological development and public sensitivity to the moral implications of scientific and technological development. Moreover, prime ministers have started forming private ABs to consider foreign and defence policies. Sato Eisaku formed one on the Okinawa reversion problem (Okinawa Kondankai) and another on the US bases (Kichi Mondai Kondankai), but the number of private ABs dealing with foreign policy and defence markedly increased during the Ohira and Nakasone premierships.[32]

Further evidence of the expanded role of ABs is the regularity of their use. For example, it has become general practice to refer draft legislation to *shingikai*. Finally, ABs are more in the public eye.

By the end of 1985, after three years in office, Prime Minister Nakasone had formed three *ad hoc shingikai*: the Temporary Advisory Council for Promoting the Implementation of Administrative Reform (Rinji Gyōsei Kaikaku Suishin Shingikai), the Supervisory Committee of the Japan National Railways Reconstruction (Kokutetsu Saiken Kanri Iinkai), and the Temporary Investigatory Council on Education mentioned earlier. Concomitantly, he formed twelve private ABs, including ones dealing with severance payments (Taishoku Teate Seido Kihon Mondai Kenkyūkai), foreign economic assistance (Taigai Keizai Mondai Kondankai), and the highly controversial issue of cabinet members' visits to the Yasukuni Shrine (Kakuryō no Yasukuni Jinja Sampai ni kansuru Kondankai). ABs' salience has risen so high that Nakasone's political style has become known as '*burēn seiji*' (brain politics) and '*shingikai seiji*' (*shingikai* politics).[33]

A second major change in public advisory bodies over the last twenty years concerns their membership. The number of state bureaucrats, officials of *tokushu hōjin*,[34] and Diet members serving on ABs has decreased, while concomitantly, there has been an increase in the membership of university academics and persons from the mass media, as well as of interest groups (notably labour, professionals and prefectural and local governments) and public-interest groups (consumers, environmentalists). Moreover, instances of members serving on more than one *shingikai* simultaneously and the numbers of *shingikai* on which a given individual serves simultaneously have also markedly decreased. As of 1978, no one has served as regular member of more than four *shingikai* simultaneously.

A further change in membership, at least in the case of permanent *shingikai*, is the continuity of members from one term to another. This has had several consequences. The members have tended to develop a long-range perception of their role and an understanding of the rules of the game and what is expected of them, such as the important part played by neutral members in resolving conflicts among interest representatives over questions of both procedure and substance. This is particularly notable in the case of *shingikai* considering prices, wage rates, etc., such as the Minimum Wage Council (Saitei Chingin Shingikai) and the Rice Price Council (Beika Shingikai). Also, recruitment to leadershp roles – chairmanships of *shingikai* and of their subcommittees – has increasingly been from among members with long tenures on the respective ABs rather than from among outsiders or newcomers. In addition there has been an increase in the proportion of chairmen and members whose association with particular *shingikai* has been longer than that of their staffs, who, like Japanese public servants generally, tend to be frequently rotated. But chairmen and members, even former bureaucrats, are less susceptible to control and manipulation by acting bureaucrats than are newly appointed members.

A third major area of change concerns the information-gathering capabilities of public advisory bodies. While the state bureaucracy has retained its primacy in information-gathering and policy analysis, nongovernment organisations have developed their own policy-related capabilities to the point where they can increasingly challenge the bureaucracy's primacy. Examples include associational interest groups (e.g. Nōkyō, trade associations, industrial unions), semi-independent research organisations (e.g. the *zaikai*-connected Sangyō Keikaku Kondankai and the government-connected Japan Institute of Labor), research institutes founded by business corporations (e.g. the Nomura Research Institute, the Mitsubishi Research Institute), groupings of local governments and Diet members' *zoku* (e.g. the Taxation Committee of the LDP Policy Affairs Research Council).

This development has had significant consequences. Members from outside the government have increased not only their contribution to the information considered by *shingkai*, but also their ability to elicit from the bureaucracy types of information they deem germane to the work of the respective *shingikai*.[35] Moreover, in addition to stepping up their formal and informal consultation with individual experts and research institutes of universities, business firms and so on,[36] bureaucrats have increasingly formed private ABs to conduct genuine and thorough research and analysis to buttress their own capabilities in these respects. Composed largely of reputable, established scholars as well as younger, up-and-coming ones, these private ABs have been used by bureaucrats to cope with challenges mounted by members of *shingikai* in the areas of research and analysis.

CONCLUSION

Despite recurring criticism of public advisory bodies in Japan it is clear that they are here to stay. Japanese ABs are used by government at the initiative of an increasing number of political actors – bureaucrats, political party leaders, interest groups, scholars and the mass media – to deal with a growing number and variety of problems. The institutionalisation of policy consultation has become part of the 'flow of history'.[37]

The perception that *shingikai* have made serious efforts to improve policy-making is widely shared among former *shingikai* members who, according to my own survey, believed that their *shingikai* had been influential. Significantly, this perception is confirmed by Muramatsu Michio's survey of élite bureaucrats and politicians. Only a small minority (15 per cent) felt that the role of *shingikai* was to legitimise the bureaucracy's policies. The remaining were divided among the roles of administrative fairness (30 per cent), adjustment of conflicting interests (30 per cent) and acquisition of expertise (25 per cent).[38] Even Sōhyō, Japan's most dissident national organisation of labour unions, which in the past has shown a strongly negative posture towards *shingikai*, has not only increased the scope of its participation in them, but has also admitted publicly that more can be gained by participating in them than by staying out. In 1983, ignoring the opposition of the Japan Socialist Party, Sōhyō decided to nominate a member to the Temporary Council for the Implementation of Administrative Reform.[39]

The ABs have acquired value and stability in the Japanese political process by increasing their level of performance in the four areas mentioned earlier: adaptability, complexity, autonomy and coherence. In terms of adaptability they have proven flexible in their response to criticism and to changes in their environment. In terms of both structure and function ABs have grown more complex. Membership is more pluralistic and subcommittees and informal study groups have emerged to handle the increasing diversity of policy problems.

The ABs have also become more autonomous. Freedom from the undue influence of both the bureaucracy and the members' constituencies is due to a number of factors. One is changes in power relations between the bureaucracy on the one hand and Diet members and interest group leaders on the other. Another factor is the enhanced policy research and analysis capabilities of organisations outside the state bureaucracy. A final factor concerns the group dynamics within the ABs. Neutral members, when necessary, play the role of conciliators and mediators of conflicting views and positions and when compromise is reached, they formally assume responsibility, enabling those who made concessions in private to avoid responsibility for them in public.

At first glance the increasing complexity of the public advisory body system in Japan appears to have decreased its coherence – the final measure of institutionalisation. Frequently ABs attached to different state bureaucratic organisations make conflicting recommendations regarding a given policy problem – a phenomenon reflecting, if nothing else, the compartmentalisation of the state bureaucracy in Japan and the existence of 'sub-governments', typical not only of Japan, but also of the USA.[40] Nevertheless, steps have been taken in Japan to add coherence to the system of public advisory bodies. There are, for example, ABs designed explicitly for this purpose, such as the *shingikai* formed to advise on the social security system and on environmental protection.

In sum, one can argue that government learning in Japan has grown directly as a result of increasing government receptivity to contributions of outsiders serving on ABs and indirectly as a result of bureaucratic efforts to diversify the sources of policy advice. The process of policy-making in Japan has accordingly become more interactive in that the bureaucracy has become more open to outside advice and has been changing its role from one of controller and manipulator to that of partner, albeit a senior partner, in the process of policy formulation. What is more, while established interests, such as business and agriculture, continue to predominate, changes in ABs' membership indicate that the policy-making process, in addition to becoming more interactive, has also become more equitable. Taken together, ABs in Japan have progressively contributed to the making of more responsive policies.

Nevertheless, it does not seem that ABs in Japan are necessarily conducive to the making of more innovative or implementable policies. While the present stage of my research prevents me from making definite judgements on this matter, it appears that in the past, subject to greater bureaucratic manipulation, ABs, and especially permanent *shingikai*, actually yielded more innovative policies than they have in recent times, though often they had not conceived these policies, but either ratified or put the final touches on policies developed by state bureaucrats. The question of implementability is even more elusive. Certain indicators of 'governability', such as the government's ability to cope with two oil crises, to keep unemployment at tolerable levels, and to maintain public order and social stability – all at low costs to the public treasury – provide evidence that, with one or two notable exceptions, Japanese policies have been generally successful from the late 1950s onwards.[41]

Viewed in comparative perspective, the available evidence shows a convergence of Japanese public advisory bodies with those in other industrialised democracies of the world. Although in Japan there may be a tendency to idealise royal commissions in Sweden and Great Britain and presidential commissions in the USA,[42] recent studies reveal that Japanese ABs may actually be more representative than the royal commissions (and departmental committees) in Britain even if the British advisory bodies are more autonomous.[43] Indeed, new research suggests that the highly vaunted royal commissions in Sweden[44] have been glorified beyond what the facts would support and that US presidential commissions are subject to criticism on various scores.[45] These studies provide further reason to reevaluate the performance of public advisory bodies in Japan and their role in policy-making.

9 Japanese Politics: Good or Bad?

J. A. A. Stockwin

The question posed in the title of this chapter may seem to many readers extraordinary. How can one apply value words such as 'good' or 'bad' to something so complex as a nation's politics? What standards of judgement could possibly be applied to the politics of Japan, when no clear and absolute standards exist for judging the quality of the politics of Western countries? Surely political scientists have no business making normative judgements since they ought to be engaged in empirical, 'value-free' research. In any case is not Japanese politics something that may only reasonably be considered in its own terms, as *sui generis* and rooted in the special cultural soil of Japan?

These questions have merit, or at least plausibility. Nevertheless, there seems a good case for raising explicitly certain normative questions which in the course of many articles and books on the politics of Japan are raised implicitly and unsystematically. Politics is widely held to be about values, and values deserve to be taken seriously in the study of politics. Moreover, ways of improving the way politics is conducted have been sought ever since people began taking an intelligent interest in the subject. It is perfectly true that no absolute standards exist, since politics is a matter of human choice. There is unlikely ever to be unanimity on what values ought to be given what priority. The extreme participatory democrat and the extreme law-and-order conservative are unlikely ever to see eye to eye, just as in economics expansionists and believers in financial stringency will always differently interpret the same set of statistics. Even so, we propose to take the position that there are a large number of broad propositions about how politics should be run which would command the assent of most reasonable people. For example, a condition of anarchic bloodletting or state-controlled mass murder is less desirable than a condition of peaceful social intercourse where the state as well as competing groups are constrained by due process of law.

Plainly there are other propositions about politics that are far more controversial than this. For instance, to what extent is inequality in the distribution of wealth tolerable in the case where such inequality accelerates the increase of total wealth? Such issues are the stuff of political debate.

When we turn to Japan, the further problem arises that the appropriate standard of reference, as suggested in the final question of our first paragraph, may possibly be different from that of Western countries because of a different cultural context. We concede that to some extent this is the case, and that normative questions need to be expressed and answered with caution in the Japanese case (as in the case of other non-Western countries). Nevertheless, we do not believe that this ought to be a reason for opting out of the important task, not only of political comparison, but also of political judgement. In recent years Japan has been the subject of both widespread criticism and of calls for emulation by Western (and non-Western) countries. It is in the possibly overbearing belief that the politics of Japan is overdue for systematic normative as well as empirical examination that this chapter is being written.

POLITICS WITHOUT CHANGE

By comparison with most other democratic political systems the feature which serves to distinguish that of Japan in the recent period is lack of change. Given that Japan is universally known for the dynamism of its economy and for the inventiveness of its industrial management, the apparently unchanging character of Japanese politics is surprising. In one sense, of course, there is constant change. The front pages of the Tokyo daily press are given over to complicated accounts of subtle changes in relationships among various political actors, most notably factions and their leaders within the Liberal Democratic Party (LDP). One has the impression of a pond whose surface is constantly disturbed by small ripples, but whose level scarcely ever changes. Occasionally, it is true, the wind will whip up quite sizeable waves (as at the time of the Lockheed revelations, or when Nakasone made some of his early speeches on defence and security), but soon the normal state of things is resumed. Political factions continue to make behind-the-scenes deals with each other and with their backers, prime ministers manœuvre desperately to stay at the top of the slippery pole, bureaucrats go about their daily business of conciliating interests, competing and confabulating with each other and running the country, while the occasional general election confirms the vast bulk of politicians in their seats, and monotonously returns the LDP to office.

We can plausibly place in the early 1970s the time when the Japanese political system, radically reshaped during the post-war Occupation, finally shook down into something very close to its present shape. This may be illustrated in a number of ways. During the 1950s and 1960s a process of massive change in electoral preference was taking place at the expense of the LDP. Traditional rural-based conservatism appeared to be of decreasing relevance to an electorate which was flocking to the large cities in response to the massive new employment opportunities provided by the economic miracle. A range of well-publicised urban problems, combined with a relatively profligate atmosphere created by ultra-high economic growth rates, gave increasing numbers of votes to parties critical of the LDP and capable of cultivating an urban base. During the 1970s, however, economic growth and with it urbanisation slowed. Serious attempts were made by government to deal with urban problems and the LDP itself made efforts (not admittedly with complete success) to improve its attractiveness to urban electorates.

The electoral system, over the same period, has been tinkered with but not radically reformed. This is despite the fact that it is widely, if not generally, recognised to have features that are both unfair and inefficient. The fundamental problem with the electoral system is a long-standing failure to institutionalise redrawing of constituency boundaries to reflect movements of population. Once in the mid-1960s, and again in the mid-1970s, a small number of seats were added in the big cities in an effort to mitigate the worst excesses of imbalance. In 1985, for the first time, there was a serious proposal before Parliament (the so-called 'six-six' proposal) to add seats in the cities while also abolishing some in the more remote and over-represented areas of the countryside. Even this, however, is a mere palliative in a situation where there is a nearly five-to-one imbalance between the value of a vote in the most over-represented constituency by comparison with the value of a vote in the most under-represented constituency. Moreover, the fact that virtually all the constituencies for the House of Representatives elect either three, four or five members whereas each elector may only cast a single non-transferable vote means that LDP candidates in constituencies where the party is strong are forced to campaign as individuals fighting against each other rather than as party members united against the opposition.[1]

There is much complaint against the electoral system as such, and indeed the courts in well-publicised verdicts have questioned the constitutionality of the vote imbalance between different constituencies. Nevertheless, a point that is less commonly made but is worth stressing here, is that failure to reform the electoral system is a crucial factor in the structural conservatism of politics itself.

This is true in at least four senses. First, the persistent failure to correct the imbalance favours the LDP to the extent that without it the party would almost certainly have been defeated in several recent elections. Second, the introduction of a list system of proportional representation into the elections for the House of Councillors (the only significant reform of the electoral system actually achieved in recent years) graphically revealed in 1983 the extent of the LDP's dependence on the 'personality voting' factor. In the 1983 Upper House elections (national constituency), where for the first time voters had to vote for the party since they had no means of expressing a personal preference, the LDP vote proportion was a mere 36.6 per cent as against more than 45 per cent in the average House of Representatives election. Third, the multi-member constituency system of the Lower House reinforces (though it does not create) factionalism within the LDP. Factions themselves, as we shall see, are an integral part of the political system as it currently operates. Fourth, the necessity to cultivate a personal machine rather than to depend on the backing of party organisation has tended to give great advantage to incumbency. It is much harder, and more expensive, to break into the charmed circle of LDP Diet Members than to keep being elected once one has been elected for the first time.

This last factor, the great stability of LDP Diet Membership, is in turn reflected in the creation of what amounts to a seniority promotion system within the LDP itself. Much as in the Japanese civil service, it is now the case that promotion to positions in the Cabinet and party organisation depends crucially on the number of times a Member has been elected to the National Diet. This is indicative of a remarkably high degree of predictability and plainly could not happen if there were a high turnover of Members from one general election to the next.

When we turn from the LDP to the opposition parties, we see again that lack of substantial change is the salient feature of the past fifteen years. By contrast, the 1950s and 1960s were decades of rapid and at times exciting change. Let us consider, first of all, the Japan Socialist Party (JSP). During the 1950s it successively split over the peace treaty settlement (1951), reunited in 1955 in a move that precipitated the formation of the LDP, and split again in 1959–60 over revision of the

Security Treaty. In the 1960s the party was first traumatised by the experience of May–June 1960, went through a moderate reformist period under Eda Saburō, but in the latter half of the 1960s lapsed into a quasi-Maoist phase (partly as a reaction to the Vietnam war), and lost no less than fifty seats in the 1969 elections. It is difficult to describe the JSP since around 1970 in terms other than 'stagnation'. As Sir George Sansom once wrote of Tokugawa farmers, the JSP has been kept in a condition where it has neither died nor lived. Possibly the leadership of Ishibashi Masashi may result in the party once more re-entering the territory of the living, but it is too early to tell.

The path taken by the other opposition parties exhibits a roughly similar pattern: a meteoric rise in popular support, resulting in up to some fifty seats in the Lower House, followed by a long period in which that support is either consolidated (but not added to) or in some cases diminished. This, with some variation, has been the case with the Democratic Socialist Party (DSP), the Kōmeitō, the Japan Communist Party (JCP) – which was not of course a new party in the late 1960s, but which rose from parliamentary near-extinction – the New Liberal Club (NLC) and the Shaminren.

What is striking about all these parties is that their successes were almost entirely confined to big-city Japan, so that the cities in contrast to the countryside became highly fragmented political territory. Moreover, the emergence of these parties and their remarkable, but in each case limited, success had the cumulative and momentous effect of fragmenting and thus weakening the total impact of the opposition within politics as a whole. It is symptomatic of this that the Prime Minister was able to retrieve a difficult political situation by bringing the NLC (eight Lower House Members) into a coalition government following the general elections of December 1983. The opposition parties, since they are all competing for much the same sections of the electorate, find it extremely difficult to co-operate with each other or contemplate merger, while substantial elements on the opposition side are tempted by the prospect of coalition with the LDP.

One of the most salient features, therefore, of Japanese politics since the early 1970s is the absence of effective challenge from a reasonably united or co-ordinated political opposition. The challenge presented by the *kakushin jichitai* ('progressive local authorities') in the 1970s was important at the time in the sphere of local politics, but ultimately the government was able to overcome it by a combination of carrot and stick. It is interesting that when the population at large began to feel the financial pinch in the late 1970s, voters in local elections quickly reverted to more conservative voting patterns. In any case the emerging multi-party coalitions of the 1980s at the local level serve to reinforce the dominant control of local government by Tokyo, which has been the underlying feature all along.

When we turn back to the LDP we find a further area of interest where little seems to have changed since the early 1970s, in contrast to quite considerable change in the fifteen to twenty years before that. With the formation of the Tanaka Cabinet in 1972 the LDP found itself with five factions of significance led at that time by Fukuda, Miki, Nakasone, Ohira and Tanaka. In 1985 the same factions still dominate the scene. Miki has been replaced as leader by Kōmoto, Ohira (who died in 1980) by Suzuki, and with the physical incapacitation of Tanaka, his faction appears likely to split into two groups, led respectively by Nikaidō and Takeshita. Kōmoto and Suzuki are both in a sense lame-duck leaders, however. Other groups, such as the tiny Nakagawa faction of the early 1980s, have made their appearance only to disappear again, but no new major faction has emerged since the realignment of factional affiliations in 1972 at the time when the long prime ministership of Satō Eisaku came to an end.

Moreover, by comparison with earlier periods, there has been surprising stability in the configuration of factional alliances, with the Tanaka–Fukuda rivalry creating a kind of underlying axis of polarisation for much of the period since 1972. The one reform which was intended by its sponsors to reduce the impact of factionalism in the LDP actually had the reverse effect. On the initiative of the Miki government (1974–6) a primary election was introduced for the presidency of the LDP with 'local members' of the LDP as the constituency. The details of operation and the subsequent history of this election need not detain us, but on the two occasions when it has been put into effect it was instrumental in extending factional rivalries to the grass roots, rather than eliminating them as seems to have been the initial intention.[2]

The prime ministership is an institution which is in certain respects difficult to interpret. The prime minister is formally the kingpin of the political system, but the evidence is strongly in favour of the proposition that his scope for independent initiative and the exercise of power is more limited than that, say, of a British prime minister. He is greatly constrained by the need to balance and relate to bureaucratic, intra-party and interest-group pressures, and the formal requirement of a biennial election for the LDP presidency (and so prime ministership as long as the LDP remains in office) makes his political survival a matter of more or less constant concern. Nevertheless, personality, including political skill, image and competence, have a significant bearing on the survivability and performance of a particular individual in the post. The combination of qualities, however, may differ at different times, and good or bad fortune may also play a crucial role.

One frequently noticed difference between the politics of the 1960s and the politics of the period from 1972 is that whereas during the 1960s the prime ministership appeared to be extremely stable, from 1972 the turnover of incumbents was much more rapid. Between July 1960 and July 1972 there were only two prime ministers, Ikeda and Satō. When Ikeda resigned in November 1964, he had recently been elected for a third consecutive term, but ill-health forced him to resign his office. It is reasonable to assume, therefore, that, had it not been for his illness, he would have remained in charge in Japanese government for at least six years. His successor, Satō, went on to serve an unprecedented seven and a half years as prime minister.

From 1972, however, a pattern of short-tenure prime ministers was established. In the twelve years from 1972 to 1984 six different holders of the position, successively Tanaka, Miki, Fukuda, Ōhira, Suzuki and Nakasone, strode the political stage. The reasons for the political demise of each of Nakasone's predecessors was peculiar to each case and need not detain us, but the effect probably was to limit the impact that a given prime minister was able to have upon events and policies.

The success of Nakasone, however, in achieving a second two-year term and then receiving a one year special extension because of his popularity and effectiveness suggests that the prime ministership may be returning to a degree of influence closer to that which it enjoyed in the 1960s. If this is so (and the case remains by no means proven), then this may possibly have more than passing significance. The potential for a strong leader to set a programme of change and carry it through to fulfilment is clearly greater if he has adequate time to do so. On the other hand the experience of the Nakasone prime ministership up to 1985 suggests an equivocal conclusion about whether the office of prime minister has been strengthened during his tenure of it. Although some (not all) policy objectives set by Nakasone have been brought towards fulfilment, there is little evidence that any of the structural constraints upon the prime minister have been significantly relaxed.

If we turn to specific policy areas, the impression is reinforced that the period from the early 1970s to the mid-1980s is one of relative consensus about a fairly narrow set of propositions, by comparison with the 1950s and 1960s, when wide divisions and frequent acrimony divided political participants. This is perhaps another way of saying that from the 1970s policy positions came to settle down into a clearly defined mould of moderate conservatism, with a detectable shift towards a more aggressive conservatism in the 1980s, and especially during the Nakasone prime ministership.

Let us take foreign and defence policy first. During the 1950s and 1960s significant political opinion was cleft on relations with China, the Japan-US Security Treaty, the status of the Self-Defence Forces, the position of Okinawa under American administration, relations with the USSR, policy towards Korea, nuclear issues and so on. Since 1970 most of these issues have either faded out as a result of new circumstances (Japan–China relations, the reversion of Okinawa), or been radically desensitised as a result either of compromises with the opposition entered into more or less willingly by government (for instance, the three non-nuclear principles, the ceiling on defence spending of 1 per cent of GNP), or again as a result of gradual assimilation of 'mainstream' views on the side of the opposition (or parts of it).

Moreover, the kinds of foreign policy issues which were emerging from the early 1970s were in themselves less susceptible to adversarial policy-making than the earlier ones. The post-oil-crisis objective of enhanced resource security, and the pro-Arab policy shift that was part of its initial stage, was hardly a contentious issue among Japanese political parties, for whom the politics of Arab–Israeli conflict was of minor intrinsic importance. The more recent question of foreign pressure on Japan to liberalise its trading stance and open its markets more convincingly to foreign imports is hardly an adversarial issue between parties (at least not in the sense that the older issues were), though it not surprisingly provokes a vigorous response from affected interest groups. On the other hand, 'old' issues, sucn as the level of defence spending, still retain much of their capacity to provoke contention when government appears ready to move beyond the constraints imposed upon it by earlier compromises. This in turn suggests that at least in the present stage of Japanese defence and foreign policy-making, it is easier to be a conservative than to be a radical of either left *or* right, though the right is probing the boundaries of constraint.

In much domestic policy, too, there has been a kind of 'degutting' process, whereby highly polarising issues, such as those of class conflict in the 1950s or environmental pollution and 'quality of life' in the late 1960s and early 1970s, have been deprived of a capacity to provoke mass dissent by a combination of stick and carrot. Adversarial unionism has been discouraged in a variety of ways and co-operative, enterprise-based unionism institutionalised. Where unions have remained a problem for government, as in the public sector, privatisation is now promoted, partly as a means of reducing union impact. The worst effects of environmental pollution were tackled in a rapid policy turnaround in the early 1970s, while alternative, left-wing solutions, which prevailed in local government for a while, were effectively squeezed out through the long term effect of financial constraints on free-spending, progressive local authorities.

The recent history of welfare policy is also instructive. Whereas in the rather euphoric days before the first oil crisis the Tanaka Administration made spectacular improvements to the welfare system (thus defusing criticism), subsequent governments have gradually cut back spending on it, with financial retrenchment being especially marked in the 1980s. The necessity for financial retrenchment, argued with great insistence by both the Suzuki and Nakasone governments, has created an atmosphere where potential new issues, such as the job status of women or the rights of the urban consumer (as against those of the rural producer, for instance), find it hard to obtain an effective hearing.

The picture of Japanese politics which we have painted so far is one in which stability and what one may broadly term 'the conservative view' have largely prevailed, and the parameters of the political system have remained remarkably unchanged for at least a decade and a half. As we have seen, there is considerable contrast between this period and the two decades which preceded it.

JAPANESE POLITICS: THE CASE IN FAVOUR

The trickiest aspect of evaluating Japanese politics is selecting which norms to apply. British or US politics (two very different political systems incidentally) are frequently used as the yardstick for measuring certain features of Japanese political behaviour, which are then found wanting. A particular example of an institution not infrequently subjected to criticism from such a point of view is the political faction, and especially the variety of factions which exists within the LDP. From the perspective of modern Western political thought, 'faction' has strong connotations of selfishness, disloyalty and fractious dissent from legitimate leadership, for reasons unrelated to voter issues or to the voters themselves, with the implication that anarchy and corruption is likely to follow from any outbreak of widespread factionalism. 'Party', by contrast, is granted the accolade of legitimacy and respectability, on the assumption that while it may be based on sectional interest, it has or should have the capacity to transcend such interest, at least when in power, in pursuit of the national interest or common good. Burke's definition of 'party' as 'a body of men united for promoting by their joint endeavours the national interests, upon some particular principle on which they are all agreed', for all its practical difficulties of application, has echoed down the years. Today 'party' also suggests the backing of an electorate, and a clear adherence to an ideology or set of policies.

Are Japanese political factions, therefore, to be placed in the rubbish basket of disreputable political institutions to which mainstream Western political theory would generally consign them? To do so would plainly be to present a false picture of the politics of Japan. LDP factions may be 'selfishly' pursuing power within the party, and not necessarily agreed upon the pursuit of a particular principle apart from that of spoils of office. They may also fractiously dissent from the party leadership and be no strangers to corruption in its various forms. Nevertheless, they impart an element of pluralism and choice into the party that has formed the government for the past thirty years. Precisely because they are power-seeking rather than ideology or policy-promoting bodies, factions have not wholly impeded the reasonably effective institutionalisation of the LDP as a political party. As personal political machines, they bargain and deal with each other in the context of a set of institutional structures which, though not untouched by personal conflict, are not normally threatened with disruption by intransigent expression of differing ideological and policy positions. Thus, in so far as the factions are more or less ideologically interchangeable with each other, their constant politicking may be contained within reasonably predictable and semi-bureaucratised structures and processes. In any case it is arguable that the politics of personal faction is such a widespread phenomenon that, whatever may be the consensus of Western political thought on the matter, it has a political rationale and even usefulness that merits serious normative consideration. Conceivably the politics of factionless party is a rather curious exception occurring only in some parts of the Western world, and there but imperfectly.

Another matter of concern is the phenomenon of one-party dominance. A standard criticism of uninterrupted rule by one party over a long period is that the business of politics and government becomes routinised, that it comes to lack the kind of political competition that places the competitors on their toes, and that it gives excessive *de facto* power to the government bureaucracy, whose various parts establish semi-permanent lines of contact with the ruling party, or with elements within it. Thus new blood and new ideas are inhibited, bureaucratism flourishes and policy dynamism is lost. Moreover, long absence from power demoralises the opposition parties, which incline to be either clients of the ministerial party, content to receive occasional crumbs from its table, or else root-and-branch opponents, concerned with ideological purity rather than with convincing the electorate to elect them to office. The electorate, in the process, is deprived of an effective choice.

This criticism, however, flies in the face of several observable facts. Although there is undoubtedly a degree of immobilism in government policy-making, there is little evidence of a gradual decline into general paralysis such as the criticism might seem to imply. Decision-making processes, on the contrary, exhibit a capacity to cope with complex and wide-ranging issues in a reasonably effective and consultative manner. This is not, it is true, equally the case in all policy areas, nor is the system noted for the speed at which decisions are taken, but in general it compares favourably with that of other comparable countries. Although, for instance, the pattern of policy response to the first oil crisis of 1973–4 was marred by serious blunders, subsequent policies on energy conservation and economic stabilisation prevented comparable disruption to the economy at the time of the second oil crisis of 1979–80. Personnel in the central ministries of government is of high calibre, and processes of achieving what is termed 'consensus' within the political élite and between it and the 'public' (in practice, largely relevant interest groups), are complex and generally understood by the participants. The LDP itself has been developing improved policy expertise of its own and the various branches of the bureaucracy have been making intelligent use of advisory bodies in order to keep in touch with significant opinion and broaden the scope of policy inputs, thus adding to flexibility and sophistication in policy-making.

Although it is possible to point to some spectacular administrative disasters, such as the siting of Narita Airport[3] and a variety of environmental pollution scandals[4] (perhaps one should now add the issue of airline safety), in the crucial area of national economic policy, Japanese government appears to have been considerably more successful than most other governments. There is no need to recapitulate here the history of Japanese economic growth and adaptability to changing circumstances since the 1950s. There is some difference of opinion about how much of this is the result of government policies and how much should be attributed to other factors, such as favourable American policies in the past, low-defence spending, a benign international trading environment, aspects of the Japanese social structure and a culture which places emphasis on diligence and thrift, as well as working for the common good.

Nevertheless, even if we state the position in a negative form, we may still allow ourselves to be impressed by the conclusion that Japanese governments, by comparison with many other governments of economically advanced states, have at least been permissive towards economic growth and development. Even though sharp differences of historical background need to be taken into account, a comparison of economic development in Japan and China over the past three decades provides impressive evidence that government policies, and not merely sociocultural factors, are crucial elements in national economic performance, and all that follows from it. There is indeed much in the argument for 'creative conservatism' presented by T. J. Pempel.[5] Whatever the criticisms that may be levelled at the Japanese political process, it seems difficult to deny that in its management of the economy, the government has done many things right in recent decades.

One area of policy where Japan has been subjected to persistent international (particularly US) criticism is defence and foreign policy. We do not have to go over familiar ground here in any detail. The crux of the complaint is that Japan has profited commercially from its one-sided reliance upon an US-led, largely US-financed regime of international security against the Soviet Union. In particular it is argued that Japan at the very minimum ought to spend enough on defence to be able to take responsibility for the practical security of its own territory, without having to rely on US protection, except for nuclear deterrence. Some versions of the argument go further and urge Japan to become more international in her defence policy, to engage seriously in such activities as sealane protection and to drop her ban on dispatch of troops overseas and on export of armaments. Some even argue that Japan should develop a nuclear capacity. Under the Nakasone prime ministership there has indeed been perceptible movement towards a more active and participatory defence policy, and defence spending has been allowed to rise significantly above the level of the general budget, so that the barrier of 1 per cent of GNP spent on defence is close to being crossed. Even so, this is not enough to satisfy some critics in Japan and elsewhere.

We shall not enter here into any moral argument about defence. We wish to argue, however, that from a domestic, political and foreign-policy point of view, Japan's security policies since the 1950s should be considered an extraordinary success story, not unconnected with the more obvious success of her economy. Let us take the domestic political aspect first. In the 1950s and 1960s issues of defence were politically highly contentious, and a government embarked on massive rearmament would have been likely to provoke political instability and unrest. Although there were arguably ostrich-like aspects to the policies actually pursued, the central purpose of calming political passions, which had been deeply aroused as a result of the horrors of war, atomic bombing and defeat, was well served by backpedalling on defence. Article 9 of the Constitution was used, not only by the opposition Socialists, but also by many mainstream conservatives (particularly those close to Ikeda and his way of thinking) as a sort of corral for defence policy. The fencing of the corral was moved outwards a little from time to time, but its restraining influence was always maintained. The benefits in terms of the stability of the political system were incalculable. By the 1970s security-related issues were less contentious, the domestic political system had settled into a mould, as we have seen, and it became possible to discuss defence more openly and frankly, though caution remains in evidence, even in the mid-1980s.

It is widely believed that the key international aspect of Japan's cautious defence policies has been the willingness of the USA to underwrite a considerable part of Japan's security. Understandably, with Japan's emergence as a global economic power of great wealth, the US reluctance to continue to play such a role without a 'reasonable' Japanese contribution has grown. Consequent pressure upon Japan has been met by some upgrading, particularly under the present somewhat hawkish prime minister. Overwhelming concentration on US interests in the matter, however, has led some observers to neglect the extent to which Japan's own interests have been served by the 'low profile' in defence. The salient feature of the recent huge increase in Japanese international influence is obviously economic. As current trade frictions graphically reveal, a power which is expanding economically while other powers are expanding less or declining is vulnerable to retaliation. In most historical examples of nations expanding economically, however, the economic expansion has been accompanied by a conspicuous increase in military capacity and involvement. The USA in the first decade after the Second World War is a good case in point.

In Japan, partly perhaps by accident, and partly by the design of shrewd post-war leaders such as Yoshida and Ikeda, spectacular and conspicuous economic growth was accompanied, not by well-remarked expansion of military capacities, but by limited military build-up projected as minimal and non-threatening self-defence through the powerful pacifist symbolism of Article 9. The article was used repeatedly in arguments with the Americans about 'contributing more to the alliance' as the reason why Japan could not accede (or could accede only minimally) to US requests. More than this, however, while attention has naturally focused on the low level of Japanese military spending, and Japan has been the target of criticism for this, it may well be imagined that massive military spending by Japan accompanied by economic expansion since the 1950s would most likely have resulted in far greater, and ultimately more damaging, criticism, not to speak of countervailing military preparations by other powers in the region.[6]

In short, Japanese politics in recent decades has produced a security policy that has served the nation's needs well both domestically and internationally. The modest but nevertheless steady build-up of defence capacity which began in the 1980s may be regarded as far less threatening either to domestic political stability or to the nation's international reputation than would have been the case had it occurred two or three decades earlier. Indeed, we may even question whether the Sino-Soviet split would have taken the form it did, thus providing a welcome respite for the US and her allies, had the Soviet Union and China in the late 1950s and early 1960s been facing a militarily resurgent Japan.

At this point in the argument, therefore, we may conclude that Japanese politics has come through the tests of the past three decades with at least three extraordinary achievements to its credit. The first is a spectacular and sustained economic transformation and the second is political stability and predictability in a nation not previously noted for either. These two goals were achieved, not through the Chinese model of ideological authoritarianism, seesawing between bureaucratic centralism and the near anarchy of the Cultural Revolution (admittedly, China is a much more complex nation to run than Japan), but within a tradition of modified liberalism and democracy. The strength of the underlying commitment to that tradition was revealed in May–June 1960 in the mass protests against the Prime Minister's introduction of police into the National Diet. Indeed, we would argue that it is Japanese politics that has kept at bay the possibility of militarist domination which brought Japan to disaster in 1945 and plagues the neighbouring Republic of Korea today.

JAPANESE POLITICS: THE CASE AGAINST

While there is much to be said in favour of the Japanese political system, it is assuredly not immune to criticism. We wish to concentrate on three areas of concern: elections, single-party dominance and bureaucratic centralism. The three are interconnected.

The electoral system for both the House of Representatives and the House of Councillors suffers from several well-canvassed imperfections. The most glaring is the failure to correct the gross imbalances that have emerged in the value of the vote between city and the countryside in the course of post-war urbanisation. It is difficult to see how this can possibly be justified except in the terms used to justify the continued existence of rotten boroughs in Britain in the nineteenth century, namely that vested interests ought to be protected, and that change was dangerous. The argument for protection of vested interests is put forward with particular insistence in the LDP, it seems, because in rural constituencies personality voting and personal networks (*kōenkai*) are so important.

This, however, takes us on to another criticism of the electoral system, the multi-member constituencies that obtain in voting for the House of Representatives and for certain seats of the House of Councillors. Multi-member constituencies enable the LDP in rural areas to elect several (three, four or, in rare cases, five) members in a Lower House seat, with the result that LDP candidates compete as much with each other as with candidates of other parties, and this in turn serves to promote personality, *kōenkai*-based, electoral campaigning. Single-member constituencies would force the LDP to fight as a party rather than as a loose combination of local notabilities, each with his own power base. Proportional representation would also, though in a different fashion, place the onus more on the party than on the individual candidate and remove much of the motivation for personality voting, though it would risk precipitating further party fragmentation. Multi-member constituencies combined with a non-transferable single vote have also been a crucial permissive factor in the fragmentation of opposition parties that has occurred since 1960.

The present Lower House electoral system, therefore, is triply beneficial to the LDP: it gives disproportionate weighting to predominantly conservative rural voters; it gives a plausible excuse for not rectifying this imbalance, namely that Diet Members who would thereby be displaced are dependent on local networks of support and could not be shunted round to other parts of the country as LDP candidates; and, finally, it has contributed to opposition ineffectiveness through fragmentation. The LDP itself, of course, has coped with the fragmenting impetus of the electoral system by instituting factionalism within a loose but cohesive party structure. It is a kind of super-party, operating a multi-party system within it, whereas the opposition is a multi-party system deprived of the co-ordinating and image-making benefits of any such super-party.

We next turn to the question of single-party dominance. It is possible to argue that the LDP has won virtually every general election since 1955 because it is popular, and that it is popular because it runs the country well and because no plausible combination of opposition parties could possibly match up to its performance. It could, however, also be argued that the LDP wins elections for some other reasons. For example, it benefits from a gerrymandered electoral system. It has also been helped by personality-based voting prevalent among the Japanese electorate, which favours LDP candidates over opposition candidates and which therefore conceals a rather low level of underlying LDP popularity, as suggested by its lacklustre performance in the national constituency contest of the 1983 House of Councillors elections, held for the first time under the newly introduced proportional representation formula and therefore probably free from the effects of personality-based voting. Finally, the LDP has done so well presumably because the opposition has been fragmented and demoralised by the electoral system and by long years in the political wilderness.

It is difficult to adjudicate between these two sets of arguments. Elements of both of them are no doubt true. What we wish to suggest, however, is that the present system has developed on the basis of a seriously inequitable and otherwise flawed system of electing the people's representatives to Parliament. In so far as the ministerial party has a vested interest in the retention of such an inequitable system, it cannot expect to remain immune from legitimate criticism.

There is, however, a further argument that can be made, namely that in Japanese conditions, alternating government, or even occasional changes of party in power, would not work; that indeed Japan has made a system of predominant party government function better in terms of policy output and long-term political stability than policies with alternating or occasionally changing government. In part this is a pragmatic argument from results, rather than from political principle, but it deserves to be taken seriously. Interestingly, however, many Japanese today go beyond this and hold that the indefinite continuation in office of a single party has demonstrated its superiority over other types of systems, and that change of government in whatever direction would be a retrograde and possibly dangerous step. The present system is seen as having taken on desirable *Japanese* features and so is immune to criticism on the basis of Western models of democratic government.

We wish to argue that there is little justification for regarding the present system as either immutable or quintessentially Japanese. There might be real difficulties in moving from the present system of election, which tends to entrench an unusually static political system, but it is not impossible. The trick would be to reform the system without de-stabilising politics or creating serious difficulties for coherent policy formation. Japanese politicians would need to learn some new skills, such as those of policy advocacy in a genuinely competitive political environment between different parties with a real hope of holding office. There would need to be less reliance on backstage deals and manoeuvres and more on open appeal to an electorate which is, after all, perhaps the most highly educated in the world. The idea, sometimes encountered, that Japanese electors are not interested in politics, and the difficulties they seem to have in exercising political influence, result from institutional rigidities rather than from any innate 'non-political' character in the Japanese people.

This takes us on to our third area of criticism, which we shall deal with more briefly, that of bureaucratic centralism. An important sub-theme of Japan's political history since the war has been persistent conflict between the gradual encroachments of an (admittedly extremely high-calibre) civil service and attempts to create autonomous areas of life or action. In various forms this can be seen in education, local government, relations between government and industry, the judiciary, agriculture, even culture. It is important to put this in perspective by making two observations. The first is that the accumulation of power in a central government bureaucracy has been a common feature of politics in many if not all advanced states in the recent period. Complexity tends to create centralisation and bureaucracy. The second is that by comparison with contemporary dictatorships or governments professing some variety of Marxist state ideology, Japan in this regard is a model of enlightenment. Nevertheless, it seems correct to observe that the Japanese civil service, working closely with the LDP and associated interest groups, has what by Western democratic standards is an exceptionally tight grip on policy initiation and control across a wide range of policy areas. The advantages in terms of co-ordination and consistency are no doubt impressive, but at the same time the range of policy choice is narrowed and the scope for independent initiative outside the central bureaucracy is restricted.

One method of attacking bureaucratic centralism is government-initiated retrenchment. The politics of President Reagan and Prime Minister Thatcher place particular emphasis on the 'privatisation' of such institutions as the Japan National Railways. Their purpose, however, is rather different from what we have in mind. The aim of making a national corporation running a deficit more efficient is no doubt laudable. Nevertheless, it does not touch the problem of opening up the system to greater scrutiny and to alternative sources of ideas.

The long-term monopoly of power by a single 'super-party' on the basis of a flawed and unfair electoral system is a key to the understanding of what we have termed 'bureaucratic centralism'. The breaking of that monopoly by the election of a responsible alternative government might seem to some a perilous undertaking, but this may well be an overly pessimistic assessment. As we saw earlier in this chapter, the polarised conflictual politics of the 1950s and 1960s have been much modified in the more sedate atmosphere of the 1970s and 1980s. What is needed, apart from electoral reform, is a realignment of Japanese party politics, whereby the LDP finally splits into two parties, each entering into coalitions with parties of the present opposition. That so little serious thought has been given to the possibilities for reform which this change might create is an indication of the mindless structural conservatism which has descended over Japanese politics as a whole in recent years.

CONCLUSION: GOOD OR BAD?

My purpose in writing this chapter has been to open up for debate certain normative issues which have become lost over the long period of structural stability briefly chronicled here. It is crucial to realise that we are discussing one of the most sophisticated societies on earth in most fields of human endeavour. In politics too, the Japanese have created a complex system of representation and governance, capable at times of impressive effectiveness. In some aspects – its stability for instance – it is the envy of other advanced polities. While giving praise where praise is due, however, we have also argued that the system has serious flaws, and that the reluctance to contemplate structural change itself indicates a possibly dangerous tendency towards sclerosis. Our tentative verdict, therefore, is 'good, but room for improvement'.

10 The Impact of Domestic Politics on Japan's Foreign Policy

F. Quei Quo

Foreign affairs affect domestic politics in Japan, but domestic politics, in turn, impinge on foreign policy.[1] Thus, following the 1983 electoral setback of the ruling Liberal Democratic Party (LDP), officials of the Foreign Ministry and top business leaders immediately voiced their concern about the possible adverse effect of the election on foreign policy-making. This close relationship between domestic politics and foreign policy has been dictated by Japan's geography, cultural traditions and historical experience. For modern Japan, national survival, not to mention growth and prosperity, has always depended on its ties with the outside world.

This essay attempts to examine how post-war party politics have been reflected in the shifts and changes in Japan's external relations. In general, Japan's foreign policies are often characterised by absence of bipartisan or supra-partisan support, lack of consensus even within the LDP itself, and frequent employment of 'dual diplomacy'. In addition, Japanese foreign policy is considered reactive rather than assertive in nature. A careful examination of reasons for these features inevitably leads us to explore three aspects of Japanese politics as they impinge on foreign policy-making: (1) party leadership and factional feuds, (2) interest groups and (3) the role played by bureaucrats.

LEADERSHIP AND FACTIONAL FEUDS

It is difficult to separate the issues of leadership and factional feuds in most Japanese political parties. A party leader dependent upon his popularity among the party membership at large is rather unusual. It was not until very recently that either of the two major parties introduced a sort of primary election for the choice of their leadership.[2] Even the new system has failed to make the election of leaders reflect grass-roots democracy. Faction bosses still manipulate the situation through their behind-the-scene wheelings and dealings.[3]

The process influences the personality of leaders as well as the formation of party policy: leaders tend to be compromisers and their policies tend to be opal-coloured or, as the Japanese call it, *tamamushiiro*. Each successive new LDP government thus consists of cabinet members representing all factions, apportioned according to their relative strength in the party. The leader's policy has to be omni-directional, offending no vociferous faction if not pleasing every one of them. In the arena of foreign policy these tendencies lead to dual diplomacy and indecisiveness in action.

The duality of 'official and unofficial' in Japanese diplomacy, therefore, is necessitated by the absence of consensus within the party and is not, as some charge, a symptom of hypocrisy. A primary example is the recent history of Sino-Japanese relations. Until September 1972 Japan maintained 'official' relations with Taiwan while at the same time keeping 'unofficial ties' and trading heavily with the People's Republic. Notwithstanding repeated overtures on the part of the People's Republic, neither Prime Minister Miki Takeo nor his successor Prime Minister Fukuda Takeo was willing to override the violent objections raised by pro-Taiwan colleagues both inside and outside of the Cabinet.[4] For that reason it took four years to finalise the Peace and Friendship Treaty with the PRC, even though the treaty consisted of only a preamble and five short articles. Clearly, treaty negotiations were sacrificed to the LDP leaders' concern about factional politics.

The personality of the leader may also play an important role in foreign policy-making. Prime Minister Yoshida Shigeru was firm in his pro-US stance over the issue of the San Francisco Peace Treaty in 1952. Likewise, Prime Minister Kishi Nobusuke stood firm in the face of violent opposition to the revised US–Japan Mutual Security Treaty in 1960. By and large the *tōjin-ha* (party politicians without bureaucratic experience) have tended to be more adventuresome in their approach to foreign affairs than the *kanryō-ha* (bureaucrats-turned-politicians). Despite their reputation for bold policies in the West, the foreign-policy achievements of ex-bureaucrat Prime Ministers Kishi, Ikeda Hayato, Satō Eisaku, Fukuda and Ōhira Masayoshi amounted to only incremental changes in the existing circumstances, whereas *tōjin-ha* leaders like Hatoyama Ichirō, Ishibashi Tanzan, Ono Bamboku, Kōno Ichirō and Tanaka Kakuei seemed less bound by existing conditions and more willing to attempt to achieve a 'breakthrough' in Japan's foriegn policy. For example, they considered the normalisation of relations with the

Soviet Union and the return of the Northern Islands no less important than the preservation of the alliance with the USA or the return of Okinawa.

Regardless of whether a leader belongs in the category of *kanryō* or *tōjin*, it is common among Japanese prime ministers to use international affairs for publicity purposes to enhance their personal reputation. Even though foreign affairs is an important factor in the minds of only 5 to 6 per cent of Japanese voters, politicians use international relations to boost their own popular image.[5] Almost every Japanese prime minister believes that he has to have a 'historic achievement' to glorify his term of office. Prime Minister Hatoyama wanted normalisation of diplomatic relations with the Soviet Union as his triumphant exit (*hana michi*), and he went to Moscow, even while very ill with a stroke and in a wheel-chair, accompanied by a medical entourage. Ikeda, dying of throat cancer, would not quit until he received worldwide attention presiding over the Tokyo Olympics. Satō hung on to his fourth term, disregarding the advice of his own brother, former Prime Minister Kishi, until he completed the task of having Okinawa returned. The achievement definitely went down to his credit in the history books of Japan. The image of *sekai no Fukuda* (Fukuda prominent on the world stage) which Fukuda tried to create by his performance at the summit, or the 'Ron–Yasu' intimacy of Nakasone and Reagan, and more recently, the 'Ivy–Nancy' friendship of their wives, which Prime Minister Nakasone has tried to project, has very little cash value in the nation's party politics.

Statements on international affairs by a Japanese leader, therefore, have to be discounted. Factional politics and the frequency of LDP presidential elections call into question not only the implementation of the prime minister's policy but even his leadership position. Fukuda did not politically survive to see the implementation of his famous Fukuda Doctrine of close co-operation with South-east Asia. Nakasone's pledges of increased defence co-operation to President Reagan caused the Japanese press to warn that 'words without action might cause friction later, domestically and internationally'.[6] The instability within the LDP leadership circle causes frequent changes of government, and the real policy-making power often falls to senior bureaucrats in various ministries, especially Foreign Affairs, International Trade and Industry, and Finance. According to an *Asahi* report, William Brock, the US Trade Representative, greeted Okonogi Hikosaburō, the new MITI minister, with 'I hope your term will be a longer one.'[7] Mr Okonogi was the fifth minister in three years with whom Mr Brock had to negotiate.

While leaders of the LDP have been able to employ dual diplomacy to satisfy both sides to a dispute in the Party, leaders of the opposition parties have been less fortunate. In the case of the Japan Socialist Party (JSP), foreign policy issues remain ideological and abstract. Conflicts of opinion led to the splitting off of the right wing to form the Democratic Socialist Party (DSP) in 1960, and to the departure of Eda Saburō in 1977 to form the Social Democratic Federation (Shaminren). The Japan Communist Party (JCP) has also suffered for a long time from bitter feuding between pro-Moscow and pro-Beijing factions. Disputes with both the Soviet and Chinese Communist parties finally led the JCP in 1967 to break with both and to begin to follow a more independent line of its own.

The continual decline of LDP electoral strength and the intensified factional feuds over the last decade have given birth to the opposition's dream of a 'coalition government' in the not-too-distant future. The opposition parties have formed electoral alliances among themselves during several general elections in recent years. To be prepared for the eventuality of the collapse of the LDP majority, they have also worked out common platforms for a possible coalition government. The JSP has had to soften its objection to the US–Japan Mutual Security Treaty so that it could become an acceptable partner to the Democratic Socialists and the Kōmeitō (Clean Government Party).

The prospect of a coalition government has also led the opposition parties to engage in more constructive acts of foreign policy instead of merely rejecting whatever the government does. The 1975 visit to Washington of a JSP delegation led by Eda Saburō, the deputy chairman of the Party, marked the first official contact between the Party and the US government in eighteen years. In 1976 the Party also returned to the Socialist International after a decade's absence. Thus, with the exception of the JCP, which has always been excluded from a proposed coalition, the opposition parties' foreign policies have become somewhat more realistic and less ideological. As the new chairman of the JSP put it recently, the opposition would like to play a role 'complementary' to the government's in foreign affairs.

The opposition's emphasis on ideological and national defence issues in the past, however, has left the field of foreign policy open to the ruling LDP's unfettered action. The only exception is the JCP, which has frequently criticised Japan's exploitation of the less-developed Asian nations, arguing that Japan has relied on their cheap labour, exploited their natural resources, destroyed their environment and indirectly supported their undemocratic regimes through economic ties. The 'Pan-Pacific' Policy proposed by Ōhira, for example, was termed to be 'serving the American military strategy of anti-communism in Asia, leading to resurrection of Japanese imperialism'.[8] During the 1985 session of the Diet, however, debates on foreign policy by the opposition were almost exclusively related to the nation's defence expenditure, the export of military technology to the US, and the port calls of nuclear-armed US ships.

From the perspective of party politics, it is therefore difficult to expect Japan to be anything but 'reactive'. Japan does not 'initiate' or 'create' changes in the arena of foreign affairs. The power structure in Japan – rule by one party ridden with constant factional feuds – prevents any Japanese leader from playing an important role in international affairs in the near future.

INTEREST GROUPS: MONEY AND VOTES

Democratic politics costs money, especially in Japan. According to the 1983 accounting of the LDP treasury the party had an income of Y24.8 billion and was still Y9.2 billion in debt. A major source of its income (Y10.9 billion) was, as usual, the *zaikai* (big-business)-supported National Political Association (Kokumin Seiji Kyōkai). The income from party membership dues accounted for only slightly less than 10 per cent of the total. Expenses for the 1983 House of Representatives and House of Councillors elections are estimated at Y7.1 and Y7.0 billion, respectively. Following the common logic of 'he who pays the piper calls the tune', it is not difficult to conclude that the LDP is the spokesman for the major industrial and business interests.

Japanese industrial–business élites exert political influence in other ways as well. They are often closely tied to political élites through marriages or 'old-boy' networks forged among former school classmates. Chitoshi Yanaga's classic study went so far as to state that 'once organised business withdraws its support, the collapse of a government follows'.[9]

The influence of business interests may be seen in the two constant themes of Japan's post-war foreign policy – economic growth and emphasis on relations with South-east and East Asian nations. These themes were adopted after careful calculation of domestic economic interests. A content analysis of major foreign policy speeches by Japanese prime ministers and other ministers in charge of foreign economic policy reveals that the first official reference to South-east Asia and economic diplomacy was made in late 1952 by Prime Minister

Yoshida in phrases such as 'since not much can be expected from China trade', and 'for the purpose of strengthening our export industries'.[10] The implementation of the policy resulted in a series of reparations agreements with South-east Asian nations. These too were viewed as good for business. On the reparations agreement with Burma, Yoshida later wrote: 'Although the Burmese called it reparations, for us it was an *investment*. Through our investment Burma would develop and it would become our *market* from which our investment would return.'[11]

Whether Prime Minister Yoshida himself held such a business-oriented vision or whether it was inspired by his political financier, the Miyashima Group, will never be known.[12] Suffice it to say that business interests helped to implement and, indeed, themselves benefited from, the reparations programme. Business and industrial leaders became more influential in government policy as they began to capture important political posts, such as chairmanships and memberships in various advisory councils and policy committees of the ministries.[13]

Nor should the role of *zaikai* as king-maker be ignored. As a freshman Diet member, Ikeda was given the Finance portfolio in the Yoshida government at the instigation of Miyashima.[14] It put Ikeda ahead of many others who were senior to him in his rise to power within the LDP. Although the zaikai leaders often say, 'what we care about is a stable government, not who is the prime minister', they have tended to favour the *kanryō*-type over the *tōjin*-type politicians. It is a well-known fact that the *zaikai* leaders publicly demanded the resignation of Prime Minister Hatoyama, disapproving of his mission to the Soviet Union in 1956. Hatoyama's major lieutenant, Kōno Ichirō, was strongly opposed by the Koba-Chū Group when he contested the LDP leadership.[15] The *zaikai* was more supportive of bureaucratic leaders like Kishi, Ikeda, Satō and Fukuda. Why was this so? One may speculate on two reasons.

First, the new leaders of the post-war *zaikai* were alienated 'outsiders' in the pre-war marriage between the *zaibatsu* (big family-controlled businesses) and politicians. Since they were not taken too seriously by the traditional established groups, they found an ally in the young bureaucrats, then known as *kakushin kanryō* (or progressive bureaucrats), who were active in building a new economic order in the Greater East Asia Co-prosperity Sphere.[16] Kishi is one example. The pre-war experience may thus account for the post-war *zaikai*'s dislike of the *tōjin*-type.

The second reason is more practical and can be given with greater certainty. The *tōjin*-types tend to be unpredictable and difficult to manipulate. Furthermore, they tend to be more expensive and yet less appreciative. The bureaucratic types are more predictable and pragmatic and provide the stability needed for economic planning and development.

After the war the *zaikai* leadership had to accommodate the leaders of new industries and revived elements of the *zaibatsu* groups. The *zaikai* also had to change some of its practices. A recent study by a Japanese journalist reveals an interesting aspect of the *zaikai*–LDP relationship.[17] On 12 August 1974 Dokō Toshio, the new president of the powerful Keidanren, announced that his federation was no longer willing to collect political funds for the LDP. The news shocked politicians as well as other business and industrial leaders. Dokō had supported Tanaka, a pure party politician, for the LDP presidency while most of his *zaikai* colleagues had favoured the former bureaucrat Fukuda. The falling-out between Dokō and Tanaka, according to the study, was caused by the former's disapproval of the latter's 'money politics'. During 1973 and 1974 the *zaikai* contribution to the LDP doubled in amount and yet LDP seats in the legislature decreased. While Tanaka thought more money would be the remedy, Dokō wondered if the *zaikai* should begin to keep a distance from the LDP, as the public's outcry against money politics had become louder and clearer.

When Tanaka's regime collapsed, Dokō's popularity among the *zaikai* leaders also declined. Between 1974 and 1977, however, the *zaikai* contribution to the 'centrist' parties almost doubled in amount. Obviously,the *zaikai* would be prepared for a second-best coalition government among the conservatives if necessary, rather than seeing the Socialists in power.

The strong influence of the *zaikai* in politics finds no counterpart in other advanced industrial nations. The typical reasons often given to explain this uniquely Japanese phenomenon are: the absence of a counterweight in labour, the style of Japanese lobbying (i.e. one lobbies *for* oneself but never *against* others) and the harmony of interests among various groups in an ever-growing economy.[18] The foregoing discussion suggests, however, that the Japanese *zaikai* cannot be viewed merely as a pressure group in a democratic political process. Its involvement in the Japanese political process is much broader and deeper than one finds in lobbyists or pressure groups elsewhere. In addition to the monetary networks there are personal networks (*jin-myaku*) which cannot be cultivated overnight. One may substitute new financial sources for the *zaikai* money, but there is no good substitute for a lasting personal network, and that may have been the political Achilles-heel of Tanaka Kakuei.

The emergence of Suzuki Zenkō as Ōhira Masayoshi's successor in the summer of 1980 and the *zaikai*'s response is another interesting case of the *zaikai*'s strong influence. 'Zenkō Who?' was a popular joke among students of Japanese politics, indicating how unexpected the succession was. None of the leaders of either the Keidanren or the Nikkeiren (Federation of Employers Organisations) was a member of Suzuki's personal support organisations. As a matter of fact, Suzuki's two small groups of supporters were mainly those involved in fisheries. The moment Suzuki became Prime Minister, however, the *zaikai* started to organise two new groups around him. The Monday Club (Getsuyō-kai) was led by Sejima Ryōzō, Chairman of C. Itoh Co., and included Morita Akio of Sony, Ishihara Takashi of Nissan and Saitō Eishirō of Shin Nittetsu (Japan Steel Corporation). The Seirei Club consisted of thirty-four senior *zaikai* leaders such as Inayama Yoshihiro of Keidanren, Nagano Shigeo of the Japanese Chamber of Commerce and Industry and Imazato Hiroki of Seiko.

The formation of these new groups showed how much the *zaikai* felt the need to be close to the apex of political power. When there is no existing personal network, the *zaikai* will quickly establish one to facilitate ties with the political world, though such a network may not be a lasting one. As one Japanese reporter has pointed out, in the pre-war period the Seiyūkai–Mitsui team and the Minseitō–Mitsubishi team took turns being the 'ins' and the 'outs', but in post-war Japan, the *zaikai* is always in power.[19]

The *zaikai* influence, however, is not unlimited, nor does it go unchallenged. By the early 1970s Japan was being severely criticised both within and outside of the country. In South-east Asia, Japan's economic activities met resistance from growing local nationalism. Japanese economic success began to be linked to problems which Japan was accused of having ignored, such as international security, the economic growth of less-developed nations and so forth. However, nothing shocked the Japanese more than President Nixon's new approach to China and his decision to retaliate against increased Japanese imports. Disliked by fellow Asians, abandoned by its ally, the USA, and ignored by Communist nations, Japan felt internationally isolated and compelled to review its entire foreign policy.

Japan's economic involvement in East and South-east Asia is as important as its ties with the USA. How to integrate Japan's interest in the two parts of the world and at the same time demonstrate that Japan would not be a 'disturbing factor' in the world economy was the main task in the nation's search for a new role in the early 1970s.[20] The concepts of 'comprehensive security' and 'Pacific Community' that emerged were welcomed by all concerned – business and industrial leaders, LDP politicians and the public at large. The report entitled *Economic Co-operation in the Pacific Area* by the Japan Economic Research Institute was jointly financed by all four major business organisations. Successive prime ministers also presented their recommendations: Miki's Asia Pacific Plan, Fukuda's Doctrine and Ōhira's Pacific Rim.

Japan's increased economic aid to Asian nations in the early 1970s provided strong evidence of willingness to share responsibility in efforts to solve the North–South problem. Business and industrial leaders viewed co-operation with Asian nations as a way to strengthen Japan's international position in the face of rising regionalism in Europe and elsewhere. Japanese leaders also hoped that such efforts would relieve the growing US pressure on Japan to contribute more to the defence of the 'free world' by increasing military expenditures. Changing international circumstances in the 1970s, such as the oil shocks, the revived US concern with the balance of military power in Asia, the Soviet invasion of Afghanistan and increased naval force in the Far East, and the revived domestic debate on national defence, forced the Japanese to re-evaluate their position on all these issues.

Meanwhile, economic realities have also been changing rapidly in Asia. In certain industries the Newly Industrialising Countries (NICs) have even become competitive with the Japanese in international markets, not only in labour-intensive, but also in some capital-intensive industries. In terms of export growth rates in manufactured goods, the NICs surpassed Japan during the decade of the 1970s. Similarly, ASEAN nations, though still one step behind the NICs, are catching up fast, especially in labour-intensive industries.

All of these changes have caused both Japanese business and government to develop a new strategy for international trade. Japan is thus considering anti-dumping legislation and other measures to protect itself against these countries. Representatives of businesses and industries which have been criticised for dumping and other unsavoury practices in the USA and the European Community will be called upon to arbitrate.

Japan proclaims itself to be a nation dependent on international trade (*bōeki rikkoku*), and the dominant influence of business and industrial groups on the nation's foreign policy is inevitable. International trade nowadays, however, often calls for reciprocity. Excessive Japanese exports and the inaccessibility of Japanese markets to foreign exporters remain serious problems for other advanced industrialised nations. So far the Japanese have found North-east Asian and South-east Asian economies complementary to theirs because of the vertical, rather than horizontal, division of labour that links one to the other. The NICs are good places in which to invest and excellent students of Japanese technology. The ASEAN nations and China are good buyers of Japanese industrial plants and suppliers of raw materials. The fact that these Asian nations are at various stages of development makes their overall relationship with Japan more complementary than competitive. It also provides Japanese industries with outlets for structural adjustment required by the advance of technology and new competition from other advanced industrialised nations.

In addition to business and industry, farm groups are said to have important influence on Japan's foreign economic policy. In a recent speech, Senator John Danforth of the USA stated:

> The relationship between politics and trade policy certainly is something that is well understood in Japan. For example, it is well known that the United States has been trying to open up the Japanese market to some of our agricultural exports, such as beef, citrus and tobacco, and that it has been very, very slow going. Why has it been so slow going? Because the Liberal Democratic Party has a solid base of support in the agricultural community in Japan and the farmers have been applying political pressure against liberalisation of imports.[21]

How important are the rural seats to the LDP? Is the electoral support given in exchange for the LDP's protection of agricultural imports? The answer to these questions can be provided with some concrete data.

Among the 511 seats in the House of Representatives, 82 of them (16 per cent) are allocated to constituencies which can be considered rural. A careful review of the electoral results in these constituencies indicates, first of all, that they are not necessarily unfavourable to the major opposition party. In 1980 the LDP captured 56 out of 82 seats (68.3 per cent) in these rural constituencies. This was higher than its national average of 56.3 per cent (284 out of 511) and is 15 per cent higher than the average in non-rural constituencies. But the same was true for the JSP. The party won 22 of the 82 rural seats (26.8 per cent) compared to its national total of 107 out of 511 (17.6 per cent). The JSP fared 7 per cent better in the rural areas than in other constituencies. The rural constituencies were strongly in favour of the LDP, but the JSP also fared well in rural areas relative to their overall national popularity. It is the minor parties which did poorly in rural constituencies; some of them did not even field any candidates.

Second, if the rural constituencies are fairly constant in terms of support for the LDP, then it must be the party's poor performance elsewhere that leads to its heavy reliance on the rural constituencies to attain a majority in the Diet. For example, in 1960, when the LDP captured 284 seats, its 56 seats from the rural constituencies accounted for one-fifth of the party's strength in the national legislature; in 1983, however, when the LDP had only 250 seats, its 56 seats from the rural areas meant 22.4 per cent of its strength. The importance of these constituencies, therefore, depends on the size of the LDP's overall majority, not on the competitiveness of the opposition.

Third, the support given to the LDP in the rural constituencies is no longer based on the party's policy of protectionism for agricultural products. Japan's agrarian policy since 1970 has been redirected away from protecting and towards subsidising the farmer's life, and in the long run, developing rural communities with government grants-in-aid. In addition, various public works projects under a succession of regional and local development plans have tied the economic life of rural areas so closely to the central government that any 'revolt' against the party in power or senior bureaucrats would be inconceivable. The amounts of grants-in-aid and the allocation of public works projects are often dependent upon the number of votes delivered by the constituency to the LDP at election time.

Fourth, the interests involved in agricultural policy go beyond farm products or the farmer's livelihood. For the 600 000 full-time farming families that are found in Japan, there are 600 000 individuals involved in the administration and management of their affairs.[22] Japanese rice, beef and oranges, no matter how expensive they are compared to international prices, must continue to be produced, no longer for the sake of consumption, but for preserving the Agricultural Empire – including the bureaucrats, the managers and the politicians. Today, the Nōkyō (agricultural co-operative), for example, is the largest insurance business and second-richest bank in Japan. One of its former presidents was asked by Prime Minister Satō to run in the House of Representatives election with a promise of the Agriculture portfolio, if elected. He refused, according to a report, on the grounds that it would be a 'demotion'.[23] The power of the Nōkyō, therefore, is not only political but also economic.

Needless to say, Japanese agriculture cannot survive by economic rationality. Most of the products are highly subsidised, but fewer and fewer people are engaged in production *per se*. An estimate shows that by 1990 there will be only about three million persons engaged in farming and more than 40 per cent of them will be over 60 years of age.[24] In the meantime, various programmes to 'restructure' the agricultural communities have been launched, but they have proved expensive and rarely successful. The Japanese government's reluctance to open up the country's agricultural products market to foreign imports is often deemed by outsiders as purely political in motivation in that the ruling LDP needs the support of the rural communities. The LDP, however, in fact can patronise and has been patronising these communities with grants-in-aid rather than with protectionism. In recent years Japanese business and industrial groups have become critical of the government policy of agricultural protectionism, because, as the main exporters, they usually become the target of foreign retaliation. The real political reason, however, lies elsewhere.

Most Japanese refuse to be convinced that the opening of the Japanese market for US beef and citrus fruits will solve the problem of trade imbalance between the two nations.[25] Nor do the Japanese believe the pressure against Japan's automobile exports is aimed at the recovery of the US auto industry. Many of them think rather that these are US ploys to force Japan's remilitarisation.[26] In this regard concern about the possible revival of Japanese militarism as well as reluctance to tamper with the constitutional limitation on rearmament have often been cited as reasons why Japan cannot yield to the US pressure. The strongest political argument against the liberalisation of the agricultural market, however, is the strategic necessity for self-sufficiency in food supply advocated by the nationalistic bureaucrats.[27] Vulnerability to a food embargo is an example used to demonstrate why Japan must not rely too heavily on others for basic commodities. Agricultural protectionism is definitely a highly politicised issue in Japan.

BUREAUCRATS AND THEIR INFLUENCE

In Japan foreign affairs have never been the career diplomats' preserved sphere of influence. The strong influence of the military before 1945 and the role of MITI in recent years are good illustrations.

However, with the broadening of international economic activities, especially on the issue of opening Japan's domestic market, the influence of the bureaucrats should now include not only that of the *keizai kanryō* (economic bureaucrats), but also of many others, e.g. those in the ministries of Transportation, Posts and Telecommunications, Agriculture, etc. It is important, therefore, to delineate the most basic characteristics of the so-called élites in Japanese government.

Owing to the pattern of their recruitment, the type of general training in their earlier appointments, and the assurance of semi-automatic promotions, Japan's bureaucrats are, by and large, sensitive nationalists. Their sense of responsibility often goes beyond what is prescribed in the book of rules and regulations. The best example is the Finance Ministry officials, who believe it is their mission to guard the state's interests.[28]

Many of the 'study groups' that surrounded Prime Minister Ōhira, including the one on the Pacific Rim, grew out of small study circles initiated by young Finance Ministry bureaucrats several years before. It was their sense of 'mission' – a young bureaucrat even called it *noblesse oblige* – that made them feel that they had to think and act for the nation and that gave them the zeal for study. These study groups, because they lead to new policy, give their members a sense of real importance. The bureaucrats, for example, believe decisions on national finance too critical to be dictated by politicians whose commitments are often particularistic. Nor do they deem Japanese politicians, especially the *tōjin* type, to be capable of understanding national finance. Although these bureaucrats are conservative in their approach, their will to study has often made them surprisingly progressive. When Prime Minister Ikeda decided to promote the famous 'Doubling the Income Plan', Finance Ministry bureaucrats were more enthusiastic than those in MITI or in the Economic Planning Agency. While the Finance bureaucrats were influenced by Keynesian theory, those in the EPA, like Okita Saburō, were experienced economic planners.[29] Thus the two walked hand-in-hand towards the common goal of building the foundation for Japan's emergence as an economic giant.

A similar attitude is prevalent among MITI bureaucrats, who once felt that Japanese business and industry lacked initiative and needed proper guidance. Hence, the famous 'administrative guidance', or, nowadays, the often criticised 'industrial targeting'. As a former deputy minister of MITI put it: 'It ["administrative guidance"] is based on the *mission* [*ninmu*], not the power [*kengen*], given to the ministry and it works on the premise of mutual trust between the administration and the industries.'[30] Still more Japanese bureaucrats will defend industrial policy by arguing that industry co-operates with the ministry on a 'voluntary basis' for the best interests of the nation.[31]

Whether it is a MITI policy or a Ministry of Agriculture scheme, it is the Finance Ministry bureaucrats who have the final say through the control of the budgetary process. Furthermore, there are about 300 Finance bureaucrats on loan to and occupying senior posts in other ministries. For the host ministries, the advantage of having a Finance bureaucrat on their senior management team is that it facilitates the budgeting and accounting process. For the Ministry of Finance the loan arrangement helps train senior officers as well as collect inside information about other ministries. The relationship between the Ministry of Finance and others is often compared to that of the Tokugawa Shogunate and the *daimyō*, who had their own domains but were always subject to the *bakufu*'s suspicion and control.[32]

The influence of the Ministry of Finance, though dominant, is not unchallenged. A skilful politician like Tanaka Kakuei was able to impose his policy upon the ministry. In 1971 Tanaka whipped the Automobile Taxation Bill through the Diet, calling the bluff of the senior Finance bureaucrats who thought Tanaka's highway projects were impossible since funds were lacking. The incident proved that politicians can 'create' money and the national budget can be altered by politicians without approval of the finance bureaucrats.

The 'raping' of the ministry by Tanaka, as the incident has since been called, caused many young Finance bureaucrats to give up their careers. Kakizawa Kōji and several others turned to politics while some others went into university teaching. They all believed, much to their regret, that the supremacy of the bureaucracy was over and it would be the politicians who would dictate the course of Japan in the future.[33] Currently there are thirty national legislators who are ex-Finance bureaucrats. Older LDP politicians like Fukuda Takeo, Miyazawa Kiichi and Hatoyama Iichirō are early graduates of the same ministry. All but one of those who have turned to politics belong to the LDP.

Because of the frequent reshuffling of the Cabinet, a minister is usually treated as an 'honorary guest of the house' in the ministry. He reads policy statements provided him by his host ministry, just as the Queen reads before Parliament the Throne Speech provided by the government in power. Most of the detailed questions in the Diet committees are answered directly by senior bureaucrats, not the minister himself. However, it is also a common practice among the ministries to use their ministers, if they are influential and capable, to enhance their bureaucratic interests or to promote a new policy which might have national significance. The relationship between the Ministry of Foreign Affairs and its ministers is a good example. In 1978 Sonoda Sunao, an ambitious Fukuda faction politician, was given the portfolio of foreign affairs. His inaugural speech was an honest appraisal of the situation:

> At this moment the most important problem is United States–Japan trade issues. Solution of these issues requires coordination with other ministries – Finance, Agriculture and MITI. However, these ministries are dominated by the nationalists (*kokunai-ha*) and that makes the coordination very difficult.
>
> Diplomacy is an important function of the government, but it has been ignored by others. My job is to elevate the status of the ministry to where it should be.[34]

The senior bureaucrats in foreign affairs saw in Sonoda an opportunity to restore their leadership in the making of the nation's foreign policy. They suggested to the minister that Japan's emphasis must be on Asia and only by asserting its leadership in Asia could Japan become influential in international politics. To demonstrate the important role of Japan in Asia they proposed to act as a 'bridge' between the USA and Vietnam and also to be an arbiter in the Vietnam–Cambodia dispute. In 1979, when the Sino-Vietnam War started, Sonoda made moves to mediate the conflict. To this day the desire to be the spokesman for Asia – the mediator between the Asians and others and among Asians themselves – remains in the minds of Japan's foreign affairs bureaucrats.

Overall, it is fair to say that the influence of the foreign affairs bureaucrats has receded into the background in recent years. Since more and more sectors of the government are now involved in external relations, co-ordination among them often requires a supra-ministerial effort. A minister's personal standing within the ruling LDP is very important in this regard. In spite of the ministry's efforts and Sonoda's dedication and enthusiasm, very little was accomplished without the blessing of the party leader. It appears that the prime minister himself must play a co-ordinating role. The trend for a prime minister to use his own 'brain trust' for special tasks as well as for the development of a comprehensive policy is worth noting.[35] Unfortunately, because of the short tenure of office of Japan's leaders, very few of these outside inputs ever bear fruit, while bureaucratic influence on policies remains strong, thanks to the permanency of the offices and all the advantages derived from it.

CONCLUSION

In a parliamentary democracy it is the party in power which is ultimately responsible to the people for the success or failure of policies. However, the discussion in this chapter has shown that Japan's parliamentary democracy has not been functioning quite the way political scientists think it should. With one party domination and without viable alternative political forces in sight, the public has not been able to enforce a system of political responsibility, except to give the ruling party a larger or smaller majority of seats according to the circumstances. Intensified factional feuds during the last decade have led to frequent changes of leaders and cabinets, including prime ministers inclined to improve relations with the Soviet Union, regimes which were staunchly anti-communist, leaders friendly to the People's Republic, and governments formally allied with the USA. Nevertheless, *none* of them was capable of making any radical change in the nation's foreign policy.

The themes of 'Asia first' and 'economics above all' developed in the early 1950s, still remain as the core of Japan's external relations. Through the years, however, these themes have gone through incremental changes. Japan's vision of international affairs has significantly enlarged. No longer is Asia considered in isolation from the rest of the world. Opinion surveys also show that Asia as such is becoming less and less 'special' in the minds of most Japanese.[36] In trade policy there has been a shift in emphasis away from exports of manufactured goods towards exports of more high-value-added technology and investments.[37] At the same time, more emphasis has been placed on human development, as evidenced by increased efforts in international cultural and educational programmes. The real cause of the Japanese success in business and industry, perhaps, lies in this adaptability or flexible accommodation to changing circumstances.

Japan's political system has facilitated the implementation of such flexibility. First of all, the continuous rule by the LDP provides basic political stability, enabling business and industry to make long-range plans. The government's industrial policy can be accepted without worry that it may change in a year or so. Second, factional politics provide opportunities for a variety of interests and opinions to be reflected in the LDP policy-making process. The duality of Japan's foreign relations, for example, makes it easier to tolerate what might appear to be contradictory or diverse policies. Third, bureaucrats' commitment to preserve the 'national interest' prevents radical changes or opportunistic measures. Fourth, the hierarchical power structure, stretching vertically downward from the factional boss to rank-and-file Diet members, prefectural assemblymen, and ward or village elders, not only makes the articulation of interests easier but also establishes a hierarchy of interests. What is good for Japan must precede what is good for Toyota or Sony, not vice versa. And, there is a common acceptance that the state is the final arbiter in deciding what is best for the nation.

Although students of Japan's policy-making process would argue against any sweeping generalisations about who or what institutions have the most influence, I would venture to say that the senior bureaucrats have more impact than others.[38] Although policies are often the results of interaction among three groups – the *zaikai*, the politicians, and the bureaucrats – it is the last group which actually works for policies, even those it does not approve of. Tanaka's success in imposing his own policy on the Ministry of Finance was accomplished only with assistance from some bureaucrats whom he had co-opted in the ministry. Politicisation and factionalisation among senior bureaucrats has sometimes been a problem for the ministries. Despite the unwritten law of seniority, politicians, as the ministers in charge, still have great influence on promotions at the higher levels. For an ambitious bureaucrat, good political connections may lead to a political career at an appropriate time. Recollecting the 1972 episode a *Mainichi* reporter wrote:

> The Finance Ministry bureaucrats are now private soldiers of Tanaka. When the Directors of the Bureau of Accounting [Mr Aizawa] and of Taxation [Mr Takagi] returned from the Prime Minister's residence, I asked them what had happened to the *mentsu* [face] and leadership of the Ministry of Finance. The answer I got was: you cannot resist the order of the Prime Minister; that is what it is to be a public servant. What was peculiarly missing in their words and expressions was the pride and confidence of the economic elites of Japan. I saw only two petty bureaucrats bowing to the political giant.[39]

Aizawa subsequently became an LDP member of the House of

Representatives and Takagi was President of the Japan National Railways a few years later.

Politicians are actors who need the bureaucrats to supply the scenario for their stage performance. In this sense the scenario-writer does have more influence on the performance than others, even when the scenario is written at the special request of the actor. Furthermore, rarely are such requests made and complied with. It takes a very strong political personality to introduce an innovative policy and impose it on bureaucrats. The *zaikai*, like a producer, gives approval or disapproval of the show but interferes very little in the details of staging.[40] When the team works in unison, it is JAPAN INC.; when it is divided, the show stalls.

Japan's slowness in responding to pressures to increase the defence budget is an example of this need for co-operation among the various groups that help determine foreign policy. While accelerated pressure from both government and non-government sources in the USA has proven to have the most effective impact on Japan's foreign policy in recent years, especially since Prime Minister Nakasone came to power, the internal politics of the LDP still place a check on Nakasone's wish to comply with US demands. Thus, Nakasone failed to lift the 1 per cent (of GNP) ceiling on defence spending. The lack of consensus within the LDP forced the prime minister to settle for a ceiling defined in terms of absolute figures rather than a percentage of GNP. Until there is a consensus on the issue, it is difficult for any single actor, Mr Nakasone included, to dominate the stage.

Like any other open society, Japan can no longer compartmentalise domestic and international affairs and, therefore, she is as much entitled as others to ask for international consideration of her domestic circumstances. In the light of the way party leadership, factional feuds, interest groups and the bureaucracy all impinge on foreign policy-making, it is realistic to expect Japan to make only incremental changes, and no radical shifts in its policy.

Part IV
Japan's Impact on the World

11 Japanese Policy-making on Issues of North–South Relations

Shigeko Nimiya Fukai

The stability and economic develoment of Third World countries is crucial to Japan's economic survival, which depends, to a large extent, upon imports of raw materials from and exports of manufactured goods to those countries. No doubt in recognition of this important fact, by 1984 Japan had become the world's second largest donor of foreign aid. Japanese aid policy nevertheless continues to be criticised on a number of grounds.

First, despite significant increases over the last few years, the total amount of Japanese aid has remained only about $31.5 per person per year, as compared to $34.1 for the USA and $51.7 for West Germany. Second, about half of Japan's Official Development Aid (ODA) is in loans, whereas the average grant component among other members of the Development Assistance Committee (DAC) of the Organisation for Economic Co-operation and Development (OECD) is about 90 per cent. This record led the DAC in late 1984 to call on Japan to improve its aid performance to meet the DAC standard.[1]

Third, Japan's aid policy has been also criticised for its geographic concentration on neighbouring Asian countries, despite some notable changes in recent years. Until a decade ago, these countries used to receive as much as 90 per cent of all Japanese foreign aid; by 1984 their share had declined to somewhat less than 70 per cent, while aid flow to non-Asian countries had increased by a corresponding ratio. In September of that year the Japanese Ministry of Foreign Affairs launched an 'Aid to Africa' campaign, targeted specifically to drought victims and refugees, and the result has been a fiftyfold increase in Japan's aid to countries in that continent. These changes doubtless reflect the Japanese government's growing awareness of problems with its aid policy.

Perhaps the least mentioned yet most significant feature of Japan's foreign aid policy is the lack of attention paid by the country's policy-makers to the distribution of political and economic power in Third World countries. Debates within the government in Tokyo continue to reveal indifference to redistribution issues despite the fact that in recent years such issues, dramatised by the demand of less-developed countries (LDCs) for a drastic restructuring of the existing international economic order, have occupied various United Nations agencies and other multilateral forums and despite the fact that the 1973 oil crisis alerted many Japanese to brewing discontent among the LDCs.[2]

Given the economic importance of the LDCs to Japan's own economic survival, this neglect of fundamental North–South issues can have serious consequences for Japan's future. The purpose of this chapter then is to explore the characteristics of the policy-making process in the Japanese government in order to explain why Japan continues to follow a much-criticised foreign-aid policy.

Past studies have tended to emphasise the impact of bureaucratic inertia, rivalries and vested interests of various ministries and the lack of genuine humanitarian concern among decision-makers for the welfare of ordinary people in the LDCs as the main factors responsible for Japan's controversial aid policy and performance on North–South issues.[3] These are important factors, but their role should be seen essentially as one of setting a general framework within which more specific self-driving forces come to play and interact. It seems necessary to make this distinction between 'framework' factors and 'driving-force' factors in order to understand the nature of Japan's North–South policy and its impact on the global pattern of North–South relationships. Since Alan Rix has already provided a detailed study of the framework factors in Japan's North–South policy-making, this study focuses on driving-force factors. To place the study in context, a brief sketch of the relevant bureaucracy follows.

I. ORGANISATIONAL FRAMEWORK

In contrast to the extensive involvement of the US Congress in North–South issues, the roles of the Japanese Diet and opposition parties are quite limited. The latter uses Diet deliberations mainly for the purpose of exposing the government's wrongdoings by investigating (and spreading) rumours of financial scandals involving one economic assistance project or another. There is no Diet committee on aid policy. The only significant decision taken by the Diet so far has been the 'Resolution on Economic Co-operation' adopted by the Foreign

Affairs Committee of the House of Representatives in April 1978 to facilitate the implementation of the ODA-doubling plan previously announced by the Cabinet.[4] Beyond declaring broad guiding principles, the Diet has demonstrated little interest in or knowledge of North–South issues or economic aid policy. This may be due to the fact that aid comprises less than 1 per cent of the General Account Budget and is believed to have little impact upon a Diet member's electoral performance.

The Japan Socialist Party (JSP) advocates a foreign policy of non-alignment and positive neutrality, but neither its party platform nor its election campaign documents present any concrete vision or policy guideline in regard to North–South issues. The Kōmeitō (Clean Government Party) and Democratic Socialist Party (DSP) are more specific: both advocate the goal of raising ODA to 1 per cent of GNP and support LDC commodity price stabilisation efforts.

The Japan Communist Party (JCP) presents the most concrete ideas and proposals. It charges that economic aid to the countries bordering East–West conflict areas constitutes intervention in domestic affairs rather than true aid. It also proposes: (1) complete suspension of aid to 'fascist military regimes', such as South Korea, (2) selection of recipients according to the values of their own programmes instead of Japan's 'national interest', (3) public access to all information on aid projects involving multinational corporations or Japan's big business, and (4) democratisation of the organisation of implementing agencies, such as the Overseas Economic Co-operation Fund (OECF).[5] These proposals demonstrate a superior knowledge and greater concern on the part of the JCP staff regarding North–South issues, but basically they constitute criticism of the existing government policy rather than innovative policy proposals. In terms of actual policy formulation JCP's influence has been very small.

Finally, even the role of the LDP is limited in the macro-policy-making process involving North–South issues. As early as 1959 the party created a Special Committee on Overseas Economic Co-operation under the aegis of its Policy Affairs Research Council (PARC). Besides acting as a 'support group' for aid ministries' policy or budget requests, an important role of the committee has been to provide opportunities for LDP Dietmen to build personal connections with agencies, firms and foreign governments involved in specific aid projects. These connections often draw suspicion and criticism of possible corruption from the opposition and the public. The actual involvement of LDP Dietmen has mostly been limited to micro-policy-making, or to specific aspects of aid budget allocations related to yen-loans projects, particularly every August when ministries discuss their budget requests with the LDP PARC committees, and during appeals negotiations (*fukkatsu sesshō*) in December or January. On most North–South issues, it is generally agreed, the bureaucracy rather than the LDP holds macro-policy-making and co-ordinating power.[6]

Ministries

Policy-making on North–South issues falls within the jurisdictions of four 'economic cooperation ministries', namely, the Ministry of Foreign Affairs (MFA), the Ministry of Finance (MOF), the Economic Planning Agency (EPA) and the Ministry of International Trade and Industry (MITI). Depending on the issues involved, other ministries, such as Agriculture, Forestry and Fisheries (MAFF), Health and Welfare, Labour, Education, Construction, Posts and Telecommunications, and Transport, may be involved. The Cabinet acts on important issues, such as budget proposals and aid agreements with LDCs. The twenty-member Advisory Council on Overseas Economic Co-operation, composed of a number of business leaders, three aid-implementing agency presidents, a few academics and a labour leader, presents proposals and opinions to the prime minister.[7]

The MFA is the official 'window' for all Japanese dealings on North–South issues and is responsible for negotiations with foreign governments. Its decisions are made, however, in consultation with other ministries. Among the four ministries, the MFA has been the most liberal and progressive voice on North–South issues, as it emphasises political and diplomatic goals in addition to Japan's economic need to secure resources and expand markets.

In 1976 Japan's ODA hit a record low of 0.20 per cent of GNP. The MFA used international criticisms of Japan's poor ODA performance for a public relations campaign, calling for a sharp increase in grant-aid and technical co-operation, in order to increase ODA and raise its grant element. The MOF (particularly its International Finance Bureau) was also eager to increase its budget for investments in and contributions to multilateral financial organisations. The MFA–MOF joint campaign aimed at the Overseas Economic Co-operation Council led the latter to recommend a substantial quantitative and qualitative improvement of Japan's ODA. The bilateral grant-aid budget was increased by 3.3 times and the total multilateral aid under MOF and

MFA jurisdiction by 2.3 times between FY 1976 and 1981. As a result of these increases, the MFA now administers almost a quarter of the total ODA budget and some 64 per cent of the bilateral grant-aid budget (the MOF manages the rest), technical co-operation and contributions to the UN- and UN-related organisations.[8]

The MFA, however, has not developed any permanent programme for educating the public on North–South issues comparable, for instance, to the Dutch programme which involves such systematic efforts as publication of a youth journal on the subject with a circulation of about 500 000 and an estimated readership of 40 per cent of all Dutch children aged 9 to 14.[9] In fact, the 1976 campaign was not exactly aimed at raising public awareness of North–South issues; it was motivated rather by a desire to expand the MFA's own interest by raising public concern over Japan's international reputation.[10]

Nor has the MFA formulated specific principles to guide Japan's aid policy comparable to those of some other donor countries. For instance, Sweden has set down egalitarian and neutralist criteria for choosing recipient countries and providing development co-operation to ensure economic and social equalisation, exclusion of reactionary regimes, and inclusion of states 'subjected to direct external pressures'.[11] The examination of MFA documents and interviews with its officials indicate that the basic motivating force comes from such external sources as the DAC, the World Bank, other multilateral bodies and some individual nations, particularly the US, rather than from a clear philosophical commitment like the Swedish 'solidarity with the poor' or the French 'inherent need to spread one's ideas and values to other parts of the world'.[12] The more recent 'Aid to Africa' campaign was also motivated by a desire to raise Japan's reputation as a donor country and to respond to the Western bloc pressure to assume a fair share of the burden of development assistance. Another reason, according to an MFA official, was to create a *medama* (attractive image-enhancing gimmick) for Foreign Minister Abe Shintarō, an aspirant for the prime ministership.[13]

On paper the EPA has a vital co-ordinating and supervising role in Japan's economic co-operation with less-developed countries. In reality its independence is seriously eroded by the presence of officials transferred from larger ministries, particularly the MOF and MITI, who occupy strategic posts and usually represent the parent ministry's viewpoint.

Legally, the EPA supervises the Overseas Economic Co-operation Fund (OECF), one of the two lending agencies along with the Export–

Import Bank of Japan (Eximbank). This responsibility fell on the EPA as a result of a 'deadly interministerial fight among the MFA, MITI, and MOF' over the administrative control of the OECF when it was established in March 1961. In spite of this unceremonious start with bureaucratic entanglement, the OECF has grown into an increasingly independent policy-making body, particularly after July 1975 when it was given responsibility for all ODA loans (i.e. loans with a grant element of 25 per cent or more). The reform has removed overlapping in the lending activities of the OECF and the Eximbank and made clearer the distinction between development aid and commercial loans in Japan's overseas loan programmes.

Through its budgeting power the MOF plays a supervisory role in and exerts restraining pressure on Japan's aid policy-making. Among all the ministries, it has been the most cautious and conservative in its attitude towards North–South dialogue at multilateral forums. Reflecting its administrative responsibility, MOF decisions are dictated by budgetary and monetary policy considerations, rather than by diplomatic or commercial goals. Since the Suzuki Administration, administrative reform and financial reconstruction to reduce the state budget deficit has made the MOF attitude on foreign-aid issues even less liberal, although it has agreed to treat the ODA budget as an exception along with the defence and energy budgets.

The MOF presently administers over 70 per cent of the ODA as Japan's 'window' for multilateral financial organisations (the IMF, the World Bank, the Asian Development Bank, etc.) and sets the budgets for the OECF and the Eximbank.

Considerations of Japan's economic security and commercial interests dominate MITI decisionmaking on North–South issues. With its jurisdiction overlapping with the MFA's, MITI deals with technical aid and loans. However, over 95 per cent of the ODA budget is managed by the MOF and MFA and less than 2 per cent by MITI. Nevertheless, MITI exerts greater influence than one might expect from this figure. Although it joins the MFA in supporting an increase in ODA spending, which amounts to an increase in guaranteed exports of Japanese goods, MITI places greater emphasis on joint government and business co-operation in its policy towards LDCs. For example, it recognises the greater value of the Other Official Flows (OOF) and Private Flows (PF) than ODA for promoting both its bureaucratic interests and Japan's commercial interests. Since the 1973–4 oil crisis, MITI has been focusing its effort on developing and applying a new 'national project' formula for large-scale economic co-operation budgets. Examples include the power and aluminum projects in Indonesia (the Asahan project) and in Brazil (the Amazon project), and petrochemical complexes in Singapore, Saudi Arabia and Iran. It has been the axis of Japan's 'commercial-interest-based economic co-operation policy'.[14]

Implementing Agencies

There are three main implementing agencies: the OECF, the Eximbank and the Japan International Co-operation Agency (JICA). Formally, policy-making power resides with the four-ministry conference. However, the high turnover in their division-level staffs has made it difficult to nurture experts in North–South issues, whereas the implementing agencies have been able to accumulate considerable amounts of technical know-how and expertise in the respective policy areas. In addition, many senior officials of these agencies come from the ministries either as transferees or after retirement. (In fact, one of the functions of these agencies is to provide post-retirement posts for these *amakudari* or 'descendants from heaven'.) These circumstances have often enabled implementing agency officials to exert substantial influence in the policy-making process.[15]

Based on expertise in project appraisal and loans policy acquired through its experience as the main source of concessional development loans (with grant element of 25 per cent or more) and contacts with LDCs, the OECF has become 'the acknowledged backbone of Japan's aid programme'. As Rix notes, its officials exert significant influence over not only 'immediate policy mechanisms' but also various 'options open to decision-makers, the scope and type of requests, and, importantly, the trends in policy as reflected in the content and direction of flows'.[16] Its activities include the managements of (1) loans to LDC governments, (2) loans to Japanese corporations, and (3) investment in Japanese corporations and contributors to such international arrangements as 'buffer stocks' maintained under various international commodity agreements.[17]

The OECF's financial resources are drawn from an annual appropriation under the General Account Budget, borrowing from the MOF's Trust Fund Bureau, which administers funds collected from post office savings and post office insurance premiums, and the OECF's own funds, including interest on and repaid principal of previous loans. Since 1966, when the OECF was authorised to borrow from the Trust

Fund, its budget has increased substantially, reflecting a growth in the volume of loans and investments abroad.[18]

The Eximbank, established in December 1950 under the name of the Export Bank of Japan, is an independent governmental financial institution designed to supplement or encourage commercial banks in financing exports, imports and overseas investments, all ultimately to promote Japanese foreign trade. Its financial resources come from paid-up capital, which is wholly subscribed and paid by the government from its Industrial Investment Special Account, borrowings from the Trust Funds and foreign financial institutions, and funds raised in foreign capital markets, loan repayments, reserve funds, etc.

Programmes covered by the Eximbank include assistance to Japanese trading and investment firms, direct loans to foreign governments and corporations for the import of equipment and technical services from Japan, and refinancing of loans to foreign governments and banks to enable them to repay their debts to Japan.[19]

The JICA was established in August 1974 as an administrative organ under MFA supervision for the management of Japan's technical cooperation programmes to promote socioeconomic progress of developing countries. Depending on projects involved, however, MITI, MAFF, MOT and other ministries exert informal but significant influence over the agency's activities which include management of technical training programmes in Japan, and of capital-grant-aid programmes for building schools, hospitals, etc., in LDCs, dispatch of Japan Overseas Co-operation Volunteers (JOCV) and of survey teams to LDCs, recruitment and training of Japanese experts to be sent abroad, and supply of equipment necessary for technical co-operation. It also provides financial aid to private Japanese firms engaged in development co-operation. One of its important objectives has been to broaden the horizon of co-operation between Japan and LDCs by providing soft loans for technical co-operation projects not funded either by the Eximbank or by OECF.[20]

Since technical co-operation is a form of grant-aid financed by the annual General Account budget, despite long-standing criticism from the OECD–DAC, MOF's Budget Bureau has restrained JICA's budget in order to keep its share in the total budget constant.

Japan's North–South Policy Administration

The dispersion of authority among the four ministries with different role perceptions has been blamed for Japan's failure to develop a consistent policy on North–South issues based on a clear statement of long-range and medium-range developmental goals. This does not mean that there is no policy consensus. The four ministries all agree that Third World stability and economic development are in Japan's self-interest.

There have been, however, significant shifts in the 'basic goals and principles' pronounced by successive prime ministers at various international forums during the past decade. The 'Fukuda Doctrine' announced in Manila in August 1977 emphasised Japan's intention to promote a 'heart-to-heart' understanding with LDCs and to contribute to world peace by diverting to LDCs the national budget surplus resulting from Japan's policy of not building a large military force. At that time the Japanese government promised to double Japan's ODA within the next three years. This was also a response to the Western pressure on Japan to reduce her balance of payment surplus.[21] Prime Minister Ohira Masayoshi's speech at the Fifth United Nations Conference on Trade and Development (UNCTAD V), in Manila in May 1979, proposed to open up Japan's market to LDC exports and to strengthen co-operation in human resource development in developing countries. However, by suspending the grant of a 10 billion (US) yen credit as a commodity loan to Vietnam (pledged by Japan in March 1978, nine months before the Vietnamese invasion of Cambodia), Ohira modified an important principle of the Fukuda Doctrine, i.e. the separation of North–South policy from East–West conflict.[22]

After the Soviet invasion of Afghanistan in December 1979 the shift away from the Fukuda Doctrine began to gather momentum. The MFA took the lead in steering the government approach to North–South issues in the general direction of supporting the US strategy to contain Soviet influence. In a document entitled 'The Idea of Economic Cooperation' (*Keizai kyōryoku no rinen*), published in December 1980, the MFA took the position that Japan should use economic aid to supplement Western defence efforts. The drafting of this document was inspired by US Defense Secretary Harold Brown's request, made in January 1980 in Tokyo, for Japan to improve its defence capability. He was reported to have indirectly demanded that Prime Minister Ohira remove the ceiling of 1 per cent of GNP which Japan had voluntarily imposed on its defence spending. Ohira told Brown that Japan would decide what to do after carefully watching how public opinion evolved. The MFA response, as formulated in the above document, was to increase economic aid to countries bordering regions of East–West conflict instead of increasing Japan's defence spending.

In Washington in May 1981, according to a senior researcher of the *Asahi Shimbun*, President Reagan pressured Ohira's successor, Suzuki, to promise a substantial increase in economic aid to South Korea as a way of sharing the US defence burden.[23] At the Ottawa summit in July 1981, Suzuki endorsed the idea that Japan should supplement Western defence efforts by increasing its economic aid. The new ODA-doubling policy should be seen in this general context. The Suzuki Cabinet also increased the yen credits given to such 'front-line states' as Turkey, Pakistan, the Caribbean countries and Thailand.

This tendency became increasingly pronounced, particularly after Foreign Minister Sonoda Sunao was replaced by Sakurauchi Yoshio on 30 November 1981. During the prolonged negotiation with South Korea on economic co-operation that preceded Sonoda's resignation, he had firmly maintained that 'security and defence issues should be discussed separately from economic co-operation'. A senior political analyst of the *Mainichi Shimbun* relates Sonoda's resignation to pressure from Tanaka Kakuei, who appears to have acted in line with the US Far Eastern strategy of encircling the Soviet Union with an alliance of China, South Korea and Japan.[24] President Reagan met South Korean President Chun Doo Hwan in February 1981, and by reassuring the latter that there would be no withdrawal of the US forces from South Korea, restored the relations that had been chilled under President Carter. Nikaidō Susumu, Tanaka's senior lieutenant, visited Washington frequently, while a number of Tanaka faction leaders visited South Korea. The press reports noted a rumour that Chun had decided to give up the Fukuda faction and the DSP in favour of the Tanaka faction as the main communication channel with Japan.[25] In July 1981 Henry Kissinger visited Tanaka and 'gave a lecture on international politics', to use Tanaka's expression.[26] In August Chun requested from Japan a huge 6 billion dollar ODA package. He emphasised that Japan should take note of the security dimension of economic co-operation. Implied was the logic that since South Korea was acting as a buffer between North Korea and Japan, Japan should support South Korea with economic assistance. Sonoda rejected the request as outrageous. In September Tanaka made a public statement which implicitly supported Chun's request, to Suzuki's and Sonoda's dismay. Other leaders of his faction also began to criticise Sonoda openly, until he resigned in November.

There was another significant development during the Suzuki Administration. MITI elaborated more focused medium-range goals for Japan's development assistance, adding to Ohira's human resource development programmes the development of agriculture and rural, energy and small and medium-sized industries. There has been some shift away from large projects and emphasis on hardware towards 'soft' technical assistance and emphasis on 'greater benefit for the population as a whole'.[27]

Prime Minister Nakasone continues the Suzuki line. On the one hand, he has increased economic aid to the 'front-line' nations. He visited South Korea in January 1983 and promised Chun a total of 4 billion dollars in aid over a period of seven years. Japanese analysts generally attributed this quick resolution of the issue to Nakasone's fidelity to the Reagan policy.[28] On the other hand, his Administration has further elaborated the contents of development aid in the area of technology transfer, especially in programmes aimed at Asian neighbours. This can be seen as a response to two forces: the desire of LDCs to obtain technology to increase their self-reliance and the need of some segments of Japanese industry to find markets for their increasingly obsolete 'intermediate technology' and/or to relocate production abroad.

Since the Fukuda Administration, the impetus for change in Japanese aid policy has come mainly from four sources: criticism and demands by the LDCs, OECD's Development Assistance Committee, the US and Japanese business. The Fukuda Doctrine was a response to LDC criticism, which had been dramatised by the anti-Japanese demonstrations during Prime Minister Tanaka's January 1974 visit to the ASEAN countries. The Western pressure on Japan to reduce its trade surplus was behind Fukuda's ODA-doubling promise. Suzuki's and Nakasone's emphasis on aid to 'nations bordering the strife-ridden regions' (*funsō-shūhen koku*) has been a response to US pressure. As already noted, Nakasone's technology transfer scheme may be understood as a response to the demands of LDCs and Japanese businesses. What may have appeared as an individual prime minister's initiative was actually devised by various ministries, with one ministry usually taking the lead, in response to pressures from one or more of the four sources noted above.

Just as there have been frequent shifts in Japan's medium-term policy goals, consistency has been notable by its absence in its North–South policy. So has been attention to the distribution of political and economic power in the world and within LDCs. This criticism of the Japanese policy has been concerned mainly with its self-centredness, its preoccupation with Japanese business interests and its indifference to the impact of its policy on the recipient country's social, economic and political development. The Japanese policy-makers have responded to this criicism in two ways: by devising various slogans, from Fukuda's 'heart-to-heart' understanding to Nakasone's 'plant renovation co-operation', complemented on occasion by introduction of mainly symbolic programmes, and by increasing the quantity of economic assistance. No systematic efforts have yet been made to examine how Japan's policy has affected employment, income distribution, social services and other conditions in the recipient country, or to reflect on the more elementary but crucial question: Has Japanese aid helped regimes willing and capable of improving grassroots welfare? It is only recently that some MFA officials began to address these questions.[29]

This may be a result, not of the decentralisation of decision-making power, but rather of the relative power relations among various forces competing or colluding to influence Japan's relations with the world market and LDCs. It may also be a reflection of the structure of Japan's domestic political and economic power relations within which the North–South policy process operates.

II. RECENT CASES

In order to identify and understand the 'forces' behind the administrative forms and rationalisations, we need to observe concrete cases. The following cases illustrate Japan's policy-making on North–South issues in the late 1970s and early 1980s.[30]

Case 1 Agricultural Development Research Centre in Honduras

The initial impetus for this project came in 1981 from a high-ranking Honduran Natural Resources Ministry official who consulted Kimura Takashige of Chūō Kaihatsu (a major consulting firm) about ways to educate agricultural civil engineers. Chūō Kaihatsu conducted a feasibility study and drew up a work-plan within the cost range of a normal Japanese grant-aid project. The Honduran government then requested from the Japanese government a capital grant of some 1.6 billion yen to implement the project; the grant was approved in June 1982 and renewed a year later.[31] Chūō Kaihatsu designed and supervised the installation of the facility. Kōnoike-gumi (a major construction company of the Kansai district), the main contractor, and fourteen subcontractors in charge of electric, water and sewage systems, worked for two years to build classrooms, dormitories and research facilities (altogether twenty-two building units), and a farm. Educational equipment and facilities were provided by Mitsui Bussan, a major Japanese trading company and the second-largest non-US firm in 1985.[32]

One of the tacit rules in Japan's aid policy is that the project must be requested by the recipient country. In reality, however, many LDC governments lack the ability to develop a suitable project and, as a result, Japanese consulting firms play an important role. As Rix has pointed out, the growth in the overseas consulting industry 'in the 1960s was closely associated with swelling Japanese government aid flows and with contracts resulting from assistance by multilateral organisations to Asian countries'.[33] Of the fifty-eight overseas consulting firms in existence in 1985, the largest, Nihon Kōei, is known for its world-wide operations and close connection with the government. Among its recent initiatives was the Asahan project in Indonesia (see below). Nihon Kōei has offices in twelve countries in Asia, the Middle East and Africa, undertaking the construction and repair of dams, rivers, bridges and roads. Some 400 people on the firm's staff are regularly engaged in project-finding in the three continents.[34]

According to a recent survey conducted by the Federation of Economic Organisations (FEO or Keidanren), the request-by-recipient rule has been one of the problems most frequently complained about by Japanese firms, due to the fact that project-finding is often undertaken in an environment of intense international competition. As a rule, although not always, project-finders get the contracts. Reflecting the FEO position, MITI advocates a proposal formula, by which the donor-side may propose projects to a recipient government. The MFA has been examining the possibility of combining the request and proposal rules.[35]

Case 2   Sale of Plant Barges

Under the terms of a special yen credit (signed on 2 February 1979) the Philippines government bought four power-generation plant barges from Japan, each with thirty-two megawatt capacity and able to supply power to 60 000 homes. The idea was first discussed by MITI officials and the Japan Plant Association in 1977 as a measure to help the depressed shipbuilding industry. The MFA suggested buying some of the power plants from the US to reduce Japan's trade surplus. MITI minister Kōmoto Toshio agreed to that suggestion as a good way to kill three birds with one stone. The first *special* yen credit deal was approved as part of the 1978 budget. A delegation of government and private-sector representatives was sent to Asian countries to find more potential buyers, and Bangladesh and Thailand bought four more. The MOF was reluctant but approved the second special yen credit deal for FY 1983. Jamaica and Eygpt are among the more recent buyers.

These deals are also typical of the Japanese aid policy in that they had a clear domestic economic policy incentive, reminiscent of the Public Law 480 of 1954 and the Food for Peace Act of 1962 of the US, both of which facilitated the utilisation of surplus grain. The Japanese government has applied the US food-assistance formula to the disposition of obsolete machines and equipment, which it buys from Japanese firms and uses for economic aid to Asian countries. The domestic goal of the policy is to facilitate modernisation of productive facilities and equipment by Japanese firms. In 1978 MITI drafted and the Diet passed the 'Structurally Depressed Industries Law' to reduce productive capacity by scrapping and rationalising plants and equipment in such depressed industries as aluminium smelting, shipbuilding, chemical fertiliser and ferroalloys; the bulk of the surplus stocks was transferred to developing countries in the name of economic aid.

The economic impact of the sale of four plant barges would be small, but as noted by a Hitachi Shipbuilding employee, 'it gave an important psychological uplift on the idle docks'.[36] The project is also seen as stimulating the new demand for barges with various facilities mounted, such as desalination barges sold by Ishikawajima Harima to a Middle Eastern country. The same formula has been used in economic co-operation projects to increase food production, to help the depressed domestic agrochemical industry.

The recipient countries, however, are often more interested in acquiring *technology and plants to produce* what they need than receiving surplus goods. Recently a Middle Eastern country requested economic aid for the construction of a fertiliser plant. The preliminary investigation conducted by the Japan Plant Association concluded that the domestic market was too small. Japanese construction firms argued that Japan could buy excess products; the Japanese fertiliser industry, however, opposed the project by pointing out the existing excess capacity in Japan. In the end the project did not materialise.[37]

Case 3 Transportation Reinforcement Project in Zaïre

The government of Zaïre decided to build a new port in Banana on the Atlantic and a railway from Matadi on the Zaïre River to the port. Japan agreed to provide 34.5 billion yen credit and technical assistance; France and Belgium agreed to provide loans for the construction of the port. In January 1976, Katase Takafumi, then Railway Division head of the Japan National Railways, was dispatched to Kinshasa and found it impossible to start the project because the post-oil crisis inflation had tripled the project costs, while the copper-price decline had sharply reduced Zaïre's export earnings and government revenue.

In view of the yen credit now hanging in the air, foreign firms, World Bank branch offices, and even Japanese tracing companies tried to sell a variety of projects, such as an oil pipe-line and roads. The Katase group wanted to build at least the Matadi bridge over the Zaïre River, an important part of the original plan. The MFA came to support the idea. Zaïre's President Mobutu also wanted the construction of the bridge. However, France and Belgium had already decided to postpone the construction of the port. Without either the new port or the railway, the bridge was nevertheless built by Ishikawajima Harima Heavy Industry and a syndicate of Japanese firms. Today, the largest suspended bridge in Africa is used each day merely by several hundred trucks and near-by people who carry things on their heads. In this case all of the 14 000 tons of steel used for the construction was purchased from Japan and some 25 million of the 34.5 million yen invested soon returned to Japan.[38]

Case 4 Economic Co-operation with the Philippines

How can a long-range strategy of a big Japanese firm affect Japan's official policy on North–South issues? How can it influence or interact with an LDC's internal power relations? The business strategy and activities in the Philippines of one of the largest trading firms, Marubeni, is illuminating.

In the early 1960s, in its effort to catch up with other Japanese trading firms which had already built bridgeheads in many parts of South-east Asia, Marubeni decided to 'infiltrate' the Philippines, which had so far been openly hostile to Japan because of the bitter memories of the Second World War. Adachi Toshio, then Marubeni's plant division head, spent half a year in Manila to cultivate friendly relations with the then Congressman Ferdinand Marcos, by, for instance, inviting him to play golf together. Marcos subsequently became a senator and was elected president in November 1965. Adachi became head of Marubeni's Manila office and maintained close relations with the Marcos family.

In 1972 President Marcos declared martial law and placed sugar under state control. Ambassador Roberto S. Benedict, a close friend of Adachi and Marcos's classmate at the Law School of the University of the Philippines, was appointed Chairman of the Philippine Sugar Commission, while serving as the ambassador to Japan. He decided to import machinery and equipment to modernise the sugar industry. Of the ten plants imported from Japan, eight were contracted by the Marubeni–Hitachi Shipbuilding group. The Eximbank paid the costs in the name of economic co-operation.

The state control of the sugar industry was aimed at breaking the back of the Lopez family, Marcos's political rival who had close ties with US business. Cultivation of ties with Japan was a logical choice for Marcos. Marubeni has since handled some 30 per cent of the trade between the two countries. The Japanese government fund was poured into the Philippines for the construction of highways, bridges, railways, harbours, irrigation systems, etc. Marubeni has been in charge of many large projects, such as the construction of the Marcos Bridge, which took four years and was financed with yen credit as a part of the Japan–Philippines Friendship Highway project. Japan's economic co-operation helped relatives and cronies of the Marcos family multiply their wealth and power.

Growing criticism of and opposition to the corruption of the Marcos rule began to shake its foundations. None the less, in March 1984, the Nakasone Cabinet decided to offer a 55 billion yen credit to the Philippines to help it cope with its economic crisis. The unpopular decision was said to have been made in response to President Reagan's request during his visit to Japan in November 1983.[39] The political instability after the assassination of Benigno Aquino in August 1983 accelerated industrial stagnation with a shortage of foreign exchange caused by capital flight. Reportedly, Marcos phoned Nakasone in January 1984 and asked for a quick decision on the yen credit issue. (Nakasone had earlier declared it his goal to build a relationship of mutual trust with ASEAN leaders, whereby they would be able 'to phone each other freely.') In April, despite widespread criticisms not only in Japan but in the Philippines, the Nakasone Administration decided to give Marcos a $140 million commodity loan just before the general elections of May 1984, which resulted in a strong showing by Marcos's opponents. This was the first large-scale loan made to Marcos after the Aquino incident; it was approved by the Japanese government even before a formal agreement was concluded between the International Monetary Fund (IMF) and the Philippine government, partly to impress ASEAN countries about Japan's 'positive' posture. In this decision Nakasone's initiative is said to have been a decisive factor. He stated in a lecture given in January that 'The litmus test for Japan's policy toward the ASEAN will be whether we make a fair contribution to the Philippines' effort to cope with its accumulated debts.' An MFA official explained at the time that Nakasone believed it to be Japan's international responsibility to take care of the Asian part of world economic problems, while the US handled Latin American problems.

Some within the Nakasone government were critical of the prime minister's decision. They argued that commodity loans should be given only to poorer countries. Others questioned the Marcos regime's future and ability to return the debt. However, the national security argument prevailed within the Tokyo Administration: it is vital for Japan to prevent a Communist takeover of the Philippines where the US naval and air force bases guard the Indochinese waters and the Malacca Strait, the 'lifeline' for Japan's oil import from the Middle East. US pressure and Nakasone's (and his supporters') responsiveness to this pressure, which may have been reinforced by his or their own perception of Communist threat to Japan's national security, overrode the public criticism and intragovernmental opposition. Nevertheless, what emerges from this episode is the shallowness of non-economic concerns among Japan's decision-making circles. Even though Japan's national security was used for rationalisation, analysts agree that it was President Reagan's request that had inspired Nakasone's 'initiative' and thereby had a decisive impact on Tokyo's decision.[40]

Case 5   The Asahan Power–Aluminium Project

This 'colossal monument of Japan–Indonesian economic co-operation'[41] completed in October 1984 at the cost of $1.6 billion (87 per cent of which was funded by Japan, 76 per cent by the Japanese government), is an outstanding example of a 'national project', in which 'private initiative and leadership encouraged government assistance necessary for overseas private investment.'[42] It involved the construction of a hydroelectric power plant along the Asahan River to supply power for the production of 225 000 tons of aluminium per year. Plans to utilise Indonesia's abundant water resources date back to Dutch studies in 1908. Japanese interest began with a survey during the Second World War by a team led by Kubota Yutaka, who later became President of Nihon Kōei. In 1967, when the Suharto government adopted a policy to import foreign capital, Nihon Kōei dispatched a survey team. In 1969 Kaiser, a US aluminium giant, submitted to the Indonesian government a report on the feasibility of an aluminium refinery plant using hydro-electric power. Japanese aluminium companies approached their US counterparts to study possibilities of joint efforts. Encouraged by the growing international interest, in January 1972 the Indonesian government decided to combine the construction of a power plant with that of an aluminium refinery and called for tenders. Both the US and Japanese companies were interested only in a refinery, not in a costly dam and a power plant.

The first oil crisis of 1973, however, changed the attitude of the Japanese companies, which faced a steep cost increase in electricity supplied by domestic petroleum-powered plants. Under MITI's 'administrative guidance', five aluminium companies led by Sumitomo Chemicals formed a united front to promote the Asahan project, which was expected to make power available at less than one-third of the prevailing cost in Japan. After securing the Japanese government's promise for financial assistance, the five Japanese companies and the Indonesian government signed a preliminary agreement on 8 January 1974; Prime Minister Tanaka visited Indonesia on 15 January in the midst of anti-Japanese demonstrations, and exchanged notes on the basic agreement on the project with President Suharto. Cost–benefit analysis had led US companies (Kaiser and Alcoa) to decide not to participate in the project.

Meanwhile, MITI pursued its own plan to develop the project into a 'national project' and cultivate broader support for the plan by consulting the Aluminium Committee of the Industrial Structure Council, presumably a neutral expert body whose proposals were made in the public interest. An ISC proposal (actually prepared by MITI officials) was drafted while negotiations were under way with the Indonesian government for a basic contract on the Asahan development. In July 1975 the Japanese business consortium and the Indonesian government signed the master agreement; in August the ISC submitted an interim report, which emphasised the difficulties faced by the Japanese aluminium industry and suggested that 'It is absolutely necessary to promote "development import" (*kaihatsu yunyū*) by relocating refineries overseas'. The report clearly revealed MITI's intention to combine aid to a structurally depressed domestic industry with overseas economic co-operation.

The production cost at the Asahan smelting factory has proved to be less than one-fifth of the prevailing cost in Japan. It is understandable that the Japanese government and business should call it 'a successful example of a national project'.[43] From the Indonesian viewpoint, however, the benefits of the project are less clear. A senior researcher of the *Asahi Shimbun* goes so far as to ask: Who benefits from the apparently useless aid project besides President Suharto?[44] A *Yomiuri Shimbun* senior researcher points out the following problems:

1. According to the basic contract, 90 per cent of power generated would be supplied to the aluminum smelting factory and only 10 per cent to the local people. The aluminum produced is handled exclusively by five Japanese aluminum companies; and three quarters of the profits of the joint venture firm, Inalum, would be taken by the Japanese according to the investment ratio. Thus most of the power, aluminum, and profits are to be sent to Japan, while Indonesia only supplies resources, water, and an industrial site;

2. The project has produced only two thousand jobs, far less than the Indonesian side had expected, because the Japanese investors gave priority to profitability and designed highly capital-intensive, that is, labor-saving factories;

3. Although Indonesia is entitled to up to one-third of the aluminum produced, there are no Indonesian factories to manufacture aluminum products. The prospects for the growth of a secondary processing industry are not bright, either, as the Indonesian government abandoned the policy of developing heavy and chemical industries in 1979. Thus, the project has had little trickle down effect in terms of employment, industrial growth, or the standard of living of the local people.[45]

III. The Nature of Japan's North–South Policy-Making

From the examples given above, it is possible to draw some general conclusions about the nature of Japan's policy-making on issues of North–South relations. The first is the importance of initiatives exercised by business, especially trading companies. The second is the willingness of the Japanese government, especially MITI, to use ODA and other forms of foreign aid as a prop for the international strategy of Japanese industries. The other side of this coin has been the relative insensitivity to LDC's needs in general and particularly to the recipient country's ability to utilise the project for achievement of its own longer-range development goals.

Chu Yukun explains these features of Japanese aid policy in terms of two motivations which underpin the government–business consensus: the desire to secure access to overseas resources and the desire to maintain international competitiveness by relocating labour-intensive production processes to labour-abundant LDCs, preferably close to sources of raw materials and cheap power.[46] Following the examples of their US, West German and French counterparts, Japanese firms have adopted the strategy of industrial relocation since the early 1970s. In the process, what Terutomo Ozawa calls development assistance packaging has emerged as a major formula from promoting smooth industrial relocation.[47] Not surprisingly, the main beneficiaries of Japanese ODA have often been Japanese trading companies, structurally depressed industries, construction firms and consulting firms.

It should be asked, however, why government–private business teamwork has become so much more dominant in Japan than in the US, West Germany or France, where ODA and industrial relocation have not coalesced to such an extent. The answer may lie in the uniqueness of multinationalism evolved in Japan, a resource-poor latecomer to the industrial world. As Galbraith has pointed out, overseas investment has been a feature mainly of activities of large oligopolistic corporations nurtured in an advanced capitalist economy like the US. Equipped with a 'technostructure, a complex of scientists, engineers, and technicians' in the fields of management, marketing and production, a mature corporation 'transcends the market internationally as it does nationally', just 'by recreating itself in other countries', in order to eliminate uncertainties in the market.[48]

Some Japanese corporations, such as Nippon Steel, Toyota, Nissan, Mitsubishi Heavy Industries and large trading companies, have reached such a 'mature' stage and have formed such a technostructure. However, nearly half of Japan's overseas investments have been made by small and medium-sized firms (with less than 300 employees or paid-in capital of 100 million yen or less). In Asia, the ratio becomes even higher; e.g. 70 per cent in South Korea. As Ozawa explains, this reflects both Japan's dual economic structure and 'the unique process by which the labour-intensive, low-productivity end of the dual industrial structure is being pushed out of Japan' into more labour-abundant neighbouring countries through direct investment.[49] This kind of industrial relocation was necessary for the 'immature' Japanese economy to remain competitive in the world market.

Without a sophisticated 'technostructure', how was it possible for the Japanese firms to go abroad? The gap has been filled largely by big trading firms, which handle not only big businesses' deals, but also play a vital role in transforming private deals in trade and direct investment involving small and medium firms into economic co-operation projects funded by the Japanese government. The commercial use of ODA and the active involvement of Japanese business interests in economic co-operation projects have thus evolved in response to the perception of the 'survival need' of the latecomer economy. This perception is widely shared by those in Japanese government and industry. At least for some of them, the primary motivation has been 'self-defence' rather than aggressive search for greater profits.

As in the case of the Asahan project, development assistance packages are also used by extractive industries for the relocation of downstream processing operations, often accompanied by the construction of a new infrastructure (power, transport and communications) and ancillary manufacturing or service industries.

The third characteristic of Japan's policy-making *vis-à-vis* North–South issues is the high sensitivity of Japanese policy-makers, particularly MFA officials, to DAC's comments on Japan's economic co-operation performance and, increasingly in recent years, to US global strategic considerations. The fourth is the reluctance of the MOF to accept and support private initiatives in developing economic co-operation projects with government funds. This has resulted in rigidity in the use of ODA.

The absence of non-economic interest groups which actively attempt to influence government policy or pursue their own activity plans in the area of North–South relations is another characteristic of the Japanese experience, which contrasts sharply with situations in some DAC nations where non-governmental organisations (NGOs), such as the National Advisory Council for Development Co-operation and the National Committee for Information on Development Co-operation in the Netherlands, actively participate in North–South policy-making and engage in their own relevant activities.[50]

The weak political support for and lack of interest among politicians in development issues, as distinguished from commercial interest, have rendered North–South issues a low-priority item in the national political agenda, and prevented the emergence of a driving force which can bring about innovations or change of direction independent from business interests. What appear as political initiatives have often been propelled by one or another of the forces listed above or else have turned out to be mainly symbolic public relations ploys to manipulate a new prime minister's public image or to pacify discontent in an LDC. The lack of interest in redistribution issues in the context of either the recipient country or the world at large is a result of the policy-making process dominated by business and US strategic interests, which may in turn reflect Japan's class relations and economic dependence upon the US market.

The future prospects for change in Japan's policy on North–South issues depends on changes in the forces identified above and also on the emergence and growth of others. First of all, strong competition from the newly industrialising countries of Asia will cause further emigration of inefficient Japanese industries, which will in turn increase the amounts of Japan's ODA and OOF budgets. It seems possible that Japan's development assistance will become even more commercial in terms of the ratio of the grant element and the selection of recipient countries and funded projects.

Second, however, the emphasis of the ODA-business strategy may shift from the export of capital goods and the securing of resources to the cultivation of LDC domestic markets and the improvement in the living standard of the poor in LDCs – fostering the middle class, as a MITI official put it, in search of a 'survival path' for the Japanese economy in the environment of growing protectionism in the US and Western Europe. As Japan is pushed increasingly into high-technology export markets by competition from the Asian NICs in the areas of smokestack industries (including petrochemicals, pulp, and artificial fibres) and mass-produced consumer electronics, trade friction with developed countries may be further intensified and provoke more protectionist measures.[51]

Another possible scenario is a decline in Japan's technical co-operation, as its competitors among developing countries move up the ladder to increasingly high-technology fields. Under such circumstances Japan may become less willing to transfer technology abroad, particularly beyond the 'intermediate technology' level.[52]

As regards the military strategic emphasis, one possible prospect is for Japanese business interests to coincide with US strategic interests, as protectionism grows in the consumer-goods market in DCs. It may be recalled that Mitsubishi Heavy Industries, Japan's largest defence contractor, has been continually campaigning for an increase in the proportion of GNP devoted to defence spending. The corporation has also been the dominant force in the FEO's Defense Production Committee, which actively lobbies for increased defence spending. In late July 1985 Nakasone announced that the 1 per cent of GNP ceiling for Japan's defence spending might have to be scrapped. If such collusion of interests were to occur between the US defence establishment and Japanese business groups (especially high-technology industries), Japan's economic assistance programmes will be influenced increasingly by US strategic considerations and Japanese (and US) defence industries' interests in disregard of the economic needs of the recipient countries. If this should happen, there is a danger that 'economic assistance' may contribute to grass-roots discontent and social unrest in the Third World and ultimately to an aggravation of global political instability.

There is also a possibility, however, that such a trend, if it becomes evident, might activate the presently latent but deep-seated anti-war sentiment among the Japanese and inspire protest movements in various forms. It is also likely to alarm Japan's neighbours. The Indonesian government recently expressed concern about Japan's defence buildup. An important new factor in this regard is the increasing ability of ordinary people to use long-distance mass-communications media. Advanced communications technology will make it not only possible but probable that such protest movements develop international networks by which otherwise isolated activities can support one another and increase their collective strength and impact.

Finally, the self-centredness of Japan's economic co-operation can be a double-edged sword. If Japan's policies should arouse sufficient resentment or even hostility in LDCs to block its own immediate goals, policy-makers may be forced to redirect their attention to the question of how to help self-sustaining development of the recipient country.[53] Developing countries' increasing self-reliance has indeed been the declared ultimate goal of Japan's North–South policies and has been used as the rationale for its preference for loans over grants. Japan's 'more enlightened self-interest' may make its policy-makers realise the need to substantiate that rhetoric in the future.

12 The Japanese Management System in Europe: Japanese Subsidiaries in the Federal Republic of Germany

S. J. Park

The Federal Republic of Germany today hosts more subsidiaries of Japanese firms than any other European country.[1] None the less, it is only recently that West German scholars began to study the operations of these subsidiaries, though a number of British research groups have for a long time been studying the investment strategies and practices followed by Japanese subsidiaries in Britain.[2] The main focus of the research project undertaken by the Research Group on Japanese Management at the East Asian Institute of the Free University of Berlin under my direction is the personnel policies of Japanese subsidiaries in the Federal Republic.[3]

The early findings of the project call into question the widely held assumption that Japanese firms are able to implement in their subsidiaries the same personnel policies that have been tried and proven effective in Japan.[4] This chapter presents a summary of the initial results of the ongoing research project in the form of four broad generalisations, followed by more detailed discussion of each generalisation.

FOUR CHARACTERISTICS OF THE PERSONNEL PRACTICES OF JAPANESE SUBSIDIARIES

First, Japanese subsidiaries in West Germany do not seem to have, as a rule, a distinctive and coherent long-range personnel plan. If one existed, such a plan would presumably be aimed at filling middle-management positions with Germans in order to reduce pressure on the relatively small corps of Japanese personnel. In reality, however, most top- and middle-level management positions in Japanese subsidiaries are occupied by Japanese all the way down to the department-head level.

Second, and following from the first point, German employees' promotion prospects are strictly limited and they seldom take part in the decision-making process. As a result, Germans who hold top management positions in their own firms are unlikely to move to Japanese firms. Moreover, those Germans with great talent and promise who are currently hired by Japanese firms are likely to leave them sooner or later for firms that offer more attractive career opportunities. Those who stay with Japanese firms are likely to do so because they lack either leadership potential or professional ambitions. Their ability and willingness to adapt to the Japanese way may fit the Japanese idea of good employees, but in the long run such a recruitment practice will cut off the Japanese firms from the best qualified personnel available in the host country.

Third, the current Japanese practice requires a large number of Japanese managers to continue to occupy central decision-making positions for a long time. This may be a strategy designed to produce quickly a large number of native managers with international experience by rapidly rotating them between positions abroad and at home. If that is the case it helps explain why Japanese transnational companies, in sharp contrast to their US counterparts, do not seem to make efforts to integrate national and foreign personnel at the management level.

It should be pointed out that a systematic personnel policy is important for any foreign subsidiary that wants to build a stable workforce of German employees so as to ensure continuities in the firm's business operations in the face of a rapid turnover among Japanese managers. From such a point of view the German managers in Japanese subsidiaries who hold *interface* positions between the Japanese management at the headquarters and German employees must play a particularly important role. (An interface position refers to a management position through which both information and directives are exchanged between Japanese managers and German employees.) None the less, few firms seem to pay special attention either to such positions or to their occupants.

Fourth, most Japanese manufacturing subsidiaries maintain technical interface positions, as well as managerial ones mentioned above. Japanese technicians who occupy these positions and who are in charge of, say, quality control instruct and train German employees in the operation and maintenance of Japanese tools and equipment. Like their counterparts in management, the occupants of technical interface positions thus perform an important 'hinge' function.

RECRUITMENT

Two different views were found to exist among the respondents of the study concerning the recruitment of German personnel by Japanese subsidiaries. One view held that a candidate's ability to do the specific type of work required by the particular position to be filled was more important than his or her ranking based on traditional Japanese criteria such as age, personal character and loyalty to the firm. The other view held that the opposite was the case.

The most accurate information on this issue was furnished by representatives of German accountant associations which often help Japanese firms find and recruit local personnel. These associations usually recommend candidates on the basis of, above all, their known ability and competence in specific areas of work. Managers of the Japanese firms then choose from among these candidates. In this selection process the Japanese apparently regard qualifications that are often not obvious to the German advisors as the most important. Preference is thus often given to younger workers without records of previous employment with a number of different firms, as if the Japanese selectors believe that such young candidates are the most likely to be willing to learn and adapt to the Japanese system.

Loyalty to the firm is also more important to the Japanese than to the Germans, presumably because the Japanese are more interested in building a dependable workforce in the long run than in immediate returns. The importance of such long-term commitment on the part of employees was emphasised both by most experts consulted in this study and by a previous study sponsored by the Japan Export Trade Organisation (JETRO).[5] The finding, however, should be further tested against data on other aspects of personnel management practised by Japanese firms.

TRAINING

It appears that only a few Japanese subsidiaries have a well-defined employee training programme. Numerous respondents mentioned occasional visits to Japan by German technicians and middle-management personnel either as reward for or encouragement of good performance. Meanwhile, rank-and-file unskilled employees receive training on the job either from German or Japanese technicians. Some receive enough training to execute tasks normally left to skilled workers. Since such skills are usually specific to the type of work available only in the Japanese firm, these employees in effect become stuck with their current employers.

The traditional Japanese practice of rotating employees from one job to another for training purposes is not common in Japanese subsidiaries in West Germany, particularly for white-collar workers. German trade unions consider the practice acceptable only if the worker is paid progressively higher wages for the new skills learned through such rotation. Otherwise, the Japanese practice would give a German employee a legal ground to resign.

Among Japanese personnel, on the other hand, the situation appears to be quite different. For example, a Japanese engineer may temporarily head the accounting department, even though this may cause trouble and require assignment of highly competent subordinates to help him discharge his unaccustomed responsibilities.

COMPENSATION FOR GERMAN EMPLOYEES

Pay in Japanese subsidiaries conforms to standards commonly accepted among German firms. In other words, Japanese firms pay wages sufficiently high to meet standards set by management–union contracts in most German firms, even though few Japanese subsidiaries are formally bound by such contracts. Japanese pay scales are in fact often considerably higher than relevant contract scales, especially in retail trades in which Japanese firms are particularly active. As a rule, lower- and middle-level management personnel are relatively well-paid, while upper-level personnel, among whom Germans are rare, earn somewhat less than in comparable German firms. This finding confirms the middle-level orientation and egalitarian pay policy commonly attributed to the Japanese management system.

Outright adoption of specific Japanese pay practices appear to be the exception rather than the rule, however. Only one firm reported payment of a bonus at Christmas time on the basis of individual performance as evaluated by the management. Provision of supplemental company pension plans was cited by some as another example of an imported Japanese practice. Most of these practices involved 'gifts' in the Japanese sense rather than 'pay', and none was in amounts much larger than those of comparable forms of compensation in German firms. Furthermore, there are few signs to suggest that these and similar practices are going to be more common in the future.

None the less, this is a very interesting subject worth a closer examination in light of the fact that wage determination is considered to be particularly susceptible to the rules of the German employment system and thus leaves only very limited leeway for innovations or deviations by Japanese firms.[6] A Japanese firm's policy and philosophy in this area may well be found in conflict with the norms of industrial relations in West Germany.

PROMOTION BLOCKAGE AND TURNOVER

Promotion opportunities for German managers in Japanese subsidiaries are quite limited, usually available only as long as the firms are expanding. Even then, German personnel quickly reach a level above which only native Japanese are expected to advance. This often makes it difficult for Japanese firms to recruit in the German employment market the best prospects for top-management positions.

There are roughly three types of German management personnel who are employed or employable by Japanese firms. First, there are top-flight managers who are often aware of the limitations placed on advancement of German personnel in a Japanese firm and therefore refuse to join one. If they do join a Japanese firm they are likely to leave it before or upon reaching the highest level open to them.[7] Second, there are those who join or stay with a Japanese firm either because they have only modest professional and social expectations or because they expect their advancement opportunities in a German firm to be no better than in a Japanese firm. For such employees the relatively attractive salaries paid lower- and middle-level managers in Japanese firms, as well as the relatively better job security they normally offer, make it worth their while to stay. Third and last, there are a few 'super-European' managers employed by Japanese firms. These are highly qualified and self-confident individuals whose intimate working knowledge of the local business scene underwrites both their competence in performance and their independence.

As a result of the conditions mentioned above, turnover among German managers in Japanese firms is relatively high in the first few years of their initial employment. This is true particularly for those who belong to the first type and some in the third type. They tend to leave a Japanese firm quickly. On the other hand, those who belong to the second type and some in the third tend to come to agreement with the Japanese and stay long enough to get used to their management methods.

DECISON-MAKING

In general, a Japanese subsidiary – whether it is a representative office, a sales subsidiary or a manufacturing unit – is completely dependent on and subject to instructions from its parent firm in Japan. Teletypes and telefaxes are the most important means of communication used in decision-making. Some experts speak of 'teletype subsidiaries' where the most important working hours are evening hours by local time when business begins in Japan.[8]

Among the firms studied there were some trading companies without a formal office co-ordinating decisions or actions of various departments and other units. In this type of firm individual departments communicate directly and separately with the headquarters in Japan where decisions are made and actions co-ordinated also on a departmental, rather than a company-wide, basis. Decision-making authority thus remains in the parent firms in Japan, which retain strong control of their subsidiaries abroad. The number of Japanese firms adopting US-style methods of supervision and accounting may be increasing, as the case of Canon Copy Lux Company suggests,[9] but they remain the exception and not the rule.[10] The testimonies of the experts we interviewed strongly contradict the conclusion of previous studies that Japanese firms give their subsidiaries abroad greater autonomy and freedom in decision-making than do American or West German multinationals.

The discrepancy between our findings and those of other authors can perhaps be best explained by the fact that their research was concerned with Japanese manufacturing firms, while our experts' experience was mainly with subsidiaries of Japanese trading companies. The perceptions of decision-making autonomy also vary between European and

US managers on the one hand and Japanese managers, on the other. The *relatively* greater freedom experienced by Japanese managers abroad must be seen in relation to the more limited freedom permitted them in Japan. 'A little more' may be perceived as a great deal more.

Another indication that real autonomy may not be as great as some other authors found it to be[11] is the great frequency and volume of reports sent by Japanese subsidiaries abroad to their headquarters in Japan. Japanese managers interviewed in our study complained that there were too many of these reports, and yet the headquarters seldom understood the problems faced by their subsidiaries abroad. This complaint makes sense if the headquarters make decisions which frequently turn out to be inappropriate.

Another problem that arises between a subsidiary and the headquarters – a problem that may be attributed to a lack of experience on the part of both in the initial phase of internationalisation – is their tendency to deal with each other at arm's length in financial matters; that is, as if they were two independent firms.

Decision-making authority within a subsidiary lies, with a few exceptions, in the hands of Japanese managers. In isolated cases German personnel may hold high-ranking positions thanks to their knowledge and competence in specific areas, such as distribution, accounting or personnel, or thanks to legal requirements, as in banking.[12] For example, we learned of a case in which Japanese and German personnel held parallel positions, although only to the department director level. It is extremely rare, however, for a German to hold a central managerial position and, even in such rare instances, it is usually not clear how closely one's formal title is matched by his or her actual decision-making authority.[13]

LANGUAGE AND NEMAWASHI

In all work discharged by a manager, speaking and writing play a critical role. There are, however, few Germans with a good command of either spoken or written Japanese. Since most Japanese do not speak German either, most business is conducted in English, except in banks where German is the standard medium of communication.

Communication between a subsidiary and the headquarters is in Japanese, as a rule. The reliance on Japanese has become even more pronounced in recent years thanks to the widespread use of telefax that can accurately transmit messages in the Japanese alphabet. This results in further exclusion of German personnel from the decision-making process. A question asked by a German employee through an English-language telex is often answered in Japanese. The answer then has to be translated by a Japanese employee or, in some cases, an additional message specifically requesting an answer in English is sent back to the headquarters so as to ease the German employee's frustration.

German employees may also be excluded from the decision-making process also because, due to the time difference between Europe and Japan, most communications between a subsidiary and the headquarters that are critical to decision-making tend to take place during evening and night hours. Japanese personnel are used to working longer hours in the first place and, moreover, most live alone without family. As a result, they usually do not mind staying on the job a few extra hours, while most Germans leave for home at the end of the normal working hours. The upshot of this is that few Germans are present in the office or at the plant when teletypes are turned on and the few who are present are likely to be barred from participation in the communication by the language barrier.

It is of considerable importance that, as mentioned above, information is exchanged between a subsidiary and the headquarters mainly during evening hours at the end of what may be called the Japanese-style happy hour. Before they reach a decision, Japanese engage in protracted discussion and conferencing, a ritual known as '*nemawashi*'. Germans do not participate in this critically important pre-decision ritual.

At the same time, since Japanese managers are usually subject to frequent transfers and, as a result, often lack competence to perform the tasks assigned to them, they are dependent on native employees to help them with technical matters. The secretary to the Japanese executive officer in a small firm, for example, is likely to wield a great deal of influence, since the executive officer changes frequently and every new one depends on her advice in performing his day-to-day duties. Most Japanese executives, typically without an adequate command of German, often become totally dependent on the secretary.

In larger firms this hinge function is often performed by Japanese who have resided in Germany for a long time. Their intimate knowledge of the firm's organisation and operations and of the German language qualify them for such a position. At the middle-management level, such a position is often filled by a German who has been with the firm for a long time and whom the Japanese trust. Should problems arise, he or she would negotiate with both Japanese and Germans and mediate between them.

MANAGEMENT–LABOUR RELATIONS

Most Japanese firms operating in the Federal Republic of Germany are very small. Like most of their German counterparts, they lack a works council (*Betriebsrat*). Larger firms, especially large manufacturing firms, usually have such a council.

Japanese executives follow a variety of strategies concerning the creation of a works council. They may, for example, contact an existing local union organisation while still looking for a site to locate the facilities. In such a case an attempt is made from the beginning to forge a social partnership relationship with local labour. Sometimes, however, they may try to establish contact with the union whose wage policy is the most acceptable. This 'offensive' strategy enables the Japanese firm to choose between several unions whose performance records are unknown. Such choice is usually facilitated by competition among the unions.

Another strategy, and one that is far more common among German firms, is to try to prevent the formation of a works council by putting pressure on or by simply dismissing potential shop activists. When a union is none the less formed, an attempt may be made to limit or otherwise influence its membership by, for example, giving support to those employees who are known to have a friendly opinion of the management.

In a Japanese firm a works council is often formed as a result of a conflict between the management and a larger labour group, a conflict that may have resulted, for example, from the hiring of a new personnel director who refuses to play by the established rules or from the move of the firm from one site to another. Depending on the reason for its formation and its membership (i.e. whether predominantly white-collar or blue-collar), a works council's working relationship with the Japanese management may vary greatly, as the following examples suggest.

In one case a works council was formed in a Japanese trading firm after a new personnel manager was hired. It continued to exist even after the controversial personnel manager left the firm, but it ceased to fight the management. All disputes, including one over the company pension plan, were solved through open and informal discussion. This suggests that some Japanese firms succeed in using a works council as a means of effective and useful communication with employees.

In a number of cases, however, serious and prolonged controversies characterised the relationships between works councils and Japanese management. Many of the controversies arose from Japanese managers' ignorance of the legal aspects of industrial relations in West Germany. Such was the case, for example, when Japanese management signed a chain of temporary wage contracts, or ignored the worker-participation rights guaranteed by the Works Council Constitutions Law (*Betriebsverfassungsgesetz*) and the Co-determination Law (*Mitbestimmungsgesetz*) in such matters as overtime, transfers, introduction of personnel information systems, etc., or misinterpreted the terms of a collectively negotiated contract that were in conflict with those of individually signed agreements.

In general, the behaviour of Japanese managers is frequently clumsy, and disagreements due to lack of information or faulty comprehension are common. One union shop steward had his wage cut for spending too much time, in the opinion of his Japanese superiors, on works council business. The role of arbitration commissions and labour courts in disputes over provisions of firm-specific management–employee contracts is often grossly underestimated by Japanese management, leading courts to hand down decisions unambiguously in favour of the works councils. Such experiences, and fear based on lack of information, in turn often lead Japanese firms to shy away from involvement with the worker participation rights legally granted West German workers. Under the Co-determination Law these rights are granted only to employees in firms with over 2000 employees, but under the Works Council Constitutions Law employees are guaranteed the right to form a works council or maintain a shop steward no matter how small the firm is. Many experts believe that the Japanese consider the optimal size of a subsidiary's workforce to be under 500 employees, apparently conscious of the fact that the rate of unionisation is generally low in such small firms.

The behaviour of Japanese managers, however, cannot be explained solely by their ignorance. Such an explanation is sometimes used by the Japanese merely as an excuse to block a works council's initiatives, as, for example, when a council is informed by the management of needs for overtime or additional shifts after a decision is already made. Such management behaviour often leads to a court action, which Japanese firms regard as a blemish on their records. They will attempt to prevent a dispute from becoming public by seeking an internal solution. An overwhelming majority of the experts interviewed pointed out that Japanese managers are wary of the risk of court actions, but often miscalculate such a risk as a result of misinformation.

One works council secretary characterised the policy followed by the management of a certain Japanese subsidiary as incompetent, stupid and stubborn. The same view was echoed by many of the experts interviewed. Many Japanese are, according to these witnesses, simply not willing to accept a works council that is not favourably disposed towards the concept of social partnership and prefers to assert its full legal rights. Japanese managers usually fight this type of works council with all means available and at all costs. Since there are works councils with considerable self-confidence that are none the less willing to co-operate with management, the reasons for the narrow-minded attitudes attributed to many Japanese managers need to be scrutinised more closely.

The Japanese try to avoid conflict over the rights of individual employees, too. When a Japanese firm wants to fire an employee it reportedly pays a generous sum of severance money, even though, should the matter be brought before a court, the decision would support the management in any case. German workers, on the other hand, tend to insist on the full recognition and utilisation of their legal rights, and that often causes bad feelings and misunderstandings between them and their Japanese employers. The latter often do not understand, say, the function of the maternity leave granted to a new mother under the German law. While a German woman uses her right to maternity leave and expects to return to work after the leave is over, it is common for a pregnant Japanese woman to resign, even though often against her will. Most Japanese managers do not understand the German practice in this regard, particularly when a German woman resigns after her maternity leave, which she regards as too short, even though the firm may have kept the position for her for as long as six months. As a result, the Japanese often try to terminate a pregnant woman's employment against her will long before the childbirth. In such a case the firm's German advisors are likely to have great difficulties in making the Japanese understand that the woman is only insisting on exercising her legal rights and that no German court would decide the case in favour of the firm.

Similar misunderstandings often arise over the treatment of employees taken ill during vacation, which they can legally extend for the time spent while ill. Another right of a German employee that is often not fully understood by most Japanese managers is the right to obtain from the employer a written and signed certificate of good conduct upon the termination of his or her employment. It was pointed out by many respondents that Japanese managers find it easy to hire German employees but difficult to fire them. The objections voiced by many works councils to the long overtime hours common in Japanese firms may stem partly from the Japanese unwillingness to hire additional employees due to the uncertainty about their long-term commitment and utility to the firm.

The success of Japanese subsidiaries in Europe in general will depend, in the long run, on both better education of Japanese personnel in the language, culture and legal practices of the host countries and on more diversified career opportunities for locally recruited management personnel. In addition, the deliberate creation and expansion of interface positions – in some ways reminiscent of the 'kachō' position in a Japanese firm – may not only help correct the deficiency of information about conditions of German employees that is so common among Japanese top managers, but also compensate to some extent for the general lack of promotion opportunities for German management personnel. If Japanese subsidiaries count solely on the 'honeymoon effect' typical of the first few years of their operations abroad, their legendary successes may well prove to be short-lived.

13 Japan as a Model for Economic Development: The Example of Singapore

Thomas A. Stanley

Studies of modern Japan have concentrated on Japan's use of Western models for its development, but a new relationship between Japan and the world has emerged in recent years: the outside world is now emulating Japan. The emergence of Japan as a major economic power has led many corporations in the US and elsewhere to consider learning from Japan methods which may improve their own competitive position in domestic and foreign markets. Even governments see the Japanese example as instructive.

This is particularly true in the Pacific area, where the newly industrialising nations are increasingly turning to Japan for inspiration and advice. Japan's position as the dominant trading partner of some of these nations and its record of high growth are only part of the reason; the use of a distinctly Asian model, with morals and social values presumed to be more amenable to Asian situations, is also strongly appealing.

The Republic of Singapore is one country in which the Japanese model of economic development is a major influence on governmental and public thinking.[1] To be sure, the government encourages the emulation of other countries in other fields, such as the US for business and finance, Israel (and more recently Switzerland) for defence and Britain for education. The Japanese model, however, is used especially in the area of industrialisation and social values.

This chapter explores ways in which Singapore has been influenced by Japan's model of industrialisation, and especially by the social and moral values presumed to be an important part of Japan's industrial success. Japanese institutional and ideological efforts to minimise conflict and direct it into economically productive channels have received special notice in Singapore and, accordingly, the adaptation of these methods in the Singapore context is the main focus of this study.

SINGAPORE'S ACCOMPLISHMENTS AND PROBLEMS: AN OVERVIEW

Singapore's leaders, especially Lee Kwan Yew and Goh Keng Swee, have effected vast changes in the quarter-century they have been in power. Singapore is rightly proud of many accomplishments: a per capita GNP second in Asia only to Japan's and so high that in 1985 New Zealand moved to reclassify it as a developed nation; public housing projects far superior to the slums they replaced; efficient harbours, roads and, planned for the near future, a rapid rail transit system; sophisticated shipbuilding, petroleum and petrochemical industries; political and social stability; and a sense of nation developed in the midst of very difficult circumstances.

Each accomplishment can, of course, be denigrated because solutions to old problems have created unforeseen new problems. For example, in the high-rise public housing projects, the racial segregation of the old neighbourhoods has been broken, reducing the likelihood of racial rioting, but there is a high degree of social isolation, resulting in new forms of social discontent and anti-social acts that are of increasing concern to residents and government alike.[2] The primary concern of the government, and probably of the people, has consistently been material well-being; the high-growth rates of the past decades have gone far to satisfy everyone's wants. Again, however, there are problems. The national wealth is not equitably distributed and income gaps are larger than in the past.

Singapore has a very good image outside of South-east Asia as well. Tourists are generally pleased by Singapore's combination of modern efficiency and a taste of the exotic East without the 'dirt' and confusion of other Asian cities. The country is stable, is aligned with the anti-communist world powers, avows democracy and supports a strong military, diplomatic, and economic presence by the US and Japan. Being much smaller than the other three newly industrialising countries of Asia (Hong Kong, South Korea and Taiwan), Singapore has generally missed being singled out as a major trading threat to industrialised nations.

LABOUR POLICY

To the outside investor Singapore has been attractive for two decades because of its labour peace and political stability. But Singapore has not always had a labour force acquiescent to the government.

At the time of independence, in 1963, Singapore suffered chronic unemployment combined with a vigorous labour movement often controlled by left-wing elements identified now as pro-communist or communist by the ruling Peoples' Action Party (PAP). In 1955, when radical elements in the labour movement frequently led strikes for political reasons, Singapore lost 946 000 man-days to strikes. By 1965 the PAP had driven the left-wing out of its ranks and established its own labour union movement (the National Trades Union Council, or NTUC) to compete with that of the leftists; in the same year 46 000 man-days were lost. By 1977 only 1000 man-days were lost. There have been no strikes since 1977.[3] Indeed, strikes have become virtually illegal.

The National Trades Union Council, a national umbrella organisation for unionised workers, has significantly helped to avoid conflict by reining in individual unions and by transmitting the policies which the government sees as essential to political and economic goals. Although NTUC was originally built on the aggressive model of the British labour movement, it has lost all the considerable power it once had, and, while it calls itself an independent organisation which supports the PAP, it is in fact subordinate to the party.[4] Wage guidelines are set by the National Wage Council (on which NTUC is represented) and strictly observed. The government has said it is in favour of a system in which labour and management bargain directly, with the government present as a secondary party. Recently, however, in response to economic contraction, the government imposed a two-year freeze on wage and salary increases. Thus the government's interests are paramount, with management's usually next and labour's interests last.

The disfavour with which the government looks on industrial action by any union was typified by the direct intervention of Lee Kwan Yew in a dispute between Singapore International Airlines (SIA) and the SIA Pilots' Association (SIAPA) in 1980. One flight was cut short in Zürich instead of its destination in London when the pilots refused, in accord with a SIA–SIAPA agreement, to work for more than twelve hours at a stretch. Lee intervened and ultimately the flight crew of four was fired and fifteen of the twenty-man committee directing the SIAPA were charged with instigating an illegal strike. All pleaded guilty.

Several months later, Ong Pang Boon, who was both Minister of Labour and Secretary-General of the PAP, was demoted to the less-important Environment Ministry for attempting to handle the SIA–SIAPA dispute in a 'British manner'; that is, through arbitration by an independent arbitrator who strikes a bargain acceptable to both sides.[5] Lee complained that his approach lacked 'productivity', which he defined as 'total cooperation [and] confidence between workers and management'. The President of the Republic of Singapore and former head of NTUC, C. V. Devan Nair, warned menacingly that 'the next time you or any other group of employees in SIA indulge in arm-twisting tactics, you will be smacked down, good and hard'.[6]

SINGAPORE AND JAPAN

If Lee found the British system of industrial relations inappropriate for Singapore, his visit to Japan in 1979, one year before the strike, left him strongly impressed with Japanese labour relations. Not long after demoting his Minister of Labour, he promoted Wee Mon Cheng, then Singapore's Ambassador to Japan, to three consecutive year-long appointments as chairman of Singapore Broadcasting Corporation, the government's public television and radio monopoly, touting him as an expert on Japan.[7]

Use of Japan as an explicit model began after Prime Minister Lee Kwan Yew's trip to Japan; thereafter, there was a virtual barrage of pronouncements eulogising Japan. Lee returned not only with his own enthusiasm about Japan, but with promises of help: the Japanese undertook to establish a Department of Japanese Studies and improve the engineering faculty at the computer training facility. Lee was particularly impressed with Japan's long-range economic planning and the high degree of consultation among representatives of government, management and labour. To help understand this new model, top economic officials went to Tokyo in 1980 to study how Japan formulates policy.[8]

In the 1980s 'co-operation between management and labour', 'house unions' and 'teamwork' became catch phrases with constant publicity. Since 1980 there have been month-long campaigns to encourage teamwork. Sponsored by the National Productivity Board, a statutory board established by the government, the campaigns gain public attention with a cartoon strip featuring, as symbol and mascot, a busy bee named 'Teamy' who originally encouraged workers to be productive, but in the 1984 campaign concentrated on management practices that limited productivity by infuriating or hindering workers. Unreconstructed workers and managers were criticised through comparison with their ideal Japanese counterparts.

There was considerable necessity for action to reduce tension between workers at the end of the 1970s. The so-called second industrial revolution initiated under the leadership of Goh Chok Tong in 1979 was designed to push Singapore from labour-intensive industry to capital and knowledge-intensive industry. In part this was accomplished when the National Wage Council raised wages about 20 per cent each year in 1979, 1980 and 1981; the stated intention was to make labour-intensive industry in Singapore uncompetitive in the international market, thus forcing workers and businesses to invest in better skills, capital equipment and technology. In 1980 and 1981 better workers were to be given even higher increases to encourage better attitudes and higher productivity. This was felt to be so divisive and threatening to so many workers that the government had added stimulus to turn to the Japanese labour model to seek additional ways of promoting teamwork and reducing discontent.[9]

In addition to the measures mentioned above, other Japanese-inspired devices and institutions for enhancing peaceful labour relations and increasing productivity have been established at the government's behest. Quality control circles were established to increase quality and productivity. Work Improvement Teams (WITS) were organised to encourage workers to study production methods and make suggestions on improving them. Companies were encouraged to undertake welfare programmes for their workers; they were allowed to retain part of the joint company–employee payment to the Central Provident Fund (CPF), invest it at returns higher than CPF pays and, after the amount has increased sufficiently, begin providing employees with welfare benefits similar to those for which large Japanese corporations have become famous in the post-war era. The hope was that workers would develop a strong emotional as well as pecuniary attachment to their firms.

An impediment to developing worker loyalty towards employers is the high frequency with which Singaporeans change jobs. Their 'job-hopping' is so famous that passing reference to it brings a knowing laugh from any audience, whether labourers, students or bankers. Officially, of course, it is viewed with displeasure since it results in labour instability and is a distinct disincentive for employers to provide on-the-job training to employees, be they plastic intrusion machine operators, machinists or computer programmers.

Various ways of limiting job-hopping have been proposed, all of them based on increased benefits to workers who stayed with their employers. Wee Mon Cheng objected that these plans amounted to materialistic incentives for loyalty to the employer while materialism was the root cause of job-hopping or disloyalty. Drawing on his knowledge of Japan, he emphasised that job-hopping could best be reduced by cultivating the workers' sense of belonging in their company and by stressing professionalism and pride in their work.[10] Nevertheless, job-hopping remains common – mute testimony to the difficulty of fostering the kind of employees' loyalty to company that is such a remarkable feature of Japan's labour relations.

The most recent step towards the Japanese labour relations system has been to establish company or house unions. In Japan's case, these have been praised for facilitating management's goals while reducing worker recalcitrance, resulting in better productivity and profits; the better profits are supposedly returned to the workers in higher wages and benefits. House unions have also been damned by critics for exposing the workers to exploitation by their companies. If the government permits, the debate will be repeated in Singapore's case as house unions become more common.

The NTUC and the government itself have been the focus of changes in union structure away from industrial or trade unionism to house unionism on the Japanese model. House unions exist in a number of statutory boards and government agencies where they were established in the absence of any union. In 1982, under the guidance of Japanophile Wee Mon Cheng, the Singapore Broadcasting Corporation established a house union which newspapers quickly labelled the 'new model'.[11] In 1984 the NTUC initiated the first major step towards house unions when it imposed them on workers at Changi Airport.

When the question of dissolving the Singapore Air Transport Workers' Union (SATU) and creating new house unions was put to the leaders of the existing union, however, significant dissent arose. Several prominent union leaders questioned or opposed the changes. Letters signed by 300 members addressed to Lee Kwan Yew and President Devan Nair requested a referendum on the issue in order to establish a mandate for or against the change. Immediately the chief leaders of the NTUC forced SATU to bring charges and pressure to bear on the opponents, threatening them with expulsion or other sanctions.[12]

The cudgelling of opponents to the principle of house unionism and to the related one of co-operation between labour and management also raises questions about the purpose of house unions: in whose interest are they being created and what is their purpose? In the case of the campaign to raise productivity, the same questions arise. A 1982 survey showed that although 94 per cent of respondents had heard about productivity, 70 per cent felt that the company and not the worker would benefit.[13]

CONFLICT CONTROL

Many of the Singapore government's actions have been directed to achieving high growth, the area where the Japanese model is so promising. Other actions of the government have been dedicated to controlling or reducing conflict, an emerging area of interest among students of Japan too.[14] In this area, parallels are pronounced and the Singaporean use of the Japanese model is often explicit. For example, the Singapore police have sent missions to Japan to study the *kōban* (local police box) system, employed Western consultants familiar with the Japanese system and invited Japanese police to Singapore to lend assistance. Whether a *kōban* system can work well in a nation of high-rise apartment blocks is debatable. To support the system, Singapore planned to add 4000 officers to the police force, nearly a 50 per cent increase in the 5400 officer force.[15]

To a larger degree, however, the Japanese experience serves to legitimise Singaporean programmes that began before the 1979 watershed in choice of Japan as model. A case in point is ethics education. When Singapore became an independent state in 1965, it had to promote loyalty to the state. Consequently, the schools increased the emphasis on patriotism in ethics education, reminiscent of pre-war Japan's *shūshin*. As the population came to identify with Singapore, explicit nationalism was reduced.

In the late 1970s and early 1980s concern about declining moral values and personal behaviour peaked at the same time that patriotic loyalty was felt to be firmly established. Increasingly, Singaporeans were warned against the permissiveness, 'unfettered' individualism, decadent materialism, and 'soft options' of the West. Lee Kwan Yew and other leaders have also frequently voiced concern about cultural rootlessness and its dangers. It is dogma that education in English alone increases rootlessness, while education in Chinese (or Tamil or

Malay, depending on race) preserves cultural traditions and morality. In Parliament in early 1977, Lee said, regarding the possibility of eliminating Mandarin in the primary and secondary schools, 'If you lose that Chinese education and you go completely English-educated, you will lose that drive, that self-confidence. That is what is wrong.'[16]

In 1979 Goh Keng Swee, then Minister of Education, initiated a study which listed desiderata for moral education in the schools: '"Sense of belonging to the community" must be taught as part of "social responsibility" and must contain elements such as "civic consciousness, respect and care for others, care for public property, respect for law and order, safety, harmony, group spirit, love for the school, cooperation, friendship, neighborliness and generosity."'[17] Lee himself was quoted as saying

> Unless we make a concerted effort and sustained effort at inculcating into [younger Singaporeans] the virtues of group discipline and the overriding calls of society upon their individual rights, more and more will be consciously influenced by the concepts of Europeans and Americans: that the rights and liberties of the individual are the first charge upon society. ... The generation now in school are nearly all in the English language stream, where the philosophy and doctrines taught are less Confucianist than the Chinese language schools; hence the importance of imparting the traditional values in moral education in the schools.[18]

The thrust towards moral indoctrination is concentrated on Confucianism. This is not surprising since Singapore is about 76 per cent ethnic Chinese. Moreover, the disproportionate percentage of the political, economic, educational and medical élites – indeed all élites – are Chinese too; moral decay among the Chinese would presumably have immediate irreversible impact.

To be fair to all Singaporeans, the government also emphasised Islam, Hinduism and Buddhism. It even lauded Christianity, because about 9 per cent of the population is Christian and even more in some élites: in 1980, 22 per cent of the members of Parliament, four of the seven 'second-generation' leaders, 30 per cent of all university students and 70 per cent of the medical students were reckoned Christian.[19] Accordingly, the government promised by the mid-1980s a compulsory moral education course under which students would study either Islam, Buddhism, Christianity, Confucianism or World Religions (a catch-all).[20]

Confucianism, however, received the greatest attention and publicity. It was presumed to be of 'natural' interest to the Chinese majority. The 1980 Census revealed that nearly all who professed no religion (13 per cent among those over ten years of age, rising to about 20 per cent among those with upper secondary education or better) were Chinese.[21] In 1982 and 1983 a series of prominent Confucian scholars from Taiwan and the USA were brought, amidst great publicity, as consultants on the Confucian curriculum. Particularly emphasised were themes in Confucianism familiar to the student of pre-war Japan: obedience, loyalty and service to the state; care of parents; esteem for the three-tiered family (children, parents and grandparents); and disdain for materialism. Although it was claimed that these values were universal to all religions, political leaders became specific when discussing Confucianism.

The promotion of values useful to a government interested in control and manipulation of the population requires no special explanation. In the case of Japan in the Meiji and pre-Second World War periods, these same moral values were encouraged in an effort to promote Japan's modernisation while easing the resulting dislocations.[22] Confucianism also served to reduce threats against the regime by encouraging loyalty and obedience to the state. These points, especially the latter, are hardly unknown to Singapore's leaders.

Some effort has been made to provide institutional support for Confucian values. In early 1982 Lee Kwan Yew, expressing shock at callous disregard of aged parents, said the government would introduce legislation requiring children to care for their parents. Ultimately the plan was dropped, but changes were made in the administration of the public housing programme which gave significant preference to three-tiered families, greatly shortening the eighteen- to thirty-six-month wait for a publicly constructed apartment.[23]

At times the urge for control exceeds the possible, especially when it seeks to promote behaviour which appears to run contrary to the general course of development in modern societies. In a television National Day rally speech in 1983, Lee Kwan Yew complained that university-educated women tended to have few children or did not marry at all. Noting that in 1980 married women who had graduated from the university had an average of 1.65 children, while women with no education averaged 3.5. Lee, accepting the hypothesis that intelligence is based 80 per cent on hereditary factors and only 20 per cent on environmental factors like education, worried that the number of highly educable people would fall, while the uneducable population would sharply rise.[24] Since government figures showed that of 117 000 women graduates, only one-half were married, efforts were made to encourage educated women to marry sooner and have more children. (One is reminded of Mori Arinori's brief hope in the 1870s of improving the Japanese race through intermarriage with Caucasians.)[25] Goh Keng Swee, Lee's right-hand man, lauded the success that Japan experienced with arranged marriages and computerised match-making. An official mission was sent to study Japan's computer match-making and bring back the software necessary to begin a similar programme in Singapore. Goh also suggested a university course on courting.[26]

Although Lee promised that no compulsory measures or disincentives would be instituted, within six months the government established incentives to encourage graduate women to reproduce while efforts to discourage others continued. The children of graduate women with three or more children were given top preference in determining school registration while 'extra' children of unsterilised, non-graduate women with three or more children were given the least preference.[27] In order to encourage other female graduates, favourable publicity was given to graduate women who decided to have a third child.

Other programmes were instituted in accord with Lee's genetic concept. The Curriculum Development Institute of Singapore was set to work producing materials to teach junior college and pre-university centre students, many of them university-bound, the importance of marriage and having children.[28] A very large tax deduction was given to graduate women who were working and had children. In early 1984 a Social Development Unit was quietly established to identify graduate women who were unmarried or university students who might not marry. These were to be taught basic social skills and the virtue of marriage and children, and many were placed in social situations alongside potential mates – boat cruises, vacation trips abroad or within Singapore and other short-term get-togethers. As of March of 1985 S\$300 000 had been spent by the Unit; 4600 people were introduced to each other and two marriages had resulted.[29] There were also rumours that unmarried graduate women were not being hired or were being passed over for promotion in the civil service.

There was considerable protest against the programme, especially by the educated élite and the university women who stood to benefit. Ultimately, in 1985, the school registration preference for prolific graduate women's children was withdrawn, leaving in limbo the few third children of graduate women conceived under the programme's stimulus. The other programmes were continued.

The genetic interests of Lee Kwan Yew must be considered not as an aberration of an aging man, but as part of the concern of the leadership with the quality of future leaders. The PAP leadership is very worried about differences between itself and the younger generation. Lee Kwan Yew constantly refers to Singapore's 'rugged' society, but worries that the younger generation appears entirely different – softened by materialism and seduced by Western decadence and individualism. The Party's worries were given reality in a 1981 by-election when, for the first time in sixteen years, a member of the opposition party, J. B. Jeyaretnum of the Workers' Party, was returned.

Confucian moral education, combined with patriotism cemented during compulsory military service, might be an excellent tool for regaining the loyalty of youth, judging from pre-war Japanese experience. Government control of the media is also put to use; SBC television has broadcast the Japanese series 'Oshin', and its own production, 'The Awakening', both in Mandarin. They are dominated by the theme that 'the young are constantly reminded of their parents' suffering and hard work, without which the Economic Miracle ... would never have occurred'. The director of 'The Awakening', Hong Kong expatriate Leung Lap-yan, admitted that the programme necessarily reflects government policy and said, 'We hope that after watching the show [the youth] will appreciate the good life they have.'[30]

CONCLUSION

Part of the appeal of the Japanese model for Asia is that Japan is Asian. It is assumed this model is more suitable to Asia than European or North American alternatives. In particular, it is assumed that the values and social factors of Japan and Asia are so similar that adoption of Japanese systems will significantly reduce the strains and dislocation of change.

Certainly the Singaporean example reflects this belief. Such thinking, however, ignores several important differences between Japan and Singapore. In Japan, there was historically a strong concept of service to the nation, but the concept of nation is new in Singapore and service to it is of low priority. Japan has a relatively high degree of social homogeneity, but Singapore has a pronounced mixture of races; the races strongly differ in traditions and harbour deep antagonism towards each other. Despite the conflicts and divisions recently documented by historians, such as peasant revolt, class conflict, labour strife and individual or local community resistance to the central state, Japan by and large has a group-oriented society in which school class, place of employment and university or school affiliation are common foci of identification. Singapore's group orientation extends only to family and racial or linguistic group in most cases. These differences suggest that merely being Asian will not make adopting the Japanese model easy.

The Japanese model attracted Singapore's attention because of Japan's present-day success, not because Lee Kwan Yew saw the development pattern as one which harnessed and muted conflict in the past 100 years. It is, however, just this harnessing and muting process where the Japanese model has been particularly effective in Singapore. The labour scene offers strong testimony to this. A new system of labour relations, artificial in the sense that it has no immediate indigenous roots and is based on the Japanese system, is being imposed on workers, primarily by the government, in a broad attempt to eliminate conflict, promote productivity and increase the freedom of management to act in response to the market without labour constraints.

The Japanese experience was quite similar. Its labour relations system can be traced back to only around 1900. It was developed by industrialists and government officials interested in capturing expensive skilled labour, stabilising and pacifying management–labour relations, and preventing political radicalism among workers. Although ties to Japanese traditions were professed, it was 'artificial' in the same sense that Singapore's use of the Japanese model is; it had no historical precedents in the labour market. Indeed, it was created for modern industry and bloomed there after 1945; traces are virtually impossible to find in small-scale traditional enterprises.

If Singapore successfully adopts a Japanese-style labour relations system, one would have to conclude that, notwithstanding cultural and historical differences, Japan's system is transferable in form, if not in spirit. Although the government, party and labour union are all willing to impose the system with a measure of force, resistance remains strong, if not vocal.

In the area of values a similar process appears to be under way. Confucianism is being promoted as a bulwark against decadent Western values, a brake on individualism, an inspiration to hard work, and a buttress for the authority of the state. Whether Confucianism can mitigate the extremely individualistic, commercial, materialistic environment of Singapore is questionable; while it does have its roots among the Chinese majority, they are shallow roots in a society that is hostile to certain aspects of Confucianism that were important in Japan, such as service to the state. At best, it appears to be useful primarily in restricting individuals and enforcing the acceptance of authority.

The authoritarian side of Confucianism draws frequent cautions from observers of Singapore who are familiar with Japan in the 1930s and 1940s, when Confucianism often served the same purpose. Like Singapore's use of Japanese-style labour relations, in the short to medium term, the Japanese model will be successful primarily as a means of increasing the state's authority and control over society and the economy and less as a blueprint for industrial development. And, as in Japan – at least until 1945 – constriction of democracy and of individual freedom and happiness is pronounced. Whether this is an inevitable result of the Japanese model may be debatable. What is certain, however, is that at least in Singapore, such a result was deliberate; indeed, it was one of the main reasons for using the model.

Conclusion

Gail Lee Bernstein and Haruhiro Fukui

The thirteen chapters that comprise this volume remind us once again of the enormously complex and multi-faceted process through which Japan has been transformed from an isolated, agricultural society to an economic world power in the past century and half. They also show, perhaps more explicitly and clearly than most previous works on similar subjects, that the complexity of the process reflects the robustness, tenacity and, above all, adaptability of Japan's native tradition in its encounter, and then perpetual contact, with the world beyond its own shores. The Japanese eagerly borrowed, adapted and exploited countless foreign ideas, techniques and institutions, even while they resisted, fought and rejected others. In the process, many aspects of the traditional Japanese culture and society have been transformed beyond recognition; many others, however, have survived remarkably intact and give contemporary Japan that distinctive flavour of an old insular culture which continues to delight and baffle not only foreign but many native scholars.

Probably the most significant change in the traditional Japanese way of life during the last 150 years has occurred in their conceptualisation of the world and Japan's place in it. An early and fascinating sign of this change is found, as Smith demonstrates, in the work of a few late Tokugawa artists. In the days of shogunal rule the Japanese were confined by numerous social and legal boundaries separating both individuals and groups from one another. Such boundaries in the traditional society, however, were by no means water-tight; they permitted a number of 'porous walls' or, as Smith calls them, 'border zones', through which individuals could pass, changing their names, professions, status and identities. The life and work of an artist like Keisai, at the vanguard of cultural change, suggest that the seemingly frozen society around 1800 was at least partially fluid. Keisai's 'higher vision', his 'sun's-eye view' capable of seeing 'beyond insularity', foreshadowed the imminent dismantling of the *sakoku* (seclusion) policy and the regime based on it, and anticipated the emergence of an island 'existing in three-dimensional space and linked in turn to the distant continent'.

If a few late Tokugawa artists and map-makers struggled to visualise the physical contours of the world beyond Japan, numerous post-Tokugawa scholars have struggled to conceptualise the social and intellectual contours of that world, especially of its most advanced and prominent regions, Europe and North America. Even that most Japanese of all modern Japenese thinkers, Nishida Kitarō, eagerly absorbed foreign influences, labouring painfully, it seems at times, to assimilate German and Anglo-American thought into his own Zen philosophy. Reading Hirai's account of his mental efforts to come to terms with Western categories of thought, one is tempted to ask, 'Why did he bother at all?' He bothered because by now the Japanese view of the world had undergone a fundamental change since the *sakoku* days, and 'civilization and enlightenment' had become Japan's official new goal, with the West its model. Nishida painstakingly attempted not to abandon the traditional Zen-derived postulates in favour of their Western counterparts, but rather to graft the latter on to the former. His was a formidable task, because the two very different systems of thought were not easily amenable to simple combination or integration.

Notwithstanding the difficulties experienced by Nishida Kitarō and numerous others, Japan negotiated the transition 'from tradition to modernity' with remarkable dispatch and apparent success. As Smith's study of a late Tokugawa artist suggests, this was due to an important extent to the flexibility and adaptability of Japan's traditional social structure. Vogel finds and highlights the same quality of adaptability in political leadership in both Tokugawa and modern Japan and attributes to that quality Japanese leaders' ability to respond rationally, and therefore by and large successfully, to both domestic and foreign crises.

The chapter by Bernstein which immediately follows Vogel's partially endorses his views by pointing to the direct and indirect aid given by the Meiji government as a critical factor in the rapid development of the silk-reeling industry in Meiji Japan and in explaining its high growth rate when compared with the Chinese and Italian industries, which did not receive comparable assistance from their own governments. Bernstein's study also shows, however, that 'modernisation' and 'development' were not achieved without considerable personal and social costs; in the specific case of the silk-reeling industry, the costs were borne mainly by young female workers in the form of low wages, hazardous and unhealthy working places and, above all, gross restrictions of personal freedoms. These restrictions, imposed by their employers, provoked women to organise protest actions, including the first-known strikes in the country's history. In the Taishō and early

Shōwa periods, however, far broader and more systematic curbs on personal freedoms, especially on the freedom of thought and speech, were imposed by governments on citizens at large. The primary victims of these official restrictions were Marxists, and especially members of the Japanese Communist Party.

Professedly a universalist and humanist ideology championing the ideals of equality and freedom, Marxism offered Japanese an alternative Western way of conceptualising the world. As such, it began to win a substantial following among university students and teachers in the 1920s, especially at the nation's foremost public universities. As Steinhoff's study shows, however, most of these pre-war Marxists had either recanted or quietly divorced themselves from the ideology by the end of the Second World War. This was a consequence not only of police pressure and brutality, but also of family ties, national or racial identity, group loyalty and a sense of common cultural heritage – i.e. those compelling traditional values which had survived 'modernisation' and 'development' remarkably intact and which continued to cause basic ambivalence in the Japanese attitude towards Western thought in general and a universalistic ideology in particular.

Tenkō, or recantation of Marxism, in pre-war Japan was thus a reflection both of the repressive hand of an authoritarian bureaucratic state and of enduring cultural values that had stood the test of time and that continued to appeal, at a deeply emotional level, to Japanese of all walks of life. The combination of these two forces effectively suppressed 'dangerous thought' in pre-Second World War Japan. It did not, however, totally wipe it out. As Steinhoff writes, a few dedicated Marxists, all either in prison or abroad in forced exile, endured and survived the repression and persecution until they were freed at the end of the war by the order of the Occupation authorities. They immediately went about rebuilding the Japan Communist Party and, for the first time, openly and freely participated in political activities in the reformed and democratised Japan. But the Occupation-sponsored reforms and democratisation no more rid post-war Japan of all the legacies of the bureaucratic state and the conformist society than the latter had rid pre-war Japan of all Marxist dissidence and criticism. Rather, the post-war period witnessed a kind of replay of the pre-war ideological clash between the paternalistic and disciplinarian state and society on the one hand, and rebellious dissidents on the other.

Krauss's study shows how and why the restrictive features of Japanese life that survived the postwar democratic reforms have drawn many young people in rebellion to Marxism. Like their prewar counterparts, post-war students have sought in the ideology of Marxism a greater sense of personal identity and autonomy and used it as a weapon with which to attack 'a society that emphasised status, success, and elite bureaucratic careers'. Their frustration and anger, which exploded in 1960 against the US–Japan mutual security pact, has since subsided. Some have in effect recanted, as most pre-war Marxists had done, but others remain critical of the bureaucratised state and conformist society. Moreover, their discontent is shared widely in contemporary Japanese society, perhaps even by the 'self-indulgent, non-political conservative youth', who may be expressing their anti-pathy to bureaucratisation and authority, not by public protest, but by withdrawal into leisure pursuits and personal fulfilment – objectives that have never gained full legitimacy in their society and are therefore 'radical' in a Japanese context.

The transformation of Japan's central political institutions during the last 150 years or so has proceeded with considerably less publicity and controversy. None the less, both the process and results of such transformation have been nearly as mixed and complex as the transfor-mation of artistic forms, philosophical postulates or socioeconomic structure. As Fukui's study suggests, political institutions in modern Japan have often evolved in directions and with consequences neither planned nor foreseen by the nation's leaders. The evolution of the House of Representatives' cumbersome election system, which since 1925 has combined a multi-member constituency and a single non-transferable vote system, is a prime example. But the failure of leaders to plan with foresight and wisdom was only one cause of the problem. More fundamental and serious in its implications was the difficulty of integrating imported foreign ideas and institutions, particularly those associated with democratic government, with the entrenched native system traditionally dominated by a strong state bureaucracy.

The chapters by Harari, Stockwin and Quo all address, directly or indirectly, this latter problem in the context of contemporary Japan under the rule of the Occupation-authored and radically democratic constitution. The general picture that emerges from their analyses is, not surprisingly, one of considerable complexity and fluidity.

Harari, while recognising the continuing power of the state bureauc-racy over the decisions and actions of public advisory groups, also points out the tendency in recent years for some advisory groups and non-government organisations, such as groups of Diet members and independent research institutes, to increase their expertise and ability to challenge the bureaucrats' primacy. Stockwin finds the political system in contemporary Japan to 'exhibit a capacity to cope with complex and wide-ranging issues in a reasonably effective and consultative manner' and to have actually done 'many things right in recent decades'. He finds, however, problems in three areas: elections, single-party dominance and bureaucratic centralism. Quo regards the state bureaucracy as the 'final arbiter in deciding what is best for the nation', and elected members of the Diet merely as 'actors' who perform on the stage according to scripts written by bureaucrats. He also argues, however, that the most effective influence on Japanese foreign policy in recent years has come, not from groups within Japan but from government and non-government sources in the USA. Quo's judgment may be correct about Tokyo's decisions on certain types of foreign policy issues, especially those directly concerned with bilateral US–Japanese relations. On other types of issues, a number of domestic groups and interests exert considerable influence. Fukai's study of Japanese foreign-aid policy, for example, shows the extensive influence of trading companies and consulting firms.

Fukai's work also raises the question of Japan's position in the overall scheme of contemporary world politics and economy, a question that echoes the concerns of artists and scholars in the earlier centuries. In fact, there is another important parallel across time: the basic foreign policy posture of post-Second World War Japan replicates the early Meiji government's – concentration on commercial expansion and avoidance of overseas military adventures and entanglements. While developing Third World countries may criticise Japan's aid policy for its moral obtuseness, and while advanced industrial countries may excoriate Japan's trade policy for its unrelenting aggressiveness, post-war Japanese leadership has based foreign policy mainly, if not exclusively, on considerations of economic security and commercial interests.

The single-minded pursuit of economic interests has now won Japan the status not only of a world economic power, but even of a model for others to emulate in the First and Third Worlds alike. As Japanese should know very well, however, an imported foreign model often causes a 'clash of cultures' and provokes hostile reaction from, if not outright rejection by, at least some segments of the population in the host society. This is likely to happen particularly in a society with a tradition and culture very different from the society being emulated. Park's study of the introduction of Japanese management methods in West Germany vividly illustrates this problem. The study leads Park to question the assumption that 'Japanese firms are able to implement in their subsidiaries [in West Germany] the same personnel policies that have been tried and proven effective in Japan'. Unlike their Japanese counterparts, German male employees will not routinely stay after hours and female employees will not automatically retire when they become pregnant. German trade unions balk at accepting such common Japanese practices as rotating employees from one job to another, relying on bonuses to supplement wages and passing up vacation time.

The 'Japanese model' may seem more suitable and attractive to a Third World country, especially in Asia. As Stanley argues in the last chapter of this volume, however, 'merely being Asian will not make the Japanese model easy' in countries that do not share Japan's cultural tradition or social structure. In the case of Singapore the model appeals to its leaders not simply as a formula for rapid economic development but, more importantly, as a justification for strong state authority and the constriction of democracy and individual freedom, political conditions which are believed, in part correctly so, to lie behind Japan's phenomenal economic growth. Social and ideological factors, such as the family system and Confucianism, are thus treated as essential components of the Japanese economic miracle. Given, however, Singapore's heterogeneous population with an 'extremely individualistic, commercial, materialistic' tradition, Stanley doubts that the Singaporean government will succeed in promoting Confucianism 'as a bulwark against decadent Western values ... (and) as a brake on individualism'.

Despite the real and serious difficulties examined by Fukai, Park and Stanley of transplanting a 'Japanese model' to another society, economically Japan has undeniably arrived with a great splash. It may have arrived politically, too, if far less dramatically. As Stockwin argues, Japan's leadership has achieved both remarkable economic growth and political stability 'within a tradition of modified liberalism and democracy'. Only in military power and status the country remains significantly inferior to the reigning superpowers and to many other countries as well. The 'failure' on this score, however, is clearly a result of deliberate abstinence and may very well represent, as Vogel believes, a perfectly rational and sensible decision, rather than either inability or ineptitude. After a 150 years of assiduous borrowing and learning from the West, the tables are turned, and it now seems to be the historical role of others, in the West and East, to learn from the Japanese, with as much care and discrimination as the Japanese have been learning from others throughout their recorded history.

The contributions to this *Festschrift* have collectively examined the cultural, social and political contours of that history and, individually, touched on some fine points of its rich and complex texture. We believe that the exercise is fully consistent in its spirit with Ishida Takeshi's own scholarship and represents a healthy, if modest, step forward in our common effort to understand and explain the modern Japanese experience more fully and accurately.

Notes and References

Introduction

* For biographical information this article relies mainly on Ishida Takeshi *et al.*, 'Zadankai: Hitotsu no kojinshi' [A round-table discussion: a personal history], 'Ishida kyōju ryakureki' [A summary of Professor Ishida's curriculum vitae] and 'Ishida kyōju chosaku mokuroku' [List of Professor Ishida's publications], in *Shakaikagaku kenkyū*, vol. 35, no. 5 (1984) pp. 277–341. We thank Professor Banno Junji of the University of Tokyo's Institute of Social Science and Shizuko Radbill of the University of Arizona's Oriental Collection for providing us with copies of the journal.

1. Takeshi Ishida, *Japanese Political Culture: Change and Continuity* (New Brunswick, N.J., and London, UK: Transaction Books, 1983) p. xi.

2. *Nihon no nashionarizumu* [Nationalism in Japan] (Kawade shobō, 1953); *Meiji seiji shisō-shi kenkyū* [A study of Meiji political thought] (Miraisha, 1954); and *Kindai nihon seiji kōzō no kenkyū* [A study of the political structure of modern Japan] (Miraisha, 1956).

3. *Gendai soshiki ron* [A theory of contemporary organisations] (Iwanami shoten), and *Sengo nihon no seiji taisei* [The post-war Japanese political system] (Miraisha).

4. See Takeshi Ishida, 'The Development of Interest Groups and the Pattern of Political Modernization in Japan', in Robert E. Ward (ed.), *Political Development in Modern Japan* (Princeton, N.J.: Princeton University Press, 1968) pp. 294–5, 335–6.

5. However, the half-dozen articles that appeared in the years immediately following Ishida's first visit to the US were concerned mainly with the norms of the US society and culture as compared, explicitly or implicitly, with those of Japanese society and culture. Typical of these efforts at comparative studies are: 'Seiō ajia nihon: kaigai kenkyū dansō' [The West, Asia and Japan: random thoughts on study abroad], *Shakai kagaku kenkyū*, vol. 14, no. 6, 1963; 'Tayōsei no kuni amerika: sono shakai to shakaikagaku dansō' [A nation of diversity: random thoughts on American society and social sciences], *Misuzu*, February 1964; 'Amerika no futatsu no kao' [The two faces of America], *Tosho*, February 1964; and 'Amerika chihō seiji no jittai: masachusettsushu no jirei wo chūshin to shite' [The reality of local politics in America: observations based mainly on the case of Massachusetts], *Reference*, no. 160, 1964.

6. A representative sample of the first type of work includes: *Heiwa no seijigaku* [The political science of peace] (Iwanami shoten, 1968); *Hakyoku to heiwa: 1941–1952-nen* [Crisis and peace: the years 1941–52] (Tokyo daigaku shuppankai, 1968); and *Heiwa to henkaku no ronri* [The logic of peace and change] (Renga shobō, 1973). The second type of work includes: *'Shūhen kara' no shikō: tayō no bunka to no taiwa wo*

252

motome te [A view from the 'periphery': in search of a dialogue with diverse cultures] (Tabata shoten, 1981); *Seiji to bunka* [Politics and culture] (Tokyo daigaku shuppankai, 1969); *Nihon no seiji bunka: dōchō to kyōsō* [Japanese political culture: conformity and competition] (Tokyo daigaku shuppankai, 1970); *Japanese Society* (New York: Random House, 1971); *Mehiko to nihonjin: dai-san sekai de kangaeru* [Mexico and Japanese: observations from the third world] (Tokyo daigaku shuppankai, 1973); *Japanese Political Culture: Change and Continuity* (New Brunswick, N.J.: Transaction Inc., 1983); and 'Conflict and Its Accommodation: *Omote-Ura* and *Uchi-Soto* Relations', in Ellis S. Krauss, Thomas P. Rohlen and Patricia G. Steinhoff (eds), *Conflict in Japan* (Honolulu: University of Hawaii Press, 1984).

7. The results of Ishida's own research on the subject were published in his 'Minamata ni okeru yokuatsu to sabetsu no kōzō' [The structure of repression and discrimination in Minamata], in Irokawa Daikichi (ed.), *Minamata no keiji: Shiranubi-kai sōgō-chōsa hōkoku*, vol. 1 (Chikuma shobō, 1983).

8. These include: '*Gukansho to Jinnō shōtō ki* no rekishi shisō; [The philosophy of history in *Gukansho* and *Jinnō shōtō ki*], in Maruyama Masao (ed.), *Rekishi shisō-shi* (Chikuma shobō, 1972); 'Josetsu: nihon ni okeru seiō seiji shisō' [Introductory notes: Western political ideologies in Japan], in Nihon seijigakkai (ed.), *Nempō seijigaku*, 1975 (Iwanami shoten, 1975); *Nihon kindai shisōshi ni okeru hō to seiji* [Law and politics in the history of modern Japanese thought] (Iwanami shoten, 1976); *Gendai seiji no soshiki to shōchō: sengoshi e no seijigaku-teki sekkin* [Organisations and symbols in contemporary politics: a political science approach to post-war history] (Misuzu shobō, 1978); 'Kawakami Hajime ni okeru itan e no michi' [The road to heterodoxy as seen in Kawakami Hajime], *Shisō*, October 1979; 'Nōkyō: Japanese Farmers' Representatives', co-authored with Aurelia George, in Peter Drysdale and Hironobu Kitaoji (eds), *Japan and Australia: Two Societies and Their Interaction* (Canberra: Australian National University Press, 1981); *Seitō to itan* [Orthodoxy and heterodoxy] (Tokyo daigaku shuppankai, 1983); and *Kindai nihon no seiji bunka to gengo shōchō* [Political culture and linguistic symbols in modern Japan] (Tokyo daigaku shuppankai, 1983).

1 World Without Walls: Kuwagata Keisai's Panoramic Vision of Japan

1. Donald Keene, *World Within Walls – Japanese Literature of the Pre-Modern Era, 1600–1867* (New York, Grove Press, 1976). Professor Keene is also the author of a pioneering book on precisely my counter-theme of 'world without walls': *The Japanese Discovery of Europe, 1720–1830* (London, Routledge and Kegan Paul, 1952).

2. Figure 1.1 represents a fine impression, in excellent condition, of what I believe to be the first state of this print, preserved in its original wrapper

in the Mitsui Bunko in Tokyo, call no. C750–12. This state may be distinguished from others by the fine line carved from the blue colour block to indicate the horizon below Korea. A common later state has completely different colour blocks, resulting in heavier overprinting on the mountain peaks, no horizon line below Korea and a differently placed moon; for an example (from the Kobe City Museum) see Hugh Cortazzi, *Isles of Gold: Antique Maps of Japan* (New York and Tokyo: John Weatherhill, 1983) pl. 60 and endcover insert.

3. The most thorough biographical investigation of Keisai is in Tanaka Tatsuya, 'Bunga no gaha, Kitao-ha', in *Nikuhitsu ukiyoe* (Shūeisha, 1983), v. 133–7, 143, 146.

4. Urushiyama Matashirō calculated that of some 250 books which Keisai illustrated, 168 were *kibyōshi*; 'Kitao Masayoshi to sono sakuhin', *Shomotsu tenbō*, 8/1 (January 1938) pp. 15–25, and 'Kuwagata Keisai no ehon', *Gasetsu*, no. 33 (1939) p. 845. A more recent catalogue of Keisai's books lists 177 *kibyōshi*; see Riccar Bijutsukan, *Uki-e Kanadehon Chūshingura – Kitao Masayoshi* (exhibition catalogue, 1979) pp. 18–31.

5. The last datable appearance of the name Masayoshi appears to be 1800, in his two final *kibyōshi*.

6. Keene, *World Within Walls*, op. cit. p. 400.

7. The term '*uki-e*' seems to have first appeared on prints of theatre interiors by Masanobu and Kiyotada in about 1739–40; the meaning was later described as referring to the visual effects of looking at such views through a lens, although there is no evidence that the first *uki-e* were so intended. For the origins and development of the genre see Suzuki Jūzō 'Uki-e no tenkai to henbō', in Riccar Bijutsukan, *Uki-e* (exhibition catalogue, 1975), and Julian Jinn Lee, 'The Origin and Development of Japanese Landscape Prints: A Study in the Synthesis of Eastern and Western Art', unpublished Ph.D. diss., University of Washington, 1977.

8. For Ōkyo's views for the *optique* see Kubota Beisen, 'Maruyama Ōkyo hitsu no megane-e', *Kottō kyōkai zasshi* (1899) pp. 39–41; Lee, 'The Origin and Development of Japanese Landscape Prints', op. cit. ch. 5; and Kōbe Shiritsu Hakubutsukan, *Megane-e to Tōkaidō gojūsan-tsugi ten* (exhibition catalogue, 1984).

9. Oka Yasumasa, 'Maruyama Ōkyo no megane-e to Utagawa Toyoharu no uki-e ni tsuite', *Kansai Daigaku Kōkogaku-tō shiryōshitsu kiyō*, no. 1 (March 1984) pp. 47–78.

10. This series consisted of at least six prints; the depiction of Nakazu in one of them dates it before 1789.

11. This painting is illustrated (but mis-identified as a view of Ryōgoku) in Ōta Kinen Bijutsukan, *Kōnoike korekushon Ōgi-e zuroku 1: Ukiyo-e hen* (Ōta kinen bijutsukan, 1981) fig. 18, and in colour in *Kobijutsu*, no. 75 (July 1985) p. 29. I am grateful to Timothy Clark of Harvard University for bringing this painting to my attention.

12. The English word 'panorama' was a product of the same era as that of Keisai, coined in about 1789 by Robert Barker to describe his invention of a circular painting which completely surrounds the viewer. I have used the term 'panoramic' here rather to describe the encompassment of a

wide and continuous topographical range of view within the limits of a conventional flat picture.

13. This scroll should not be confused with the famous gazetteer of the same name (but different characters for 'Edo') of 1834–6, edited by Saitō Gesshin.

14. The connections proposed here follow the suggestions of Kano Hiroyuki, 'Kitao Masayoshi to sono jidai – Kare o meguru hitobito', in Riccar Bijutsukan, *Uki-e Kanadehon Chūshingura – Kitao Masayoshi*, p. 3.

15. Kano Hiroyuki, 'Kuwagata Keisai ehon no kentō', *Museum*, no. 338 (May 1979) p. 23, claims that this drawing was taken from *Kōmō zatsuwa*; in fact it is of a different type and must have come from some other source.

16. Figure 1.11, from the Mitsui Bunko (call no. 604–1) represents the earlier of two separate editions of Keisai's *Edo meisho no e*; in the later one, the key block is essentially the same except for the addition of the Kayaba-chō Yakushi Hall, about 1½ inches below and to the left and Nihonbashi Bridge, and the deletion of the carver's signature to the lower right. The later colour blocks omit the cloud on the left slope of Mt Fuji, and show a solid rising sun rather than one crossed by clouds. The seal of the publisher Seiryōkaku (Suwaraya Ihachi) is normally found in the lower left margin of the later edition. Within each edition there are alternate states, with variant colour blocks; the pristine impression of the Mitsui Bunko copy suggests that it is the earliest state of the first edition; it may be distinguished from later states by the pattern of the clouds across the rising sun. The Mitsui Bunko collection also includes a painting which is larger in scale but otherwise almost identical, except for the absence of written labels, to the print; it is undated and unsigned, but ascribed by the library to Keisai. Across the top of the painting in an unidentified hand is a series of Chinese poems celebrating the sights of Edo, composed in pairs by Confucian scholars Hayashi Razan (1583–1657) and Hori Kyōan (1585–1642). Since this painting includes a depiction of the Kayaba-chō Yakushi Hall, I would propose that it post-dated the first edition and was hence copied from the print, rather than vice versa. See note 32 for reference to two other painted versions of the Edo view.

17. I have been unable to locate a surviving copy of the wrapper itself, but the information on it is recorded in 'Shōshin-hitsu Edo ichiranzu no gendai', *Ukiyoe no kenkyū*, no. 9–10 (May 1924) p. 39.

18. *Edo hon'ya shuppan kiroku*, iii (Yumani shobō, 1980) pp. 440–1. The first to draw attention to this source appears to have been Iwata Toyoki, 'Edo jidai no chōkanzu', *Gekkan kochizu kenkyū*, no. 12 (February 1971) p. 7.

19. For a collection of important essays on the evolution of urban views and bird's-eye views in Japan see Yamori Kazuhiko, *Kochizu to fūkei* (Chikuma shobō, 1984).

20. The most elaborate such screen is the 'Screen of Twenty-eight Cities', in the Imperial Collection; see *Genshoku Nihon no bijutsu* (Shōgakkan, 1968–76), xxv, pls 22–3.

21. Saitō Gesshin, *Bukō nenpyō*, entry for 3/21/1828' see Kaneko Mitsuharu (ed.), *Zōtei Bukō nenpyō*, Tōyō bunko 117–18 (Heibonsha, 1968), ii, 73–4. Gesshin included the same allegation in his revision of the *Ukiyo-e ruikō*. The word '*ichiranzu*' in the title of Kazan's view (as printed on the wrapper in which it was sold) may well have been used here for the first time, and corresponds fairly well to the English 'bird's-eye view' (for which the earliest *OED* citation is 1762–71).

22. Masamune Isoo and Wakabayashi Shōji (eds), *Kinsei Kyōto shuppan shiryō* (Nihon kosho tsūshinsha, 1965) p. 21; I am indebted for the reference to Iwata, 'Edo jidai no chōkanzu', p. 7.

23. Ōkyo's view of Kyoto is introduced in Cal French, *Through Closed Doors: Western Influence on Japanese Art 1639–1853* (Rochester, Mich.: Meadow Brook Art Gallery, Oakland University, 1977), entry 45 (pp. 109–11). For the date on the box see Ikenaga Hajime, *Shiritsu Kōbe bijutsukan shūzō Nanban bijutsu sōmokuroku* (Kobe: Shiritsu Kōbe bijutsukan, 1955) p. 187.

24. Sasaki Jōhei, 'Maruyama Ōkyo no sansuiga ni tsuite', *Bijutsushi*, no. 120 (April 1986) pp. 113–31.

25. See French, *Through Closed Doors*, op. cit. p. 109, for an excellent stylistic analysis of Ōkyo's Kyoto view.

26. Ōkyo also painted a similar view of Osaka, now in the collection of Nanba Shōtarō; see *Edo jidai zushi*, vol. xviii (Chikuma shobō, 1978) fig. 4. A view of Nagasaki harbour in the Nagasaki Prefectural Art Museum is signed by Ōkyo and dated 1792, but its authenticity is in doubt; see fig. 6, Hosono Masanobu, 'Yōfū hanga', *Nihon no bijutsu*, no. 36 (Shibundō, 1969), translated as *Nagasaki Prints and Early Copperplates* (Kodansha International and Shibundo, 1978).

27. Louise Norton Brown, *Block Printing and Book Illustration in Japan* (London: George Routledge & Sons Ltd, and New York: E. P. Dutton & Co., 1924) p. 123. Brown asserts that Masayoshi visited Kyoto 'about 1786', apparently on the assumption that the designs in *Ehon Miyako no nishiki* (1787) were based on first-hand experience, when in fact they were adapted from *Miyako meisho zue*. Her reconstruction of Keisai's contact with Ōkyo through the kyōka volume *Haikaika Miyako manshu* (which she mis-reads as '*Haikai Kato Manshu*') is also suspect, since surviving editions of this work make it clear that the illustrations were by the 'late' (not 'old age') Ōkyo himself rather than Keisai, and that the preface is not by Shinra Banshō but by Shinratei II; the date of the preface (*ne hazuki*) must be, given the circumstances described, the Eighth Month of 1804. Brown's assertions (and errors) are all repeated by Nakada Katsunosuke, *Ehon no kenkyū* (Bijutsu shuppansha, 1950) p. 96.

28. For the trip to Tsuyama see Tanaka, op. cit. p. 135.

29. The commentary on this print in Nakamura Hiroshi (ed.), *Nihon kochizu taisei* (Kōdansha, 1964) pl. 77, identifies this as a setting sun, which seems unlikely.

30. This painting is now mounted as a screen, in the collection of the Tsuyama shiritsu kyōdokan; for a good reproduction see Suwa Haruo and Naitō Akira, *Edo zu byōbu* (Mainichi shinbunsha, 1972) pl. 107,

where it is called 'Edo keikan zu byōbu'. Still another painted version of the Edo panorama survives in the Japan Ukiyoe Museum Collection in Matsumoto, reproduced in Nihon Ukiyo-e Hakubutsukan, *Nikuhitsu ukiyo-e senshū* (Gakken, 1986) pl. 116. It is signed in a style identical to that of the printed version, but the composition is different. It is undated, but I would guess that it came after the print, in response to a request for a painted version. Finally, a large painting of presumably the same view hung for many years in the Ema Hall of Kanda Myōjin Shrine and was finally destroyed in the Kanto Earthquake of 1923; see Kaneko (ed.), *Zōtei Bukō nenpyō*, ii, 74; Mori Senzō, 'Kuwagata Keisai no kotodomo', *Gasetsu*, no. 33 (1939) pp. 829–30; and Mimura Seisaburō, 'Keisai ni kanshite', *Gasetsu*, no. 33 (1939) p. 838 (which however mistakes Keisai's painting for a separate one of the shrine festival procession).

31. Among the many later panoramas of Edo which are modelled after the original Keisai view are: a copperplate etching by Aōdō Denzen, before 1815 (see Hosono, op. cit. fig. 103); an eightfold screen by *ukiyo-e* painter Shuntoku, now lost (Narazaki Muneshige, 'Shuntoku kenkyū no zenshin tashō', *Ukiyoe-kai*, 4/1 [January 1939] pp. 35–6); a copperplate etching by an unknown European illustrator in Siebold's *Nippon*, 1832–51 (ii, 39); a crude *ukiyo-e* print by Kunimori, 1843–6; a careful copy of Keisai's original by his grandson Keirin, after 1854 (see, for example, Chikuma shobō, *Edo jidai zushi*, suppl. vol. 2, pp. 104–5, and Mildred Friedman (ed.) *Tokyo: Form and Spirit* [Walker Art Museum, 1986] p. 33); and a *sugoroku* board-game print by Hiroshige II, 1859 (see, for example, Shinji Yoshimoto (ed.), 'Edo happyaku yachō', *Nihon no kochizu*, vol. ix [Kōdansha, 1977] p. 1, and facsimile reproduction in Iwata Toyoki (ed.), *Ō-Edo ezu shūsei* [Kōdansha, 1974]).

32. On the basis of the entire argument which I have presented I here make the assumption that the view of Edo preceded the view of Japan, although there is no documentary evidence for dating the latter. Given the similarity of style between the two views, I would judge that the view of Japan followed that of Edo within a year or two.

33. Sasaki Jōhei, 'Maruyama Ōkyo no kaigaron' (Kyōto daigaku bungakubu bigaku-bijutsushigaku kenkyūshitsu) *Kenkyū kiyō*, no. 3 (1982) pp. 7, 13.

34. Saitō Gesshin, *Edo meisho zue*, v (1836), s.v. 'Kanda Daimyōjin no yashiro'. A depiction of the same large telescope appears in Keisai's *Edo meisho zue* of 1785.

35. For the complex character of Sadanobu himself see Haruko Iwasaki, 'Portrait of a Daimyo – Comical Fiction by Matsudaira Sadanobu', *Monumenta Nipponica*, 38/1 (Spring 1983) pp. 1–48.

36. For Bunchō's Izu paintings see Tani Bunchō, *Kōyo tanshōzu* (Meicho shuppan, 1975), *kaisetsu* by Hosono Masanobu.

37. Denzen himself produced a panoramic view of Edo; as cited in note 33, I believe that Denzen followed Keisai, although the reverse possibility has been considered (but finally discounted) in Unno Kazutaka, 'Edo chōkanzu no sōshisha', *Gekkan kochizu kenkyū*, 8/9 (June, 1970) pp. 2–11.

38. 'Shokunin-zukushi ekotoba', 3 painted handscrolls, Tokyo National Museum; see Asakura Haruhiko (ed.), *Edo shokunin-zukushi* (Iwasaki bijutsu sha, 1980) for a half-tone reproduction.
39. Iwasaki, 'Portrait of a Daimyo', op. cit. p. 19.
40. Haga Tōru, 'The Western World and Japan in the Eighteenth Century', *Hikaku bunka kenkyū* (Tōkyō daigaku kyōyō gakubu) no. 16 (March 1978) p. 22. I have provided my own translation of the poem.
41. Suien's comments are attached to a copy of *Nihon meisho no e* in the National Diet Library, call no. GAI [*inoshishi*] 125.

2 Anglo-American Influences on Nishida

1. Yamada Munemutsu, *Nihongata shisō no genkei* (San'ichi shobō, 1961) p. 94.
2. Takeuchi Yoshitomo, *Nishida Kitarō, kindai nihon no shisōka* (Tokyo daigaku shuppankai, 1966) passim.
3. Valdo H. Viglielmo, 'Nishida Kitarō', in Donald Shively (ed.), *Modernization of Japanese Culture* (Princeton, N.J.: Princeton University Press, 1971) pp. 530–2.
4. Takeuchi, *Nishida Kitarō*, op. cit. p. 240.
5. Ibid. pp. 107–8.
6. Yamada, *Nihongata shisō*, op. cit. p. 49.
7. Takeuchi, *Nishida Kitarō*, op. cit. p. 111.
8. Nakajima Rikizō, 'Eikoku shin Kanto gakuha ni tsuite', *Tetsugaku zasshi*, vol. 7, no. 70 (December 1892); vol. 8, no. 71 (January 1893); and vol. 8, no. 72 (February 1893).
9. Nishida Kitarō, 'Gurin shi rinritsugaku no tai'i', *Kyōiku jiron*, vol. 36, no. 362 (5 May 1895); vol. 36, no. 363 (15 May 1895); vol. 36, no. 364 (25 May 1895).
10. Nishida Kitarō, *Nishida Kitarō zenshū* [hereafter cited as *Zenshū*] (Iwanami shoten, 1953) Supplementary vol. v, p. 33.
11. For example, Nishida confuses *intellect* and *knowledge*. See Nishida, 'Gurin shi', vol. 36, no. 363, p. 25.
12. Nishida, *Zenshū*, op. cit. Supplementary vol. v, p. 31.
13. Nishida, 'Hyūmu no ingahō', *Zenshū*, op. cit. Supplementary vol. ii, pp. 26–33.
14. Ibid. pp. 34–63.
15. For instance, see William James, *The Writings of William James*, ed. John J. McDermott (New York: Random House, 1967) especially chs ii and iii.
16. Nishida, 'Junsui keiken sōgo no kankei ni tsuite' [On the relations among pure experiences], *Zenshū*, op. cit. Supplementary vol. ii, p. 64.
17. Shimomura Toratarō, 'Nishida Kitarō and Some Aspects of His Philosophical Thought', in Nishida Kitarō, *A Study of Good*, trans. Valdo H. Viglielmo (The Printing Bureau of Japanese Government, 1960) p. 201.
18. William James, 'Radical Empiricism', *The Writings*, op. cit. p. 134.
19. *Zen no kenkyū* (Iwanami, 1975) p. 6.

20. Ibid. p. 57.
21. Palpable throughout *Zen no kenkyū* is Nishida's determination not to be considered a Kantist.
22. Nishida, *Zen*, op. cit. p. 62.
23. Ibid. p. 71.
24. Ibid. p. 62.
25. Ibid. p. 95.
26. Ibid. pp. 57–8.
27. Viglielmo translates *tōitsuteki arumono* as 'certain unified thing'. Nishida, *Good*, op. cit. p. 76.
28. Nishida, *Zen*, op. cit. p. 75.
29. Ibid. p. 60.
30. Ibid. pp. 63–70.
31. Ibid. pp. 63 and 70.
32. Ibid. p. 80.
33. Ibid. p. 60.
34. Ibid. p. 71.
35. Ibid. p. 79.
36. Ibid. p. 73.
37. Ibid. p. 80.
38. Ibid. p. 73.
39. Ibid. p. 80. All citations in this paragraph are taken from pp. 80–2.
40. Ibid. chs 6 and 7.
41. Ibid. pp. 86–7.
42. Ibid. p. 78.
43. All references in this paragraph are to ibid. ch. 10.
44. Ibid. p. 99.
45. Ibid. p. 84.
46. Ibid. p. 85.
47. Ibid. p. 102.
48. Ibid. p. 91.
49. Ibid.
50. Ibid. p. 92.
51. Ibid. p. 94.
52. Ibid. p. 91.
53. Ibid. p. 92.
54. Ibid. p. 84.
55. Ibid. p. 96.
56. Ibid. p. 98.
57. Ibid. p. 96.
58. Thomas Hill Green, *Prolegomena to Ethics*, ed. A. C. Bradley (Oxford: Clarendon Press, 1906), 5th ed., pp. 58–61.
59. Ibid. p. 78.
60. Ibid.
61. Green makes this point numerous times. For instance, see ibid. p. 15.
62. Ibid. p. 18.
63. Ibid. pp. 29–31.
64. Ibid. p. 91.
65. Nishida, *Zen*, op. cit. p. 96.

66. Viglielmo, *Nishida*, op. cit. p. 555.
67. Nishida, *Zen*, op. cit. p. 160. *Das Veilchen* is one of Goethe's enigmatic and controversial poems in which a violet dies happily under the crushing foot of a young shepherdess whom the flower adores. It easily lends itself to a Freudian interpretation of masochistic love that ends in tragedy. It is extremely doubtful if the poem represents the 'true feelings of all humans' and the idea of true good, as Nishida contends.
68. William James, 'The Continuity of Experience', *The Writings*, pp. 292–301.
69. Ibid. p. 293.
70. Nishida, *Zen*, op. cit. p. 14. Reference is to William James, *The Principles of Psychology*, vol. i, ch. vii. The three works of James which Nishida used extensively were *The Principles of Psychology*, *A World of Pure Experience* and *The Stream of Consciousness*.
71. Nishida, op. cit. Reference is James, *A World of Pure Experience*.
72. Nishida, op. cit. p. 23. Reference is James, op. cit.
73. Nishida, op. cit. p. 19.
74. Ibid. p. 33. Cf. William James, 'Attention and Will', *Psychology, Briefer Course*, in William James, *The Moral Philosophy of William James*, ed. John K. Roth (New York: Thomas Y. Crowell Co., 1969) pp. 72–102.
75. Nishida, op. cit. p. 39.
76. Op. cit. p. 44. Cf. F. C. S. Schiller, 'Axiom as Postulates', *Personal Idealism*, ed. Henry Sturt (London: Macmillan & Co., 1902) p. 92.
77. Nishida, op. cit. p. 29. The text is paraphrased freely, rather than translated verbatim, for the sake of the clarity of meaning. Nishida's reference to Hegel is the latter's *Wissenschaft der Logik*.
78. Nishida, op. cit. p. 16.
79. Ibid.
80. Nishida himself does not give the example of tea ceremony. The idea, however, is expressed thus: 'When one is learning an art, what is at first conscious becomes unconscious as the skill develops.' *Zen*, op. cit. p. 20.
81. Ibid. p. 45.
82. Ibid. pp. 47–9.
83. Ibid. p. 29.
84. James, 'Pure Experiences', op. cit. p. 212.
85. Nakajima Tokuzō, 'Gurin shi chishiki tetsugaku wo yomu', *Tetsugaku zasshi*, vol. 9, no. 94 (December 1894); Mizobuchi Shinma, 'Gurin shi chishiki tetsugaku ron', *Tetsugaku zasshi*, vol. 10, no. 101 (July 1895); Fukasaku Yasubumi, *Rinri to kokumin dōtoku* (Kōdōkan, 1916).
86. Nakajima, 'Eikoku shin Kanto gakuha', p. 650.
87. Ibid.
88. Takeuchi, *Nishida*, op. cit. p. 178.
89. James, 'The Continuity', op. cit. p. 292.
90. Takeuchi, *Nishida*, op. cit. p. 196.
91. Nishida, *Zen*, op. cit. p. 61.
92. Thomas Hill Green, 'Essays on Christian Dogma' and 'Conversion of St. Paul', *Works of Thomas Hill Green*, ed. R. L. Nettleship (London: Longmans, Green & Co., 1888), 3 vols, vol. iii, pp. 161–89.
93. Nishida, *Zen*, op. cit. p. 27.

94. Because Green's ethical philosophy was famous in Japan as the doctrine of self-realisation, scholars have speculated on its relationship to Nishida's view of nationalism. Elsewhere I have demonstrated that the complex idea of self-realisation was made to accommodate the philosophies of the nationalists even more effectively than those of their opponents during the Meiji era. Regarding Nishida, my view is that he was no exception to the Meiji rule. Although he used the term 'self-realization', the meanings he attributed to it were those of the Meiji nationalists, not the liberal meaning Green had given it. Incidentally, in the late 1930s, when the Japanese government intensified suppression of liberal opinions, Nishida attempted to rescue one victim, Kawai Eijirō, who was the most renowned protagonist of Green in the post-Meiji era. His stance on 'the Kawai Eijirō Case' was perhaps a belated acknowledgement of his indebtedness to Green. See Atsuko Hirai, 'Self-Realization and Common Good: T. H. Green in Meiji Ethical Thought', *The Journal of Japanese Studies*, Winter 1979, pp. 107–36; Atsuko Hirai, 'Thomas Hill Green in Modern East Asia with Special Reference to the Thought of Mao Tse-tung', *Proceedings*, 30th International Congress of Human Sciences in Asia and North Africa (Mexico, 1982), China 4, pp. 145–63; Atsuko Hirai, *Individualism and Socialism: The Life and Thought of Kawai Eijirō (1891–1944)* (Cambridge, Mass.: Harvard University Press, 1986) chs 4 and 8.

3 A Non-traditional View of Japanese Modernisation

1. Masao Maruyama, *Studies in the Intellectual History of Tokugawa Japan* (University of Tokyo Press, 1974) p. 9.
2. Ibid. p. 15.

4 Women in the Silk-Reeling Industry in Nineteenth-century Japan

1. I should like to acknowledge my debt to the Social Science Research Council and the Japan Foundation for generous research grants in 1981–2. I am also extremely grateful to Nagahara Keiji and Nakamura Masanori for facilitating my research while I was a visiting scholar in the Department of Economics, Hitotsubashi University. Their assistance was indispensable. Nagahara Kazuko lent valuable bibliographic suggestions, and Itō Masakazu, director of the Okaya Silk Reel Museum, served as a genial guide through the museum's exhibit of silk-reel equipment. At the University of Arizona's Oriental Collection I benefited from the research and translation skills of Shizuko Radbill and from Mary McWhorter's ready willingness to help me locate and acquire research materials. By carefully reading the first draft of this chapter, Mikiso Hane and Nakamura Masanori saved me from several errors of fact and interpretation. Haruhiro Fukui offered stimulating suggestions for developing the comparative and analytical dimensions of the study.

A shorter version of this chapter was presented in 1984 at the Western Conference of the Association for Asian Studies, where Anne Walthall made helpful comments that were incorporated into the present version. Any remaining problems are, of course, solely my own responsibility.

2. Among the exceptions are Mikiso Hane, *Peasants, Rebels, and Outcasts: the Underside of Modern Japan* (New York: Pantheon, 1982); Sharon L. Sievers, *Flowers in Salt: the Beginnings of Feminist Consciousness in Modern Japan* (Stanford, Calif.: Stanford University Press, 1983) chap. 4; Gary R. Saxonhouse, 'Country Girls and Communication Among Competitors in the Japanese Cotton Spinning Industry', in *Japanese Industrialization and Its Social Consequences*, ed. Hugh Patrick (Berkeley, Calif.: University of California Press, 1976) pp. 97–125; and Yasue Aoki Kidd, *Women Workers in the Japanese Cotton Mills: 1880–1920* (Ithaca, N.Y.: Cornell University East Asia Papers no. 20, 1978).

3. The Japanese textiles industry consisted primarily of cotton and silk production. The silk industry was divided into two separate processes: reeling silk thread and weaving silk cloth of various kinds. Silk filatures, where silk thread was produced, shared some of the characteristics of the cotton mills, but because they were less mechanised and used a unique wage system, they posed special problems for their employees.

4. William Jones Chambliss, *Chiaraijima Village, Land Tenure, Taxation, and Local Trade, 1818–1884* (Tucson, Ariz.: University of Arizona Press, 1965) p. 17 n. 9.

5. Kajinishi Mitsuhaya, Furushima Toshio, Tatewaki Sadao and Oguchi Kenzō (eds), *Seishi rōdōsha no rekishi* (Iwanami shoten, 1955) pp. 4–5. A late eighteenth-century book on sericulture laments male farmers' unwillingness to care for silkworms, which they viewed as 'women's work', and their 'consequent ignorance of the subject'. See Thomas C. Smith, *Nakahara* (Stanford, Calif.: Stanford University Press, 1977) p. 152 fn e.

6. See, for example, Yanagida Kunio, *Japanese Manners and Customs in the Meiji Era*, transl. Charles S. Terry (Obunsha, 1957) p. 246; and Alice Mabel Bacon, *Japanese Girls and Women* (Boston, Mass.: Houghton Mifflin, 1902) p. 246.

7. Thomas C. Smith, *Agrarian Origins of Modern Japan* (New York: Atheneum, 1966) p. 167 n.

8. William B. Hauser, *Economic Institutional Change in Tokugawa Japan: Osaka and the Kinai Cotton Trade* (Cambridge: Cambridge University Press, 1974) pp. 138–40.

9. Kajinishi, *Seishi rōdōsha*, op. cit. pp. 4–5. Women of Okinawa wove to fulfil Okinawa's tribute payment to Satsuma *han* until 1902. From the ages of 14 to 50 they paid a compulsory cloth tax. See Morosawa Yōko (ed.), *Onna no hataraki* (Heibonsha, 1978) p. 83.

10. William B. Hauser, 'The Diffusion of Cotton Processing and Trade in the Kinai Region in Tokugawa Japan', *Journal of Asian Studies*, vol. xxxiii, no. 4 (August 1974) pp. 637–8.

11. Smith, *Agrarian Origins*, op. cit. pp. 166–7.

12. Kajinishi, *Seishi rōdōsha*, op. cit. p. 6.

Notes and References 263

13. Smith, *Agrarian Origins*, op. cit. p. 169.
14. Stephen W. McCallion, 'Silk Reeling in Meiji Japan: The Limits to Change', unpub. Ph.D. diss., Ohio State University, 1983, p. 37.
15. Grace Hutchins, *Labor and Silk* (New York: International Publishers, 1929) p. 13. See also 'Silk', *Chambers's Encyclopedia*, vol. 12 (London: International Learning Systems Corp., Ltd, 1973), pp. 558–9; *Silk and Japan* (The Japan Silk Association, n.d.) pp. 1–7; Takizawa Hideki, *Mayu to kiito no kindai shi* (Kyōikusha, 1979) pp. 20–1.
16. Sasaki Junnosuke, 'Endogenous Technology and Society in Japan' (The United Nations University, 1981) pp. 26–33. Because the age, height and kind of mulberry-tree affects the quality of the leaves fed to silkworms, considerable effort was devoted to tree husbandry in rural Japan. See Kajinishi, *Seishi rōdōsha*, op. cit. p. 4.
17. McCallion, 'Silk Reeling in Meiji Japan', op. cit. pp. 31–2. See also Hutchins, *Labor and Silk*, op. cit. pp. 13–14; and Iwajiro Honda, *The Silk Industry of Japan* (The Imperial Tokyo Sericultural Institute, 1909) pp. 156–7.
18. The Okaya Silk Reel Museum in Nagano prefecture has a display of the evolution of silk-reeling equipment in Japan. See the museum's booklet, 'Okaya seishi hakubutsukan' (Okaya: Shiritsu Okaya seishi hakubutsukan, 1955). See also photographs in Kajinishi, Mitsuhaya (ed.), *Gendai Nihon sangyō hattatsu shi*, vol. xi: Sen-i (Rojunsha, 1964).
19. Kajinishi, *Seishi rōdōsha*, op. cit. pp. 10–11. In addition to foreign steam-powered reels, described below, treadle reeling-machines (*ashibumi*) operated by a pedal were widely in use in cottage industries in the Okaya area after 1873. See 'Okaya seishi hakubutsukan', pp. 7 and 24; and Yagi Haruo, 'Seishigyō', in *Nihon sangyōshi taikei*, comp. Chihōshi kenkyū kyōgikai (Tokyo daigaku shuppankai, 1961) vol. i, pp. 236–8. In China the treadle reeling-machine was probably in use as early as the Sung period if not earlier, according to Lillian M. Li, *China's Silk Trade: Traditional Industry in the Modern World, 1842–1937* (Cambridge, Mass.: Harvard University Press, 1981) p. 35.
20. McCallion, 'Silk Reeling in Meiji Japan', op. cit. pp. 34–5.
21. Ibid. pp. 38 and 42. The cost and availability of cocoons dictated limits to the scope of silk-reeling operations and determined the number of silk-reelers and the number of reeling days. See Kajinishi, *Seishi rōdōsha*, op. cit. pp. 11–12.
22. Ibid. p. 6.
23. Ibid. p. 9.
24. Yanagida, *Japanese Manners and Customs*, op. cit. p. 234.
25. Kajinishi, *Seishi rōdōsha*, op. cit. pp. 19–21; Takeshi Hayashi, *Japanese Experience*, no. 2 (Oct 1979) p. 9; and Morosawa Yōko, *Onna no hataraki*, op. cit. p. 102. See also Wada (*née* Yokota) Ei (Hideko), *Tomioka nikki* (Sōjusha, 1976).
26. In 1874, continuing its efforts to encourage the silk-reeling industry, the Meiji government established a sericulture research centre under the Industrial Promotion Bureau of the Ministry of Home Affairs.
27. McCallion, 'Silk Reeling in Meiji Japan', op. cit. pp. 118–19. McCallion

cautions, however, that it is 'highly unlikely that their role as diffusers of new techniques was at all extensive since they returned home to work in filatures run by other *shizoku.*

28. For example, see Robert Cole and Ken'ichi Tominaga, 'Japan's Changing Occupational Structure and its Significance', in *Japanese Industrialization and Its Social Consequences*, op. cit. p. 61. The definition of 'skilled' and 'unskilled' is open to interpretation. My discussion of the technology of sericulture and silk-reeling was intended to demonstrate that a great deal of skill was involved.

29. Kajinishi, *Seishi rōdōsha*, op. cit. pp. 5–9. Suwa factory workers were immortalised in Yamamoto Shigemi's classic memoir, *Aa Nomugi tōge*, originally published in 1968.

30. Ishii Kanji, *Nihon sanshigyō shi bunseki* (Tokyo daigaku shuppankai, 1972) p. 210.

31. Ibid. pp. 261–4.

32. Nakamura Masanori, *Nihon no rekishi*, vol. 29: *Rōdōsha to nōmin* (Shōgakukan, 1981) p. 91.

33. Kajinishi, *Seishi rōdōsha*, op. cit. p. 34. A Tokyo newspaper reported in 1876 that children between the ages of 8 and 13 were being hired in Jōshū (Gumma prefecture). The impoverished backgrounds of female workers is confirmed by data compiled in *Shokkō jijō*, the official survey of factory conditions commissioned by the government in 1897 and originally published in 1903. The three-volume work was reissued by Shinkigensha in 1976.

34. Nakamura, *Rōdōsha to nōmin*, op. cit. pp. 222–3.

35. Ibid. p. 91.

36. Ibid. p. 42. 'Wily farmers sometimes made contracts with labor recruiters from two or three different companies in order to collect the money that was given upon the signing of the agreement, and ... factories thus defrauded had little recourse.' See Yanagida, op. cit., *Japanese Manners and Customs*, op. cit. p. 76.

37. Kajinishi (ed.), *Gendai Nihon sangyō hattatsu shi*, op. cit. p. 154.

38. Nakamura, *Rōdōsha to nōmin*, pp. 94–5.

39. *Nōgyō keizai jijō* (Nōshōmushō Nōshōkyoku, 1909) pp. 30–1. Fluctuations in the price of rice might result in the percentage varying from as little as 6 to as much as 9 per cent.

40. *Shokkō jijō*, vol. i, p. 192, drawn from a survey of 205 factories in Nagano prefecture.

41. A reeler named Watanabe Ruiko, who worked as an instructor in a filature employing 280 women in 1905, wrote, 'However little money I received, I sent half home to my parents.' See Takizawa, *Mayu to kiito no kindai shi*, op. cit. pp. 178–9.

42. Nakamura writes that statistics on the factory girl's percentage contribution to the small cultivator's farm income are not available for the Meiji period, but he estimates the amount as approximately 20 per cent. Statistics for the Taishō period suggest the amount exceeded 20 per cent. Personal letter, 16 August 1985.

43. Hane, *Peasants, Rebels, and Outcasts*, op. cit. p. 177.

44. Laura S. Strumingher, 'Women's Work and Consciousness: Lyon, 1830–50', *Societas*, vol. vi, no. 4 (Autumn 1976) p. 288.
45. Nakamura Masanori, 'Seishigyō no tenkai to jinushisei', *Shakai keizai shigaku*, vol. 32, nos. 5–6 (1967) p. 54.
46. Yamada Moritarō, quoted in Izumi Takeo, 'Transformation and Development of Technology in the Japanese Cotton Industry', working paper (The United Nations University, 1980) p. 36.
47. Yamaguchi Kazuo, *Nihon sangyō kinyūshi kenkyū: seishi kinyū hen* (Tokyo daigaku shuppankai, 1966) p. 151.
48. Nakamura Takafusa, *Economic Growth in Prewar Japan* (London and New Haven, Conn.: Yale University Press, 1971) pp. 131–2. Filatures geared their wage scales to the level of the region's lowest-paid wage-labourers – agricultural day-workers.
49. The best source in English for the cotton-spinning mills is Kidd, *Women Workers in the Japanese Cotton Mills*, op. cit. See also Hane, *Peasants, Rebels, and Outcasts*, op. cit., for excerpts from *Aa Nomugi tōge* on Suwa factory girls. In Japanese see *Shokkō jijō.*
50. Nakamura, *Rōdōsha to nōmin*, op. cit. p. 82. A 1910 survey of factory girls in 28 prefectures found that over 10 per cent had serious diseases, such as tuberculosis, by the time they returned home. See Ishihara Osamu, *Jokō to kekkaku* (1914), quoted by Hiroshi Hazama, 'Historical Changes in the Life Style of Industrial Worker', in *Japanese Industrialization and Its Social Consequences*, op. cit. p. 32 n. 17.
51. E. Patricia Tsurumi, 'Female Textile Workers and the Failure of Early Trade Unionism in Japan', *History Workshop*, no. 18 (Autumn 1984) pp. 3–27.
52. Yamaguchi, *Nihon sangyō kinyūshi kenkyū*, op. cit. p. 151.
53. Takeshi Hayashi, *Japanese Experience*, no. 2 (October 1979) pp. 8–9.
54. Morosawa, *Onna no hataraki*, op. cit. p. 19; Nakamura, *Rōdōsha to nōmin*, op. cit. pp. 87–9.
55. Corrado Molteni, 'The Development of the Silk Reeling Industry in the Process of Japanese Industrialization (1868–1930)', *Rivista Internazionale di Scienze Economiche e Commerciali*, vol. 30, no. 8 (August 1983) p. 745.
56. The most important financial institution for silk filatures in Nagano prefecture between Meiji and early Taishō was the Nineteenth National Bank, which put almost all its efforts into financing the silk industry, especially in the Suwa region. See Yamaguchi, *Nihon sangyō kinyūshi kenkyū*, op. cit. pp. 151 and 180–1.
57. Li, *China's Silk Trade*, op. cit. pp. 182–3.
58. *Chambers's Encyclopedia*, vol. 12, pp. 558–9.
59. Li, *China's Silk Trade*, op. cit. p. 83.
60. Ishii, *Nihon seishigyō shi bunseki*, op. cit. pp. 244–5.
61. Molteni, 'The Development of the Silk Reeling Industry', op. cit. pp. 744–9.
62. Ibid. pp. 751–2.
63. Li, *China's Silk Trade*, op. cit. pp. 163 and 200.
64. Ishii, *Nihon seishigyō shi bunseki*, op. cit. p. 247.

266   *Notes and References*

65. Molteni, 'The Development of the Silk Reeling Industry', op. cit. p. 748 n. 19. International comparisons can only be approximate, owing to differences in standard of living, inflation rate, and so forth.
65. Personal interview with Ishii Kanji, 28 March 1982, Tokyo. Mills producing the highest quality silk thread, such as the Gunze filature in Kyoto, required fewer working hours each day in order to promote quality.
67. W. D. Darby, *Silk, the Queen of Fabrics* (New York: Dry Goods Economist, 1924) p. 17. See also Li, *China's Silk Trade*, op. cit. pp. 83–4.
68. Hutchins, *Labor and Silk*, op. cit. pp. 13–14.
69. Warren P. Seem, *Raw Silk and Throwing* (New York: McGraw-Hill Book Co., 1929) pp. 26–7. The seriplane method of grading rested ultimately on the subjective judgement and honesty of the checker and was not a reliable standard because 'unevenness does not naturally grade itself into seven evenness pictures'.
70. Nakamura, *Rōdōsha to nōmin*, op. cit. p. 85.
71. Ishii, *Nihon seishigyō shi bunseki*, op. cit. pp. 271–8.
72. Preface to Kidd, *Women Workers in the Japanese Cotton Mills*, op. cit. p. xi.
73. Nakamura, *Rōdōsha to nōmin*, op. cit. p. 91. This was known as 'yome iri mae no kuchi berashi' (reducing the number of mouths to feed before getting married).
74. Ibid. See also Ishii, *Nihon seishigyō shi bunseki*, op. cit. pp. 269–70.
75. Hane, *Peasants, Rebels and Outcasts*, op. cit. p. 180.
76. Yanagida, *Japanese Manners and Customs in the Meiji Era*, op. cit. p. 76. Over half of the factory girls surveyed in 1910 did not return home. See Hiroshi Hazama, 'Changes in Life Style of Industrial Workers', op. cit. p. 32 n. 17.
77. Nakamura, *Rōdōsha to nōmin*, op. cit. pp. 83–4. One of Nakamura's informants, who went to work in the filatures at the age of 18, in 1904, married a fellow worker five years later and remained in Suwa. Since she came from a poor mountain village where her parents barely eked out a living cutting wood and cultivating a small paddy field, we can assume that her standard of living improved as a result of being able to remain in the town of Suwa rather than returning to farming.
78. Personal interview, 25 April 1982, Uwa-cho, Higashiuwa-gun, Ehime prefecture.
79. Because the price of silk thread had fallen, wages had also declined, and the workers required loans to help them and their families through the hard times.
80. Yoneda Sayoko, 'Meiji sen-kyūhyaku nen no Kōfu seishi kōjō sōgi ni tsuite – Nihon ni okeru saisho no sutoraiki', *Rekishi hyōron*, 105.5 (May 1959) pp. 70–1 and 78. See also *Nihon fujin mondai shiryō shūsei*, vol. 3: *Rōdō* (Domesu, 1981) pp. 377–8.
81. Kajinishi, *Seishi rōdōsha*, op. cit. pp. 36–9. The working day was increased to 14.5 hours, and the pay for the highest-paid workers was decreased from 32–33 *sen* per day to 22–23 *sen*. See also Mitsui Reiko, *Gendai fujin mondai undōshi nempyō* (San-ichi shobō, 1976) p. 27.

82. *Shimbun shūsei: Meiji hennenshi* (Zaisei keizai gakkai, 1940) vol. 6, p. 289.
83. *Seishi rōdōsha*, op. cit. pp. 36–9.
84. Ishii, *Nihon seishigyō shi bunseki*, op. cit. pp. 356–7.
85. Yoneda, 'Meiji sen-kyūhyakunen no Kōfu seishi kōjō sōgi ni tsuite', op. cit. pp. 71–7.
86. Ibid.
87. Ishii, *Nihon seishigyō shi bunseki*, op. cit. p. 357.
88. Sievers, *Flowers in Salt*, op. cit. p. 64.
89. *Shokkō jijō*, vol. iii, op. cit. pp. 190–1.
90. Gary R. Saxonhouse, 'The Supply of Quality Workers and the Demand for Quality in Jobs in Japan's Early Industrialization', *Explorations in Economic History*, 15, 1 (1978) pp. 45–7.
91. *Shokkō jijō*, op. cit. vol. iii, pp. 182–91.
92. Mitsui, *Gendai fujin mondai undōshi nempyō*, op. cit. p. 71. Other stipulations prohibited children under the age of 12 from working, required two days off each month, outlawed 'dangerous work' and made special provisions for sick or pregnant women. The law was not enacted until 1916.
93. Molteni, 'The Development of the Silk Reeling Industry', op. cit. p. 754 n. 32; Ishii, *Nihon sanshigyōshi bunseki*, op. cit. **p**. 357.
94. Laura Strumingher, *Women and the Making of the Working Class: Lyon 1830–1870* (St Alban's, Vt: Eden Press, 1979) pp. 104–8.
95. Wanda F. Neff, *Victorian Working Women, An Historical and Literary Study of Women in British Industries and Professions, 1832–1850* (London: Frank Cass & Co. Ltd, 1966) pp. 70 ff., and Takamure Naosuke, *Nihon bōsekigyōshi josetsu*, 2 vols (Hanawa shobō, 1980) vol. i, pp. 301 ff.
96. For a discussion of this question, see Saxonhouse, 'Country Girls and Communication Among Competitors in the Japanese Cotton-spinning Industry', op. cit. pp. 97–125. In England production did not decrease after the ten-hour work day was enforced, according to Neff, *Victorian Working Women*, op. cit. p. 74.
97. Strumingher, *Women and the Making of the Working Class*, op. cit. pp. 2 and 7.
98. Nora Lan-Hung Chiang Huang, 'Spatial and Bahavioral Aspects of Rural–Urban Migration – The Case of Female Movement in Taiwan', Research Report (Taiwan: Population Studies Center, National Taiwan University, April 1982) p. 21, quoting Yin Chien-Chung, University of Hawaii unpub. Ph.D. doc. diss., 1975.
99. Sung Jae Koh, *Stages of Industrial Development in Asia, a Comparative History of the Cotton Industry in Japan, India, China, and Korea* (Philadelphia: University of Pennsylvania Press, 1966) p. 64.
100. Mark Fruin, 'Peasant Migrants in the Economic Development of Nineteenth-century Japan', *Agricultural History*, 54.2 (1980) p. 264.
101. Susan B. Hanley and Kozo Yamamura, *Economic and Demographic Change in Preindustrial Japan, 1600–1868* (Princeton, N.J.: Princeton

University Press, 1977) pp. 254–5; and Mark Fruin, 'Peasant Migrants', op. cit. p. 264.

102. Alice Mabel Bacon, *Japanese Girls and Women*, rev. and enlarged ed. (Boston, Mass.: Houghton Mifflin Co., 1902) p. 246.

103. Diane L. Wolf, 'Making the Bread and Bringing it Home, Female Factory Workers and the Family Economy in Rural Java', *Women in the Urban and Industrial Workforce: Southeast and East Asia*, Development Studies Centre Monograph no. 33 (Canberra: The Australian National University, 1984) p. 216.

104. Ibid. p. 219.

5 Tenkō and Thought Control

1. The research for this paper was supported by an NDEA-related Fulbright–Hays fellowship, intramural grants from the University of Hawaii and its Center for Asian and Pacific Studies, and a grant from the University of Hawaii Japan Endowment Fund, which is funded by a gift from the Japanese government.

2. For detailed analyses of thought-control policies see Lawrence Ward Beer, *Freedom of Expression in Japan* (Kodansha International Ltd, 1984); Richard H. Mitchell, *Censorship in Imperial Japan* (Princeton, N.J.: Princeton University Press, 1983); and Richard H. Mitchell, *Thought Control in Prewar Japan* (Ithaca, N.Y.: Cornell University Press, 1976).

3. Ikeda Katsu, *Chian iji hō*, in *Shin hōgaku zenshū* (Nihon hyōronsha, 1939) vol. xix, p. 24.

4. A departmental directive of 16 May 1928, outlining the duties of thought procurators, is reprinted in Shihōshō, keiji-kyoku, *Shisō jimu ni kansuru kunrei tsūchōshū*, in *Shisō kenkyū shiryō tokushū*, vol. xxi (May, 1935).

5. Data from Shihōshō, keijikyoku, *Chian iji hō ihan jiken no saihan ni kansuru kenkyū*, in *Shisō kenkyū shiryō tokushū*, vol. xlvi (December 1938), pp. 20–1.

6. Figures taken from a mimeographed table produced by the Thought Bureau, Criminal Affairs Division, Ministry of Justice, 9 March 1935. It is reproduced in Shakai bunko (ed.), *Shōwaki kanken shisō chōsa hōkoku* (Kashiwa shōbō, 1965) p. 3. The total used in this table is persons against whom charges were entertained, which already represents a 15 per cent reduction from the total number of persons arrested.

7. Calculated from data in Shihōsho, keiji-kyoku, *Chian iji hō ihan jiken no saihan ni kansuru kenkyū*. For a more complete discussion of these administrative practices see Patricia G. Steinhoff, 'The Legal Control of Ideology in Prewar Japan', paper presented at the 1970 Congress of Orientalists, Canberra, Australia.

8. See W. Allyn Rickett, 'Voluntary Surrender and Confession in Chinese Law: The Problem of Continuity', *Journal of Asian Studies*, vol. xxx, no. 4 (August 1971).

9. The official orders and forms for these requirements are reprinted in Shihōshō, *Shisō jimu ni kansuru kunrei tsūchōshū*, op. cit.

10. Mizuno Shigeo, 'Nihon kyōsantō dattai ni saishi tōin shokun ni "kansō".' Mimeographed manuscript, 23 May 1929.

11. Shihōshō, keiji-kyoku, *Shisō jimu ni kansuru kunrei tsūchōshū*, op. cit. pp. 118–19, contains a directive from the July 1931 Thought Procurators' conference entitled 'Item concerning weighing the offense of the JCP Kaitōha defendants and inspection policy for group organization of said faction'. (my translation).

12. Nabeyama Sadachika, *Watakushi wa kyōsantō o suteta* (Taitō shuppansha, 1949) pp. 145–60.

13. Gail Lee Bernstein, *Japanese Marxist, A Portrait of Kawakami Hajime, 1879–1946* (Cambridge, Mass.: Harvard University Press, 1976) p. 163.

14. Figures for 1933 from Yamamoto Katsunosuke and Arita Mitsuho, *Nihon kyōsanshugi undōshi* (Seiki shōbō, 1950) p. 382; for 1934 from Shakai keizai rōdō kenkyūjo, *Kindai nihon rōdōsha undōshi* (Hakurinsha, 1947) p. 137; and for 1936 from Takabatake Michitoshi 'Ikkoku shakai shugisha', in *Tenkō*, ed. Shisō no kagaku kenkyūkai, ɪ (Heibonsha, 1959) p. 192.

15. Chief Administrator of Prisons, Directive No. 1731, December 1933. Reprinted in Shihōshō, *Shisō jimu ni kansuru kunrei tsūchōshū*, pp. 178–9.

16. See Tosawa Shigeo, 'Shisō hanzai no kensatsu jitsumu ni tsuite', reprinted in *Shakai shugi undō*, III, *Gendai shi shiryō*, vol, xvi (Misuzu shobō, 1965).

17. The process of *tenkō* is analysed in detail in Patricia G. Steinhoff, *Tenkō: Ideology and Societal Integration in Prewar Japan* (Ann Arbor, Mich.: University Microfilms, 1971) ch. 4.

18. Germaine Hoston, '*Tenkō*: Marxism and the National Question in Prewar Japan', *Polity*, Autumn 1983; and Shisō no kagaku kenkyūkai (ed.), *Tenkō*, 3 vols (Heibonsha, 1959).

19. Matsuzawa Hiroaki argues for a different sort of emotional response linked directly to the organisational structure of the Party. See his '"Theory" and "Organization" in the Japan Communist Party', trans. J. Victor Koschmann, in J. Victor Koschmann (ed.), *Authority and the Individual in Japan* (University of Tokyo Press, 1978) pp. 108–27.

20. See Takeshi Ishida, 'Conflict and its Accommodation', in Ellis S. Krauss, Thomas P. Rohlen and Patricia G. Steinhoff (eds), *Conflict in Japan* (Honolulu: University Press of Hawaii, 1984), for a succinct description of this social structure.

21. For fuller documentation of the types of *tenkō* outlined below see Steinhoff, *Tenkō*, op. cit. ch. 5.

22. See ibid. ch. 6.

23. Tokuda Kyūichi and Shiga Yoshio, *Gokuchū jūhachinen* (Jiji tsūshinsha, 1947).

6 The 1960s' Japanese Student Movement in Retrospect

1. Parts of this chapter were taken from 'Marxism and the 1960 Anpo Students: Ideology Revisited', presented at the 1971 Western Conference of the Association for Asian Studies and 'Japanese Student Protesters and Movements: Theoretical and Comparative Perspectives', presented at the 1981 Association for Asian Studies Annual Meeting. I should like to thank Gail Lee Bernstein for her comments and suggestions on the original version of the 1971 paper, and Patricia G. Steinhoff and the other participants on the 1981 panel for their feedback on the latter paper. As always, I owe a great debt of gratitude to Professor Kazuko Tsurumi of Sophia University, whose work first stimulated my interest in the student movement and who so generously enabled me to do my research on former students in 1969–70.

2. Robert A. Scalapino and Junnosuke Masumi, *Parties and Politics in Contemporary Japan* (Berkeley and Los Angeles, Calif.: University of California Press, 1962) p. 1.

3. See George R. Packard III, *Protest in Tokyo* (Princeton, N.J.: Princeton University Press, 1966) passim, for a description of the major role of students in the movement and its important events.

4. For example, see Nishibe Susumu, 'Rokujūnen Anpo: Senchimentaru Jyānī', *Shokun*, July 1985.

5. See Patricia G. Steinhoff, 'Student Conflict', in Ellis S. Krauss, Thomas C. Rohlen and Patricia G. Steinhoff (eds), *Conflict in Japan* (Honolulu: University of Hawaii Press, 1984) pp. 174–213; and David E. Apter, *Against the State: Politics and Social Protest in Japan* (Cambridge, Mass.: Harvard University Press, 1984).

6. In my *Japanese Radicals Revisited: Student Protest in Postwar Japan* (Berkeley, Calif.: University of California Press, 1974) I found that at least as of 1970, most former leaders and activists of the 1960 movement that I interviewed had not 'converted' to the right.

7. The following portrait of 1960 Anpo students is based upon Kazuko Tsurumi, *Social Change and the Individual: Japan Before and After Defeat in World War II* (Princeton, N.J.: Princeton University Press, 1970) chs ix, x and xi; Kazuko Tsurumi, 'Student Movements in 1960 and 1969: Continuity and Change', Research Paper (Series A–5) of the Institute of International Relations, Sophia University, n.d.; Robert Lifton, 'Youth and History: Individual Change in Postwar Japan', in Erik H. Erikson (ed.), *The Challenge of Youth* (Garden City, N.Y.: Anchor Books, 1965); and Ellis S. Krauss, *Japanese Radicals Revisited*, op. cit. chs 2 and 3.

8. On family backgrounds and politicisation in adolescence see especially Krauss, *Japanese Radicals Revisited*, op. cit. chs 2 and 3.

9. Lifton, 'Youth and History', op. cit.

10. Tsurumi, 'Student Movements in 1960 and 1969', op. cit. p. 14.

11. Ibid. pp. 13–15.

12. See Takahashi Akira, 'Nihon gakusei undō no shisō to kōdō', *Chūō Kōron* (May, June, August 1968); and Tsurumi, 'Student Movements in 1960 and 1969', op. cit.

13. Tsurumi, op. cit. pp. 33–6.
14. Ibid.
15. Otto Klineberg, Marisa Zavalloni, Christiane Louis-Guérin and Jeanne BenBrika, *Students, Values, and Politics: A Cross-Cultural Comparison* (New York: The Free Press, 1979).
16. Ibid. p. 108.
17. Ibid. pp. 146 and 174.
18. Ibid. pp. 121 and 135.
19. Ibid. pp. 81 and 95.
20. See Krauss, *Japanese Radicals Revisited* op. cit.; and Tsurumi, *Social Change and the Individual*, op. cit.
21. Ibid. especially ch. 4.
22. These findings in Japan, incidentally, are very similar to those of follow-up studies conducted by James Fendrich on southern civil rights activists of the early 1960s in the US. See Ellis S. Krauss and James M. Fendrich, 'The Adult Political Identification and Behavior of Former Student Activists: A Comparative Study of Japanese and White and Black Americans', *The Japan Interpreter*, vol. xi, no. 3 (Winter 1977).
23. These factions include the 'Bund' (Communist League), Revolutionary Communist League, Socialist Student League, Socialist Youth League, Democratic Youth League, Structural Reform, Anti-Mainstream and Yoyogi.
24. Aside from the two leaders quoted above, at least three others have gone on to graduate school, become interested in quantitative economics and rejected Marxism. Two of the three came to the USA for advanced study. One died in a tragic fire at the University of Pennsylvania, the other taught at Harvard. The remaining example received his Ph.D. from Tokyo University. See Tachibana Takashi, 'Rokujū anpo eiyū no eikō to hisan', *Bungei Shunjū*, xlvii, 2, Feb. 1969, p. 250; Mainichi Shinbun Shakaibu, *Anpo: Gekidō no kono jūnen* (Bungei Shunjū, 1969) pp. 12–13.
25. Ronald Inglehart, 'The Silent Revolution in Europe: Intergenerational Change in Post-Industrial Societies', *American Political Science Review*, vol. 65 (December 1971) pp. 991–1017.
26. Scott C. Flanagan, 'Value Change and Partisan Change in Japan: The Silent Revolution Revisited', *Comparative Politics* (April 1979).
27. Nobutaka Ike, 'Economic Growth and Intergenerational Change in Japan', *American Political Science Review*, vol. 67 (December 1973).
28. I define 'postindustrial' society as one in which a high level of affluence has been attained, mass higher education has been expanded, communications and 'knowledge-intensive' industry are important and the once Utopian ideals of equality, abundance and personal and political freedom have been legitimised and at least partially achieved.
29. For the role of government in creating the fractionalisation and extremism of the student movement in the 1970s and more on the process by which this takes place, see Steinhoff, 'Student Conflict', op. cit.
30. Ike, 'Economic Growth and Intergenerational Change in Japan', p. 1202, citing Masao Maruyama, 'Patterns of Individuation and the Case of Japan: A Conceptual Scheme', in Marius B. Jansen (ed.), *Changing*

Japanese Attitudes Toward Modernization (Princeton, N.J.: Princeton University Press, 1965).

31. Ike, op. cit. pp. 1196–7. Ike also sees youth rebellion in the West as antithetical to the tradition of individualism, because it takes the form of a search for collectivity, while in Japan the rebellion is against the tradition of collectivism and thus takes individualistic forms. See p. 1203.
32. On *tenkō* see Tsurumi, *Social Change and the Individual*, op. cit.

7 Electoral Laws and the Japanese Party System

* In preparing this chapter I received generous assistance particularly from two colleagues. Professor Banno Junji of the University of Tokyo Institute of Social Science not only lent me the original copy of his Master's thesis on electoral laws and party politics in mid-Meiji Japan, but also drew my attention to Minobe Tatsukichi's 1930 article on a related topic. Dr William D. Hyder of my department at the University of California, Santa Barbara, did all the computation used in the statistical analysis in the latter part of the chapter and also prepared all the appended figures. I am deeply grateful to both friends for their assistance.

1. See Maurice Duverger, *Political Parties* (New York: John Wiley & Sons, 1954).
2. Stein Rokkan, *Citizens, Elections, Parties* (New York: David McKay Co., 1970); and Vernon Bogdanor and David E. Butler (eds), *Democracy and Elections: Electoral Systems and Their Political Consequences* (Cambridge: Cambridge University Press, 1983). See also Seymour M. Lipset and Stein Rokkan (eds), *Party Systems and Voter Alignments: Cross-national Perspectives* (New York: Free Press, 1967); and Leslie Lipson, *The Democratic Civilization* (New York: Oxford University Press, 1964).
3. Bo Särlvik, 'Scandinavia', in Bogdanor and Butler, *Democracy and Elections*, op. cit. p. 123.
4. Bogdanor, 'Conclusions', in Bogdanor and Butler, *Democracy and Elections*, op. cit. p. 261.
5. See Douglas W. Rae, *The Political Consequences of Electoral Laws* (New Haven, Conn.: Yale University Press, 1967) p. 138.
6. Ibid. pp. 70–3, 134.
7. Ibid. p. 138.
8. Ibid. pp. 114–7.
9. For relevant statistics see tables in ibid. pp. 121, 123.
10. For explanations of the different PR formulae see ibid. pp. 28–30, 36–8. For explanations of the particular electoral formulae used, currently or in the past, by twenty-four democracies, see the introductory remarks preceding each country section and appendix A in Thomas T. Mackie and Richard Rose, *The International Almanac of Electoral History*, 2nd ed. (New York: Facts on File Inc., 1982).
11. Rae, *The Political Consequences*, op. cit. pp. 23–8.

12. Richard Rose, 'Elections and Electoral Systems: Choices and Alternatives', in Bogdanor and Butler, *Democracy and Elections*, op. cit. p. 41.
13. See Robert A. Newland, *Comparative Electoral Systems* (London: Faber & Faber, 1982) p. 33.
14. Enid Lakeman, *How Democracies Vote: A Study of Majority and Proportional Electoral Systems*, 4th ed. (London: Faber & Faber, 1970) p. 86.
15. See Rose, 'Elections and Electoral Systems', in Bogdanor and Butler, *Democracy and Elections*, op. cit. p. 33; and Arthur S. Banks and William Overstreet (eds), *Political Handbook of the World 1982–1983* (New York: McGraw-Hill Book Co., 1983) p. 453.
16. On the element of uncertainty see ibid. pp. 80–4, and on the Japanese gerrymander see J. A. A. Stockwin, 'Japan', in Bogdanor and Butler, *Democracy and Elections*, op. cit. p. 219, and *Japan: Divided Politics in a Growth Economy*, 2nd ed. (London: Weidenfeld & Nicolson, 1982) pp. 108–14.
17. See Shūgiin and Sangiin (eds), *Gikai seido shichijūnen-shi: shiryō-hen* (Okurashō insatsu-kyoku, 1962) p. 196.
18. See Umetani Noboru, *Oyatoi gaikokujin: seiji hōsei* (Kajima kenkyūjo shuppankai, 1971) pp. 84–5.
19. Ibid. p. 202.
20. Shūgiin and Sangiin, *Gikai seido shichijūnen-shi: shiryō-hen*, op. cit. pp. 204–5.
21. Ibid. pp. 209–10.
22. Mackie and Rose, *The International Almanac*, op. cit. p. 366.
23. Peter Pulzer, 'Germany', in Bogdanor and Butler, *Democracy and Elections*, op. cit. pp. 84–5.
24. Eda Sagarra, *An Introduction to Nineteenth Century Germany* (Burnt Mill, Harlow, Essex: Longman, 1980) pp. 145–6.
25. Hugo Preuss quoted in Koppel S. Pinson, *Modern Germany: Its History and Civilization*, 2nd ed. (New York: Macmillan, 1966) pp. 159–60.
26. Sagarra, *An Introduction*, op. cit. pp. 145–6.
27. See Max Beloff and Gillian Peele, *The Government of the United Kingdom: Political Authority in a Changing Society* (New York and London: W. H. Norton, 1980) p. 130.
28. Lakeman, *How Democracies Vote*, op. cit. pp. 80–4.
29. William Harbutt Dawson, *The German Empire 1867–1914 and the Unity Movement*, reprint ed. (Hamden, Conn.: Archon Books, 1966) vol. 1, p. 388. The second-ballot system, however, was not a German invention but was borrowed from the French, whose experience and ideas also influenced the authors of the 1889 Japanese electoral law. France under the Third Republic (1870–1940) used either single-member constituencies (*scrutin d'arrondissement*) with the second-ballot or multi-member constituencies (*scrutin de liste*) with a majority formula and with or without the second ballot. Incidentally, Italy, too, used the second ballot in single-member constituencies in the election of its Chamber of Deputies during much of the period between 1861, when it was unified, and 1919. See Lakeman, *How Democracies Vote*, op. cit. pp. 200, 206–7.

30. Shūgiin and Sangiin, *Gikai seido shichijūnen-shi: shiryō-hen*, op. cit. pp. 197, 223.
31. See Yamagata's statement of 19 December 1899 before the House of Representatives in Shūgiin and Sangiin, *Gikai seido shichijūnen-shi: shiryō-hen*, op. cit. p. 218.
32. See Ichiki Kitokurō's statement in ibid. p. 220.
33. Shūgiin and Sangiin, *Gikai seido shichijūnen-shi: shiryō-hen*, op. cit. p. 219.
34. On relevant developments see Masumi Junnosuke, *Nihon seitōshi ron*, vol. 2 (Tokyo daigaku shuppankai, 1966) chs 5 and 6.
35. See Shūgiin and Sangiin, *Gikai seido shichijūnen-shi: shiryō-hen*, op. cit. pp. 232–3, 236.
36. Ibid. p. 239.
37. Ishikawa Masumi, *Sengo seitō kōzōshi* (Nihon hyōronsha, 1978) p. 18.
38. See T. A. Bisson, *Prospects for Democracy in Japan* (New York: Macmillan, 1949) pp. 57–8.
39. See statements by Minister of State Horikiri Zenjirō, Chairman Kiyose Ichirō of the House of Representatives committee in charge of the bill, and House of Peers member, Count Hayashi Hirotarō in *Shūgiin and Sangiin, Gikai seido shichijūnen-shi: shiryō-hen*, pp. 279–82, 285–6.
40. Nishihira Shigeki (ed.), *Naigai senkyo dēta* ('78 Mainichi nenkan bessatsu) (Mainichi shimbunsha, 1978) pp. 3, 11. See also Sakagami Nobuo, *Nihon senkyo seido ron* (Seiji Kōhō Sentā, 1972) pp. 166–7. .
41. On such attempts under the Hatoyama Cabinet in 1956 and the Tanaka Cabinet in 1973 see ibid. pp. 169–70, and Masumi Junnosuke, *Gendai seiji: 1955-nen igo*, vol. 1 (Tokyo daigaku shuppankai, 1985) pp. 229–31.
42. See Rae, *The Political Consequences*, op. cit. pp. 56–7.
43. The average vote and seat shares won by the largest two parties are not given in the table because the rank order of these shares was found to be identical with that of the shares won by the largest parties alone.
44. See Kōmei Senkyo Renmei (ed.), *Shūgiingiin senkyo no jisseki: dai l-kai–dai 30–kai* (Kōmei senkyo renmei, 1967) pp. 53–4, 123–4.
45. For an introductory explanation of the method see Michael S. Lewis-Beck, *Applied Regression: An Introduction* (Sage University Paper, 22; Series: Quantitative Applications in the Social Sciences) (Beverly Hills: Sage Publications, 1980).
46. Bogdanor, 'Conclusion: Electoral Systems and Party Systems', in Bogdanor and Butler, *Democracy and Elections*, op. cit. p. 251.
47. See, *inter alia*, Scott C. Flanagan, 'Voting Behavior in Japan: The Persistence of Traditional Patterns', *Comparative Political Studies*, i (1968) pp. 399–410. See also his 'National and Local Voting Trends: Cross-level Linkages and Correlates of Change', in Kurt Steiner, Ellis S. Krauss and Scott C. Flanagan (eds), *Political Opposition and Local Politics in Japan* (Princeton, N.J.: Princeton University Press, 1980) pp. 153–72.
48. Minobe Tatsukichi, *Gendai kensei hyōron: Senkyo kakuseiron sonota* (Iwanami shoten, 1930) pp. 13–15. See also pp. 36–7. I am indebted to Professor Banno Junji for drawing my attention to this most valuable source.

49. For a more complete account of the relevant developments see Shūgiin and Sangiin (eds), *Gikai seido shichijūnen-shi: Seitō kaiha-hen* (Okurashō insatsu-kyoku, 1961).

50. For a recent discussion of the LDP factions see Haruhiro Fukui, 'The Liberal Democratic Party Revisited: Continuity and Change in the Party's Structure and Performance', *The Journal of Japanese Studies*, Summer 1984, pp. 397–407.

8 The Institutionalisation of Policy Consultation in Japan

1. Samuel P. Huntington, *Political Order in Changing Societies* (New Haven, Conn.: Yale University Press, 1969) pp. 12, 18, 20 and 22.

2. For a bibliography on policy consultation in North America, Western Europe, Australia, Israel and Japan see Ehud Harari, 'Turnover and Autonomy in Japanese Permanent Public Advisory Bodies', *Journal of Asian and African Studies* (Leiden) vol. xvii, nos 3–4 (1982) pp. 246–9; and 'Policy Concertation in Japan', *Occasional Paper*, no. 58/59 East Asian Institute, Free University of Berlin (Berlin: Verlag Ute Schiller, 1986).

3. *Gekkan seifu shiryō*, no. 3, pp. 127–30. The most recent unofficial estimate, based on a survey of the private ABs mentioned in the daily newspapers from January 1984 to September 1985, is 299. The official and unofficial estimates are mentioned in Sone Yasunori, 'Yarase no seiji: shingikai hōshiki o kenshō suru', *Chūō kōron* (January 1986) p. 151.

4. *Shingikai sōran* (Okurashō insatsukyoku, 1983).

5. Murakami Naofumi, 'Hōsei shingikai no kikō to ninmu', *Jurisuto*, no. 510 (15 July 1972) p. 18; Byron K. Marshall, 'Professors and Politics: The Meiji Academic Élite', *Journal of Japanese Studies*, vol. 3, no. 1 (Winter 1977) pp. 82–4.

6. Iwao F. Ayusawa, *A History of Labor in Modern Japan* (Honolulu: East West Center Press, 1966) pp. 106–11; Sumiya Mikio, *Nihon rōdō undō shi* (Yūshindō, 1966) pp. 84–7; Ronald P. Dore, 'The Modernizer as a Special Case: Japanese Factory Legislation 1882–1911', *Comparative Studies in Society and History*, vol. 2, no. 4 (October 1969) pp. 433–50; Koji Taira, *Economic Development and the Labor Market in Japan* (New York: Columbia University Press, 1970) pp. 90–2, 135–7; Kenneth B. Pyle, 'Advantages of Followership: German Economics and Japanese Bureaucrats, 1840–1925', *Journal of Japanese Studies*, vol. 1, no. 1 (Autumn 1974) pp. 149–50.

7. Marshall, 'Professors and Politics', op. cit. pp. 81–2.

8. Rōdōshō (ed.), *Rōdō gyōsei shi* (Rōdō hōrei kenkyūkai, 1961), op. cit. vol. i, pp. 9–10; Ikeda Akira, *Nihonteki kyōchōshugi no seiritsu: Shakai seisaku shisō shi kenkyū* (Keibunsha, 1982) pp. 22–30.

9. Kishimoto Eitarō, *Nihon rōdō seisaku sōshi* (Yūhikaku, 1948) pp. 102–4; Morita Yoshio, *Nihon keieisha dantai hatten shi* (Nikkan rōdō tsūshin-sha, 1958) pp. 124–31, 423–69; Rōdōshō, *Rōdō gyōsei shi*, op. cit. pp. 430 ff.; Ikeda, *Nikonteki kyōchōshugi*, op. cit. pp. 48–66; Robert A.

Scalapino, *The Labor Movement in Prewar Japan* (Berkeley, Calif.: Institute of Asian Studies, 1985).

10. Ronald P. Dore, *Land Reform in Japan* (London: Oxford University Press, 1959) pp. 80–1; Ann Waswo, *Japanese Landlords: The Decline of a Rural Élite* (Berkeley, Calif.: University of California Press, 1977) pp. 118–23.

11. Harada Tomohiko, 'Dōwa gyōzaisei no enkaku to sono seikaku' in Isomura Eiichi (ed.), *Dōwa gyōsei ron* (Akashi shoten, 1983) vol. i, p. 54.

12. Chalmers Johnson, *MITI and the Japanese Miracle* (Stanford, Calif.: Stanford University Press, 1982) pp. 102 ff.

13. Ide Yoshinori, *Nihon kanryōsei to nihon bunka: nihon gyōsei kokka ron* (Tokyo daigaku shuppankai, 1982) pp. 81–2.

14. Ibid. 82–90; Tanaka Tokihiko, 'Okada naikaku', in Hayashi Shigeru and Tsuji Kiyoaki (eds), *Nihon naikaku shi roku* (Daiichi hōki shuppan, 1981) pp. 359–64; Johnson, *MITI*, op. cit. pp. 123–6.

15. Ide, *Nihon kanryōsei to nihon bunka*, op. cit. p. 82.

16. Shōkō Gyōsei Shingikai (ed.), *Shōkōshō yōran* (Shōkō gyōsei sha, 1941) pp. 79–154, cited in Chalmers Johnson, *Japan's Public Policy Companies* (Washington, D.C.: American Enterprise Institute, 1978) p. 66, n. 7.

17. In addition to the sources referred to above, see *Asahi Shimbun*, 30 December 1952 and 17 December 1956; Satō Tatsuo 'Iinkai, shingikai kinmu hyōtei', *Sankei shimbun*, 20 February 1961; Rōdōshō, *Rōdō gyōsei shi*, op. cit. p. 682; Rinji Gyōsei Chōsakai, 'Tōshin', *Jichi kenkyū*, vol. 40, no. 11 (October 1964) p. 87; Katō Kazuaki, 'Shingikai ni tsuite', *Toshi mondai kenkyū*, vol. 23, no. 4 (April 1971) p. 45; Miyoshi Shigeo, 'Shingikai seido ni kansuru shomondai', *Toshi mondai kenkyū*, vol. 23, no. 4 (April 1971) p. 39; Abe Hitoshi, 'Shingikai seido no suii', *Chiiki kaihatsu*, no. 160 (January 1978) pp. 8–14; Kawaguchi Hiroshi, 'Shingikai seido ron no hensen', *Chiiki kaihatsu*, no. 161 (February 1978) p. 32; Satō Atsushi, 'Shingikai no yakuwari', *Chiiki kaihatsu*, no. 160 (January 1978) p. 3; Ogita Tamotsu, 'Chihō seido chōsakai no ayumi', in Nihon Gyōsei Gakkai (ed.), *Chihō jichi no sanjūnen* (Gyōsei, 1979) pp. 39–40; Ide, *Nihon kanryōsei*, op. cit. pp. 77–82; Johnson, *MITI*, op. cit. p. 166; Shindō Muneyuki, 'Seisaku kettei no shisutemu: shingikai – shimon kikan – shinku tanku no yakuwari', *Jurisuto*, no. 29 (January 1984) pp. 246–51; Sheldon M. Garon, 'The Imperial Bureaucracy and Labor Policy in Postwar Japan', *Journal of Asian Studies*, vol. xliii, no. 3 (May 1984) pp. 441–57; Ernest J. Notar, 'Japan's Wartime Labor Policy; A Search for Method', *Journal of Asian Studies*, vol. 24, no. 2 (February 1985) pp. 311–28.

18. Article 8 of the National Government Organisation Law, passed 10 July 1948, came into effect 1 June 1949.

19. A legislative package regarding ABs came into effect on 1 June 1951. See Rinji Gyōsei Chōsakai, 'Tōshin', p. 87; Gyōsei Kanrichō (ed.), *Gyōsei kanrichō no nijūnen shi* (Daiichi hōki shuppan K.K., 1973) pp. 68–89, 643–65.

20. Philip H. Trezise and Yukio Suzuki, 'Politics, Government and Economic Growth in Japan', in Hugh Patrick and Henry Rosovsky (eds), *Asia's New Giant: How the Japanese Economy Works* (Washington,

Notes and References   277

D.C.: The Brookings Institution, 1976) p. 769. For unqualified rejection of their argument see Johnson, *Public Policy Companies*, op. cit. pp. 65–6, n. 7.

21. For review of the major arguments of these studies see Kawaguchi, 'Shingikai seido', op. cit. pp. 27–32.
22. Especially Ebata Kiyoshi, 'Kore ga seifu shingikai da', *Jiyū*, August 1965, pp. 131–41.
23. Very good summaries in English appear in Yung Ho Park, 'The Governmental Advisory Commission System in Japan', *Journal of Comparative Administration*, vol. 3, no. 4 (February 1972) pp. 435–57; T. J. Pempel, 'The Bureaucratization of Policymaking in Postwar Japan', *American Journal of Political Science*, vol. 28, no. 4 (November 1974) pp. 656–62; and T. J. Pempel, *Patterns of Japanese Policymaking* (Boulder, Colo.: Westview Press, 1978) pp. 68–74.
24. Gyōsei Kanrichō, *Gyōsei kanrichō; Jiji shimbun*, 10 February 1951.
25. See n. 3.
26. *Asahi Shimbun*, May 23, 1957, editorial; Ebata, 'Kore ga seifu shingikai da', p. 165; Hayashi Shūzō, in 'Zadankai: Shingikai', *Jurisuto*, no. 510 (15 July 1972) p. 39.
27. For example, *Yomiuri shimbun*, op. cit. 3 May 1967.
28. See, for example, the special issues of *Chiiki kaihatsu*, no. 160 (January 1978) pp. 1–20 and vol. 161 (February 1978) pp. 1–151, and of *Zaikai tembō*, vol. 23, no. 12 (December 1979) pp. 56–102; also James Elliott, 'The 1981 Administrative Reform in Japan', *Asian Survey*, vol. 23, no. 6 (June 1983) pp. 765–79.
29. For analyses of these changes see Ōtake Hideo, *Gendai nihon no seiji kenryoku keizai kenryoku* (San'ichi shobō, 1979); Muramatsu Michio, *Sengo nihon no kanryōsei* (Tōyō keizai shimpōsha, 1981); Inoguchi Takashi, *Gendai nihon seiji keizai no kōzu: seifu to shijō* (Tōyō keizai shimpōsha, 1983); Satō Seizaburō and Matsuzaki Tsunehisa, 'Jimintō kōchōki seiken no kaibō', *Chūō kōron*, November 1984, pp. 66–100.
30. This summary is based on: (a) an aggregate data analysis of *shingikai*'s structure and membership composition. The data were generated from published *shingikai* membership lists, primarily *Shingikai sōran* and *Shokuinroku*; various *Who's Who*, such as *Jinji kōshinroku* and *Asahi nenkan bessatsu*; and published lists of business firms, *tokushu hōjin*, labour unions, etc.; (b) analysis of 693 responses to a questionnaire I mailed in December 1974 to members of *shingikai* (response rate 35 per cent); (c) case studies conducted by others and myself in several policy areas; and (d) recent analyses of various aspects of the advisory system (Muramatsu, *Sengo nihon no kanryōsei*; Tanaka Yoshitaka, 'Rōdō kumiai to kanchō to no kankei', *Hōgaku seminā zōkan: kanchō to kanryō*, no. 23 (August 1983) pp. 237–45; Shindō, 'Seisaku kettei no shisutemu', op. cit.; and William G. Ouchi, *The M-Form Society* (Reading, Mass.: Addison-Wesley, 1984).
31. The most notable example of the latter is the formation in 1979 of the National Land (Kokudo) Shingikai, merging 13 out of the 19 *shingikai* then in existence in the National Land Agency. Of these 13, 8 were concerned with the development of particular regions, 4 with areas

sharing a certain characteristic (mountainous areas, for example) and 1 with the development of local industries. *Shingikai sōran*, op. cit. 1975, 1979; Satō Hidetaka, 'Shingikai seido kaikaku to kokuminteki kadai', *Keizai*, no. 174 (October 1978) pp. 68–74.

32. Sone, 'Yarase no seiji', op. cit. p. 150.
33. Sone, 'Yarase no seiji', p. 150; Uenishi Akio, 'Burēn seiji' (Kōdansha, 1985); *Asahi shimbun* (morning), 12 December 1985, p. 2.
34. These include public corporations and national enterprises, even before the recent privatisation of two of the three public corporations – the mammoth Denden Kōsha (NTT) and the Senbai Kōsha (Public Monopoly Corporation).
35. It should be pointed out, however, that bureaucrats screen information whenever they deem fit and can get away with it. See, for example, the newspaper report to the effect that bureaucrats of the Economic Planning Agency refused to comply with requests for information by the drafting subcommittee of Nakasone's Maekawa study group mentioned earlier, arguing that the requested information would have embarrassing repercussions for Japan's international relations. *Asahi shimbun* (morning), 8 April 1986, p. 3.
36. For one vivid account of these developments see Ronald P. Dore, 'A Case of Technological Forecasting in Japan' (London: Technical Change Centre, 1983, mimeo).
37. James C. March and John P. Olsen, 'The New Institutionalization: Organisational Factors in Political Life', *American Political Science Review*, vol. 78, no. 3 (September 1984) p. 739.
38. Muramatsu, *Sengo nihon no kanryōsei*, op. cit. p. 125. His discussion, however, reveals that he holds the widespread view of *shingikai* as being largely the handmaiden of the bureaucracy. See pp. 126–8.
39. *Nihon no rōshi kankei* (annual) (Nihon rōdō kyōkai, 1984) pp. 80–1.
40. About 'sub-governments' in Japan see John C. Campbell, 'Policy Conflict and its Resolution within the Government System', in Ellis S. Krauss *et al.* (eds), *Conflict in Japan* (Honolulu: University of Hawaii Press, 1984) pp. 294–334.
41. Two notable exceptions, the recent shift to deficit financing and the growing dissatisfaction with various features of the education system, have been studied by the Second Rinchō and the Education Rinchō respectively.
42. For example, Muramatsu, *Sengo nihon no kanryōsei*, op. cit. p. 128.
43. Thomas J. Cartwright, *Royal Commissions and Departmental Committees in Britain: A Case Study in Institutional Adaptiveness and Public Participation in Government* (London: Hodder & Stoughton, 1975).
44. Rune Premfors, 'Governmental Commissions in Sweden', *American Behavioral Scientist*, vol. 26, no. 5 (May/June 1983) pp. 623–42.
45. Michael Cardozo, 'The Federal Advisory Committee Act in Operation', *Administrative Law Review*, vol. 33, no. 1 (Winter 1981) pp. 1–62.

9 Japanese Politics

1. See J. A. A. Stockwin, 'Japan', in Vernon Bogdanor and David Butler (eds), *Democracy and Elections: Electoral Systems and Their Political Consequences* (Cambridge: Cambridge University Press, 1983).
2. For a comprehensive discussion of parties in Japan, see 'Nihon no seitō', *Jurisuto sōgō tokushū*, no. 35 (Summer 1984).
3. David Apter and Nagayo Sawa, *Against the State: Politics and Social Protest in Japan* (Cambridge, Mass., and London: Harvard University Press, 1984).
4. Margaret A. McKean, *Environmental Protest and Citizen Politics in Japan* (Berkeley and Los Angeles, Calif., and London: California University Press, 1981).
5. T. J. Pempel, *Policy and Politics in Japan: Creative Conservatism* (Philadelphia: Temple University Press, 1982).
6. For recent works on foreign and defence policy see J. W. M. Chapman, R. Drifte and I. T. M. Gow, *Japan's Quest for Comprehensive Security: Defence, Diplomacy and Dependence* (London: Frances Pinter, 1983), and Robert S. Ozaki and Walter Arnold (eds), *Japan's Foreign Relations: A Global Search for Security* (Boulder, Colo., and London: Westview Press, 1985).

10 The Impact of Domestic Politics on Japan's Foreign Policy

1. An earlier version of this paper was presented at the Nitobe–Ohira Memorial Conference, held 22–25 May 1984, at Vancouver, Canada. I wish to thank the Japan Foundation and the Social Science and Humanities Research Council for their financial support of this research project. Thanks are also due to Dr Frank Langdon for his critical comments on the earlier draft of the manuscript.
2. The first LDP primary was introduced in 1978. The JSP had its first membership ratification of a leadership race in 1977.
3. See Kosakai Shōzō, *Jimintō sōsaisen* (Kadokawa shoten, 1982).
4. For details see Hong N. Kim, 'The Fukuda Government and Politics of the Sino-Japanese Peace Treaty', *Asian Survey*, vol. xix, no. 3 (March 1979) pp. 297–313.
5. For example, in the 1983 pre-election survey the public ranked the importance of foreign affairs seventh among the ten items they wanted the government to work harder on. The percentage of the respondents who placed emphasis on different types of issues were: cost of living 24 per cent; less taxation 24 per cent; welfare 17 per cent; external affairs 7 per cent.
6. *Japan Times Weekly*, 24 December 1983, p. 4.
7. *Asahi shimbun*, 1 February 1984.
8. See the JCP 1979 campaign booklet, *Sōsenkyo no sōten to nippon kyōsantō no seisaku*. See also Maitani Ichiro, *Shin daitōa kyōeiken*

hiteiron (Aki shobō, 1970) for an earlier criticism of the LDP's Asia policy.

9. Chitoshi Yanaga, *Big Business in Japanese Politics* (New Haven, Conn.: Yale University Press, 1968) p. 148.
10. Watanabe Ryōichi, 'Sengo nihon keizai seisaku bunseki', in *Gendai keizai kōza* (Chikuma shobō, 1968) pp. 212–44.
11. Yoshida Shigeru, *Jūnen no ayumi*, quoted in Katō Yoshinori, *Zaikai* [*Gendai no keizai*, vol. 14] (Kawade shobō shinsha, 1967) p. 42.
12. Miyashima Seijirō (1879–1963), President of the Nichibo Co., was a classmate of Prime Minister Yoshida's at Tokyo Imperial University. In the early post-war period, many new industrial leaders gathered around Miyashima with a view to participating in the reconstruction of the Japanese economy.
13. Watanuki Joji, 'Political Process of Japan's High Economic Growth and Her Emergence as an Economic Giant 1955–1977', *Annals of Japanese Political Science Association*, 1977.
14. Katō Yoshinori, *Zaikai*, op. cit. p. 158.
15. Ibid.
16. Ibid.
17. 'Inayama Yoshihiro: President of Keidanren', in Tahara Sōichirō, *Nihonshiki shihaishatachi* (Chūōkōronsha, 1981) pp. 296–311.
18. T. J. Pempel, 'Japanese Foreign Economic Policy: The Domestic Bases for International Behavior', in Peter J. Katzenstein (ed.), *Between Power and Plenty: Foreign Economic Policies of Advanced Industrial States* (Madison, Wis.: University of Wisconsin Press, 1978) pp. 139–90. See also Ishida Takeshi, 'Wagakuni ni okeru atsuryoku dantai no rekishiteki jōken to sono tokushitsu', in Nihon seiji gakkai (ed.), *Nihon no atsuryoku dantai* (Iwanami shoten, 1960).
19. Mori Kishio, *Shushō kantei no himitsu* (Chōbunsha, 1981) pp. 156–63.
20. See Tesse Morris-Suzuki, 'Japan and the Pacific Basin Community', *The World Today*, vol. 37, no. 12 (December 1981) pp. 454–60.
21. John C. Danforth, 'The Politics of Trade', in Edward R. Fried, Philip H. Trezise and Shigenobu Yoshida (eds), *The Future of U.S.–Japan Economic Relations* (Washington, D.C.: The Brookings Institution, 1983) p. 47.
22. Tahara, *Nihonshiki shihaishatachi*, op. cit.
23. Ibid.
24. Zenkoku nōkyō chūōkai, 'Nihon no nōgyō wo kangaeru', *Bungei shunjū* (January 1984) p. 142.
25. It is often argued that the opening of the Japanese agricultural market probably would be more beneficial to Australia than to the US.
26. See, for example, Kotani Hidejirō, *Dai-niji nichi-bei jidōsha sensō* (Nippon kōgyō shimbunsha, 1982).
27. Interview with a Ministry of Agriculture and Forestry senior bureaucrat reported in Kakizawa Kōji, *Kanryōtachi to nippon maru* (Gakuyō shobō, 1978) pp. 94–126. Muramatsu Michio's study also indicates that bureaucrats themselves perceive their influence in industrial and agricultural policies as much stronger than in such other policy areas as health care. See his *Sengo nihon no kanryōsei* (Tōyō keizai shimbunsha, 1980).

28. Sakakibara Eisuke, *Nippon wo enshutsu suru shinkanryōzō* (Yamate shobō, 1977).

29. See Sakaguchi Akira, 'Zaikai, seitō, kanryō: zaikai wo chūshin ni mita pawā erīto shūdan no hensen', in Masamura Kimihiro (ed.), *Gendai nihon no keizai seisaku* (Chikuma shobō, 1974). The influence of Shimomura Osamu, a Keynesian in the Ministry of Finance, has been mentioned by many former bureaucrats. See also Saburo Okita, *The Developing Economies and Japan* (University of Tokyo Press, 1980), esp. pp. 195–225.

30. See Yano Toshihiko, *Nippon kabushiki kaisha no hansei* (Nippon kōgyō shimbunsha, 1972) pp. 84–8.

31. See, for example, Masutaro Urata, 'New Approaches to Competition Policy', in *U.S.–Japan Relations: Towards a New Equilibrium [Annual Review, 1982–3]* (Cambridge, Mass.: The Program on U.S.–Japan Relations, Center for International Affairs, Harvard University, 1983).

32. See Zin Ikkō, *Ōkura kanryō* (Kōdansha, 1982).

33. See Kakizawa Kōji, *Kasumigaseki sanchōme no ōkura kanryō* (Gakuyō shobō, 1977) pp. 53–65.

34. Watanabe Ryōjirō, *Sonoda Sunao: Zenjinzō* (Gyōsei mondai kenkyūsho, 1981) pp. 256–7. See also 'Gaimushō', in Tahara Sōichirō, *Nihon no kanryō 1980* (Bungei shunjūsha, 1979).

35. See 'The Nakasone Brain Trust', in *Japan Times Weekly*, 10 March 1984.

36. Gaimushō, *Gaikō ni kansuru seron chōsa 1970–82* (Sōrifu kambō kōhōshitsu: annual). See also Japan Center for International Exchange (ed.), *The Silent Power: Japan's Identity and World Role* (Simul Press, 1976) pp. 176–7.

37. See Tsūshōsangyōshō (ed.), *Tsūshō hakusho* (Ōkurashō insatsukyoku), 1980, 1981 and, especially, 1982. The last is sub-titled *Japan's Role in the Revitalization of the World Economy*.

38. See T. J. Pempel (ed.), *Policymaking in Contemporary Japan* (Ithaca, N.Y.: Cornell University Press, 1977) p. 310.

39. Quoted in Tahara, *Nihon no kanryō*, op. cit. p. 149.

40. In their 'Bureaucrats and Politicians in Policymaking: The Case of Japan', *American Political Science Review*, vol. 78, no. 1 (March 1984) p. 144, Muramatsu Michio and Ellis S. Krauss argue that 'if business, bureaucracy, and the LDP are the three legs of a tripod supporting the Japanese state, then one leg [meaning business] is shorter than the other two'.

11 Japanese Policy-making on Issues of North–South Relations

1. Fujita Kimio, '1985-nen wagakuni keizai kyōryoku tembō', *Kokusai kyōryoku tokubetsu jōhō*, vol. 11 (January 1985) pp. 4–7.

2. See Shigeko N. Fukai, 'Japan's North–South Dialogue at the United Nations', *World Politics*, vol. 35, no. 3 (October 1982) pp. 73–105.

3. See Alan Rix, *Japan's Economic Aid* (New York: St Martin's Press, 1980); and Haruhiro Fukui, 'Policy-making in the Japanese Foreign

Ministry', in Robert A. Scalapino (ed.), *The Foreign Policy of Modern Japan* (Berkeley, Calif.: University of California Press, 1977). For the West European cases see Christopher Stevens, 'Policy-making on North–South Issues: The Importance of Administrative Organization', *Millennium*, vol. 11, no. 1 (September 1982) pp. 14–26.

4. It listed three principles: no intervention in a recipient country's domestic affairs; promotion of the recipient country's economic and social development and stabilisation, promotion of the people's welfare and avoidance of action likely to invite suspicion of wrongdoing; and refusal to give aid to be used for military purposes or contribute to international conflict. In 1981, upon the commencement of the second ODA-doubling plan, a similar resolution was adopted. For the evolution and general overview of Japan's aid policy see also William L. Brooks *et al.*, 'Japan's Foreign Economic Assistance', *Asian Survey*, vol. 25, no. 3 (March 1985) pp. 322–39. For international comparison of recent years see Ministry of Finance, International Finance Bureau (ed.), *Ōkurashō kokusai kinyū-kyoku nempō*, 1985, ch. 11.

5. Nihon Kyōsantō (ed), *Kokumin no tame no zaisei hyakka* (Nihon kyōsantō shuppan-kyoku, 1982).

6. See, for example, Rix, *Japan's Economic Aid*, op. cit. p. 16; Samejima Shinsuke, *Nihon no taigai enjo seisaku* (Asahi shimbun-sha, internal report, 1982) p. 111; *Asahi shimbun* (hereafter *Asahi*), 6 February 1985.

7. *Shingikai sōran*, 1984, pp. 30–1.

8. Samejima, *Nihon no taigai enjo*, op. cit. pp. 112–13.

9. Steven H. Arnold, *Implementing Development Assistance: European Approaches to Basic Needs* (Boulder, Colo.: Westview Press, 1982) p. 78.

10. Samejima, *Nihon no taigai enjo*, op. cit. p. 113.

11. Arnold, *Implementing Development Assistance*, op. cit. pp. 108–9, 124.

12. Ibid. p. 11.

13. Interview with a Ministry of Foreign Affairs official, 8 January 1985.

14. See Matsui Ken, *Keizai kyōryoku* (Yūhikaku, 1983) p. 153; Rix, *Japan's Economic Aid*, op. cit. p. 26; and Samejima, *Nihon no taigai enjo*, op. cit. pp. 90–103, 113–14. See also Terutomo Ozawa, *Multinationalism Japanese Style: Political Economy of Outward Dependency* (Princeton, N.J.: Princeton University Press, 1979), and William E. Bryant, *Japanese Economic Diplomacy: An Analysis of Business–Government Linkages* (New York: Praeger, 1975).

15. For information on the implementing agencies see Ministry of Foreign Affairs (ed.), *Kokusai kyōryoku handobukku* (hereafter *Handbook*) Kokusai kyōryoku kenkyū-kai, 1983).

16. Rix, *Japan's Economic Aid*, op. cit. p. 258.

17. JICA, *Japan International Cooperation Agency*, 1984, pp. 1–2.

18. Hassan Selim, *Development Assistance Policies and the Performance of Aid Agencies* (New York: St Martin's Press, 1983) p. 125.

19. Ibid.; *Handbook*, pp. 137–58.

20. JICA, 1984, p. 22.

21. Samejima, *Nihon no taigai enjo*, op. cit. p. 24; interviews with Ministry of Foreign Affairs officials, January 1985.

22. Fukai, 'Japan's North–South Dialogue', op. cit. p. 90; Atarashi Kinju, 'Japan's Economic Cooperation Policy towards the ASEAN Countries', *International Affairs*, vol. 61, no. 1 (1985) pp. 115–16.
23. Samejima, *Nihon no taigai enjo*, op. cit. p. 129.
24. Iwami Takao, *Kakusan no hanauta ga kikoeru*, part III (Ushio Publishing Co., 1982) pp. 138–47.
25. Shimizu Shinzo, 'New Channel of Japan–ROK relations', *Japan Times Weekly*, 12 September 1981.
26. Iwami, *Kakusan*, op. cit. p. 143.
27. Atarashi, 'Japan's Economic Cooperation Policy', op. cit. p. 117.
28. Kubota Akira, 'Foreign Aid: Giving With One Hand?', *Japan Quarterly*, vol. 32, no. 2 (April–June 1985) p. 142.
29. Interviews with Kubota Akira, 9 January 1986, and Suzuki Yūji, 21 January 1986. For a recent MFA study of ODA, see MFA, ODA Study Group, *Seifu kaihatsu enjo (ODA) no kōkateki kōritsuteki jisshi ni tsuite: ODA kenkyūkai ripōto* (December, 1985).
30. The information has been compiled mainly from press reports, especially the *Asahi shimbun*'s special series, 'Enjo tojōkoku, Nihon', government documents, journal articles and interviews.
31. Tsūshō Sangyō-shō (ed.), *Keizai kyōryoku no genjō to mondaiten*, 1984, p. 666; *Asahi*, 5 January 1985.
32. *Asahi*, 29 January 1985; *Forbes*, 16 July 1985.
33. Rix, *Japan's Economic Aid*, op. cit. p. 201.
34. *Asahi*, 8 January 1985.
35. Interview with Ōta Hajime, Economic Co-operation Section, Keidanren, 4 February 1985; *Keidanren Geppō*, November 1984, January 1985, February 1985. Keidanren's 'Opinions on Economic Cooperation Administration', submitted to the relevant ministries as well as to the Cabinet, in August 1984, listed changing this rule as a priority item to be considered.
36. *Asahi*, 29 January 1985.
37. Ibid.
38. *Asahi*, 10 January 1985.
39. Kubota, 'Giving With One Hand', op. cit. p. 142.
40. *Asahi*, 19 January 1985.
41. *Keizai kyōryoku no genjō to mondaiten*, 1979, cited by Samejima, *Nihon no taigai enjo*, op. cit. p. 95.
42. Rix, *Japanese Foreign Aid*, op. cit. p. 236.
43. Samejima, *Nihon no taigai enjo*, op. cit. p. 95.
44. Kubota, 'Giving With One Hand', op. cit. p. 142.
45. Shimizu Yoshinori, 'Tojōkoku no nīzu to surechigau nihon no keizai enjo', *World Review* (Yomiuri shimbun-sha), vol. 5, no. 9 (September 1983) p. 38.
46. Chu Yukun, *Namboku mondai o miru me* (Yūhikaku, 1980) p. 198.
47. Ozawa, *Multinationalism*, op. cit. p. 230.
48. John K. Galbraith, *Economics and the Public Purpose* (Boston, Mass.: Houghton Mifflin, 1973) p. 167.
49. Ozawa, *Multinationalism*, op. cit. p. 82.

50. Arnold, *Implementing Development Assistance*, op. cit.
51. Jonathan B. Tucker, 'Managing Industrial Miracle', *High Technology*, vol. 5, no. 8 (August 1985) p. 30.
52. On this topic see ibid.; *Creative Computing*, vol. 10, no. 8 (August 1984) pp. 12–125; and also Kubota Akira, *'Ajia seichō chiiki' to nihon: heizon suru 'hikari' to 'kage'* (Asahi shimbun-sha, internal report, 1985) pp. 140–8. A MITI official noted that some companies had shown increasing reluctance in accepting trainees from NICs. Interview, 10 January 1986.
53. See Kikuchi Yasushi, 'Bunka-kōritsu naki taigai-enjo o haise', *Chūō kōron*, vol. 100, no. 10 (October 1985) pp. 153–65.

12 The Japanese Management System in Europe

1. The distribution of subsidiaries of Japanese manufacturing firms in Europe at the end of 1984 was as follows: West Germany 34, Great Britain 32, France 30, Spain 22, the Netherlands 16, Belgium 15, Ireland 11, Italy 8, Portugal 8, Denmark 2.
2. For British works on the subject, see K. Thurley *et al.*, *The Development of Personnel Management in Japanese Enterprises in Great Britain: Comparative Industrial Relations* (International Centre for Economic and Related Disciplines, London School of Economics, April 1980); K. Thurley, M. Trevor and P. Worm, *Japanese Management in Western Europe: Comparative Industrial Relations* (International Centre for Economic and Related Disciplines, London School of Economics, July 1981); M. Trevor, 'Does Japanese Management Work in Britain?' *Journal of General Management*, vol. 8, no. 4, 1983/29; M. Trevor's *Japan's Reluctant Multinationals: Japanese Management at Home and Abroad* (New York: St Martin's Press, 1983); and M. White and M. Trevor, *Under Japanese Management: The Experience of British Workers* (London: Heinemann, 1983). For a study of Japanese subsidiaries in the US, see R. Johnson, 'Success and Failure of Japanese Subsidiaries in America', *Columbia Journal of World Business*, Spring 1977, pp. 30–7. For studies in West Germany see B. Kumar, H. Steinmann and Y. Nagamura, *Japanische Führungskräfte in Deutschland – Ensendung, Einsatz und Arbeitszufriedenheit* (Nürnberg: University of Erlangen, 1984); I. Schendel and B. Wilpert, *Management Development Scheme (MUS): Fallstudien zur Praxis japanischer und deutscher Unternehmen in Deutschland* (Berlin: Technical University of Berlin, 1984); S. J. Park (ed.), *Japanisches Management in der Praxis* (Berlin: Verlag Express Edition, 1985).
3. The project is supported by a Volkswagen Foundation grant.
4. See H. Demes *et al.*, 'Japanische Unternehmen in der Bundesrepublik Deutschland: Ergebnisse einer Expertenbefragung zu Investitionsmotiven, Managementpraktiken und Arbeitsbeziehungen', *Occasional Papers*, no. 55 (Berlin: Ute Schiller Verlag, 1984). This article is based on interviews with economic advisers, lawyers and labour representatives dealing with Japanese subsidiaries in the Federal Republic.

5. Japan Export Trade Organization, *Japanese Manufacturing Companies in Europe* (JETRO, 1983).
6. H. Demes, *Ist das japanische Industrial Relations System auf die Bundesrepublik Deutschland Übertragbar* (Berlin: Ute Schiller Verlag, 1983).
7. Countermeasures adopted by Japanese firms usually prove to be inadequate. One firm reported the creation of an elaborate system of titles exclusively for German managers.
8. This tendency is reinforced by the introduction of telefax which makes international communications in Japanese much easier than previously.
9. The 'Big Ten' Japanese firms in Düsseldorf have recently increased the ranks of their Japanese customers and hired Japanese accountants.
10. See, however, *Der Spiegel*, no. 46, 1982. The control of this firm by its parent firm in Japan has ended.
11. N. K. Welge, with the collaboration of I. K. Johansson *et al.*, 'Entscheidungsprozesse in komplexen, international tatigen Undernehmungen', *Zeitschrift für Betriebswirtschaft* (*ZFB*) vol. 52, 1982; B. Kumar and H. Steinmann, 'Netzspinner in der Fremde', *Manager Magazin*, no. 11, 1983; B. Kumar *et al.*, *Japanische Führungskräfte in Deutschland*, op. cit.
12. Here the appointment of a German director is legally required.
13. There are, however, a number of cases in which Germans in formally subordinate positions make decisions on the basis of their personal competence and knowledge.

13 Japan as a Model for Economic Development: The Example of Singapore

1. It is not easy to define 'the Japanese model', for even experts are not agreed. For my purposes, however, I will use the model that Singaporean authorities emphasise. The model centres on factors which have fostered Japan's high-growth economy since 1945. These factors include the guidance provided by the government to the economy and to individual industries; the 'Japanese employment system' of lifetime employment for permanent employees, extensive fringe benefits and salary based on seniority; the Japanese industrial relations system that minimises labour–management conflict through company unions which co-operate intimately with management; and the sequence of development of industries of increasingly higher capital or technological investment. Social stability is seen as an important contribution to economic performance. Therefore, factors like the family system, paternalism and even Confucian ideology are incorporated into the model.
2. *The Straits Times*, 3 January 1979, p. 7.
3. *Far Eastern Economic Review*, 25 June 1982, p. 58. There was, however, a strike in early 1986.
4. In 1983 the secretary-general of the NTUC, Lim Chee Onn, was one of the rising stars of the PAP's 'second generation' leaders and a technocrat appointed to NTUC from the bureaucracy. Lim was suddenly removed

from his office in April 1983 in a public exchange of letters with the prime minister, who appointed Ong Teng Cheong as a replacement (*Far Eastern Economic Review*, 28 April 1983, pp. 14–16). While Lim's sudden disgrace and elimination from the 'second-generation' group underlined the penalty of political missteps, it also underlined how little independence NTUC has. It is Lee Kwan Yew and the PAP who appoint and remove NTUC leaders, not the NTUC itself. The NTUC does 'elect' leaders after Lee appoints them (*Far Eastern Economic Review*, 11 August 1983, p. 17).

5. *Asiaweek*, 16 January 1981, p. 16.
6. *Asiaweek*, 30 October 1981, p. 19.
7. Wee was tried and found guilty of tax evasion on 31 January 1984, the final day of his tenure as chairman of SBC. His son later faced related charges. This kind of disgrace following political patronage led Goh Kian Chee (son of Goh Keng Swee, Singapore's economic wizard and Lee Kwan Yew's right-hand man) to observe that he could not recall anyone leaving the higher echelons of the PAP 'without (a) having defected to the communists, (b) having gone crooked, (c) having been pronounced incompetent, unreliable, weak, brainless, lacking in intellectual depth, enjoying laxity in amoral lifestyle, reckless and ambitious, and (d) having gone somewhat gaga' or dying (*Far Eastern Economic Review*, 15 February 1980, p. 26). Wee Mon Cheng was replaced with another former Ambassador to Japan, Wee Kim Wee (*Asiaweek*, 24 February 1984, p. 62).
8. *Far Eastern Economic Review*, 15 May 1981, pp. 34–6.
9. *Far Eastern Economic Review*, 15 May 1981, pp. 34–6.
10. *Far Eastern Economic Review*, 20 February 1981, p. 60.
11. *Far Eastern Economic Review*, 25 June 1982, p. 58.
12. *Asiaweek*, 6 July 1984, p. 23.
13. *Asiaweek*, 10 December 1982, pp. 41–2.
14. For example, see Ellis S. Krauss, Thomas P. Rohlen and Patricia G. Steinhoff (eds), *Conflict in Japan* (Honolulu: University of Hawaii Press, 1984); Tetsuo Najita and J. Victor Koschman (eds), *Conflict in Modern Japanese History: The Neglected Tradition* (Princeton, N.J.: Princeton University Press, 1982); and George de Vos (ed.), *Institutions for Change in Japanese Society* (Berkeley, Calif.: Institute of East Asian Studies, University of California Press, 1984).
15. *Asiaweek*, 18 February 1983, p. 49.
16. *Far Eastern Economic Review*, 22 March 1984, p. 23.
17. Ibid. 1 August 1980, p. 54.
18. Ibid. p. 83.
19. Ibid. p. 77. The 1980 Census recorded Christians as 10.3 per cent of the population over 10 years of age. Among those with tertiary education, 35.9 per cent were Christian. See *Asiaweek*, 7 September 1984, p. 31. The percentages are perhaps higher in 1986.
20. *Far Eastern Economic Review*, 22 March 1984, p. 26.
21. *Asiaweek*, 7 September 1984, p. 31.
22. See virtually any study of late Tokugawa and Meiji Japan, especially Byron K. Marshall, *Ideology and Industrialization in Japan, 1868–1941:*

The Creed of Prewar Business Elite (Stanford, Calif.: Stanford University Press, 1965).

23. *Far Eastern Economic Review*, 22 March 1984, p. 26. Over three-quarters of Singaporeans own or rent apartments built by the public Housing Development Board. For all but the élite, private apartments and houses are prohibitively priced. HDB is an efficient instrument for enforcing officially condoned behaviour since there is no viable alternative housing for the vast majority and since the government retains broad powers to evict even those who purchase their living quarters.
24. *Far Eastern Economic Review*, 8 September 1983, pp. 23–4.
25. Ivan P. Hall, *Mori Arinori* (Cambridge, Mass.: Harvard University Press, 1973) pp. 185–6, 250–1.
26. *Asiaweek*, 9 September 1983, p. 33; and 16 September 1983, p. 33.
27. *Far Eastern Economic Review*, 2 February 1984, p. 8. Ultimately, the school registration programme was also offered to women with A-level examination qualifications (equivalent to high-school education) and graduates of non-university tertiary institutions like the Institute of Education, a teacher-training facility.
28. Ibid. 22 March 1984, p. 10.
29. *The Straits Times*, 7 March 1985, p. 12.
30. *Far Eastern Economic Review*, 18 October 1984, p. 46; and *Asiaweek*, 23 September 1983, p. 22.

Index